TABLE OF CONTENTS

Menu Design

MERCHANDISING AND MARKETING

Menu Design
MERCHANDISING AND MARKETING

SECOND EDITION REVISED

Albin G. Seaberg

Seaberg Menu Research Service
Highland Park, Ill.

Jule Wilkinson, Editor

CAHNERS BOOKS INTERNATIONAL, INC.
221 Columbus Avenue
Boston, Massachusetts 02116
Affiliated with the Publishers of
Institutions/Volume Feeding Magazine

MENU PRICES IN THIS BOOK

Since October of 1975 to October of 1976, the U.S. city average consumer price index for restaurant meals has gone from 176.8 to 188.1. From 1967, when the index was 100, the inflation factor has boosted the index nearly double, and a year when inflation is only 5 percent is considered good. No book, therefore, such as this one, unless published monthly could keep up with the rapid price rise factor.

Figures, charts and even menu examples should be looked at, therefore, from a comparison viewpoint. For up-to-date information U.S. Department of Labor publications, such as the *Monthly Labor Review*, should be consulted.

Copyright © 1973 by Cahners Books International, Inc.
Second Edition, Revised
First Edition Copyright 1971 by Medalist Publications, Inc.
Subsidiary of Cahners Publishing Co., Inc.

ISBN 0-8436-0572-3

Library of Congress Catalog Card Number 72-149403

Fourth Printing

Printed in the United States of America

INTRODUCTION

In terms of food service systems engineering, the menu is probably the key focal point of the entire operation, and in terms of selling it is very often the number one food service salesman. It should be examined, changed, analyzed and improved constantly from the viewpoint of design, merchandising and marketing.

As a printed communication, the menu should be looked at in terms of a piece of paper on which words, drawings, designs, colors, illustrations, etc., are printed. It should look attractive, that is colorful, clean and reflective of the quality, style and general appearance of the establishment.

A dirty, soiled, poorly printed, hard to read menu creates a first impression that can be disastrous. An attractive, colorful, clean and sparkling appearing menu which, in addition, is easy and entertaining to read, sets up the proper mood for the customer. He is inclined to like your operation and its cuisine before he even orders.

And, the mere appearance of your menu can condition the customer to order more, building the check higher than he probably intended. Selection of the proper paper, type selection, printing, design and illustration are fields that may seem "afar" to the average food service operator who is, in addition, required to know how to cook like a chef, promote like a showman, balance a set of books, deal with personnel and the public, and, finally, perform the ultimate miracle of showing a profit at the end of each month.

But, as in all phases of the food service business, there are experts to help and actually produce and print the menu. The purpose of this menu book is to help you in all of the problems of the menu. With this book, plus the use of the professional expert, writer, artist and printer, you should produce a better, more effective menu.

The Menu That Sells

As a merchandising tool, the menu should be written and produced to sell. It should sell what you want it to sell the most of, in terms of specific items—entrees, appetizers, drinks, desserts—no matter what the category of your food and drink offering. Considering popular tastes, what the public will actually "go for," order and reorder, plus what is a high profit item for you, your menu should be written, organized and designed to sell what you want it to sell. There are some basic rules developed in advertising, propaganda and publicity that will help you sell more and more of what you want to sell. But, in addition, experimentation is necessary to merchandise effectively. Tastes change, prices vary, and what was popular today, may be less so tomorrow.

The menu is not just a selling tool for food and drink. It can sell many other things—catering, take-outs, party-banquet facilities, etc. One of the most common faults of many menus is the blank page. These are pages that have been paid for, but not used.

You should consider every page or panel of the menu in terms of a magazine advertisement; you would not buy two pages of magazine advertising (at an enormous cost) and leave one blank. Yet, your menu is just like an ad. It is read by a considerable number of people every day. If you add up the number of readers for a period of a month or more, you can see that your menu has considerable advertising space value. This space value should be exploited to the fullest and used for every profitable communication purpose possible.

In addition to a well designed, well printed and effective selling tool, the menu is a marketing print-out of your particular food and drink service operation. It is the end result, whether carefully planned and checked out or haphazardly assembled, of your selection of (1) what items of food and drink to serve, (2) how many food and drink items to serve, and finally, (3) how much to charge or the price of everything you serve. A study, therefore, of what other restaurants serve, how many of each category of items they serve, and what they charge cannot help but be of value in making these vital marketing decisions in your own particular operation.

Help in Menu Production

The plan of this menu book is to give as many different food service operators as possible "help" in a practical, realistic sense. In the case of the big operator in a major metropolitan center who can afford top professional talent—writers, artists, printers, etc.—help is less needed, although sometimes an excellent artist-designer, as well as a creative writer may violate some of the basic rules of menu design and production due to lack of knowledge of the special problems of menu communication. In the case of the restaurateur who operates in a small town or away from the main centers of the graphic arts and advertising skills, the need for help can be much greater.

For this group of food service people, the menu book is designed to give the most complete help. Charts, diagrams and examples are given in profusion. A section of "clip art" is also included. Your printer can "lift" this art work directly from the book and use it on your menu, either as a cover design or for decoration and color on the inside.

Printing and producing the menu can be an expensive item in the over-all budget of a restaurant. As a result, you want to get as much "bang from your buck" as possible. The thing to keep in mind is that you are communicating first and producing a work of art second. This consideration can reduce cost while improving sales.

But the menu should not be the place where you are "penny wise and dollar foolish." Failure to change a menu, both in content (items and prices) and in design and layout, when it is not effectively merchandising, because you have a stack of menus that you want to "use up," can be a most disastrous economy.

What this means in the final analysis is that you are in charge. The printer, artist, designer and writer can help you, but the success or failure of your menu as well as of your operation is up to you. Your general knowledge of the food service business must be translated through the above people into the proper sales tool.

No printer can tell you what to list, what to charge, what to feature, etc., and no artist or writer is qualified to write or list a selection of "high profit, fast moving" food and drink items. But working together with the help of the information in this menu book, you should be able to solve every menu problem in every area—design, merchandising, and marketing.

PRODUCING A MENU

To begin a menu, you have to begin somewhere, and you need help from qualified people to design, write and print your menu. Before you call in help, however, you should have an idea of what you want to serve and what you want to charge. In the case of a new menu, starting from scratch, you should make a written or typewritten list. Depending on your type of operation, the following is a chart to help you list what you want on your menu:

FOOD

Appetizers	Description	Price

Soups	Description	Price

Salads	Description	Price

FOOD (cont.)

Sandwiches

Description	Price

Entrees

Description	Price

Side Orders

Description	Price

Desserts

Description	Price

	Description	Price
Beverages		

DRINKS
Cocktails

	Description	Price

	Description	Price
Beers		

	Description	Price
Wines	Red	
	White	

Wines	Description	Price
Rose´		
Champagne		

After Dinner Drinks	Description	Price

After you have listed what you want to serve, to help clarify your menu in your own mind, and to help your designer and printer, make up a list of "Specials." These are items you want to feature, sell more of and in general use to create "menu excitement." Your designer or printer must know what you want to feature before he even begins on your menu. Some typical Specials are:

1. "For Two" combinations—dinner, drinks or desserts.
2. Continental Type Specials—French, German, Italian, etc.
3. Family Specials—this can be almost any entree item that you can offer, usually on an "all you can eat" basis, to the whole family.

4. Daily or Weekly Specials—these can be special nights, Friday Fish Fry, Captain's Table, Sunday Buffet.

5. Special Drinks—a special Martini or Manhattan or some other.

This is only a small list of "Specials." The subject is covered in more detail in a separate chapter. The main thing is to think in terms of some Specials. You may even want to illustrate them as well as feature them in bolder type, more complete copy and inside a box, circle or some other graphic device, and this also should be discussed with your printer-designer.

Rate Items for Popularity and Profit

Next, take your list as indicated above and rate each category in numerical order. For example, under Appetizers, if you are listing six of them, rate them in order of priority 1, 2, 3, 4, 5, 6 as to what you consider (1) popularity with the customer from your experience or from your menu surveys, (2) profit, that is, the appetizer from which you make the biggest profit.

Now, you are ready to call in the artist-designer, writer, printer or menu company to begin to create a menu for you. If you do not build your menu in this fashion, your outside help cannot intelligently design a menu that does what you want it to do.

The selection of a designer, writer, printer and producer of a menu can be a problem for you depending on the size and location of your restaurant. Your possibilities are as follows:

1. An Advertising Agency

If you are big enough to have an ad agency at present which handles advertising, publicity and promotion for you, people at the agency can design and write a menu for you. Agencies usually have competent artists, writers and merchandising people who can put together a menu for you. And they have printing production experience that they can apply to your menu problem.

2. A "Specialist" Menu Printer

These are printing companies who over the years have come to specialize in the printing of menus. There is a wide selection of these specialists across the country. The best of these specialists will have a complete staff to serve you—artists, designers, writers, etc. The range of competence varies, however, from company to company. To insure a good job, ask about their services and capabilities and also ask to see samples of menus they have produced in the various stages from start to finish.

The advantages of a "menu house" are several. First, they have the printing equipment—presses and typesetting—to produce your menu. Not every printing plant is set up to print menus. And secondly, they usually have had a great deal of experience in the problems of producing a menu.

3. The Artist-Designer

Any commercial artist or graphic designer can give you help in creating an attractive looking menu and probably will give you a functional layout. He cannot, however, write your menu. This you must do yourself under this type of menu production arrangement or get a writer to work with the artist or designer.

4. A Writer

A competent advertising copywriter can help you write your menu. He can usually add sparkle to your descriptive wording, and he may have "ideas" for a different, creative menu. But he will have to work together with an artist or designer.

5. A Printer

Practically any printer can produce a menu for you. But many printing plants do not print menus because printers are specialists. They vary considerably in the types of printing equipment they have—one-color, two-color and four-color presses, the size of piece of paper the press can print on and the various kinds of presses. Also, there are two basic kinds of printing—letterpress and offset. The printer who produces your menu should generally be geared for smaller job, short-run printing, except for large chain or franchise operations where an order of 100,000 menus may be common.

Your menu printer should also have typesetting facilities since most of your menu is words and figures. Check with him to see what selection and variety of type faces he has so that he can set up a readable and attractive listing. Also, remember that your menu is a changing list—the prices change and the items change; so you should have a very close arrangement with your printer for constant quick service.

Menus can be designed to fit printing equipment, but this is putting the cart before the horse. If at all possible, design your menu to sell your cuisine, select the paper (from samples furnished by a printer or by a paper merchant) and then have the printer adapt his equipment with possibly some variation in size, fold and cut to accommodate his plant and produce the menu economically.

THE MENU COVER

Your menu cover is a symbol of your identity plus part of your restaurant decor. Give it all the attention that it deserves to make it effective. A well designed, colorful, attractive and serviceable menu cover is usually one of the visible signs of a good restaurant, but it should not be the first consideration in creating your menu. A good menu should be designed from the inside out, so to speak. This means that you should start with your actual list of what you want to sell. This list, plus prices and descriptive copy, makes up the heart of your menu.

Have a layout, or make a layout yourself, of the internal listing of your menu. This will tell you how many pages and what size your menu should be—2 pages, 3 pages, 4 pages or more. Then have this listing set up in type and see what it looks like. If there is any evidence of crowding or of type too small or hard to read, increase the size of your menu. Most menus are too small for the number of items listed.

Then after you have decided on the size and number of pages in your menu, design your cover. Do not start with a pre-printed or stock menu cover and try to make your food and beverage listing fit. This is false economy in most cases.

Selecting Art and Design

In considering your cover art and design, several things should be taken into account—cost, number of colors, paper, selection of an artist or designer and the suitability of the cover design to the decor and style of your restaurant.

The more colors you print on your cover, the more expensive it will be. The most economical cover design will be one color on colored paper (black on blue or red, for example, on white or light colored paper or gold, yellow or orange on black paper). Next comes 2, 3 and 4 colors. A 4-color printed cover will give you all the colors in the spectrum. Usually, 2 colors on white or colored paper will give you all the color you need on a well designed menu.

Paper is also very important for a good menu cover. It should be a heavy, durable. grease-resistant paper unless you are printing a daily, throw-away menu. In fact, the paper can be selected first and your designer's layouts made right on the paper you are going to use.

The selection of an artist-designer is no problem in a large metropolitan area. If one is not known, a selection can be made from the yellow pages of your phone book. But, if your restaurant operation is off the beaten path, you will have more difficulty. For your operation, contacting a city artist or using preprinted menu covers from stock are possibilities. There are other possibilities, however, such as using a photograph for your menu cover art. Local photographers (professional or amateur) may have photos or can take photos suitable for menu covers. A good photo of a local scene, a food still life, or some other eye-catching subject, if printed in black and white with the name of the restaurant in a second bright color, can make an attractive menu cover.

Another inexpensive source of art for menu covers is old prints, woodcuts, engravings or drawings. They are usually in "line" and, therefore, easy and inexpensive to reproduce.

A little research in old bookstores or at the public library can very often turn up interesting and unusual art that is suited to certain types of restaurants. Woodcuts or engravings that are in black on white can be reproduced in other colors and increased or decreased in size.

In addition, going to art fairs and exhibitions can result in the finding of a print drawing, watercolor or oil painting that would be suitable.

Design Must Fit Operation

Your cover design, however, should be suitable to your type of operation. If yours is a Colonial Inn restaurant, your menu art and cover should reflect this, and, with the large amount of Colonial and Early American art available, this should be no problem. Likewise, if yours is a sophisticated Supper Club restaurant, your cover art should reflect this to the extent of going Abstract, Op or even Pop!

Then, too, your menu cover should be considered as decor. Circulated among your customers, the color of your menu should either blend or contrast pleasantly with the color scheme of your restaurant. In a well designed restaurant operation, the menu cover design is usually planned to harmonize with the theme and color of the decor as well as to illustrate the name appropriately.

There are certain basic items of copy that can be on the front cover such as address, phone number, hours of service and credit cards honored. But rather than clutter the cover with too much copy, just the name of the restaurant on the front cover is adequate for copy on the cover, with the rest of the copy on the back cover. In addition, the back cover is an ideal place to feature such sales points as party, banquet, meeting facilities, take-out service, history of your restaurant and a map of your location.

The long, narrow design of this menu cover fits the name of the restaurant—Belt 'N Buckle. It is printed in two colors, black and metallic gold, on white stock.

The name of your establishment may dictate the artwork and design on your cover. For Herb Traub's *PIRATE HOUSE*, it had to be pirates. The combination of high quality artwork plus humor make this an especially good cover. It is in full color which also adds to its charm and appeal.

HERB TRAUB'S *Nationally Famous*

Pirates' House

"...what foods these morsels be!"

In two colors, black and orange, on white paper, this cover establishes a supper club mood in a very effective manner.

This is an unusual cover. The artwork, a drawing in full color, is of very high quality. But, in addition, this cover has a great deal of copy, in both English and French. In most cases, too much copy on the cover spoils the design and makes for a cluttered appearance, but this cover "works" despite type in two languages.

The Meson Madrid Restaurant uses a "gate" design on the cover in two colors, black and brown, on cream colored paper. The "gate" folds open in a gate fold with the top part die cut so that name of restaurant is not cut in half when the menu is opened.

The "Yankee Drummer" Restaurant achieves an interesting and different menu cover that reflects the "flavor" of the operation as well as advertising its "Tavern Tap." The colors are green, brown and orange with a golden ribbon.

An old print can be used for menu cover art. This line cut of an old sailing vessel is a "natural" for a seafood restaurant—the Cape Cod Inn. This cover in two colors, blue-green and black on white.

CAPE COD INN

An attractive, interesting treatment of just the name of the establishment can make a good cover. This cover of Alioto's with its big fancy "A" and the rest of the word in script in white on a dark red background has impact.

The cloisenne Flower Urn, salvaged from the ruins of old Waverly now graces the Victorian Table in the main lobby.

WAVERLY INN

CHESHIRE, CONNECTICUT

The Waverly Inn uses a full color photo on the cover of its menu. This happens to be a cloisonne flower urn within the restaurant (part of the decor) with flowers in it. Stock photos in color or in black and white can be used in a similar manner.

Rosoff's

Times Square Theatre Landmark since 1899

TIMES SQUARE AS IT LOOKED WHEN ROSOFF'S SERVED ITS FIRST MEAL

Rosoff's Is Proud To Have Grown With Broadway

"The Vanderbilt Cup" 1906   JOHN BARRYMORE "Hamlet" 1922   WEBER & FIELDS Weber & Fields Music Hall 1899   "Cyrano" 1923   "Fedora" 1902

ROSOFF'S Restaurant and Hotel · 43rd Street, just East of Broadway · New York City · JU 2-3200

Rosoff's Restaurant specializes in before- and after-theater dinners. They, therefore, use this motif plus an historical approach on their menu cover. The main illustration is a photo of Times Square in 1899, the year Rosoff's was established. Below this are individual photos of famous actors and actresses in their most famous roles. Historical photos and photos that associate with the style and atmosphere of the restaurant make good menu cover art. This cover is in two colors, black and blue, on white.

A clever, humorous drawing, the name of the restaurant big and bold and the restaurant's specialty (steak by weight) are all combined in this effective menu cover. It is done in only one color (black) on white stock, but it shows the impact a one color cover can have if the idea is creative.

This menu cover for a Pancake specialty restaurant uses a geometric design approach. The name of the restaurant Pancake Corner is large and dominant, and the address is easy to read as placed in the lower right hand corner. The colors are three shades of green and two shades of yellow on white. The paper stock is heavily laminated.

THE

INTERNATIONALLY KNOWN

COACHMAN'S

INN

10350 MAIN STREET (Route 5)

CLARENCE, NEW YORK 14031

•

PHONE: 759-6852

In two colors, red and black, on tan paper stock, this menu cover is attractive while containing considerable information. The coach design is good, the name is large and bold and the address and phone number are included. The tan paper stock is attractive and is also serviceable and grease resistant.

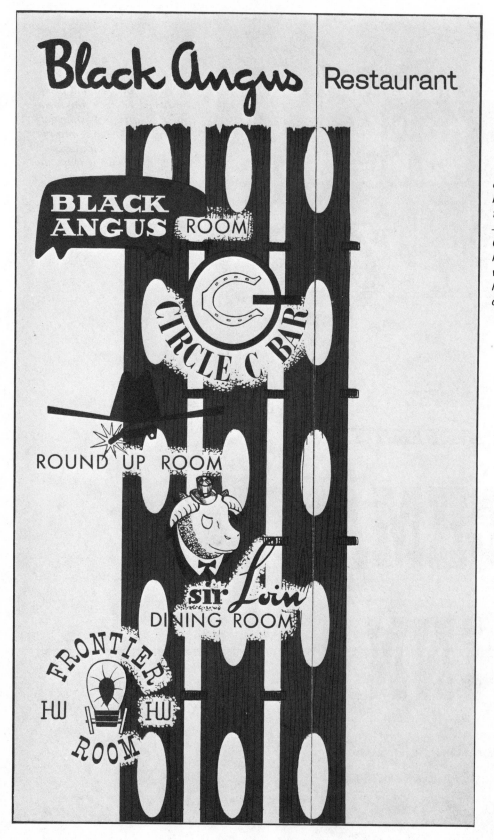

This menu cover in two colors, black and brown on white, has an unusual feature since it features five "special" rooms —Black Angus Room, Circle C Bar, Round Up Room, Sirloin Room and Frontier Room with appropriate art for each listing. And yet through good design, the cover works well.

This menu cover is very rich and elegant looking. It is in gold on black. The cover material is a plastic, imitation leather which adds to the quality appearance of this menu.

Sophisticated design with an oriental, South Seas flavor is the feature of this cover for Mark Thomas' Outrigger Restaurant. It is in two colors, blue and green, on white paper. Top professional design talent will insure a cover as attractive as this one.

Marrell's Restaurant uses simple but effective graphics. They have taken ads from an old newspaper and reproduced them leaving a panel for printing the restaurant's name. The old ads provide "human interest" and make for conversation. This cover is in black and white.

The Waterfront Restaurant has an interesting and unusual logotype. It has worked its name into the drawing of the fish. Since this is a restaurant specializing in seafood, the trademark is very appropriate. The cover is in one color (blue) on white stock and illustrates how much can be done with only one color.

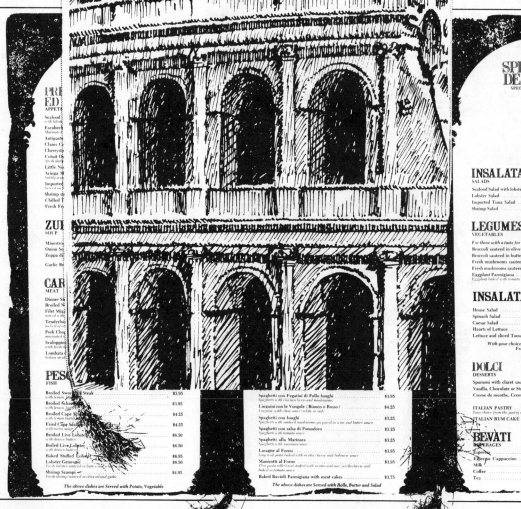

This menu shows a creative, imaginative use of paper. The cover is heavy coated stock, red on one side, white on the other. The insert is parchment paper with the edges actually burned to create a special effect. The back cover has a special insert wine list that can be changed without changing entire cover.

SPECIALITA DEL GIORNO
SPECIALTY OF THE DAY

INSALATA
SALADS

Seafood Salad with lobster, shrimp, King crabmeat and tuna fish	$5.25
Lobster Salad	$5.50
Imported Tuna Salad	$4.95
Shrimp Salad	$5.25

LEGUMES
VEGETABLES

For those with a taste for the unusual

Broccoli sauteed in olive oil and garlic	$ .95
Broccoli sauteed in butter	$ .95
Fresh mushrooms sauteed in butter	$1.25
Fresh mushrooms sauteed in olive oil and garlic	$1.25
Eggplant Parmigiana	$ .95

Eggplant baked with tomato sauce and parmesan cheese

INSALATA DEL CASA

House Salad	$ .60
Spinach Salad	$ .65
Caesar Salad	$1.00
Hearts of Lettuce	$ .75
Lettuce and sliced Tomato	$ .60

With your choice of Italian, Oil and Vinegar, Roquefort, French or Russian Dressing

DOLCI
DESSERTS

Spumoni with claret sauce	$ .65
Vanilla, Chocolate or Strawberry, parfait	$ .75
Creme de menthe, Creme de cacao, Creme almond, parfait	$1.25
ITALIAN PASTRY	$ .75
Your choice from the pastry cart	
ITALIAN RUM CAKE	$ .75

BEVATI
BEVERAGES

Espresso	$ .65
Espresso Cappuccino	$ .75
Milk	$ .25
Coffee	$ .25
Tea	$ .25

The above dishes are Served with Potato, Vegetable

The above dishes are Served with Rolls, Butter and Salad

This attractive menu shows how a menu, since it is a piece of paper, can be die-cut into unusual shapes and folded as many times as needed.

SALAMI
SAUSAGE
LINGUISA
CHEESE
BEEF
GREEN PEPPER
MUSHROOM
ONION
ANCHOVY
PEPPERONI 2.45
BACON 2.05
CONFUSION 3.45

(for any combination — no additional for each item)

Pizza on French Bread
Served on crisp sour dough French bread with your choice of:

CHEESE .... 1.25   SALAMI 1.35
SAUSAGE .... 1.45   MUSHROOM 1.35
ANCHOVY .... 1.35   BEEF 1.35
PEPPERONI .... 2.45   CONFUSION 1.95

(for any combination — 50c additional for each item)

RIGATONI 1.55
RIGATONI with meat ball 1.90
A delicious wide flat noodle in our own meat sauce.
Spaghetti, Ravioli or Rigatoni ... ¹⁄₂ order 1.10
Mushrooms with Pasta .... .80

All above served with French Bread and Butter.

On the Side
French Bread and Butter .... .35
Oven Hot Garlic Bread .... .45
Polpette (Two meat balls) .... .70
Grilled Mushrooms with Butter .... .80
Italian Sausage .... .90

.55
1.90
1.85
2.00
1.85
1.85
.... RAVIOLI with meat ball 2.20

caffè giovanni

SANDWICHES

Steak Sandwich   French Dip Sandwich
Bistecca Italiana served   Choice beef on
on French roll with sauteed   french roll dipped
mushrooms, tossed salad   in our special broth and served
and fruit garnish.   with potato or tossed salad.
2.15   1.65

American Cheese (Grilled) .... .70
Roast Beef, Italian Style 1.10
Served hot on French roll with sauteed bell peppers
Polpette (Meatballs on French bread) .... .95
Italian Sausage, Mama Savaria Style .... .95
Grilled with our special sauce on French roll.

IL HAMBURGO
Hamburger .... .95
The finest fresh ground beef done to perfection.
Cheese Burger 1.05
Topped with tasty cheese melted to mouth-watering goodness.
Mushroom Burger 1.45
Smothered in delicate Italian mushrooms—Delicious!
Mozzarella Burger 1.15
Light, golden Italian cheese—melts in your mouth.
Onion Burger 1.15
Smothered in onions, sauteed to golden goodness.
Pizza Burger 1.50
Covered with Giovanni's own secret sauce—Magnifico!

MAMA SAVARIA'S SPECIALTY
Homemade Minestrone Soup— .45
A Specialty of the House, rich, hot and filling!

SALADS
CRISP, TOSSED GREENS — .45   (with anchovies) — .65
GIOVANNI'S POTATO SALAD .... .40
Made with sour cream.
COTTAGE CHEESE .... .40
COMBINATION SALAD .... .95
Crisp greens mixed with fresh, cherry tomatoes, salami, tangy pepperoncini and black olives.

Choice of our dressings:
Italian, French, Thousand Island, Blue Cheese, Garlic.
Please Pay Cashier

LUNCHEON
Served daily from 11:00 a.m. to 4:30 p.m.

LINGUISA SANDWICH 1.55
A smoked sausage smothered in green peppers and melted cheese. Served with fresh green salad.
POLPETTE SPECIAL 1.15
Meatballs perfectly seasoned and sauced for a man with French bread and butter.
Served with fresh green salad.
ITALIAN SAUSAGE SANDWICH 1.35
Served open-face—Mama Savaria Style in Giovanni's special sauce. Served with fresh green salad.
GROUND ROUND STEAK 1.95
Covered with our Special Sauce, sauteed mushrooms, and served with spaghetti, garnish, bread and butter.
RIB EYE STEAK 2.35
Served with spaghetti, garnish, bread and butter.
VEAL ALLA POMADORO 2.95
Thinly sliced veal sauteed with cherry tomatoes, mushrooms and green peppers. Served on a bed of Rigatoni with bread and butter.
SLIMLINE 1.35
Broiled ground beef served with cottage cheese and fruit.
ARROSTO FREDDO 1.15
Cold roast beef sandwich served with hot, hot soup or crisp salad.
POOR BOY SANDWICH .... (For One) .95
                          (For Two) 1.65
Made with cappacola, salami, cheese, tomato, shredded lettuce, and our Italian dressing on French bread — garnished with cherry tomato, black olive and tangy pepperoncini.
All Luncheon items above served until 4:30 p.m. daily.

GIOVANNI'S CHAMPAGNE BRUNCH
11:00 a.m. to 3:00 p.m. — Sunday
Giovanni invites you to a complimentary glass of champagne served with any food on our menu for your enjoyment during a Sunday Brunch — Italian Style.
Additional Glass of Champagne .65
Sunday Brunch Special
THREE EGG OMELETTE
Cheese, Salami, or Mushrooms 1.50
Served with garnish and toasted french roll.

caffè giovanni

SEQUENCE–THE SECRET OF MENU ARRANGEMENT

Like a novel or a symphony, a meal has a beginning, a middle and an end. And this is the key to the way a menu should be designed. The size of the menu and the fold of the pages and the number of pages will, of course, make for a different problem in each case, but if the menu layout follows the meal sequence, you will usually be doing the right thing. The order of reading on the menu is from outside pages to inside pages, from top to bottom and from left to right. On a rectangular piece of paper, for example, the starting point is the upper left hand corner where you would usually start a letter.

The meal sequence is as follows, or some portion of the following depending on how large or extensive your menu is: Appetizers, Soups, Entrees and Desserts. Within this sequence there are items such as Side Orders, Salads, Sandwiches, Beverages and Children's Menu. The position of salads and sandwiches can present a problem depending on how the establishment wants to treat or sell them. When salads and sandwiches are considered entree and the children's menu problem is best solved by a separate menu. An example of the above sequence is shown in Figure A, a 1-panel menu:

FIGURE A

On this menu, the time sequence is followed by placing the before items, appetizers and soups, at the top; the middle items, entrees, at the center, and the after items, desserts, at the bottom. Salads and side orders are placed to the right on panel 4. Even the sequence or order that you list your entrees in is important. The top item on any entree listing has the best chance of being ordered and the top group, steaks, seafood, etc., also has the best chance of being ordered. So select and list in the number one position what you want to sell best.

Another example of the time sequence layout for a somewhat larger menu is shown in Figure B, a 4-page insert in a 4-page cover:

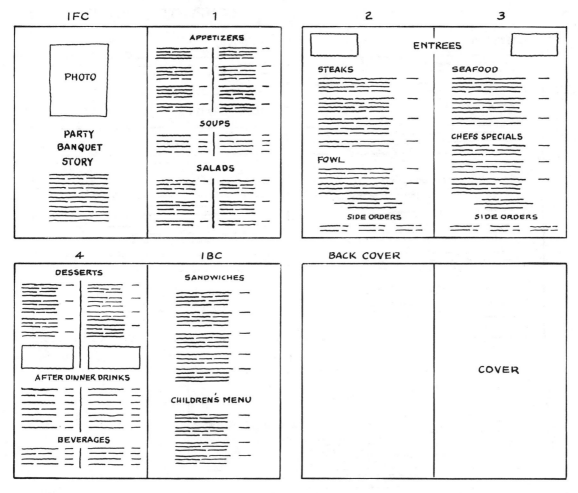

FIGURE B

On page 1 of the 4-page insert, the appetizers, soups and salads are listed. This gives room for these to have a large listing with good descriptive copy, especially if they are big, expensive items. The entrees are listed on pages 2 and 3 using the headings—Steaks, Fowl, Seafood and Chef's Specials. In all cases, entrees should be given top billing—best position, largest, boldest type and most descriptive copy. Desserts and Beverages are listed on page 4. Side orders are listed at the bottom of pages 2 and 3 under the entree listing. A separate page or even better a dessert menu enables the waitress to present this after part of the menu listing to the customer without asking him if he wants a dessert—positive instead of negative selling.

The 4-page cover (Figure B) is used for the items and services outside of the time sequence. Sandwiches and the children's menu can be listed on the inside back cover. The inside front cover can be used to tell and sell your party-banquet-meeting facilities, illustrated with a photo.

If you list and sell your entrees both a la carte and complete dinner, another element is added to the entree listing problem. It can be solved in two ways, as shown in Figures C and

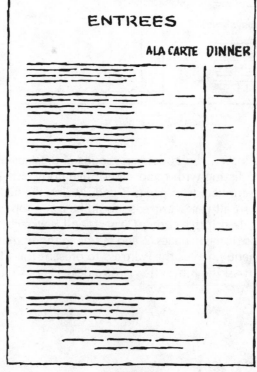

FIGURE C

FIGURE D

D. Figure C shows two separate listings, one a la carte and one dinner. These can be two identical listings with different prices or the dinner listing can include some of the a la carte items and some "daily" items not offered a la carte. For this type of separate listing, the dinner items can be printed on a tip-on for daily changes.

The layout in Figure D shows a la carte and complete dinner entrees listed once with two prices. When listing this way, be sure the difference between the two prices is the same in all cases since the "extras" on the complete dinner are always the same.

In both methods of listing, Figure C and D, be sure to list clearly and boldly what is included a la carte and what is included in the complete dinner so that the customer can choose intelligently from either one or the other.

The food service operation that serves alcoholic beverages—cocktails, wines, beers, etc.—has an additional menu layout problem, but the sequence formula works again here. Some drinks are before dinner drinks (cocktails), some drinks are with-dinner beverages (wines, beers), and some are after dinner (brandies, cordials, dessert wines, some cocktails). The idea is to list the beverage item in its proper order so that it will sell itself at the proper time. The cocktail, bourbon, scotch, gin, vodka, etc., list should be what the customer sees first when he picks up the menu since this is what you want him to order first. The beer and

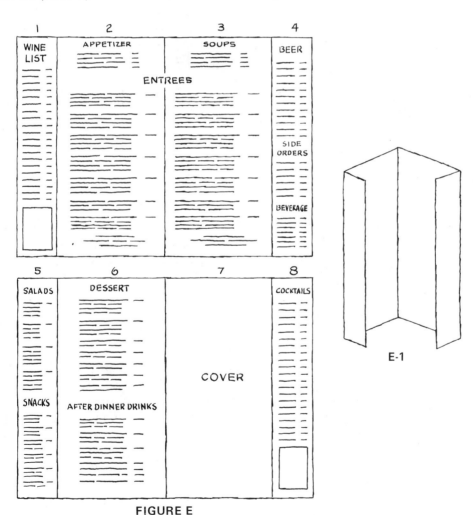

FIGURE E

wine list should be next to the entree list since he will order these items to be drunk with his meal. The after dinner list should be with the dessert listing which presents the other after dinner items of the menu. Figure E, preceding page, shows one solution to the drink sequence listing.

This menu folds as shown in Figure E-1. Therefore, the first panel the customer sees after the cover is panel 8 which is the cocktail plus other "before" drinks listing. The wine list is printed on panel 1 next to the entree listing, and beer is listed on panel 4 also next to the food selection. Finally, the after dinner drink selection is printed on panel 6 with the dessert selection. Another way to list your bar selections on the menu, following the sequence pattern, is shown in Figure F.

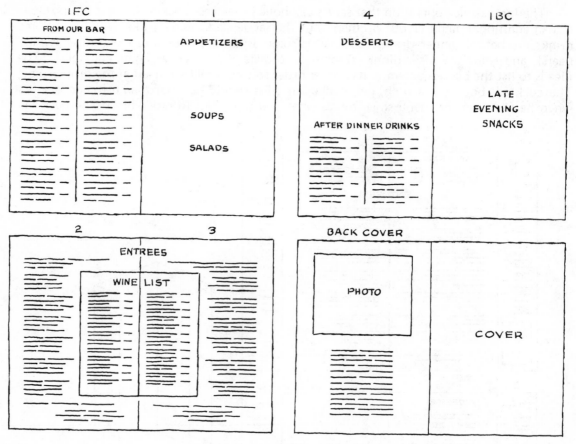

FIGURE F

This menu is a 4-page insert bound into a 4-page cover with a smaller wine list bound into the center. A complete before dinner, From Our Bar listing is printed on the inside front cover. This includes cocktails, bourbons, scotches, vodkas, gins, rums, etc. The wine list is a smaller 4-page insert bound into the center of the menu between pages 2 and 3. Notice that it is right in the middle of the entree listing.

A separate wine list that is not made an integral part of the menu will not work for you. The customer will not ask for it and the waiter or waitress cannot be depended on to present it to the customer. Finally, on Figure F the after dinner drinks are listed on page 4 with the desserts.

The After Dinner or Dessert menu shown in Figure G is another excellent method of making the menu follow the eating sequence of the customer:

FIGURE G

The desserts are listed on page 2, the after dinner drinks on page 3 and the dessert wines on page 4.

Every food service operation has its own menu problem and no two are alike. But if the sequence plan is kept in mind while planning the menu layout, the placement of the various categories of food and drink will be correct. And a correct, working layout will help merchandise and sell your product.

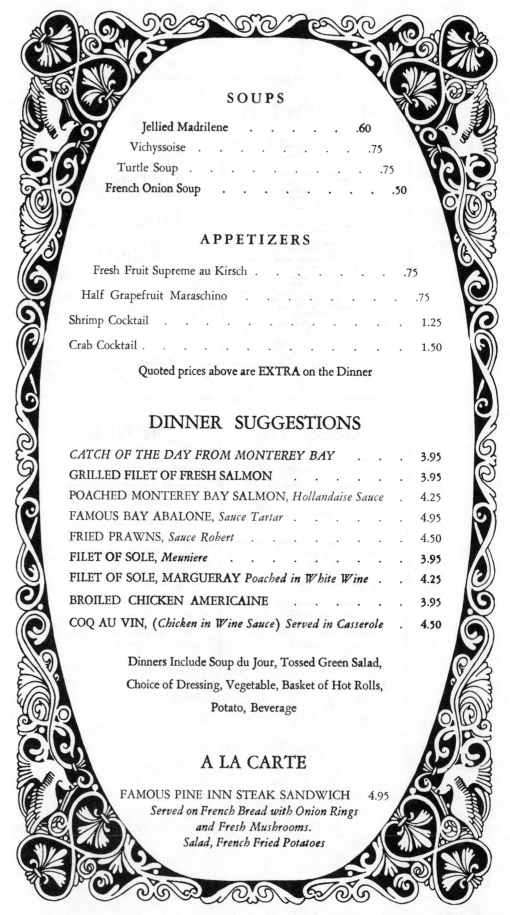

SOUPS

Jellied Madrilene 60
Vichyssoise 75
Turtle Soup 75
French Onion Soup 50

APPETIZERS

Fresh Fruit Supreme au Kirsch 75
Half Grapefruit Maraschino 75
Shrimp Cocktail 1.25
Crab Cocktail 1.50

Quoted prices above are EXTRA on the Dinner

DINNER SUGGESTIONS

CATCH OF THE DAY FROM MONTEREY BAY . . . 3.95
GRILLED FILET OF FRESH SALMON 3.95
POACHED MONTEREY BAY SALMON, *Hollandaise Sauce* . 4.25
FAMOUS BAY ABALONE, *Sauce Tartar* 4.95
FRIED PRAWNS, *Sauce Robert* 4.50
FILET OF SOLE, *Meuniere* 3.95
FILET OF SOLE, MARGUERAY *Poached in White Wine* . 4.25
BROILED CHICKEN AMERICAINE 3.95
COQ AU VIN, (*Chicken in Wine Sauce*) *Served in Casserole* . 4.50

Dinners Include Soup du Jour, Tossed Green Salad,

Choice of Dressing, Vegetable, Basket of Hot Rolls,

Potato, Beverage

A LA CARTE

FAMOUS PINE INN STEAK SANDWICH   4.95
*Served on French Bread with Onion Rings
and Fresh Mushrooms.
Salad, French Fried Potatoes*

A two-panel menu with the listing in the proper time-ordering sequence. The deco-

OUR CHEF SUGGESTS

VEAL OSKAR 5.25
*Tender Veal Steak sauted in Butter
Topped with King Crab Meat, served
with Asparagus and Bearnaise Sauce*

SWEET BREADS, *Saute* 4.50

TERI YAKI STEAK, *Rice Pilaf* 4.95

PRIME RIB OF BEEF 6.25

BEEF STROGANOFF IN CASSEROLE 4.50

SPECIAL EDITION 3.95
*Every night the Pine Inn features a Dinner Special. Look thru the
Victorian Door on your table and find out what the Chef has pre-
pared for you tonight.*

FROM THE BROILER

SHISH KEBAB (*Marinated Lamb on a Skewer*) 4.50

BROILED LAMB CHOPS 5.50

FILET "QUEEN VICTORIA" — *a house specialty* 5.25

NEW YORK CUT SIRLOIN 7.00

TAVERN'S TREAT (*Broiled Ground Round with Chef's Garni*) . 3.95

TOURNEDOS OF BEEF, *Maitre D'Hotel* 6.50

FILET MIGNON AU CHAMPIONS 6.95

BEEF BROCHETTE (*Marinated Beef on a Skewer*) . . . 4.95

Dinners Include Soup du Jour, Tossed Green Salad,
Choice of Dressing, Vegetable, Basket of Hot Rolls,
Potato, Beverage

DESSERTS

Cheese — Choice of Monterey Jack, Camembert,
    Porte Salute, Roquefort, Edam 60
Choice of Ice Creams 40
    Choice of Sherbets 40
      Creme de Menthe Parfait 70
      Creme de Mocca Parfait 70
      Cointreau a la mode, A real delight . .75
      Fresh Fruit in Season 50
      Homemade Pie du Jour . . .60

BEVERAGES

Coffee, Tea, Sanka, Milk .25

rative border plus the type selection make for an attractive menu as well.

★ **Traditional Southern Favorites** ★

★ Appetizers

Chincoteague Oysters on Half Shell .90
Select Backfin Crabmeat Cocktail 1.00
Supreme of Fruit with Port .40
Melon in Season with Smithfield Ham 1.25
Cream of Sussex Peanut Soup .30

Jumbo Gulf Shrimp Cocktail, Sauce Louisa 1.10
Cherrystone Clams, Cocktail Sauce .85
Chilled Fruit Juices .30

Chicken Broth with Caroline Rice .30

★ Seafoods

Centennial Seafood Platter, Pittsylvania Butter, Sauce Louisa 2.90
Pan Fried Botetourt Trout, Princess Anne Potatoes, Garden Vegetables 2.40
Golden Fried Jumbo Shrimp filled with Crabmeat Madison 2.65
Richmond Imperial Crab on Smithfield Ham, Crisp Potatoes and Cole Slaw 2.35

★ Entrees

(Choice of Vegetables from the Du Jour Menu)
Broiled Bedford Sirloin Steak, Country Butter 4.95
Breast of Capon Chimborazo, Julienne Potatoes 3.25
Filet of Albemarle Beef, Churned Butter 4.60
Grilled Augusta Lamb Chops on Toast, Green Salad 3.50
Smithfield Ham Steak, Red-Eye Gravy, Hot Grits 3.40

★ Salads

Fresh Fruit Salad Plate 1.25
Jumbo Shrimp and Garden Tomatoes 2.40
Waldorf Salad .80

Gulf Shrimp and Crabmeat 2.65
Hearts of Lettuce and Tomatoes. .75
Tossed Salad .60

CENTENNIAL COLD SEAFOOD PLATTER 2.90

(Crabmeat, Shrimp, Lobster, Clams, Cole Slaw, Cocktail Sauce, Lettuce and Tomatoes)

★ Sandwiches

Smithfield Ham and Turkey, Cole Slaw, Mixed Pickles 1.35
Albemarle Chopped Steak on Toasted Bun, French Fries, Lettuce and Tomatoes 1.05
King George French Toasted Ham and Cheese, Potato Salad, Pickles 1.25
Sliced Rockingham Turkey .80   Smithfield Ham 1.10
Richmond Club Sandwich 1.10 . . . . . Jr. .90

★ Desserts

Richmond Cream Pie .35   Peach Melba .40
Chilled Ripe Albemarle Peaches .35
Nesselrode Parfait .40   Pie du Jour .30
Fresh Berries in Season
Specially Prepared Ice Cream and Sherbet .30

★ Beverages

Centennial Room Coffee .25   Milk .20   Tea .25   Sanka .25

A one-page menu listing in a logical sequence with attractive headings.

FIGURE 1

WIGS RESTAURANT
Carry Out Service
Anything on our menu can be packaged
to take home
We have special cartons
which keep food piping hot

One-fourth Fried Chicken, Salad, French Fries, Roll .90

SINGLE ORDER, 2 Pieces _____ $ .50
ONE WHOLE CHICKEN, 8 Pieces _____ $1.89
TUB O'CHICKEN, 16 Pieces _____ $3.49
(Feast for Five)
Large TUB O'CHICKEN, 21 Pieces _____ $4.45
(Enough for Eight Hungry People)

Wig's Special Salads and Salad Dressings

	Pt.	Qt.	Gal.
Potato Salad	.45	.85	$3.40
Cabbage Salad	.40	.80	$3.00
Baked Beans (hot or cold)	.35	.70	$3.00

	Pt.	Qt.
Mild French Salad Dressing	.75	$1.40
Thousand Island Salad Dressing	$1.00	$1.85
Blu Cheese Salad Dressing	$1.00	$1.85
Vinegar and Oil Salad Dressing	$1.00	$1.85

From Our Own Pastry Shop

(One Day Notice Required)

Dinner Rolls	.50 Dz.	Whole Pies ____ $1.00
Large Cinn. Rolls	1.20 Dz.	Coffee Cake (round) ___ .80
Small Dinner Cinn. Rolls, Iced	.60 Dz.	Oatmeal Coffee Cake-Sheet ___ 2.10

PHONE ED 1-0930

WIGS RESTAURANT
We Have Banquet Facilities for
Gatherings from 15 to 250
We Also Cater Parties Outside our
Restaurant for Gatherings from
100 to 2500.

These Facilities Include . . .

● COMPLETE AIR CONDITIONING
● A COMPLETE SOUND SYSTEM
● NEW STORY & CLARK PIANO
● CONTROLLED LIGHTING

After you have completed your meal . . .

Please Look Over Our Restaurant Including
Our Kitchen. We Are Always Pleased to
Show Our Guests Our Facilities.

We Hope You Have Enjoyed Your Visit with
Us. If You Have Any Suggestions for Improving Our Food or Service Please Tell Us.

YOUR HOSTS,
Georgia and Jack Wiggins

HOURS:
Weekdays _____ 5 a.m. to 8 p.m.
Sundays and
Holidays _____ 11 a.m. to 2 p.m.
Buffet Only

WE ARE NOT RESPONSIBLE FOR ARTICLES
LOST OR STOLEN

FIGURE 2

FIGURE 3

This menu covers a lot of subjects in a small space through the full use of all panels plus the clever fold. Fig. 1 shows the cover. Fig. 2 shows the first fold when the menu is opened. The Carry Out and general information about the operation—hours, days open, etc. are listed here. In Fig. 3, panels 3, 4, 5 and 6 are shown with Sandwiches on panel 3 (plus fountain items). Steaks and Specials are listed on panel 4. On panel 5 Lunches, Salads and Specials of the Day are listed. On panel 6, the Breakfast menu plus drinks and assorted specials are listed. Putting specials on the back page gives them maximum exposure.

FIGURE 1

App

Escargots 1.95
Imported snails in the shell
sauteed to a gourmets delight

California Fruit Cocktail Supreme
with Wedge of Fresh Lime 1.40

Iced Tangy Tomato Juice with Lemon Wedge .45

French onion soup au croutons ....

Gourmet

— PREPARED AT

Caesar Salad 1.50
Crisp hearts of romaine, golden brown croutons,
anchovies and parmesan cheese, tossed at your
table with a dressing of fresh lemon juices,
olive oil, coddled egg and finished with
freshly ground pepper.

Marine

BROILED AUSTRALIAN ROCK I
A large juicy lobster tail prepared in the sh
enchaning seafood treat served with golde
drawn butter and lemon wedge

FOR THE UNDECIDED
An exotic treat of a moderately sized sirloi
plus one-half rock lobster tail. Truly a uniqu

ROCKY MOUNTAIN RAINBOW T
From the streams and lakes of Montana hig
Three-quarters of a pound of fighting 'Bow
sauteed in butter, and served with a rasher c

FRESH JUMBO PRAWNS
Dipped in our own oriental batter and fried
golden brown .Served with Rainbow cole s
tangy cocktail sauce and lemon wedges.

GRILLED FILET OF HALIBUT ...
Served with lemon wedge and tartar sauce

Flamed at

BUTTERFLY NEW YORK STEAK
A large choice New York steak superbly pr
in a skillfully blended sauce, laced in flamir
and served with a large baked potato.

BEEF STROGANOFF
Thin strips of beef tenderloin and mushroom
sauteed in butter and wine and a dollop of
sour cream—added at just the right momen
served with homemade noodles with sesame

MALAYAN TENDERLOIN TIPS ..
Choice beef tenderloin tips, skillfully braised
Flamed with brandy and served on a bed of

Above entrees served with soup du jour, relish trays, dinner salad

---

Desserts

CHERRIES JUBILEE 1.25
Prepared at your table in a chafing dish,
with large pitted cherries flamed in select
liqueurs and brandy. Served over large
mounds of vanilla ice cream in
supreme bowl.

CREME DE MENTHE PARFAIT .... .75
Creamy rich ice cream mingled with
green Creme de Menthe, topped with
fresh whipped cream.

OLD FASHIONED STRAWBERRY PIE ... .50

HOT APPLE PIE .... .50
An old Dutch treat, served with
your choice of cheddar cheese or
mounds of whipped cream.

ICE CREAM OR SHERBET .... .40

COCONUT SNOWBALL with
CHOCOLATE SAUCE SUPREME ...... .50

After Dinner Drinks

Creme de Menthe	.90	Black Russian	1.30
King Alphonse	1.00	Stinger	1.10
Cognac	1.00	B & B	1.10
Brandy Alexander	1.10	Galliano	1.00
Drambuie	1.00	Grasshopper	1.10
Creme de Cocao	.90	Pink Squirrel	1.10

Steaks and Chops

BIG SKY T-BONE STEAK 6.50
A favorite cut from our specially
aged beef loins.

FILET MIGNON 6.25
The queens choice, the most
tender of all red meats.

NEW YORK STRIP STEAK 6.00
The finest cut of beef, selected for tenderness
from our best strip loins.

FRENCH CUT LAMB CHOPS 4.50
These extra thick chops are selected from
the choicest Montana spring lamb.

CLUB SIRLOIN STEAK 4.25
Always a favorite, cut from
the finest Montana beef.

CENTER CUT PORK CHOPS 3.75
Grilled until well done, served with
fresh apple sauce.

Best in Montana

ROAST PRIME RIB OF BEEF
Aged prime roasted slowly
to retain all natural juices.
Our most popular entree.
4.00

CATTLEMAN'S CUT
Sliced extra heavy
for the hearty appetite.
5.00

All Entrees served with soup du jour, large fresh crisp tossed salad and
relish trays, fluffy baked potato, hot rolls and butter
choice of beverage

FIGURE 2

App

Escargots 1.95
Imported snails in the shell
sauteed to a gourmets delight

California Fruit Cocktail Supreme
with Wedge of Fresh Lime 1.40

Iced Tangy Tomato Juice with Lemon Wedge .45

French onion soup au croutons ....

Gourmet

— PREPARED AT

Caesar Salad 1.50
Crisp hearts of romaine, golden brown croutons,
anchovies and parmesan cheese, tossed at your
table with a dressing of fresh lemon juices,
olive oil, coddled egg and finished with
freshly ground pepper.

Marine

BROILED AUSTRALIAN ROCK I
A large juicy lobster tail prepared in the sh
enchaning seafood treat served with golde
drawn butter and lemon wedge

FOR THE UNDECIDED
An exotic treat of a moderately sized sirloi
plus one-half rock lobster tail. Truly a uniqu

ROCKY MOUNTAIN RAINBOW T
From the streams and lakes of Montana hig
Three-quarters of a pound of fighting 'Bow
sauteed in butter, and served with a rasher c

FRESH JUMBO PRAWNS
Dipped in our own oriental batter and fried
golden brown. Served with Rainbow cole s
tangy cocktail sauce and lemon wedges.

GRILLED FILET OF HALIBUT ...
Served with lemon wedge and tartar sauce

Flamed at

BUTTERFLY NEW YORK STEAK
A large choice New York steak superbly pr
in a skillfully blended sauce, laced in flamir
and served with a large baked potato.

BEEF STROGANOFF
Thin strips of beef tenderloin and mushroom
sauteed in butter and wine and a dollop of
sour cream—added at just the right momen
served with homemade noodles with sesame

MALAYAN TENDERLOIN TIPS ..
Choice beef tenderloin tips, skillfully braised
Flamed with brandy and served on a bed of

Above entrees served with soup du jour, relish trays, dinner salad

Complete Dinners

which include

Soup of the day	Tossed Salad
	with choice of dressing

BREAST OF CAPON CORDON BLEU 4.50
Savory breast of capon filled with lightly smoked ham
and swiss cheese. Served with fluffy white rice,
spiced peach and supreme sauce.

BEEF AND BACON 3.25
Choice ground sirloin of beef, topped with crisp bacon,
and encircled with onion rings.

FILLET OF DOVER SOLE 3.25
Dipped in egg batter and grilled to a golden brown,
served with Rainbow tartar sauce.

FRIED CHICKEN 3.25
Country style, golden brown and done to a turn.

GRILLED BABY BEEF LIVER with BACON or ONIONS 2.95

Above items served with
Large baked potato or fluffy white rice.
Fresh dinner rolls with butter.
Choice of beverage.
Ice cream or Sherbet

House Specialty

NEOPOLITAN SPAGHETTI DINNER
Real Italienne Spaghetti with a delightfully rich
meat sauce. Served with ravioli, and
shredded parmesan cheese.
3.25
Served complete with tossed salad and
choice of dressing.
Dinner rolls with butter. Choice of beverage.

nd Chops

.... 6.50

.... 6.25

.... 6.00
tenderness

.... 4.50
from

.... 4.25

.... 3.75

Montana

RIB OF BEEF
oasted slowly
atural juices.
ular entree.
0

AN'S CUT
ra heavy
ty appetite.
0

, large fresh crisp tossed salad and
otato, hot rolls and butter
beverage

Appetizers

Escargots 1.95
Imported snails in the shell
sauteed to a gourmets delight

California Fruit Cocktail Supreme
with Wedge of Fresh Lime 1.40

Iced Tangy Tomato Juice with Lemon Wedge .45

French onion soup au croutons .... .40

Alaskan King Crab Legs on Ice 1.95

Gulf Prawn Cocktail Supreme 1.50

Seafood Cocktail Supreme 1.50

Marinated Herring 1.50

Gourmets Delight
— PREPARED AT YOUR TABLE —

Caesar Salad 1.50
Crisp hearts of romaine, golden brown croutons,
anchovies and parmesan cheese, tossed at your
table with a dressing of fresh lemon juices,
olive oil, coddled egg and finished with
freshly ground pepper.

Innkeeper's Salad 1.60
Originally created in our kitchens,
prepared at your table with fresh
hearts of lettuce and romaine. Served
with a hot sweet and sour dressing
and crisp bacon chips.

Mariners Choice

BROILED AUSTRALIAN ROCK LOBSTER TAIL 7.25
A large juicy lobster tail prepared in the shell. An
enchanting seafood treat served with golden
drawn butter and lemon wedge

FOR THE UNDECIDED 7.25
An exotic treat of a moderately sized sirloin steak
plus one-half rock lobster tail. Truly a unique taste treat.

ROCKY MOUNTAIN RAINBOW TROUT 3.50
From the streams and lakes of Montana high country.
Three quarters of a pound of fighting "Bow,"
sauteed in butter, and served with a rasher of bacon.

FRESH JUMBO PRAWNS 3.25
Dipped in our own oriental batter and fried to a
golden brown. Served with Rainbow cole slaw,
tangy cocktail sauce and lemon wedges.

GRILLED FILET OF HALIBUT 2.95
Served with lemon wedge and tartar sauce

Flamed at Your Table

BUTTERFLY NEW YORK STEAK 6.25
A large choice New York steak superbly prepared
in a skillfully blended sauce, laced in flaming brandy
and served with a large baked potato

BEEF STROGANOFF 5.25
Thin strips of beef tenderloin and mushrooms,
sauteed in butter and wine and a dollop of
sour cream—added at just the right moment—
served with homemade noodles with sesame seed

MALAYAN TENDERLOIN TIPS 5.25
Choice beef tenderloin tips, skillfully braised in a mild curry sauce.
Flamed with brandy and served on a bed of fluffy white rice.

Above entrees served with soup du jour, relish trays, dinner salad, large baked potato or rice, rolls, butter and choice of beverage.

Wine
"A meal without wine is like a day without sunshine"

Champagnes

	Bottle	½ Bottle
Mumm's Extra Dry	10.50	6.65
Taylors New York	6.50	4.50

Sparkling Burgundy

Taylors New York	6.50	4.50
Christian Brothers	6.00	4.50

Red Wines

Paul Masson Burgundy	3.50	2.90
Martini Pinot Noir	4.40	3.30
Charles Krug Cabernet Sauvignon	4.35	3.25
B and G Prince Noir	4.30	3.40
B and G Beaujolais	4.85	

Chablis

Wente Pinot Blanc	3.85
Chenin Blanc Krug	3.90
Paul Masson	3.65

Rhine

Paul Masson Rhine Castle	3.90	3.00
J. Kayser, Glockenspiel	5.00	3.65
Charles Krug, Gray Riesling	4.00	3.00

Rose

Lancers Crackling Rose	6.10	4.25
Nectarose, Vin Rose d' Antou	4.50	
Masson Rose	3.65	2.95

Italian

Italian Swiss Tipo-Red	3.45	2.85

nd Chops

.... 6.50

.... 6.25

.... 6.00
tenderness

.... 4.50
from

.... 4.25

.... 3.75

Montana

RIB OF BEEF
oasted slowly
natural juices.
pular entree.
0

AN'S CUT
ra heavy
ty appetite.
0

large fresh crisp tossed salad and
otato, hot rolls and butter
beverage

FIGURE 3

The full use of a center insert is demonstrated with this menu. Fig. 1 shows the main panel at left and the Wine List. Fig. 2 shows the insert—Complete Dinner and House Specialty, and Fig. 3 shows the Dessert Menu and the right hand main panel. Note that the narrower center panel never completely covers the two large main panels so the patron is always aware of the variety of choices available.

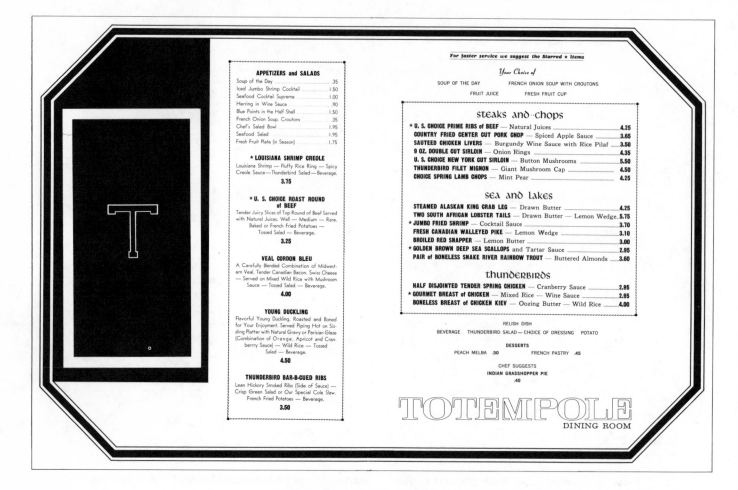

This menu has three tip-on panels. One is a Wine List, one includes Appetizers, Salads and Specials, and the third is the main Dinner menu. This is a highly flexible menu.

MENU COPY

Every menu is a written communication. Some are just a list—a bill of fare. Some list the items for sale with haphazard description. The best menus describe, romance and sell what is being served. A menu should be compared with an advertisement in a national magazine, and as much time and effort should go into the writing of a menu as a 4-color ad. In addition, the menu is an ideal place to sell your operation, its unique character and cuisine, and through this institutional sell help to create atmosphere and good publicity—the sort of publicity that makes for repeat business.

The copy in a menu can be broken down into three main categories: (1) listing of food items; (2) description and sell of food listing; and (3) institutional copy about the restaurant, its service and cuisine.

To begin with, just the listing of food is not the simple matter it would seem at first. For example, let's consider a common item such as potatoes. Is a potato, a potato, a potato, per Gertrude Stein? The following is a sample listing of potatoes taken from many menus:

Hashed Brown Potatoes
Brabant Potatoes
French Fried Potatoes
Lyonnaise Potatoes
Parsley Potatoes
Baked Idaho Potatoes
Au Gratin Potatoes
Whipped and Creamed Potatoes
Parisienne Potatoes
Escalloped Potatoes
Country Fried Potatoes
Potato du Jour
Boiled Potatoes
Mashed Potatoes
Cottage Fried Potatoes
Potato Salad

There are several observations to be made from the above list. First, the name of the food item is important. A rose by any other name may smell the same, but the name rose conjures up a definite mental picture; the same is true of the name of a food item. Every item on the bill of fare, therefore, must be named with care and exactness. Second, the name of a food item is not an exact scientific label. From the above list of potatoes, for example, how many people could describe exactly what they would get if they ordered Brabant Potatoes or Parisienne Potatoes? A short survey in your own dining room could show more than one word on your menu that the general public does not understand. How many customers know that au jus means served in gravy or juice of the meat? Or how many people know that lyonnaise means cooked with flaked or sliced fried onions?

For a chef, or an experienced restaurateur, all the above terms are well known, but unless the customer has been educated to all the foreign, uncommon words, he needs help. The alternative is a Berlitz blitz course in all foreign words used in menus as part of the American Language!

The next consideration, therefore, is the descriptive copy covering the individual menu item. This can be simple or elaborate, but, in any case, it usually adds interest and sales value to a menu. For example, bread and butter can be described better as "Oven Fresh Rolls and Creamery Butter." This is a short but mouth watering description. Some other descriptions that add to the menu mental picture are as follows:

"TENDER THICK PORK CHOPS" . . . cut from the loins of finest native pork and broiled to perfection. A unique experience that will long be remembered."

"DANISH BROOK TROUT . . . from cold Scandinavian waters by way of the gentle savory heat of the hearth coals . . . to you . . . truly the perfect fish. Served with lemon butter."

"OYSTERS AND BACON EN BROCHETTE . . . ten of the most delicious, salty, fresh Gulf Oysters we can find, skewered with bacon, brushed with butter and broiled. Served with crisp brabant potatoes, baked tomato and mushroom."

"BONELESS FRIED CHICKEN . . . TRANSOCEAN AIRLINES. Something to remember Hawaii by. Tender halves of chicken in which all the bones have been carefully replaced with pineapple sticks, then dipped in fresh coconut cream and rolled in grated coconut. Baked to a golden crunchy brown and sauced with coconut cream giblet gravy. Served with baked banana."

From the above appetizing adjectives, dripping with flavor and taste, it's easy to see that a few extra, well chosen words are in order.

The meal does not have to be described in a list-description manner, however, as shown by the following description (on the menu, not in a travel brochure) of a breakfast (served until midnight) at Brennan's French Restaurant in New Orleans.

"A TRADITIONAL BRENNAN BREAKFAST
    This is the way it was done in leisured antebellum days; first an absinthe Suissesse to get the eyes open, then a fresh Creole cream cheese. Now an egg Benedict, followed by a hearty sirloin with fresh mushrooms. Hot French bread and marmalade, and a chilled Rose wine. For the finale, crepes Suzette, cafe au lait, and a Cognac snifter. Important:

DON'T HURRY!"

If the above doesn't start a "Better Breakfast" trend in America, words have lost their power to fire the imagination.

It's not just food, though, that warrants a good word. If you have a Wine Cellar worth a Wine List, a bit of descriptive copy such as the following from The Old Mill Wine List is appropriate:

"Wine is wholesome food which stimulates digestion, makes fine foods taste better, and lends an air of festivity and congeniality at the dinner table; it's natural, therefore, that the enjoyment of a bottle of wine with dinner is fast becoming an American tradition."

And here is a listing from Canlis' Charcoal Broiler Restaurant:

"FRESH SALMON STEAK . . . Volumes and volumes of words have been written about salmon. You've had it a la this and a la that. All we can say is praise be to Allah for bringing this fish to us. We just charcoal broil it."

The third broad copy category covering menu writing is institutional copy. Just as a company has a "Corporate Image", which is the total picture the public has about it, so a food service operation has a public image. And the menu is one of the best places to build the image. The approach varies with every establishment because each has its special feature, character, service or history which makes for interesting copy material.

The El Rancho restaurant builds its institutional approach around a local industry, a glassware company. The glassware is used in the restaurant and sold to the public. This copy, therefore, serves two purposes. It adds local color to the restaurant and it merchandises and sells the glassware. Tie-ins with local industries are a natural for a certain type of restaurant.

Henrici's restaurant in Chicago uses, for their point of departure on institutional copy, the historical approach. The restaurant was established in 1868; so in copy and illustration, they sketch some of the great historical events of the last 100 years, such as the Chicago Fire of 1871 and the Columbian Exposition; the history of a great city adds to the fame of Henrici's restaurant.

The decor of a restaurant can have publicity value. The Pontchartrain Hotel, New Orleans, as an instance, has a series of Murals (The Marfield Murals), that they describe in the first page of their menu. Special decorations, paintings, sculpture and other objets d'art can very appropriately be referred to in a menu.

The Ranch Kitchen in Gallup, New Mexico, features a short history of Gallup and the surrounding country. Then they give a thumbnail sketch of the Navajo, Zuni and Hopi Indian tribes of New Mexico. They describe the silver work, turquoise jewelry and rugs of the Navajo weavers, which they just happen to have for sale!

Kolb's restaurant in New Orleans has a new approach in restaurant merchandising through the menu. They have taken a magazine article from Down South Magazine and reprinted the entire article (with photos) on the inside front and back covers of the menu. On the cover of the menu they describe the four dining rooms of the restaurant. This makes the menu a complete merchandising piece which can be used as a give-away or mailing brochure.

A more common copy approach which can be used by almost every restaurant is to feature and romance the specialty of the house. Al Farber's restaurant in Chicago, for example, calls their introductory copy "MUCH ADO ABOUT STEAK" with such phrases as "discriminating epicureans—prepared to delight the palate of all—the eye of the beef is an 'eye opener' and a taste sensation." Any specialty of the house worth its salt is worth some special "hard sell" copy to establish authentic character for the operation.

A location which is out of the way can be used as an asset to hang your sales message to. The White Turkey and the Red Barn restaurants in Connecticut use their country location to advantage in their menu institutional promotion. The copy begins . . . "If You Love the Country . . . But Live in the City . . . '' and leads into the pleasures of a trip into the New England countryside which ends at one of these restaurants for a relaxing, pleasant and gracious meal, with appetites keener and more appreciative because of the ride. This approach is really creative meal merchandising.

Another institutional approach is the "Our Philosophy—Our Creed—The Tradition of This Restaurant" approach. This type of "Cafe Editorial" is a good general method of presenting the restaurateur as a serious student of the customer's gastronomic needs. Vic's Tally Ho restaurant in Des Moines, Iowa, begins their story along this line with . . . "You're on the board of directors . . . '' From this they lead into a description of the goals and ideals of the restaurant.

From the above mentioned and the reprinted examples of institutional copy, it can be seen that there is a great variety in points of departure for merchandising and publicizing the particular quality, flavor or specialty of almost any restaurant.

As for the actual writing of menu copy, the putting together of words, phrases and apt expressions, the best advice for a food service operator (unless he is a writer himself) is to secure the use of professional talent, usually through his advertising agency, or the services of a free lance writer. The writing of a menu is too important to be left to an amateur.

This is original, creative copy all the way through from beginning to end—from appetizers to desserts.

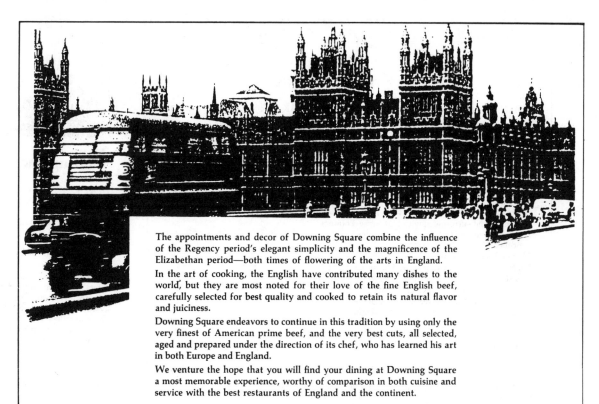

The appointments and decor of Downing Square combine the influence of the Regency period's elegant simplicity and the magnificence of the Elizabethan period—both times of flowering of the arts in England.

In the art of cooking, the English have contributed many dishes to the world, but they are most noted for their love of the fine English beef, carefully selected for best quality and cooked to retain its natural flavor and juiciness.

Downing Square endeavors to continue in this tradition by using only the very finest of American prime beef, and the very best cuts, all selected, aged and prepared under the direction of its chef, who has learned his art in both Europe and England.

We venture the hope that you will find your dining at Downing Square a most memorable experience, worthy of comparison in both cuisine and service with the best restaurants of England and the continent.

Donald R. Bergman
Prime Minister

Inside front cover.

Opening menu page.

The shadow of Big Ben falls on the heart of royal and aristocratic London—Westminster Abbey, Charing Cross, Parliament Square and Downing Street.

Downing Square was inspired by the traditions and atmosphere of this part of London, as well as the recollection of an era when the great Escoffier reigned supreme as maitre chef at the Savoy and British chefs were the best in the world.

Introduction of Business

Marinated Herring in Cream w. Onion . . 1.25
Shrimp, Scampi, ... 2.75
Blue Point Oyster Cocktail (in season) . . 1.95
Jumbo Shrimp Cocktail 2.50
Lobster Cocktail 2.75
Littleneck or Cherrystone Clams 1.50
Crablump Cocktail 2.95
English Potted Shrimp, Maison 1.95
Seafood Cocktail Supreme 2.95
Smoked Nova Scotia Salmon 1.95
Portuguese Boneless Sardines 1.50
Baked Clams Casino or
    Oysters Casino (in season) 2.75
Hot Shrimp Balls, Sauce Remoulade 1.75
Chopped Chicken Livers,
    w. Bermuda Onion 95
Grapefruit Supreme 85
Melon in Season 1.00
Chilled Tomato, Clam or V-8 Juice 60
Fresh Fruit Cocktail 1.00

What Precedes Debate

Onion Soup au Gratin 85
Chicken Consomme w. Fine Noodles
    and Matzoh Ball 75
Soup du Jour 75

Center spread, Downing Square menu.

Main or Principle Motions

DOWNING SQUARE PRIME BONELESS SIRLOIN STEAK 7.95

The usually unflappable British can get very excited about their beef. Portly Henry VIII, who knew a good piece of beef when he tasted it, was so delighted with a particularly appetizing one that he drew his sword and knighted it on the spot. Ever since, that cut has been known as Sir Loin. Our Boneless Sirloin Steak is true heir to the title.
Just the very best prime quality beef, aged to develop the flavor fully in our own aging box.

Jr. Prime Sirloin Minute Steak	6.95
Filet Mignon, with Mushroom Cap	7.95
Double Prime Sirloin Steak (for two)	15.75
planked and surrounded with Dutchesse Potatoes and Bouquet of Fresh Garden Vegetables, Broiled Mushrooms Cresson	16.95
Chopped Sirloin Steak	4.95
Chateaubriand, Sauce Béarnaise, Mushroom Caps (for two)	15.75
with a Bouquet of Fresh Vegetables & Duchesse Potatoes	16.95

DOWNING SQUARE ENGLISH MIXED GRILL 6.95
(Lamb Chop, Calf's Liver, Chopped Steak, Bacon Strip, Filet Mignon & Grilled Tomato)

Jersey Pork Chops, Apple Sauce	5.50
Calf's Liver, Saute or Broiled, Bacon or Onions	5.95
Two (2) Broiled Triple Rib Lamb Chops (25 minutes)	6.95

DOWNING SQUARE THICK MUTTON CHOP WITH KIDNEY 7.00

The English are pretty particular about their mutton too. Charles II earned the epithet "The Mutton Eating King," and Shakespeare's Falstaff gorged upon a succulent joint of mutton. Downing Square's magnificent mutton chop is skewered around a kidney and broiled just to perfection.

DOWNING SQUARE FILET MIGNON EN BROCHETTE, Wild Rice	6.75
Broiled Half Spring Chicken, Grilled Tomato, Spiced Apple Ring	4.75
Steak Tartar, Garni	6.95

Putting the Q[...]

HEAVY CUT ROAST PRI[...] OF BEEF, AU JUS . . . . .

DOWNING SQUARE ENGLISH CUT . . . . both with Yorkshire Pudd[...] Baked Potato, Caesar or M[...] Green Salad

The English are colloquially [...] eaters" . . . with good reas[...] rather stuffy about insisting [...] quality beef, such as our Ro[...] The name Beefeaters origina[...] the beruffled Yeomen of th[...] still stand watch at the Tow[...] Way back in the 17th centu[...] obstinately insisted on their [...] stone of beef a day" prefera[...] here, in its own succulent jui[...]

BONELESS CHICKEN PA[...] Potato, and Caesar or Mi[...] Green Salad . . . .

Braised Brisket of Beef, Pot[...] Pancake, Apple Sauce & V[...] Caesar or Mixed Green Sa[...]

Final pages (see foldout p. 50).

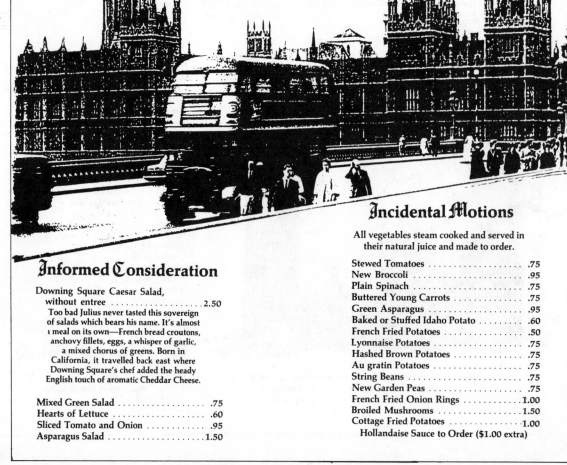

Informed Consideration

Downing Square Caesar Salad, without entree 2.50
Too bad Julius never tasted this sovereign of salads which bears his name. It's almost a meal on its own—French bread croutons, anchovy fillets, eggs, a whisper of garlic, a mixed chorus of greens. Born in California, it travelled back east where Downing Square's chef added the heady English touch of aromatic Cheddar Cheese.

Mixed Green Salad	.75
Hearts of Lettuce	.60
Sliced Tomato and Onion	.95
Asparagus Salad	1.50

Incidental Motions

All vegetables steam cooked and served in their natural juice and made to order.

Stewed Tomatoes	.75
New Broccoli	.95
Plain Spinach	.75
Buttered Young Carrots	.75
Green Asparagus	.95
Baked or Stuffed Idaho Potato	.60
French Fried Potatoes	.50
Lyonnaise Potatoes	.75
Hashed Brown Potatoes	.75
Au gratin Potatoes	.75
String Beans	.75
New Garden Peas	.75
French Fried Onion Rings	1.00
Broiled Mushrooms	1.50
Cottage Fried Potatoes	1.00
Hollandaise Sauce to Order ($1.00 extra)	

Rules of Order

All entrees served with Downing Square Caesar Salad or Tossed green salad, (Choice of dressing) and choice of either baked potato, baked stuffed potato, or french fried Idaho potato.

Announcing the Vote

MEDALLION OF VEAL CORDON
  BLEU 6.25
  The Medallion is the very finest cut of veal, taken from the fillet. Our chef, a very fussy fellow, insists on this sort of thing. . . . He prepares it a la cordon bleu with cheese and a spicy Italian ham called prosciutto sealed between two slices of veal. Samuel Pepys, 17th century English diarist, was equally vain about his veal, noting in his diary that he served it to his guests along with "a dozen larks" at "a pretty dinner, most neatly dressed by our own, only maybe."

Boiled Beef, in Pot with Noodles,
  Matzoh Ball & Vegetables 5.50
Boiled Spring Chicken in Pot with
  Noodles, Matzoh Ball & Vegetables . . 5.25
Veal Cutlet Parmigiana 5.50
Schnitzel Holstein, Garni 5.50

ROAST STUFFED ROCK CORNISH HEN
  Wild Rice & Montmorency Sauce 5.95

Miscellaneous

Fresh Seafood Downing Square with
  Lobster, Shrimp, Crabmeat 5.50
Special Chef's Salad Bowl 4.75
Shrimp or Lobster or Crabmeat Salad . . .4.75
Assorted Cold Cuts, Potato Salad,
  Sliced Tomatoes 4.75

uestion

..ME RIB
. . . . 6.95

. . . . 5.75
..ing,
..lixed

..called "Beef-
..on. They are
..on the highest
..ast Prime Rib.
..lly applied to
..e Guard who
..er of London.
..ry the guards
..ration of "six
..bly served, as
..ces.

..RMIGIANA
..ked
. . . . 5.25

..a?o
..egetable,
..ad 5.50

Subsiding Motions

ENGLISH DOVER SOLE, Broiled or
  Saute Meuniere or Amandines 5.95
  Incomparable Dover Sole has been called the wonder of the fish world. The sole served at Downing Square is snatched from British waters and cooked à la meunière or broiled or Amandines, seasoned, and served with a delicate butter sauce—to reveal the natural flavor at its best.

Broiled Swordfish Steak, Lemon Butter . .4.95
Broiled Scampi, Downing Square Sauce . .5.50
Broiled Digby Bay Scallops 5.50
King Crabmeat Saute, Rice and Peas 5.25

BROOK TROUT SAUTE,
  AMANDINES or BROILED 5.75

Broiled Salmon Steak, Maitre D'Hotel . .4.95
Broiled Filet of Sole 4.75
Lobster a la Newburgh 6.25
Shrimp a la Newburgh 5.95
BROILED STUFFED LOBSTER TAILS,
  WILD RICE, PEA PODS 6.95
BROILED LIVE LARGE MAINE
  LOBSTER 7.95
Stuffed with Shrimp or Crabmeat 1.75 extra

Nominations to Close

Coffee (Pot) 50
Milk 40
Tea (Pot) 50
Espresso 75
Buttermilk 40
Irish Coffee .1.50

Reconsider

Special Downing Square Creamy
  Cheese Cake 1.00
Melon in Season 1.00
Rice Pudding Chantilly 90
Frozen Ice Cream Cake Melba 1.10
Downing Square Chocolate Rigo Cake . .1.25
Nesselrode Pie 1.00
Home Made Apple Pie 85
Coup au Marons 90
Imported Cheese with Toasted Crackers . .85
Snow Ball, Kahlua 1.25
French Ice Cream 75
Peach Melba .95
Jello with Whipped Cream 85
Jumbo Peaches 85
Fruit Compote 85
Assorted Sherbet 65
Coup St. Jacques 90
Fresh Strawberries with Whipped Cream 1.50
French Pastry 1.00
Fresh Fruit Pies 75
Bisquit Tortoni 65
Spumoni 75
Macedoine of Fresh Fruit 1.25

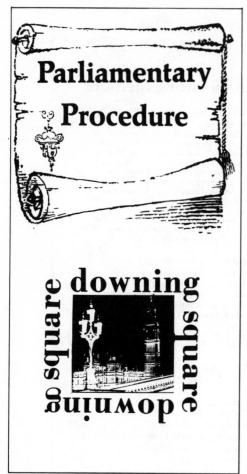

Theme is carried through to flap on inside of back cover of Downing's menu; for other details of this menu see pp. 46-49.

Mammy knows how to cook and write.

★
MAMMY'S FAMOUS FRIED CHICKEN
Half Fried Disjointed, Delicious, Delectable Milk Fed Chicken,
cooked a golden brown with oodles of French Fried Potatoes,
Vegetable Salad and Home Made Rolls—ummm
$2.30
★
FRIED JUMBO SHRIMP IN SHORT PANTS
From the clear, blue Atlantic, come our especially Selected
Jumbo Shrimp, Batter Dipped and Fried in deep fat,
Cocktail Sauce, Cole Slaw, and never-to-be-forgotten
Mammy's Hush Puppie
Coffee or Tea
$2.35
★
FRIED OCEAN-FRESH OYSTERS
Rolled in cracker crumbs and fried all succulent and brown
created for hungry landlubbers with a sea going air,
Cole Slaw, Cocktail Sauce, French Fried Potatoes,
and Hush Puppie!
Coffee or Tea
$2.35
★
FRIED FRESH DEEP SEA SCALLOPS
A treat to the palate that sends taste buds soaring! Cole Slaw,
Cocktail Sauce, French Fried Potatoes, and Hush Puppie
Coffee or Tea
$2.25
★
FRIED RED SNAPPER STEAK a la MAMMY'S
Caught not too many miles off Daytona at the World's Famous
Snapper Banks in the deep Atlantic, served with Cole Slaw,
Cocktail Sauce, French Fried Potatoes and
Hush Puppie as only we serve them!
Coffee or Tea
$2.95
★
MAMMY'S SEA FOOD PLATTER
For all those who can't make up their minds about our Famous
Sea Foods, Fried Jumbo Shrimp, Fried Oysters, Fried Sea Trout,
Fried Scallops, French Fried Potatoes and add a
Hush Puppie for a true fisherman
Coffee or Tea
$2.60
★
STUFFED TOMATO WITH SHRIMP SALAD
Stuffed Tomato with Shrimp Salad, Hard Boiled Eggs,
Potato Chips, Pickles, Saltines
Coffee or Tea
$1.60
★
ICED SHRIMP
Truly a Shrimp Connoisseur's Delight, Tomatoes, Lettuce,
Pickles and Sea Food Sauce, Saltines
Coffee or Tea
$1.60

DINNERS

Crisp Romaine Salad with choice of dressing (Roquefort, French, 1000 Island, Vinegar and Oil) Baked Potato with Sour Cream, Butter, Cheese and Chives (French Fries Optional). Garlic Cheese Toast   Coffee or Tea

Extra Portion of Dressing .25 Additional

S2S2S2S2S2S 2S 2S 2S 2S2S2S2S2S2S2S2S2S2S2S2S2S2S 2S 2S 2S 2S 2S 2S 2S

SAS-KA-BOB, Sirloin of Beef en Brochett $3.50

Charbroiled on a skewer to suit your taste. After this Webster will delete the word Shish-ka-bob.

S2S2S2S2S2S 2S 2S 2S 2S2S2S2S2S2S2S2S2S2S2S2S2S2S 2S 2S 2S 2S 2S 2S 2S

PRINCE OF DESCANSO, Jumbo Deluxe Top Sirloin $5.95

For he man appetites and discriminating tastes.

MR. BIG TOP, Deluxe Top Sirloin $4.25

Using only prime beef. A mouth watering taste.

CHOICE FILET, Prime Eastern Beef $4.75

A taste will tell you this was worth coming for, but you still must leave by 4 A.M. (see you again tomorrow).

NEW YORK CUT, A national favorite....................$4.75

One taste and you will say more, more, more and it will be there, a generous portion.

GROUND SIRLOIN, Fresh ground to order $2.25

Our chef will not divulge the secret of such succulent flavor, please do not ask him. Only one to a customer, please.

STEAK AND LOBSTER COMBINATION $3.95

Variety is the spice of life: This succulent combination will add spice enough to make this an unforgettable banquet.

BROILED LOBSTER, Salt water delicacy....................$3.50

Only freshly netted lobster plus meticulous preparation could guarantee this taste tingling delight.

BROILED LAMB CHOPS $2.95

Fresh from the Montana Buttes, if you're undecided try these. Your appetite will be delightfully appeased.

BROILED PORK CHOPS, Corn fed stock....................$2.75

How long since you've had a dinner down on the farm? This Saska specialty will help you relive those delightful, if all but forgotten memories.

FRENCH FRIED JUMBO SHRIMP $1.90

Creole Babies, Darkies on the wharf, Absinthe House. This delicacy will whisk you to New Orleans in fantasy and flavor. Try it!

PAN FRIED CHICKEN (one half chicken) $2.25

When you are being served this Southern delight, close your eyes and listen; You may hear the faint strains of a Stephen Foster melody drifting up from the Swanee River.

S2S2S2S2S2S 2S 2S 2S 2S2S2S2S2S2S2S2S2S2S2S2S2S2S 2S 2S 2S 2S 2S 2S 2S

SASKA SPECIAL STEAK, Using Prime Top Sirloin only $3.50

Cooked to a turn, using Saska's original method. After trying this gourmet's delight you will spell steak as follows: S-A-S-K-A.

S2S2S2S2S2S 2S 2S 2S 2S2S2S2S2S2S2S2S2S2S2S2S2S2S 2S 2S 2S 2S 2S 2S 2S

Good, straightforward, informative copy.

OLE!

You'll shout "Ole!" when you first taste this treasure of Early California. Tender chunks of Choice Lamb, Tiny Onions, fresh California Peppers, red Garden Tomatoes and broiled Mountain Mushrooms—all skewered on a sword. Charbroiled to your taste, served over Rice Pilaf with a Crisp Green Salad.

4.25

EL PESCADOR

Large succulent Gulf Shrimp deep fried to a Golden Brown served with **TIA MARIA** special Sauce. French Fries and a Crisp Green Salad.

2.95

EL TORITO

Chopped Tenderloin of Beef. Served with French Fries and a Crisp Green Salad.

3.25

SENOR TORO

Originally known in Early California as the "Trail-steak" and now famous as the "New York Cut." Subtly seasoned with Spicy Black Peppercorns and lightly brushed with Golden Butter. Charbroiled to your taste over the **TIA MARIA** hearth. Served with French Fries and a Crisp Green Salad.

5.95

Featuring Spanish or English cuisine, the right words help to sell.

Literary Delights $1.35

freshly ground beef with a variety of trimmings and potatoes — choose your favorite

CHARLES DICKENS—*bacon, tomato and onion make this our favorite; served on an English muffin*

WILLIAM WORDSWORTH—*melted tangy cheese and mushrooms top this specialty*

OLIVER GOLDSMITH—*a plain and juicy burger cooked to perfection; served on a homemade bun—your choice of a bleu or Swiss cheese topping if you desire.*

ROBERT BURNS—*a delightful caper for those young at heart; green pepper, onion and a special sauce with capers*

Fried Chestnut Shrimp
3.50

When first we rubbed our magic lamp and our Geni came up with our Baked Garlic Shrimp, nearly every good restaurant tried to copy its tantalizing taste (it's still one of our best sellers). But NOW . . . after a new appearance of our Geni, we take five of the Biggest, Most Colossal Shrimp ever spawned in old Neptune's Kingdom and married them to the spices of the ages, fry them a Chestnut brown in butter and broil a whole Tomato to add zest. And NOW . . . and NOW . . . to make every gourmet drool like Niagara, we make a mess of Fried Rice-India Chutney for the palate's sake, Assorted hot breads, Coffee or Tea. Confucius say . . . "Ah me!"

Famous Lobster Platter
4.75

People are sometimes called 'Lobsters', and in most cases, my sympathy would be with us tired, old people.

But, 'Ole Man Lobster', free from worry, just lazies around all day, in the azure sunlit waters, off the incomparable keys, just getting fat to grace, (who's Grace?) your Succulent Lobster Platter at Creighton's . . . and 'Sir' Lobster to you, Pal . . . You get it three ways . . . Broiled Lobster, Lobster in rich Cheese Sauce, and Tropical Lobster Salad, with Piquant Dressing. A frying pan of French Fried Potatoes . . . Deviled Eggs, Pickles, and Lettuce and Tomatoes.

But Wait !!! That ain't all . . . Assorted hot breads, Coffee or Tea.

Baked Shrimp
3.50

With Garlic Butter Sauce in a Covered Casserole a la Creighton's

Giant Shrimp or Prawns selected from all the big catches of our Great Gulf Fleet of Mexico. Pure creamy butter combined with Aromatic Garlic Slices and served hot in a covered Casserole. Tossed Green Salad, Cottage Fried Potatoes au Gratin with Bleu Cheese, Assorted hot breads and more Butter, Tea or Coffee.

This Gourmet's Gustatory Treat would make Old Mussolini (The Shrimp) rise from his grave!

Who's a Lira ? ? ?

ROAST MILK FED TURKEY WITH DRESSING . . . .

This is our best selling Dinner. And there is a reason! The tender lean meat is delicious because the birds are fed on milk and grain, which is bound to produce the finest turkey meat. And our Tuskegee Chefs roast each bird to perfection. The dressing is a recipe of our Grandmother which was good then and even better today. Now it is Turkey Dinner **EVERYDAY!**

O'BRIEN'S FAMOUS FRESH PORK (LEAN) SAUSAGE . . . .

Served with Corn Fritter and Maple Syrup. This is the Sausage that won two First Prizes in New York City. Made from young pigs not weighing over 180 lbs. Made with Hams and Shoulders so it has to be lean. Deliciously mild seasoned.

BROILED PORK CHOPS . . . .

With modern refrigeration Pork is wonderful the year aound. Like with the Sausage these Pork Chops are on the Lean side. Well done to a golden brown under the Broiler, yet full of tasty juice which is bound to tickle the taste-buds.

CHICKEN SHORTCAKE
Natchez
$1.65

When crinoline and hoop skirts were in vogue and Jean LeFitte was pirateering around New Orleans, it wasn't gold he was looking for. No suh, he was looking for a Natchez Negro Mammy who could make Chicken Shortcake. This old recipe has been handed down as it was in the Good Old Days. Succulent young chicken cooked in its own juices in a black iron pot until tender. Mushrooms and seasoning added, then placed between hot egg bread slices (eggs, shortening, and water-ground meal) for your ultimate eating delight. Served with shoestring potatoes cooked for this order (not when LaFitte helped save New Orleans).

Our own chef's salad, coffee or tea, and Mammy's Famous Apple Pie simply drenched with whipped cream.

No wonder LaFitte fit!

FAMOUS LOBSTER PLATTER
$4.25

People are sometimes called 'Lobsters,' and in most cases, my sympathy would be with us tired, old people.

But 'Ole Man Lobster,' free from worry, just lazies around all day, in the azure sunlit waters, off the incomparable keys, just getting fat to grace your succulent lobster platter . . . and 'Sir' Lobster to you, Pal . . . You get it three ways . . . Buttered Lobster, Lobster in rich cheese sauce, and tropical lobster salad, with French dressing. A frying pan of French Fried Potatoes . . . deviled eggs, pickles, lettuce and tomatoes.

But Wait!! That ain't all . . . Hot rolls, Coffee or Tea, and to top off 'The World's Best Meal,' a slice of 'Mammy's Apple Pie.' Can I say more ? ? ? ? ?

BAKED SHRIMP
$2.50

With Garlic Butter Sauce in a Covered Casserole a la Mammy's Shanty

Giant Shrimp or Prawns selected from all the big catches of our Great Gulf Fleet of Mexico. Pure creamery butter combined with Aromatic Garlic Spices and served hot in a covered Casserole. Tossed green salad, cottage fried potatoes au gratin with Blue Cheese, Hot Rolls and more butter, Tea or Coffee.

This Gourmet's Gustatory Treat would make Old Mussolini (The Shrimp) rise from his grave!

Who's a Lira ? ? ?

Recommended by The Management

A lot of good words about a lot of good food.

TYPE SELECTION FOR A MORE READABLE, ATTRACTIVE MENU

A study of the correct type face is vital to creating a more readable and more attractive restaurant menu. The obvious purpose of a restaurant menu is to communicate the food items served and their price to the customer; this must be done in words that must be set in type, if not lettered by hand.

It may seem to some that a study of type is a small detail in the operation of a restaurant, but since there is very little verbal communication between the server and the served, as well as a general reluctance to ask questions, written communication becomes very important. Also, a study of thousands of menus has shown many where the type was too small for easy reading, set too close together (which creates confusion and obstructs readability) and where listings of dinners, appetizers, salads, sandwiches, desserts and beverages were jammed together in such an illogical manner as to make selection a job instead of a pleasure.

Type comes in many faces. Your printer will have a type book from which a selection can, and should be made. The basic varieties of type which we will discuss here are Roman, Modern and Script.

The Roman type faces are the older types which are patterned after Roman inscriptions carved on statues. They are a thick and thin type with much grace and beauty and are extremely readable. Most books, magazines and newspapers are set in some version of Roman style type face such as Bodoni, Garamond, Caslon, Century Schoolbook and other variations.

Modern type faces are newer faces which do not have the thick-thin character of Roman face types. They are cleaner looking without serifs, more regular in shape and, therefore, more modern looking. A comparison between Modern type faces and Roman type faces might be made by comparing the United Nations building (Modern) and the Capitol building in Washington, D. C. Some Modern type faces are Futura, 20th Century, Spartan and Venus.

Script type faces are generally an imitation of handwriting or lettering. The free flow of the hand is achieved to a certain extent in these type faces. Generally speaking, script type faces should be used for headings and subheads. A continued use of script type becomes hard to read, but an occasional use adds variety and beauty to a menu. Some script faces are Commercial Script, Lydian Cursive and Brush.

Within the many type faces there are two sub-divisions. Almost all type comes in upper and lower case. Upper case are the capitals (A, B, C, D, E). Lower case are lower case letters (a, b, c, d, e, f). The important rule for the menu builder to remember is that it is easier to read lower case type than upper case. The reason is the irregular appearance that the line of lower case type presents. This catches the eye as it moves swiftly along in the process of reading.

Proof of the easier readability of lower case type is the fact that the body copy of books, magazines and newspapers is always set in lower case type. This does not mean that upper case capitals do not have their use. For headings, subheads and special emphasis, upper case is most effective. It provides a change of pace from the lower case type and estab-

SOLID

The main purpose of letters is the practical one of making thoughts visible. RUSKIN says that "al l letters are frightful things, and to be endured o nly upon occasion, that is to say, in places wher *The main purpose of letters is the practical one of making thoughts visible. Ruskin says that "all* THE MAIN PURPOSE OF LETTERS IS THE PRACTICAL O THE MAIN PURPOSE OF LETTERS IS TH

Type set solid—no leading.

3 PT. LEADED

The main purpose of letters is the practical one of making thoughts visible. RUSKIN says that "al l letters are frightful things, and to be endured o nly upon occasion, that is to say, in places wher e the sense of the inscription is of more importa *The main purpose of letters is the practical one of making thoughts visible. Ruskin says that "all*

Same type set with 3 points of leading.

BODONI REGULAR

36 POINT

ABCDEFGHI
abcdefghijklm

Caps and Lower case

BODONI REGULAR ITALIC

36 POINT

ABCDEFGHI
abcdefghijklm

Caps and Lower case

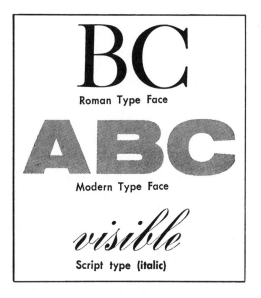

BC
Roman Type Face

ABC
Modern Type Face

visible
Script type (italic)

lishes categories and breaks in the menu listing which should generally be in lower case type face.   In addition to lower and upper case, most type faces have an italic variation. This simply means that, while the regular type face is designed straight up and down, the italic variation is designed on a slant or angle. The italic type face should be used only for accent or special emphasis. It should never be used in large doses because it becomes tiring to the eye and hard to read.

Next, we must consider type sizes. Type is measured by points. Starting usually with 6 pt., the size of a particular face will increase in size from 6 pt. on through 8, 10, 12, 14, 16, 18, 24, 48 and 72 points. The important consideration for the restaurateur building a menu is never to set any part of his menu in type smaller than 12 pt. (The type face of this article is 11 pt.) Remember that your menu is going to be read by members of the general public who have a great variation in their seeing ability. Generally, older people have trouble reading small type. Also, the person who wears glasses for reading only is reluctant to take out his glasses when in a public place such as a restaurant. So, if you want to be considerate of all of your customers, set your menu in large, easy to read type.

The next consideration in the typesetting of your menu is the space between lines or, as it is called in the printing trade, leading. Leading, like type, is measured in points. Type set without any leading between lines is set solid. As a rule of thumb for menu typesetting, 3 points of leading should be the minimum between lines. This gives air or white space around the type so that it is readable and easy on the eye.

In the discussion so far of type for menus, the emphasis has been upon readability, and this is as it should be. Communication is the primary purpose of a menu and any other considerations, such as design, character or color, while they are important, are secondary to the basic consideration of smooth, easy communication of the message.

Of secondary consideration, however, when selecting type for a menu, should be the style or character of the type. To begin with, you have to consider the character of your restaurant.   This should determine the character and appearance of your menu and the styles of type you use. If your restaurant is of modern design--concrete, lots of glass, clean simple lines and decor--then the type for your menu should be modern, set in a clean simple manner to compliment your decor.

If your restaurant has a different character--Old English, Rathskeller, Chinese, Italian, Greek--a type face should then be considered which will match the character and cuisine. As a rule, with the wide selection of types available, one can be found that will enhance your bill of fare. A word of warning, however; strange, exotic and unusual types are usually more difficult to read, and, therefore, should be used sparingly. Just as seasoning is used to add flavor to food, unusual type is used to add flavor to a menu. But, as you well know, seasoning must be used with care.

Typesetters, when discussing type faces, will refer to "color" even when they are talking about black type on white paper. What they are referring to is the weight, lightness, grayness or open or closed character of the type. Some type is heavy, thick or very black due to bold design, while other type is open, light and airy in character. Selecting type for its character is important for your restaurant menu. If your type is all bold and heavy (shouting in a loud voice) while your restaurant is a quiet, elegant place that caters to the "carriage trade," the result will be a sour note.

Type should usually be printed black or white on light tinted paper (cream, tan, ivory, gray, etc.), but type may be printed in colored ink on white or colored paper. If your type is printed in green, blue or brown, for example, be sure it is a very dark green, blue or brown. The rule, again, is readability. Copy printed in a light color on a grey or dark paper will be hard to read. Section headings such as "Sandwiches, Salads, Appetizers, Beverages, Complete Dinners", can very often be printed in a second color from the general black or dark-colored type. As a rule, reverse type (white type on black background) should be avoided.

This discussion on type is, of course, elementary. It is not intended to make the reader a type expert, but it is intended to help the restaurateur to be aware of the type problems in menu design. For functional, effective menu type design, the services of an expert designer and printer should be employed, especially a printer with an adequate type selection.

---

*Petit Tenderloin Steak . . . 6.75   6.00

A smaller cut of Filet Mignon broiled and served with mushroom cap.

#22 St. Emilion—$3.50   Paul Masson Gamay Beaujolais—$2.75

*Heavy Steer Sirloin Steak . . 7.75   7.00

Beautifully grained heavy cut sirloin trimmed to perfection broiled with buttered herb sauce.

#27 Pommard-Épenots—$7.00   Almaden Pinot Noir—$3.00

*Delmonico Steak 6.75   6.00

An excellent cut of eye of the rib with its own distinct flavor.

#23 Haut Medoc—$3.25   Paul Masson Burgundy—$2.50

*Chopped Sirloin Steak . . . 4.50   3.75

A large patty of beef ground from our choice cuts, served with butter.

#26 Beaujolais—$3.00   Paul Masson Gamay Beaujolais—$2.75

*Broiled Spring Chicken . . . 4.00   3.40

One half young broiler rubbed with butter and broiled to a golden brown served with currant jelly.

#12 Soave Bolla—$3.00   Paul Masson Emerald Dry—$2.50

Breaded Veal Cutlet, Parmesan . 4.75   4.00

A delightfully breaded cutlet fried in butter covered with rich tomato sauce, Parmesan cheese and served in an au gratin dish.

#30 Valpolicella Bolla—$3.00   Almaden Chianti—$2.25

*Broiled Double Lamb Chops . 6.95   6.25

Two thick chops cut from young lamb and served with mint jelly.

#24 St. Julien—$3.75   Almaden Cabernet Sauvignon—$2.75

The old-looking antique type in a nice variation of light and bold fits in with the style, decor and cuisine of this Colonial style eatery.

To recapitulate, the following are some general rules to follow in selecting type for an effective menu:

1. Do not set type less than 12 pt.
2. Use lower case type for most of the menu listing for readability.
3. Use upper case type for heads and sub-heads.
4. Have at least 3 pts. leading between lines.
5. Select type faces which match the character of your restaurant.
6. Use strange, exotic faces sparingly.
7. If type is in color, be sure it is a dark color.
8. Avoid reverse type.

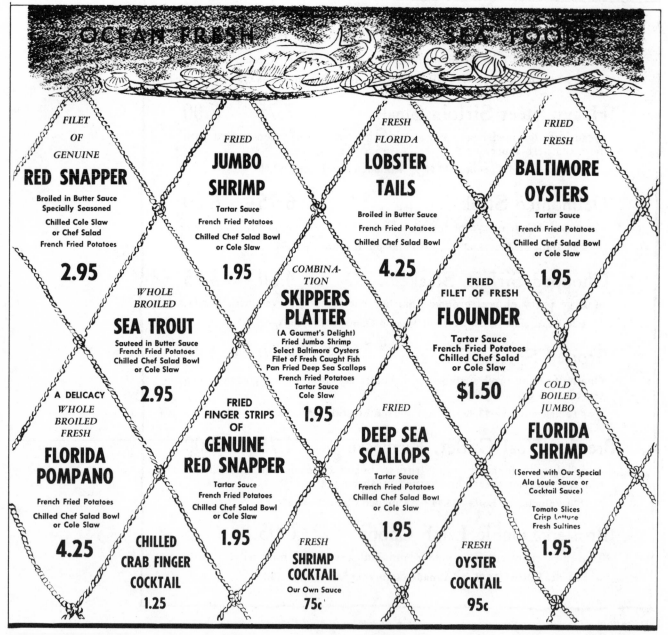

Unusual "special" type listing with appropriate graphics lift the seafood selection out of the ordinary and make it a faster moving entree.

THE UPSTAIRS ROOM

To Begin...

May We Suggest a Cocktail
From Our Rolling Cart

Glass of Wine .70   Imported Beer .75

FROM THE IRON KETTLE

French Onion Soup .60   Soup du Jour .50

OUR LUNCHEON FEATURES

Your Choice — Hot Dishes

3.00

MONDAY		TUESDAY
Short Ribs of Beef		Roulade of Beef
Boneless Chicken Parmigiana		Chicken a la King

THURSDAY	WEDNESDAY	FRIDAY
Baked Ham and Sweets	Lobster a la Newburg	Seafood Creole
Chicken Livers	Salisbury Steak	Savory Meat Loaf
in Wine Sauce		

Your Choice — Cold Platters

3.00

Mayflower Salad   Chef's Seafood Salad

Served with Coffee or Tea

THE SANDWICH BOARD

Your Choice

2.50

Roast Beef   Roumanian Pastrami   Corned Beef

Nova Scotia Salmon and Cream Cheese

Above Served with German Potato Salad, Tomato Wedge, Dill Pickles
and Coffee or Tea

THE SWEET CUPBOARD

Your Choice

.50

Fruit Pie   Melon in Season

Chocolate Seven Layer Cake

Creamy Rice Pudding   Cheesecake   Fresh Fruit Cup

ANOTHER *Mayflower* ENTERPRISE

Type selection and decorative border compliment each other.

SANDWICHES

BARB BURGER   1.65
An original Barb Creation . . . a grilled double deck sandwich on rye, choice ground beef with sauted onions and sharp Cheddar cheese, French fries, tossed green salad.

SPECIAL DELUXE
HAMBURGER   1.30
Served on toasted bun with relish, tomato, lettuce, French fries and tossed green salad.

CHEESEBURGER   1.05
Served open-faced with relish, tomato and lettuce. Onion if desired.

HAMBURGER   .95
Served open-faced with relish, tomato and lettuce. Onion if desired.

CHEESE 'N FRUIT   1.25
Grilled cheese sandwich, a nest of chilled fruits, honey lime dressing.

GRILLED CHEESE   .80

HOT ROAST BEEF
SANDWICH   1.95
Open-face sandwich served with potato; Barb-Q sauce or brown gravy and tossed green salad.

HOT TURKEY
SANDWICH   1.95
Open-face sandwich served with turkey dressing, potato, cranberry sauce, giblet gravy and tossed green salad.

RUEBEN SANDWICH   1.85
Grilled double-deck sandwich on rye with Swiss cheese, corned beef and sauerkraut, tossed salad.

KOSHER CORNED BEEF
SANDWICH ON RYE   1.75
Served with tossed green salad and French fries.

CLUB HOUSE SANDWICH 1.95
Served with potato salad.

DUNGENESS CRAB
SANDWICH   1.95
Fresh crab meat with melted cheese, served on toasted English muffin with tossed green salad or cole slaw.

SPECIAL TREAT
HAMBURGER   1.65
Our own choice chopped sirloin, fresh daily, served on crusty French bread with Barb-Q dip or au jus, French fries and tossed green salad.

OUR FAMOUS
FISH'N CHIPS

Dipped in our special batter, French fries, tartar sauce, cole slaw or tossed salad.
1.50

LOW CALORIE PLATE   1.55
Broiled chopped sirloin patty with cottage cheese, peach slices and Melba toast.

SPAGHETTI ITALIANE   1.75
Featuring the Barb's popular meat sauce, combination green salad with garlic bread.

HAM or BACON & EGGS   1.85
Served with hash brown potatoes, toast and jelly.

OUR POPULAR
DIP SANDWICHES

BEEF DIP   1.45
BREAST OF TURKEY   1.45
PREMIUM HAM   1.45
The above sandwiches are served on hot French bread with Barb-Q dip or au jus. Choice of tossed green salad, cole slaw or French fries.

SALADS

CRAB OR SHRIMP   2.85
LOUIE   *Small Order* 2.50
Choice Dungeness crab or Alaskan shrimp on crisp shredded lettuce, tastefully garnished with sliced tomato, hard-boiled egg and ripe olives, Thousand Island dressing.

CHEF'S SALAD   1.85
Julienne of ham, turkey and cheese, served on crisp tossed salad, garnished with egg, tomato, olives and your favorite dressing.

BARB'S MIXED GREEN   1.35
SALAD   *Small Order* 1.05
Special chef's dressing topped with bacon and Parmesan cheese.

Type and graphics go together exceptionally well on this menu. Notice

BROILED STEAKS

Includes tossed green salad, choice of dressings, choice of potato or spahetti, hot French bread.

**U.S.D.A. CHOICE
TOP SIRLOIN STEAK**   2.95
"Tender and Juicy"

**U.S.D.A. CHOICE
NEW YORK STEAK**   3.95
"Cattlemen's Favorite"

CHOPPED SIRLOIN STEAK 2.45
Choice lean ground beef—excellent RARE.

**U.S.D.A. CHOICE TOP SIRLOIN
STEAK SANDWICH**   2.45
Served on toast, tossed green salad, choice of dressing and French fries.

When ordering please indicate your preference:

RARE — Dark red inside
MEDIUM RARE — Light red inside
MEDIUM — Pink inside
WELL DONE — Brown inside
(It breaks our heart to do it!)

CHILDREN'S MENU

UNDER 12

SPAGHETTI   1.15
Includes Salad and Hot French Bread.

FISH and CHIPS   1.15
With Salad.

COMPLETE DINNERS
Includes French Fries, Tossed Green Salad, Choice of Beverage and Dessert.

TURKEY   1.75

GROUND SIRLOIN   1.55

SIRLOIN OF BEEF   1.85

APPETIZERS

Crab or Shrimp
Cocktail Supreme   1.85

Dinner Size Crab or
Shrimp Cocktail   .95

SOUP OF THE DAY
BOWL .35   CUP .25

POPULAR DINNERS

Our dinners are served with chef-made soup or tossed green salad with choice of dressing, choice of potato or spahetti Italiane, hot French bread.

SPARERIBS   3.75
Western style Barb-Q spareribs with our delicious tangy Barb-Q sauce.

**ROAST SIRLOIN
OF BEEF**   2.95
The heart of roast, expertly seasoned, served with natural juices.

**ROAST BREAST
OF TURKEY**   2.95
A traditional holiday feast that is a year-round favorite.

GULF PRAWNS   2.95
Dipped in our special batter, deep fried to the peak of their natural flavor.

QUILCENE OYSTERS   2.95
Direct from the cool waters of Quilcene Bay, prepared to a delicious golden brown.

**DEEP FRIED
EASTERN SCALLOPS**   2.95
Dipped in our special batter, deep fried to a golden brown.

CAPTAIN'S PLATE   3.75
Combination of shrimp, scallops, halibut and oysters. A perfect assortment for seafood lovers.

that items are listed in large, bold caps while descriptive copy is in lower case type.

FIVE COURSE DINNERS INCLUDE - *Relish plate, soup or juice, salad and choice of dressing, bread and butter, coffee or tea, dessert:*

1. Sauerbraten - Tender Cut of Beef - *marinated at least 48 hours - roasted and served with a deliciously different sauce and potato dumplings.* $3.50

2. Wienerschnitzel - *Choice Veal breaded with farm fresh eggs and cracker meal, sauteed to a rich golden brown.* $3.55

3. Knackwurst - *Spicy Beef Sausage - country style served with our special German style sauerkraut and choice of potatoes.* $3.35

4. Bratwurst - *A Delicious Sausage served hot off the grill (one part pork two parts veal) served with our special German style sauerkraut and choice of potatoes.* $3.35

5. Kasseler Rippchen - *Truly different Smoked Pork Chops served with our special German sauerkraut & choice of potatoes* $3.45

6. Pilsner Huhn - *Half of a Golden-brown Caponette dipped in our unique batter served with spicy beets & choice of potatoes.* $3.25

7. Shrimp - *Large Dinner Shrimp - golden brown in special batter with cocktail sauce and choice of potatoes.* $3.25

8. Steak - *Filet Mignon 8 ounce - bacon wrapped - garnished with onion rings and served with choice of potatoes.* $4.50

9. Rind Rouladen - *FRIDAY & SATURDAY ONLY - Rolled and Stuffed Top Round braised in its own gravy Bavarian style - served with choice of potatoes and sweet-sour red cabbage.* $3.45

CHILDRENS PORTIONS (under 12 years) - $2.00

APPETIZERS   •   SIDE ORDERS   •   ALA CARTE

1. Shrimp Cocktail - 85¢   3. Herring - Creamed (marinated) - 85¢
2. Onion Rings   -   45¢   4. Clam Chowder   Friday Only - 90¢

The type selection indicates a German menu.

A La Carte Dining
Continued

FRIAR TUCK'S CORNISH HEN
WILD RICE, BLACK CHERRY SAUCE
3.25

BROILED PORK CHOPS
Two center cut chops chosen from tender
young stock. Applesauce.
3.75

LAMB CHOPS
(TWO EXTRA THICK CENTER CUT)
Tender young spring lamb chops done to just
the right turn; garnished with mint jelly and
all dressed-up in the latest of French "panties"
4.25

VEAL SCALLOPINI, MARSALA
Cutlet of milk fed veal and fresh mushrooms
with our own special sauce
3.50

BROILED FLORIDA LOBSTER
Large "Select" Lobster, stuffed with our special
dressing, and served with hot drawn butter.
4.50

BROILED
FILET OF RED SNAPPER
Freshly caught in the Gulf of Mexico, with
Almandine or Lemon Butter
3.95

MEDIEVAL
MORSELS OF THE SEA
A creation of Fresh Florida Seafood, including
Scallops, Oysters, Shrimp, Deviled Crab Patties,
plus Half Broiled Lobster. Your choice of
Cocktail or Romoulade Sauce.
4.95

BOUNTIFUL RELISH TRAY, SALAD, VEGETABLE, POTATO, HOT ROLLS,
BUTTER AND BEVERAGE ARE SERVED WITH ENTREE.

Specialties of Our Master Chef

A La Carte Dining

Headings should be bolder and in a different type face (or hand lettering) from the descriptive or listing copy.

Roast Long Island Duckling a la Orange (½ Duck) $4.25

Always crisp. Our duck is considered by many to be the finest available, served either with a flavorful orange sauce or a tasty brown gravy.
Recommended wine: #12 Neumagener ''Moselle'' or #42 Beaujolais

Baby Beef Liver $3.25

(Served either with fried onions or crisp bacon slices) Long famous here at the Inn due to the extra care we take in the selection and preparation of this delicacy.
Recommended wines: #43 Fleurie or #33 Tavel Rose

Sauerbraten and Spatztles $3.50

A German pot roast of beef marinated in wine and spices for several days. The marinade, our own recipe, adds a deliciously different flavor to the roast. Served only on Wednesdays and Saturdays, this savory treat is delightfully complimented by the Spatzles and Red Cabbage.
Recommended wine: #12 Neumagener ''Moselle'' or #42 Beaujolais

The Couplet $6.75

Filet Mignon coupled with South African Lobster Tail provide a new taste sensation.
Recommended wine: #13 Schloss Vollards or #43 Fleurie

Crabmeat Au Gratin $5.00

Fresh backfin crabmeat is embraced by our own cheese sauce. A delectable treat you will enjoy.
Recommended wine: #27 Pouilly Fuisse or #33 Tavel Rose

Broiled Seafood Combination $6.00

Lobster Tail, Trout, Jumbo Shrimp, Scallops and Haddock, broiled to perfection.
Recommended wine: #26 Montrachet

Benetz Inn Stuffed Shrimp $3.75

Jumbo shrimp stuffed with our famous deviled crab stuffing.
Recommended wine: #32 Mateus or #23 Chablis

This is clean, simple sans-serif type, but the heavy, bold type of the name and price of the entree stand out well from the descriptive copy which is still large enough to be read with ease.

THE MENU IS
A PIECE OF PAPER

Your menu will last longer and look better if you take the time to select a good, suitable paper. The design of a menu should begin with the selection of the paper on which it will be printed because paper is as integral to creating good design and, thereby, an effective menu as copy, typography and art. Also, since paper represents about one-third of the printing cost of a menu (exclusive of art and copy), the selection of the paper (or papers) on which a menu is printed is well worth the consideration of all parties concerned in menu design—the designer, typographer, printer and food service operator.

What is paper? One answer might be that paper is the ideal printing surface, and, of course, nearly all menus are printed on some kind of paper. Papers (up until the modern industrial revolution) were made almost completely from rags and by hand. With the invention of machinery and with the development of chemistry, modern paper-making processes were developed. Most modern papers used at present for printing purposes are machine-made from wood pulp.

For the restaurateur, there are two basic approaches to the selection of paper for his menu. This paper selection depends upon how the menu is used or whether immediate obsolescence or maximum permanence is desired.

For a menu that changes every day, it is obvious that immediate obsolescence is the criteria. This menu can be printed on a lighter weight, non-coated stock since it is going to be printed, used only one day, and then thrown away. A light, inexpensive paper stock, however, can still have color, texture and good tactile qualities that will enhance the design of the menu. No concern, however, need be given on this type of menu for resistance to stain, handling and rough usage since it is practically a throw-away item comparable to the daily newspaper. In fact, some menus of this type have been printed on newsprint.

The second basic paper approach to the menu is the one designed for maximum permanence. This type of menu is usually printed on a heavy, durable, coated paper that will last a long time despite much handling by the customer. It should probably be on a water resistant type of paper that can be wiped clean with a damp cloth. This type of paper is usually a heavy Cover, Bristol or Tag stock which is coated or treated with clay, pigment, varnish or plastic. This coating makes the paper water and grease resistant and gives it longer life, even with constant customer handling.

Compromise Solutions that Work

There are variations or combinations, of course, to these two approaches. A menu does not have to be printed entirely on the same kind of paper. A common solution to the immediate versus the permanent menu problem is to design the cover of the menu on heavy, coated stock while the inside pages are of lighter, less permanent (and less expensive) paper. This type of paper selection can be tailored to fit the permanent and the daily items on the menu.

The permanent items on the menu—usually beverages, sandwiches, salads, specials of the house, etc., will be on the heavy paper part of the menu, while the special daily menu will be on an insert or insert pages which will be on lighter paper.

The use of different kinds of paper in the same menu can serve a design and functional purpose, also. Papers of different texture, thickness and color can emphasize a particular part of the bill of fare which the restaurateur wishes to give an extra sales push.

Selecting the right paper for the menu is a no less complicated problem than selecting the right silverware, dishwasher or china to be used in a restaurant. First, there are the physical and esthetic qualities of paper such as strength, dimensional stability, opacity, ink receptivity, smoothness and whiteness. Then, there is texture. Paper comes in textures varying from very coarse to the most smooth. Considering that the menu is held in the customer's hand, as well as read, the texture or "feel" of a menu can be important.

Color can be added to the menu through the use of paper which comes in the purest white, through the softest pastels to the richest solids. It can, too often, become the habit to think of color as something added to white paper via printing when color can be in the paper as well as in the ink.

Some of the printing and design techniques which can be used in connection with paper and menu design are:
1. Opaque and transparent inks on colored and white paper.
2. Embossing.
3. Light inks on dark paper.
4. Tints and metallics on tinted paper.
5. Three-dimensional use of paper.
6. Printing on transparent (cellophane) or semi-transparent stock.
7. Textural, tactile and other sensorial effects.
8. Varieties of paper within the same menu.

Printing Process Determines Paper

The printing process also dictates the kind of paper to be used in successful menu design, although the quality of the paper itself will largely determine the success of the finished product. Most menus are printed by Letterpress or Offset Lithography methods of printing or by a combination of the two. Menu covers are usually printed by the Offset Lithography method, while the inside listings are usually printed letterpress since the type can be left standing, and day-to-day changes can be made in prices and the bill of fare without making new plates.

For the selection of paper for these two printing processes, the following characteristics should be taken into consideration:

Letterpress—
1. Type and line cuts bite into paper.
2. Almost any paper is suitable for type and line printing surfaces.
3. Hairlines will increase in weight materially.
4. Halftones require smooth, plate-finished or coated papers.

Offset Lithography—
1. The process allows for greater latitude in paper selection and printing.
2. There is no impression or bite into the paper.
3. There is enough flexibility or give to compensate for textured surfaces.

In addition, paper can be folded in many different ways to create interesting configurations, and paper can be die-cut into unusual shapes other than the conventional square or rectangular form most used. These two characteristics of paper—foldability and the fact that it can be cut into almost any shape—should be used to advantage to create interesting menu design.

In conclusion, it must be repeated again that paper is important to the success of a good menu. For the restaurateur, it is vital to have the printer or designer show a variety of papers for selection. The right paper will do a better job and do it for less money. Make paper part of the operation's menu picture.

BASIC PAPER DEFINITIONS

ANTIQUE PAPER—paper with a rough, textured surface.

BOND—paper for letterheads, forms and business uses.

BOOK PAPER—papers having characteristics suitable for books, magazines, brochures, etc.

BRISTOL—cardboard of .006 of an inch or more in thickness (index, mill and wedding are types of bristol)

COATED—paper and paperboard whose surface has been treated with clay or some other pigment.

COVER STOCK—a variety of papers used for outside covers of menus, catalogs, booklets, magazines, etc.

DECKLE EDGE—a rough-edge paper formed by pulp flowing against the frame (deckle) providing a feathered, uneven edge when paper is left untrimmed.

DULL-COATED—paper with a low gloss coated surface.

EGGSHELL—a semi-rough surface paper similar to the surface texture of an egg.

ENAMELED—any coated paper.

ENGLISH FINISH—book paper with a machine finish and uniform surface.

GRAIN—a weakness along one dimension of the paper—folding of papers should be with the grain.

MACHINE FINISH—book paper with a medium finish—rougher than English finish but smoother than eggshell.

OFFSET PAPER—coated or uncoated paper suitable for offset lithography printing.

VELLUM FINISH—similar to eggshell but from harder stock with a finer grained surface.

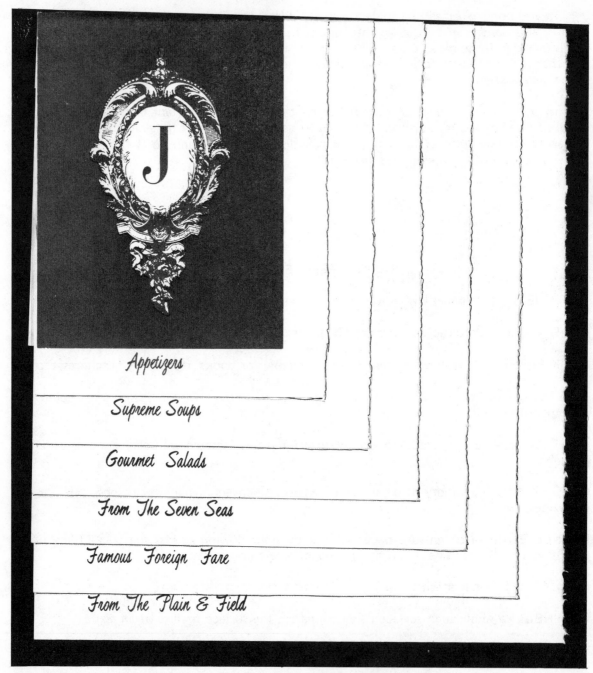

A great deal can be done with paper. This unusual fold treatment uses paper of different size for each page of the menu. Folded over, it allows the customer to lift up and look at each panel or page. Also, each page is identified with a heading at the bottom—appetizers, supreme soups, gourmet salads—for easy identification when the menu is closed.

FOR A MORE CREATIVE MENU

Most food service operators will admit the importance of creativity in the success of a food service business, creativity in the selection and preparation and serving of foods and drinks and in the decor and general appearance and operation of the establishment. Equally of value, the menu itself, in appearance, design and style, can be more creative, to attract attention, create comment and increase business. The following are some creative suggestions to help stimulate your imagination. Some of the ideas are taken from interesting, creative menus, and some are just "top of the head" ideas.

First, let's consider what your menu is printed on. Most often it is paper of varying kind and quality. But menus do not have to be printed on paper. They have successfully been printed on cloth, plastic and even wood. Several restaurants print (silk screen) their menu on a wooden board shaped like a bread board with a hole for hanging on the wall. This is an expensive menu, of course, but the restaurant usually sells this menu as a souvenir. In fact, one restaurant operator with this type of menu is supposed to have made the facetious remark that he made more money out of selling his menu than selling food and drink.

One type of printing surface not seen by this writer that would seem to me a "natural" for a Steak House or a restaurant featuring wild game would be a menu printed on real or imitation leather so that it looked like the "skin" of an animal. This could be die-cut as in Figure 1.

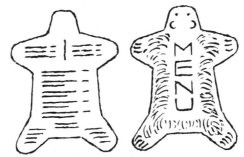

FIGURE 1

Paper, itself, of course, comes in a great variety of kinds, sizes, textures, colors, etc. Most menus do not take advantage of the many kinds and colors of papers available. For example, a menu consisting of a four-page cover, a four-page insert and an additional four-page smaller insert as shown in Figure 2, can be put together from three different papers of three different colors and textures to create an interesting "creative" effect.

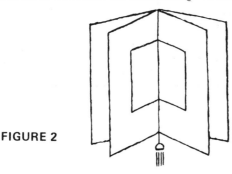

FIGURE 2

An interesting combination of menu and decor is to use wallpaper for the cover of your menu if you have an interesting paper on the walls of your establishment.

Since most menus are printed on paper, consideration should be given to the ways paper can be used. First, paper can be folded, and second, paper can be die-cut into various shapes and configurations. First, let us consider folding, because too meny food service operators, printers and designers take the easy way out and just take a piece of paper, fold it in half and there is their menu. But there are other ways.

A piece of paper can be folded to look like a napkin. A very simple way is to take a square piece of paper and fold it twice from corner to corner and you have a menu that looks like a napkin—(see Figure 3).

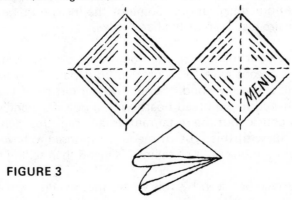

FIGURE 3

Another simple fold that can be used with a menu is shown in Figure 4:

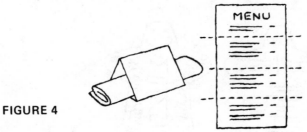

FIGURE 4

This menu is just a long piece of paper folded three times into the shape of a triangular tent and then the napkin is placed inside to hold it down securely. Another interesting way to fold a piece of paper for a menu is to fold it unevenly into different sized panels as shown in Figure 5:

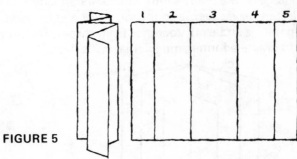

FIGURE 5

This menu has five panels and four folds. Panel No. 3 is the largest, panels 2 and 4 are smaller and of the same size, and panels 1 and 5 are the smallest and also of the same size. The menu folds up "accordion" style.

A simple irregular fold used by some restaurants is a good method for visualizing the index for a large menu, by folding each insert in the menu a little off center as shown in Figure 6:

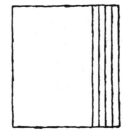

FIGURE 6

A word of caution is in order on the subject of folding paper for a menu. All paper does not fold well, even when scored. Certain papers crack when folded, leaving a ragged, unsightly edge and one that will soon wear out and cut down on the life of a menu. Check the "foldability" of your paper before the printer prints up 10,000 menus!

The second characteristic of paper is that it can be cut into various shapes—geometric, squares, circles, triangles, octagons, as well as irregular shapes. Among examples of varied shapes used successfully are Pancake House menus which are printed on a round sheet that corresponds to the shape of a pancake. Steak Houses have printed menus in the shape of steaks and an Oyster House has printed a menu in the shape of an oyster (see Figure 7).

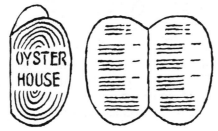

FIGURE 7

A die-cut menu is, of course, more expensive, but once you have paid for the original die, it is yours and at a one-time cost only.

A few dining rooms print their menu in the form of a newspaper. This is an idea that can be expanded. In addition to a newspaper format, why not a magazine format? The idea is to give more information than just the listing of the food and drink served. The menu becomes a merchandising-advertising vehicle. If your restaurant is in a theater district, theater news printed in a newspaper-magazine format menu is a good idea. And, if your operation is in a financial district, financial or stock-market news makes good editorial copy.

The problem with this kind of menu is that it usually takes professional journalistic personnel to write it and keep it current. And if it contains changing up-to-date information, the menu must be printed anew fairly often—daily, weekly, or monthly. But many food service operations have a daily or weekly menu anyhow, so this is not an unusual problem.

Another menu possibility is the three-dimensional menu. A menu need not be a flat, two-dimensional piece of paper. It can be in the form of a cube, pyramid, etc., as shown in Figure 8:

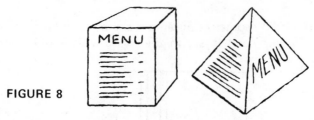

FIGURE 8

This kind of menu would sit in the center of the table. An especially appropriate use of a three-dimensional menu is a three-dimensional Wine List using the actual bottle of wine as shown in Figure 9:

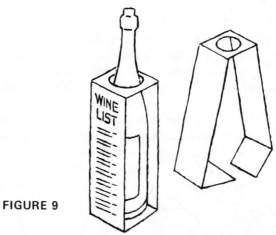

FIGURE 9

Finally, let's look at some really "way-out" menu ideas. How about a "Gambler's Menu," not really encouraging gambling for money or profit, however. This type of gambling would just be taking a chance on which menu entree to order. This menu could have a dial that could be spun around until it stopped at a number which would correspond to a numbered entree, Figure 10:

FIGURE 10

Another unusual kind of menu would be a "Dial An Entree" type of menu. This menu would be printed on a circular dial which could be rotated from a central pivot and menu items "selected" one at a time. Figure 11 shows how this menu would be designed:

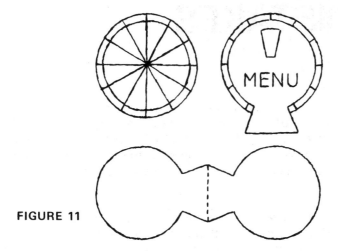

FIGURE 11

Menu items, entrees, appetizers, desserts, etc., could be printed on both sides of the circular dial.

The few "different" menus presented here are only a small selection of the possibilities in menu design. Creative food service operators will continue to make new, different and unusual menus to sell more food and drink, build the check and advertise an eating place equally creative in all respects.

MOST COMMON MENU MISTAKES

A careful study of over a thousand menus over a period of two years has resulted in the observation of a certain pattern of errors and mistakes in menu design, listing and merchandising which repeat themselves. A list of these cardinal mistakes and what should be done to correct them follows. This list should be of interest to the menu conscious food service operator and if any of these mistakes appear on your menu, you should take a second, critical look at it.

A general observation, however, can be made before listing the common errors and that is that it is obvious in too many cases that important design and merchandising decisions are being made by the printer of the menu and not the food service operator himself. Such matters as layout (which items should be given the most importance and where they should be listed), type size and style, size of the menu and kind of paper it is printed on are too often determined by the limitations of the printer's presses and type selections plus the stock of paper he happens to have in his storeroom.

The food service operator should put himself, not his printer, in charge of his menu.

The first, most common menu mistake is a menu too small (physically) to accommodate the large (or even small) listing of items from appetizers to entrees to dessert. The result is crowding, type usually too small to read, no descriptive copy and no "specials" merchandised in larger, bolder type. This kind of menu is hard to read and harder to order from. Very often it will include a large listing of excellent (and expensive) entrees that do not get the treatment they deserve simply because the menu is not big enough.

The next very common menu mistake is listing items in too small type. What is too small type? It is type your customers cannot read easily (preferably without glasses if they are far sighted) in the lighting conditions of your restaurant. Too many menu planners assume that everybody has the eyesight of a jet fighter pilot (20/20 vision under twilight conditions). Actually, only a minority of people have perfect vision (without glasses) and they don't always bring their glasses with them when they eat out.

The answer to this menu problem is simple too. Set your menu in larger type.

Another common menu problem is lack of descriptive copy. Strangely enough, if you were to ask a restaurant man about the food he serves, he could probably "talk" fluently about it. He is proud of it. He can describe it. He can tell you how it is prepared, the originality of the recipe, the quality of the ingredients, etc., etc. But when he comes to list these same items in cold type on the menu, he is struck dumb and says nothing.

This does not mean that a menu should be a literary creation. "Just the facts, ma'am" are enough; but too often just the facts (which can usually be contained in one average length sentence) are left out.

A professional writer, of course, will give you the best menu copy (if properly informed about what you serve), but any restaurant menu builder can write copy. Answer the following questions (some or all) about the entrees that are your specialties, and also about expensive and unusual drinks, appetizers, salads, sandwiches and desserts.

1. What is it?
2. How is it prepared?
3. How is it served?
4. Does it have unusual taste and quality properties?

Foreign menu items—French, German, Italian, Chinese, etc.—especially need descriptive copy or translations so that the customer can order intelligently.

Do you treat every item on your menu the same? That is, do you list everything in the same size type and give no "special position" to any item? If so, you are committing another menu mistake. It's just common sense that a $5.00 steak and a 10¢ cup of coffee should not be given the same importance on the menu, but in a surprising number of cases, this is so.

The answer to this problem is easy too. List your "big" items, usually your entrees, either dinners or a la carte, in bigger, bolder type than the other "smaller" items on the menu. Give them better position (usually center) and give them the most descriptive merchandising, sell copy. The situation is simple. You decide which items of those listed on your menu you would like to sell the most of (big profit, most popular, etc.) and treat them accordingly.

Another strange but common menu mistake is one of omission. It usually involves liquor, a big profit, easy to serve and store item. Many a menu will sell this big item with the line, "Ask for your favorite cocktail." This philosophy, carried to its ultimate conclusion, could result in a menu that consisted of a piece of paper on which the following informative message was printed, "Ask for your favorite food and drink, we may have it."

If you serve liquor, list it, all of it, cocktails, tall drinks, mixed drinks, coolers, bourbons, scotches, gins, vodkas, rums, beers, wines, etc., etc. Then list the price per drink (or bottle, split, etc.) because you wouldn't list a T-bone steak without listing the price. And, finally, list brand names when possible. Brand names mean quality plus; they represent millions of dollars of advertising that the food service operator ignores at his own expense.

Another menu mistake area is sequence. This means that food and drink is consumed in a time sequence and should be listed in that order on the menu. Cocktails, soups and appetizers are before items, entrees (dinners or a la carte) and most wines are middle items, and desserts, after dinner drinks (brandies, cordials, etc.) cigars, coffees, etc., etc., are after items. The menu should be organized in this time sequence (for the above items) and side items, such as sandwiches, salads, side dishes, etc., should literally be listed on the side or in some less important place, unless you specialize in sandwiches or salads, in which case, they become entree items.

A common menu mistake for which there is no excuse is tip-ons, clip-ons, or daily menus which, when attached to the menu, cover some printed portion of the menu. If you use tip-ons or have a changing daily menu that is attached to the regular menu, design your menu to allow for these tip-ons. Customers, in most cases, will not lift up a tip-on to read under it.

And while on the subject of the daily, special, changing portion of the menu, we have arrived at another common menu mistake or more often catastrophe. Many a menu, which otherwise is well designed and printed, will have a daily menu, luncheon or dinner, done on a typewriter, poorly organized, poorly printed (mimeographed) on poor paper. Very often these "daily" items are repetitions of regular items on the permanent menu which makes them a double menu mistake.

The solution to this menu problem can be achieved in three steps as follows:
1. Cut down on the number of your daily specials.
2. Do not repeat "regular" items already listed on the menu.
3. Print in regular type on good quality paper.

Finally, to wrap up this list of most common menu mistakes (not all of the menu mistakes could be covered at this time), here is a common group of errors of omission. This is the failure of too many restaurants to list somewhere on the menu the following basic information: address, phone number, days open, hours of business and credit cards honored.

HOW MANY MENUS SHOULD YOU HAVE?

Every food service operation has a different menu problem depending upon the number of meals it serves and the type of operation it has. The basic separation of menu types is in-to the breakfast, lunch and dinner menu, but there are many more. A list of possible differ-ent, separate and distinct menus is listed here:

1. Breakfast menu
2. Luncheon menu
3. Dinner menu
4. Late Evening Snack menu
5. Sunday Brunch menu
6. Children's menu
7. Dessert or After Dinner menu
8. Room Service menu
9. Poolside menu
10. Banquet menu
11. Take-Out menu
12. Wine List

No restaurant and hardly any hotel or motel would create and print twelve menus, but the fact that it is possible to print and use twelve different menus for twelve different pur-poses shows the scope and importance of how you use the menu. The other possibility is to have only one menu and cover all twelve subjects on that one menu. There are problems, however, in combining too many subjects in one menu, and there are times when a separate menu will do a better job. Let's examine the problem.

First, there is the Breakfast, Luncheon and Dinner problem. An establishment that serves all three meals can either print three separate menus or one menu that combines all three or some combination such as a separate Breakfast menu and the Luncheon and Dinner menu together. Visually, the three combinations work out as shown below:

BREAKFAST MENU   LUNCHEON MENU   DINNER MENU

FIGURE A

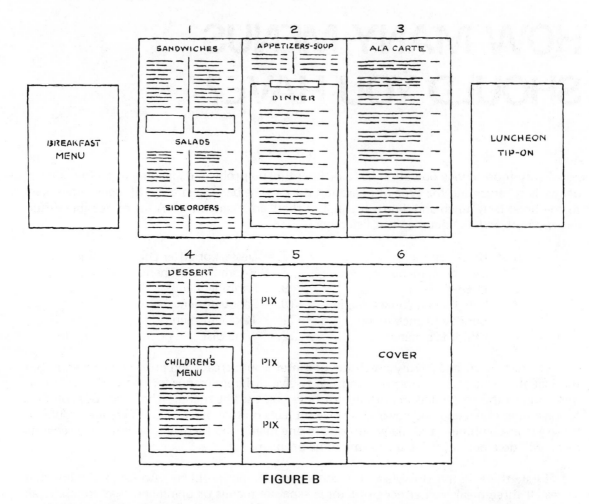

FIGURE B

Figure A illustrates three separate menus. Figure B shows a separate Breakfast menu and the Luncheon and Dinner menu combined on one menu. If you have a cut-off time for serving breakfast, it is almost mandatory that you have a separate breakfast menu since the customers will continue to order the breakfast items after you have stopped serving them. On the other hand, it is always good communications to list the hours the Breakfast menu is served, even if it is served 24 hours a day.

The key to listing both the Luncheon and Dinner menu on one menu is the tip-on. This means that the Luncheon menu can be removed and the Dinner menu placed in the same space. The Luncheon and Dinner (complete Dinner or Dinner Specials for the Day) listing, however, must be small enough to fit into the space allowed. If you have a big, varied and complicated Luncheon or Dinner listing, a separate menu for each is recommended. The menu should fit what you serve, not the other way around. Also, since the tip-on is the key to the functioning of this type of menu, care should go into its preparation and printing. The typesetting should be as good as the rest of the menu, and the printing and paper should be of the same good quality.

Figure C illustrates one possible combination of all three meals—Breakfast, Luncheon and Dinner on one menu. The Dinner-Luncheon combination is the same as in Figure B, but, in addition, the Breakfast menu is printed on panel 5 (back) of this 2-fold, 3-panel menu. This allows the breakfast part of the menu to be presented to the customer without exposing the rest of the menu when folded up. Combining all three meal listings on one menu and using tip-ons can save you money in printing, but the menu must be designed with care so that each part functions separately.

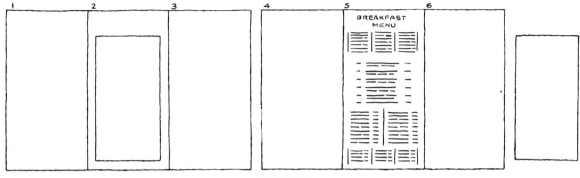

FIGURE C

Consideration should be given to future changes in the menu. When all three menus are combined in one, the only change that can be made without changing or reprinting the entire menu is on the tip-ons. And there is a limit to the number of tip-ons that can be put on a menu. Another menu possibility that works for the three-meal problem is shown in Figure D below:

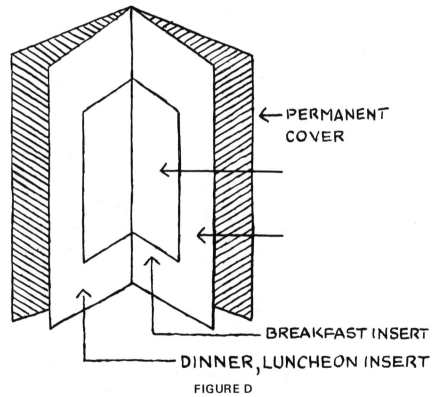

FIGURE D

Figure D is the type of menu where you have a permanent cover and you bind into this cover listings as needed—luncheon, dinner or even breakfast. In Figure D, insert A could be one of the three menus, and Figure B could be the Luncheon or Breakfast menu. The main advantage of this type of menu, besides its flexibility, is that the cover (4 pages) can be of heavier, more expensive, coated paper while the inserts which change more often can be of lighter, less expensive paper. Also, your expensive 2, 3 or 4 color printing can be on the cover and the run can be larger to bring the unit cost down.

One factor to keep in mind when using a semi-permanent cover is to use all four pages (front cover, back cover, inside front cover and inside back cover). In too many cases only the front cover is used and the other three pages are left blank. This is a waste of valuable advertising, selling space. Some of the possible uses for these three pages are:

1.   From Our Bar Listing
2.   Wine List
3.   Party-Banquet Story
4.   Late Evening Snacks
5.   Weekly Menu
6.   Take-Outs
7.   History of Establishment

If you are worried about price changes on this semi-permanent part of the menu (Liquor Listing, Wine List, Take-Outs, Late Evening Snacks) you can utilize a tip-on here also as shown in Figure E:

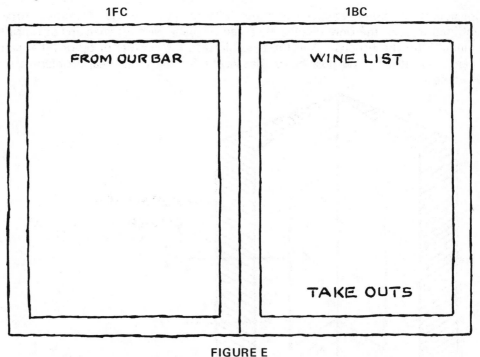

FIGURE E

These tip-ons, however, since they will not be changed very often, can be pasted right on the menu. Then when a change is required, the new listing can be pasted right over the old one and the cover can continue to be used.

Children's menus are very often separate menus. There are a great variety of these entertainment type menus on the market. Any menu house or printer can show you samples of this type of menu. If you have a large, or desire a larger, "family" business, a separate Children's menu that entertains as well as lists the food for children is a good idea. If your service to children is not sizable, a small listing on the menu is enough, or in some cases merely the statement, "children's portions available at half price." The emphasis you put on this part of the menu depends on your market and type of restaurant.

A separate Wine List is often printed by restaurants, but this is one case where there should not be a separate menu. The problem is to get the list to the customer at the right time. A separate Wine List, unless it is asked for or is on the table and used, will not sell anybody except the customer who orders wine regularly. Even a Wine List on the table can get overlooked; unless the customer opens it, and looks at it, he is not exposed to wine merchandising. The Wine List as an integral part of the menu and located next to the entree listing is a selling part of the menu. The idea is to make it impossible to ignore the wine listing. Figures F and G below show two possible methods of making the Wine List part of the menu by placing it next to the entree listing: In Figure F the Wine List is a panel or separate fold of the menu next to the entree listing, and in Figure G the Wine List is bound into the center of the entree listing.

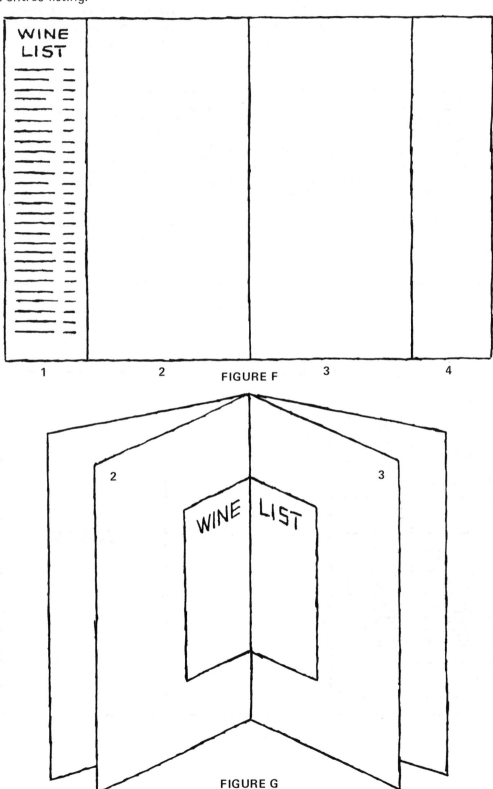

FIGURE F

FIGURE G

In the case of Desserts and After Dinner Drinks, a separate menu is an exception. And in this case, a separate menu can do a better job. The effectiveness of an After Dinner menu is in how it is used. The menu must be presented to the customer after he has finished his meal or entree without asking if he wants dessert or an after dinner drink. Only after he has had time to look at the menu and be exposed to the sell on it should the question be asked.

The Dessert and After Dinner Drinks listing can be part of the total integrated menu as well as a separate menu, but when this is the case, it should get separate treatment. Figures H, I and J show three possibilities for listing the "after" portion of the menu:

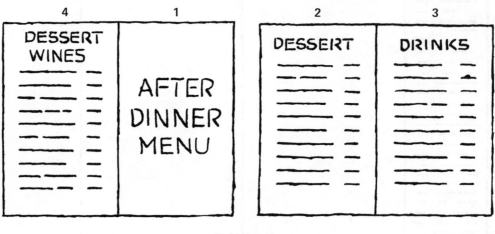

FIGURE H

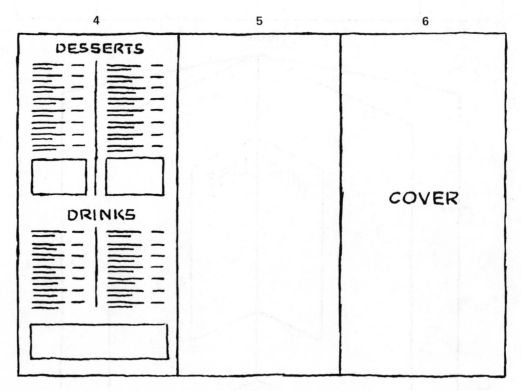

FIGURE 1

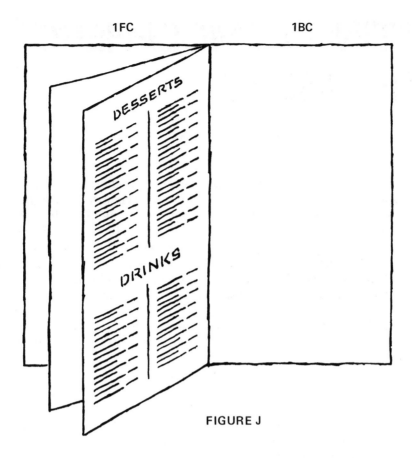

FIGURE J

Figure H is the separate After Dinner menu with Desserts listed on page 2, After Dinner Drinks on page 3 and Dessert Wines on page 4. Figure I is a 3-panel, 2-fold menu with the Dessert and After Dinner Drink listing printed on panel 4. Figure J is a 4-page insert bound into a 4-page cover with the Dessert and After Dinner Drink listing on page 4. The two menus illustrated in Figures I and J should be used the same way the separate After Dinner menu is used, that is, presented to the customer after he has finished his entree. Another advantage of the separate Dessert and After Dinner menu is that changes in price and item selection (and experimentation) can be made without changing the rest of the menu.

Specialty menus, such as Banquet, Room Service, Poolside, Take-Out, Sunday Brunch and Late Evening Snack menus, are used depending upon the type of specialized services you offer. In most cases, if you want to increase any one of these specialized parts of your menu, a separate menu or separate treatment on your regular menu is the answer. This means presenting information, items, prices, etc., selling with good copy, good art (illustrations) and good printing. In other words, any list of items or services that you sell as part of your food service should be sold somewhere on the menu or on a separate menu.

CREATING ATMOSPHERE ON THE MENU

The success of many a food service establishment is based on its friendly atmosphere as well as the good food it serves. The decor, the attitude of the host, waitresses and other employees will to a large extent determine the atmosphere of the operation. Most operators are friendly, out-going, extroverted people or they would not be in the food service business. But, in addition to people, decor and general atmosphere, the menu can reflect a more friendly environment. A few, well chosen words on the menu can help create an atmosphere of hospitality and welcome. The following examples are chosen from actual "in use" menus, and they show how the imaginative use of words can create a happy menu.

Down South in Atlanta, Ga. the people who run Mammy's Shanty like to pose as simple, country folk, not like their smart city friends, but the following shows that they are a lot smarter than most:

"GEORGIA CRACKER"
Sampler Plate
$3.25
(an assortment of foods us natives like)
Us crackers always got a chicken, and a pig or two.
Nearly any place there's water,
You can find some crabs. (How true. How true.)
And shrimp! we have as many as taxes.
Apples grow in most backyards (as well as 5 or 6 brats).
    Add 'em all together, and they really spell eating.
(Everything except the brats.)

    So we decided, for our perspicacious Northern cousins, to let them try all our good easy eating at one sitting, by arranging in our best Georgia Manner a selected piece of Fried North Georgia Chicken, one South Georgia Pork Chop, one deviled Crab, and a Florida Avocado, stuffed with Fresh Texas Shrimp Salad, French Fried Idaho Potatoes, rolls and butter, coffee, and
THE WORLD'S BEST PECAN PIE

Michel's Restaurant in Harlan, Iowa, is happy that the customer came, and says so:

Yes, We're Glad You Came
Thanks for visiting us! We're happy,
gratified and complimented.
    Happy to prepare for you the finest
food in town.
    Gratified for this opportunity to demonstrate
our service and hospitality.
    Complimented that you chose us to satisfy
your appetite. We appreciate your confidence
and will always do our utmost to deserve your
friendship and patronage.

Copy need not be long or involved to brighten up a menu. The Gay Nineties Restaurant in Rock Island, Illinois, for example, heads its fountain listing—Ice Cream Saloon, a bit of imaginative menu copy.

A few words about steak—other than the actual listing and description of the steak—is possible, as The Look-Out Below Restaurant menu shows:

"Like a timeless work of art, steaks demand the perfection that only European trained chefs, working with the finest beef and years of experience, can create."

"The result? A true masterpiece as prepared by our chefs that you'll savor and remember until your next visit . . ."

One of the best pieces of menu copy of a general nature that this writer has run across in a long time is the Ode to Dining as it appears on Saska's menu:

> We may live without poetry, music and art
> We may live without conscience and live without heart
> We may live without friends, we may live without books
> But where is the man who can live without cooks?
> We may live without books, what is knowledge but grieving?
> We may live without hope, what is hope but deceiving?
> We may live without love, what is passion but pining?
> But where lives the man who can do without dining?

Many establishments have names that are of historical or topical interest. It makes good advertising sense to take advantage of the situation, and The Epicurean Restaurant does just this, as shown below:

EPICURUS (341-270 B. C.)

The Greek philosopher to whom the phrase "Eat, drink, and be merry for tomorrow we die" has been ascribed. Though his philosophy taught that pleasure or happiness is the goal of all morality, it made a distinction between pleasures, advising the cultivation of the most enduring ones. Stressing the pleasures of the intellect and particularly those of friendship, it was held that genuine pleasure is derived from a life of prudence, honor and justice.

The word "epicure" has become the term used for one who displays fastidiousness in his tastes or enjoyments.

A topical reference, in an election year, appears on the dessert menu of Latz's Knife and Fork Inn. It says, "Where Hungry and Thirsty Democrats and Republicans Are Always Welcome."

A few words about your restaurant, its cuisine, history, etc., is always good on the menu. The following example from the Smith Farm Restaurant in Maine, is good, friendly, hospitality copy:

Years ago . . . having a surplus of vegetables and fruits, the Smiths erected a simple highway vegetable stand. It prospered. Home-made ice cream was added . . . it too became popular . . . and more popular. Then home grown turkeys were added in the form of luscious home-made sandwiches. The demand was so great that real farm style turkey dinners were added to the growing business. More room was needed and the barn was "fixed up" so that customers could "set 'n eat."

The Smith Farm reputation for good food grew and grew. More dining space was made available . . . more additions made and the menu increased . . . until today . . . Smith Farm customers come from all over the nation for our now famous "New England Cookin'."

From East, South, West and North, thousands who have been guests here have discovered a certain character at the Smith Farm, and a certain excellence in the service that they like.

In every city of any distinction there are hotels and eating places that stand out and give it a memorable character. Pity the town, no matter how large and important, that has no restaurant that people tell each other about and plan to revisit.

It has been said that Smith Farm is such a restaurant, and it is our intention to deserve that reputation . . . and preserve it. It's a two-way street, of course. So long as we bring credit to Maine, our friends in Maine will make Smith Farm Restaurant a frequent rendez-vous. You who are reading these lines are the final judge and arbiter, and we invite your judgment in presenting this menu of the dishes we are prepared to serve—many of them are old family recipes—all of them tested by discerning people.

Even such pedestrian copy as what credit cards you honor and what the various food and travel guides think of you can be said in a better way, as shown by the following from Poor Richard's Restaurant:

To all our esteemed customers
At this point we urge you to use your Carte Blanche or American Express credit cards whenever you like. Further, we beg you not to leave hats, coats, and other stuff behind. We can't be responsible for them. And finally, to toot our horn a little, we remind you that Poor Richard's is approved by the A. A. A., is listed in Mobil's "Northwest Travel Guide," and has been given the full-page treatment from "Ford Times." However, we do not sell gasoline or autos, just superb food.

For the hotel-motel restaurant, this copy about "The Innkeeper" from the Surf and Surrey menu is good, friendly and informative copy:

Arriving by stagecoach, bareback or mule, hungry and thirsty they came in from the harsh, hot, dusty roads in summer and the cold, soggy and wet trails of winter. Often they had been traveling difficult distances at great personal peril. Bandits and highwaymen waited around almost every crook in the road to harm them and steal their money.

The Inn was a refuge. It was a place of cheer, warmth and generous hospitality. The Innkeeper was ready with a quick greeting, a friendly smile, a haunch of mutton and a gill of kill-devil. The fireplace was large and warm. The pub was a cacophony of laughter and good conversation. The kitchen sent out its magical odors and culinary masterpieces, while the resting wayfarer was safe, happy and well fed as well as being protected from the storm and the dangers of the highwayman.

A hearty Appetite . . English

Bon Appetit . . . . . French

Buon Appetito . , . . . Italian

Guten Appetit . . . . German

Buen Apetito . . . . Spanish

Bkychot Kywahgr . . Russian

B'et E-Avon . . . . Hebrew

Smaeznego . . . . . . Polish

Smak-lig-Målted · · Swedish

Gourmet information creates atmosphere on the menu.

A Warning   La Serviette Au Cou   Dinner Rules

Since the "Les Amis d'Escoffier" Society is dedicated to the art of good living only, it is forbidden, under threat of expulsion, to speak of personal affairs, of one's own work or specialty, and more particularly to attempt to use the Society as a means of making business contacts. It is unnecessary to elucidate further upon this delicate subject which everyone understands. Furthermore, at these dinner-meetings reference will never be made on the subjects of: politics, religious beliefs, personal opinions of either members or guests irrespective of their profession or social status.

Too often we find, as we come
  to the table,
an elegant "rag" no larger
  than a hand,
That futilely and preten-
  tiously means to supplant
That napkin of old, so ample
  and comfortable.
The dining room lacks the
  grandeur of yore:
Varnished floors, mirrors
  clear and of tinted glass
Give the illusion of hospital,
  clinic, or bath.
Bring back the large table-
  cloth, we humbly implore.
So flattering to gleaming
  arms, softening to the
  sounds,
A background sublime for the
  flowers and fruits,
Whose whiteness enchants the
  guests sitting 'round.
If a toast to your health you
  would enjoy,
Madame, bring out that
  entrancing linen
For then indeed would we
  abound in joy!

The napkin must be tucked under the collar. There will be no reserved seats. Persons under the influence of liquor will not be permitted to sit at the table. Members and guests will attend the dinner-meetings in informal dress.

The wines, carefully selected to accompany and enhance the delicacy of each course, must be drunk during the course for which they are intended. To enforce this ruling, the glasses—even if full —will be removed at the end of each course.

Smoking is absolutely forbidden up to the time dessert is served. A person who smokes while eating does not deserve the title of "Gourmet."

The Wine Does It...

*Liberal amounts of fine California wines add
extra flavor and excitement to these savory dishes*

ENTREES:

Stroganoff of Beef Tenderloin Burgundy 3.90
*tenderloin tips in our own rich and delightfully
tasty sauce—with buttered noodles and a splash of BURGUNDY*

Veal Scaloppini Burgundy 3.95
*tender veal steak sauteed with parmesan cheese and
served in a tomato-mushroom-BURGUNDY wine sauce with rice pilau*

Veal Scaloppini Marsala 3.95
*prepared the same as the scaloppini above, however,
the MARSALA wine makes it a sweeter and richer combination*

Tournedos of Beef Tenderloin Burgundy 5.60
*fine broiled tenderloin tournedos, broiled tomato, mushroom caps
and our own elegant BURGUNDY wine sauce*

Broiled Sweetbreads in Sherry 3.85
*an unusual dinner of sweetbreads broiled in SHERRY
and served with crisp bacon*

Chicken Livers, Sauteed 3.95
*fresh chicken livers sauteed with mushrooms
and SHERRY wine on toast points*

SEAFOOD SPECIALTIES WITH WINE:

Roulades of Sole Bordeaux 4.25

Filet of Red Snapper Chardonnay 4.50

Alaskan King Crab Newberg 3.90

*"The Wine Does It . . . " food cooked in wine creates its
own atmosphere.*

oysters

	small	large
natural	$0.65	$1.25
mornay	$0.75	$1.35
kilpatrick	$0.85	$1.45
fried with sauce tartare	$0.85	$1.45

prawns

	entree	dinner
edwardian	$1.25	$2.25

marinated with french dressing, celery and shallots — served with asparagus

butterfly with sauce tartare	$1.10	$2.10
new orleans on rice	$1.10	$2.10
prawns cavill avenue	$1.10	$2.10

cold curried prawns on pineapple shell — delicious

crab

served on the shell

local crab vinaigrette	$2.25

served cold with lemon juice, oil and herbs

st. louis	$2.25

served cold with tabasco sauce, creme tomato and chopped olives

lobsters

mornay	$2.25

grilled with a rich cheese sauce

thermidor	$2.25

piping hot garnished with a spicy mustard sauce

grilled lobster	$2.25

broiled on our charcoal grill — basted with fresh butter

fish

grilled fish of the day	$2.00

(whole) grilled over flaming charcoal — served with lemon

fillets of fish en papillote	$1.75

wrapped in alfoil, grilled over flaming charcoal and garnished with maitre butter, lemon juice and parsley

grills

t-bone steak lyonnaise	$2.25

a man sized delicious steak — charcoal grilled, buttered and garnished with onions poached in white wine

rump steak with mushroom sauce	$2.25

grain fed selected local beef — served with fresh mushrooms and whole roasted potato in alfoil

fillet steak pacific	$2.30

thick choicest eye fillet grilled to your taste over flaming charcoal, served with grilled pineapple and whole roasted potato in alfoil

filet mignon	$2.30

the tenderest cut of fillet wrapped in bacon garnished with maitre butter and served with grilled stuffed tomato and whole roasted potato in alfoil

steak bermuda	$2.50

a gourmet's treat — succulent fillet stuffed with bananas and bacon

carpet bag steak	$2.50

for those who like a mixture of land and sea — thick fillet stuffed with oysters and bacon

tournedos piedmontese	$2.50

thick fillet pieces basted in butter, served on a bed of fried rice, garnished with whole stuffed tomato

shish kabob	$2.25

chunky cubes of fillet steak marinated in wine, bacon, capsicum and fresh mushrooms grilled on a skewer in traditional turkish style and served on a bed of fried rice

pork chops tahitian	$2.25

thick pork chops slowly grilled and garnished with fried bananas, corn on the cob, grilled pineapple and candied sweet potato

ham steak hawaiian	$2.25

thick ham steak freshly cut grilled over charcoal and served with delicious raisin sauce and grilled pineapple

all grills can be served with mushroom, bearnaise, chasseur or barbecue sauce on request $0.20

Unusual headings such as Grills and Prawns help to create a foreign atmosphere.

This unusual menu cover designed from newspaper stories and illustratious of 100 years ago creates an old time atmosphere.

The OPEN HEARTH INTELLIGENCER

Philadelphia, Penna. - Summer 1876   One Cent

PHILADELPHIA, "The Centennial City"

Transcontinental Hotel of Philadelphia

The luxurious new *Transcontinental Hotel* has been built especially for *the Centennial*, it has accommodations for a thousand guest at five dollars per day. To right of picture is a corner of the sprawling *Hotel Globe* with room for two thousand guest. The crowded intersection shown is at Elm (Parkside) and Belmont, close by *the Centennial* and the route of the official parades.

Philadelphia is host to travelers from throughout the world during Centennial

The *Great Exhibition* opened on May 10th and thousands continue to converge on city. The fair is a challenge to the hardy visitor who wishes to see it all on foot. There are 25 miles of outdoor walks which cover the entire 236 acres and eleven miles of indoor walking.

The main attraction, the great Corliss engine, which was started on opening day by *President Grant* continues to be the star attraction. Its fourteen hundred horsepower engine could, if necessary, drive the entire shafting machinery required to operate the exhibits.

ULYSSES S. GRANT

PRESIDENT GRANT IN PHILA, PA.

On May 10, President U. S. Grant led a procession officially opening the *"Centennial."* Flags of all nations whipped in the breeze and all buildings in Philadelphia were gaily decorated. The many bands played a march written for the occasion by Richard Wagner and the poet Whittier and a chorus of six hundred voices singing Handel's "Hallelujah Chorus."

A reception followed honoring *President U. S. Grant* and other officials at the *Original Open Hearth Restaurant*, which is located at nearby Belmont and City Line Avenues. The elegant banquet menu featured Saddle of Mutton, Potted Pigeon with Mushrooms, Gallinteen of Quail with Truffles and Mr. Segal's own . Romanian Garlic Rib Steak.

Elegant New DINING SALOON Open...

Upon returning from the Centennial, *Harper's* warned that at *the Open Hearth's Dining Saloon...*" you shall find the mere fragments from a roast brisket of beef or the segment of a lobster so bedecked and so dressed with piquant sauces, and so flanked with savory vegetables that you shall come to a new knowledge of the triumphs of cookery." At an official dinner held at this fine dining saloon,

Philadelphia's Mayor Wm. S. Stokley warned . . . "if any of the attractions which have made this Exhibition so great is to survive for future generations enjoyment, let's hope it is the *Original Open Hearth*. If a century from now there be a *Bi-Centennial*, let us hope that our offsprings dine as well as we do tonight. I propose toast to Mr. Segal and his Excellent staff."

Original Open Hearth

Mr. Segal recalls playing host to James Buchanan Brady, better known as Diamond Jim. In the days of the fifteen-course dinner, he was recognized as Number One eater, the man whom restaurateur Al Segal admiringly designated "the best twenty-five customers the Open Hearth has." After a recent party held in the Wedgewood Room, Mr. Segal recalled, "When Diamond Jim pointed at a platter of French pastry, he didn't mean any special piece of pastry. He meant the whole platter of pastry."

LABRADOR
French Steamship arrives.

The French Motor Steamship "LABRADOR," which docked in Philadelphia on March 24th was the largest vessel to ever navigate the Delaware River. Most of its cargo was goods for *the Centennial Exhibition*, however there were 200 cases of J. Goerg & Co., La Perie de la Cuvee Champagne aboard and destined for the *Open Hearth's* wine cellar.

CONTINENTAL RAILWAY

Philadelphia, May 1 — A new era has begun in the field of modern transportation with the opening of the Continental Railway. Eight beautiful enclosed four-wheeled carriages have been put into use and eleven more are to follow. A stable of twenty healthy, vigorous horses will be used on the Continental Railway line, which extends from Front and Market Streets to the Centennial grounds. The ride from Belmont and Elm (Main entrance to the fair) to City Hall can be made in only one hour and fifteen minutes. The fee for a round-trip being 7¢.

COLOR ON THE MENU

Advertising in America vividly illustrates the effectiveness of color as a sales and merchandising tool for products of all kinds. Because people are known to respond to it, color fills our magazines, books, newspapers and even TV.

Color photography plus modern methods of color reproduction have made color illustration commonplace in printed media. Today there is an accelerating trend to colorful menus.

Color on the menu can function in many ways. First, it can act as decoration, making the menu more attractive and interesting. Second, it can be used through color photography reproduction to *illustrate* your food and drink, and third, color can set the mood and style for your restaurant.

Using color as decoration or design on your menu can be done simply, with the use of one additional color plus black, or all of the colors of the rainbow can be used. Color can also be added to the menu through the use of colored paper.

The *amount* of color used on a menu for design purposes will depend on two factors—cost and the effect desired. The more colors used on a menu, the more expensive it is to print. One color on colored paper is the least expensive. Next comes two colors down, then three and finally four, which gives you all the colors of the spectrum. Four colors are necessary to reproduce illustrations developed from food photography.

Color will also produce an *ef-*

Albin G. Seaberg

fect on your menu. If you use many bright colors in panels, headings and illustrations, you will create a menu that characterizes a certain type of restaurant, usually a sandwich shop, pancake house, short order, fast service type of restaurant. If, on the other hand you use pastel shades or tans, buffs, ivory, gray or blue plus black with gold, etc., and use any bright colors sparingly, you will create a more sophisticated mood. This use of color is typical of the supper club, the continental, more expensive type of restaurant.

The simplest and easiest way to use a second color in the design of your menu is to print your headings, Seafood, Steak, Appetizers, Desserts, etc., in color—red, blue, brown, green, or gold—while printing the rest of the food listing in black.

As a rule, however, only a limited amount of type should be in a second color since any large amount of type in color becomes hard and tiresome to read. The human eye seems to *read* black and white best of all.

The selection of colored paper can enhance the appearance of your menu without adding to the printing cost. There is an almost

These two attractive tip-ons, one for a dessert and the other a side order, illustrate the most versatile, flexible and inexpensive way to use color on the menu. They can be clipped, stapled or glued to the menu. If printed on Kleen-Stik, the color tip-on can be attached and removed as desired.

unlimited selection of papers available in every color imaginable, including metallic gold, silver and copper.

In selecting colored paper, however, be careful of two things. First, if you are going to print a considerable amount of readable copy, be sure that the color is not too dark. Some reds and blues are too dark to allow for black type to be read when printed over these dark colors.

In addition, some papers are chosen for cover stock use that are the same color, red, black and blue for example, on both sides. This usually means that the inside front cover, inside back cover and back cover cannot be used for merchandising either in the form of a printed message or illustrations. Paper can be obtained that is colored on one side and white on the other. This is more practical for menu use.

Another simple and inexpensive method of adding color and elegance to a menu is to use wide, colorful ribbons as part of the design. A wide red or blue ribbon, for example, glued to the front cover or "wrapped around" from the front to the inside front cover, adds color and texture to the menu and creates a rich-appearing menu.

Full color food illustrations with menu listings are a natural merchandising combination. Color photography means that your food and drink can be presented exactly the way it looks when served in your restaurant. And food illustration needs *color*.

No food advertiser would think

OLD FASHIONED STRAWBERRY SHORTCAKE

FRENCH FRIED ONION RINGS

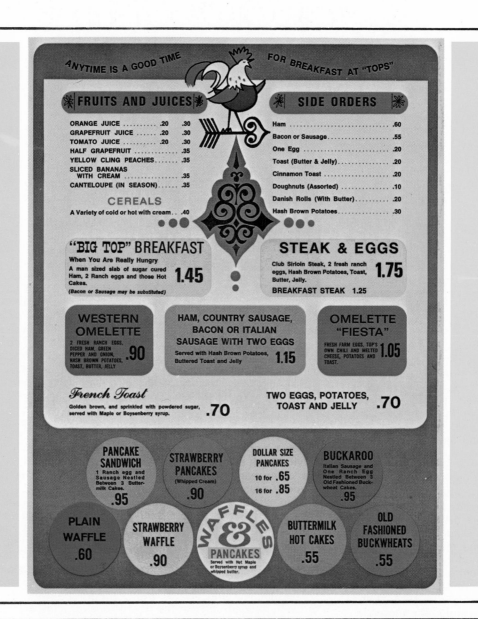

ANYTIME IS A GOOD TIME FOR BREAKFAST AT "TOPS"

FRUITS AND JUICES

ORANGE JUICE	.20	.30
GRAPEFRUIT JUICE	.20	.30
TOMATO JUICE	.20	.30
HALF GRAPEFRUIT		.35
YELLOW CLING PEACHES		.35
SLICED BANANAS WITH CREAM		.35
CANTELOUPE (IN SEASON)		.35

CEREALS

A Variety of cold or hot with cream .. .40

SIDE ORDERS

Ham	.60
Bacon or Sausage	.55
One Egg	.20
Toast (Butter & Jelly)	.20
Cinnamon Toast	.20
Doughnuts (Assorted)	.10
Danish Rolls (With Butter)	.20
Hash Brown Potatoes	.30

"BIG TOP" BREAKFAST
When You Are Really Hungry
A man sized slab of sugar cured Ham, 2 Ranch eggs and those Hot Cakes.
(Bacon or Sausage may be substituted)
1.45

STEAK & EGGS
Club Sirloin Steak, 2 fresh ranch eggs, Hash Brown Potatoes, Toast, Butter, Jelly.
1.75
BREAKFAST STEAK 1.25

WESTERN OMELETTE
2 FRESH RANCH EGGS, DICED HAM, GREEN PEPPER AND ONION, HASH BROWN POTATOES, TOAST, BUTTER, JELLY
.90

HAM, COUNTRY SAUSAGE, BACON OR ITALIAN SAUSAGE WITH TWO EGGS
Served with Hash Brown Potatoes, Buttered Toast and Jelly
1.15

OMELETTE "FIESTA"
FRESH FARM EGGS, TOP'S OWN CHILI AND MELTED CHEESE, POTATOES AND TOAST.
1.05

French Toast
Golden brown, and sprinkled with powdered sugar, served with Maple or Boysenberry syrup.
.70

TWO EGGS, POTATOES, TOAST AND JELLY
.70

PANCAKE SANDWICH
1 Ranch egg and Sausage Nestled Between 3 Butter-milk Cakes.
.95

STRAWBERRY PANCAKES
(Whipped Cream)
.90

DOLLAR SIZE PANCAKES
10 for .65
16 for .85

BUCKAROO
Italian Sausage and One Ranch Egg Nestled Between 3 Old Fashioned Buck-wheat Cakes.
.95

PLAIN WAFFLE
.60

STRAWBERRY WAFFLE
.90

WAFFLES & PANCAKES
Served with Hot Maple or Boysenberry syrup and whipped butter.

BUTTERMILK HOT CAKES
.55

OLD FASHIONED BUCKWHEATS
.55

CHICKEN COUNTRY FRIED
Three generous pieces of tender, juicy chicken cooked to our own formula, rich gravy, fluffy whipped potatoes, creamy cole slaw, cranberry-orange relish, served with warm roll and butter.
1.89

STEAK "SIZZLER" SANDWICH
7 ounces of U.S. choice butt sirloin broiled and on buttered toast makes this a real bargain with tossed salad and choice of dressing.
2.19

FISH 'N FRIES
Golden brown Lake Perch fillets from icy waters, firm and sweet with crisp French fries, creamy cole slaw and lots of tartar sauce, warm roll and butter.
1.49

of picturing his product in black and white or with line drawings. If a picture is worth a thousand words, a color reproduction is the closest thing there is to the actual food entree, appetizer or dessert itself.

The main objection to color halftones on the menu, of course, is cost. First, there is the cost of color photography. Unless the restaurant operator can use stock photographs of food set-ups similar to what he serves, he will have to buy the services of a photographer. The cost of a good (professionally competent) color photograph can vary from $50 to $250 or more.

Then there is the cost of positives, color separations and plates (the process of making the color photograph ready for printing). An 8½ by 11 four-color positive costs around $250 in Chicago. Smaller color positives cost somewhat less, but the cost of 4 or 6 color illustrations on a menu will not be small.

Finally, the printing of a four-color menu will be more expensive. A restaurant operator can figure on his printing costs alone to be 35 per cent more for color than for his present one or two-color menu. So, if color reproduction is so much more expensive, why consider it at all?

In the first place, color is in. From color TV to decor and even to the way men and women dress, color is being used more and more in our society. Therefore, the dull and drab gray of yesterday is just not good enough for today.

In the second place, nothing illustrates and thereby sells food as well as a good color illustration. You can describe your steak, roast beef, chicken or shrimp with the best copy in the

Opposite page, top: This menu shows an effective use of color panels—squares, circles, rectangles, plus other color design uses. Notice how breakfast "specials" are given the color panel treatment.

Opposite page, bottom: Color food illustrations do not have to be photographs. These three color drawings of chicken, steak and fish are very effective and attractive.

Right: Cocktails, wines, beers and after dinner drinks can also be illustrated in color. Considering their "high profit" value, perhaps more drinks should be illustrated, and in color!

world, and it will never do the communication job that a color illustration will do.

Color illustration is especially effective as a selling tool in the restaurant that wants to make the customer decide quickly what he wants, order it, eat it, pay his check and leave so that a new customer can take his place. The agonizing slowness that some customers exhibit when ordering, which can cost the restaurant operator money, can be partly eliminated by color photography.

Of course, not every item on the menu can be illustrated in color. First, there are too many items, and, second, the cost is prohibitive. The most commonly color illustrated items on the menu are:

1. Appetizers
   a. Shrimp cocktail
   b. Antipasto
2. Salads
   a. Tossed or Chef
   b. Fruit
   c. Caesar
3. Sandwiches
   a. Hamburger
   b. Cheeseburger
   c. Club
4. Entrees
   a. Steaks
   b. Shrimp
   c. Chicken
5. Desserts
   a. Pie
   b. Cake
   c. Sundaes

The selection of what you illustrate in color on your menu, of course, should be based on what you want to sell most. The items you illustrate in color will get the most attention and probably the fastest action.

This brings up another aspect of the use of color illustrations. Because of the high cost of color, your selection of items to be illustrated should be made with care. You will have to live with your selection for some time unless you want to go to the considerable expense of new photography, positives and color printing. Items that are proven sellers and profitable should be the ones selected for color illustration.

Color food illustrations are used in two basic ways on the menu—a square or rectangular picture including some background and the vignette picture,

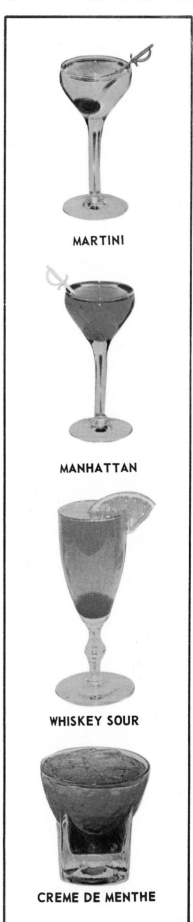

MARTINI

MANHATTAN

WHISKEY SOUR

CREME DE MENTHE

Willkommen to

Frankenmuth Bavarian Inn

where the gemuetlichkeit of Old Bavaria
blends with the hospitality of New America

Speise Karte

or only the food on the plate.

The vignette illustration will be more expensive since the engraver has to eliminate the background from the color photo, but it does concentrate the viewer's attention on the food. The square or rectangular illustration, however, can be just as effective if the background is simple and does not interfere with the main subject, the food being served and sold.

Another important factor relative to color illustration is the quality of the illustration and the quality of the printing reproduction. The entire effort and cost of color illustration on the menu can be defeated by poor reproduction.

The appetite appeal of food illustration depends upon accurate color reproduction. A greenish steak, salad with brown lettuce or a gray apple pie is worse than no illustration at all. Many menu items, especially French-fried shrimp or fried chicken, tend to look more like brown lumps of nothing rather than appetizing entrees.

Care and competence in color reproduction are essential requirements. Your printer and your photographer should be professionals who know what they are doing, or else you could be wasting a good deal of money.

A common error in the use of color illustrations is failure to list the items sold and price next to the color illustration. Just an illustration of a steak at the top of your steak listing is not good enough. You cannot illustrate a steak without it being some spe-

Opposite page: This beautiful as well as colorful cover illustration sets the mood for this restaurant specializing in German food. The glass of beer looks real and appetizing enough to drink!

Above: This attractive menu cover is in full color on white stock. In addition to the name shown prominently, it has a drawing of the restaurant plus color photos of 4 *feature* items—shrimp, chicken, fruit salad and steak. This cover illustrates that many merchandising factors can function on a menu cover, if it is well organized.

Below: Ozzies restaurant uses a four color illustration nearly actual size of a steak with french fried onion rings and a baked potato on its cover. This gives "number one" position to this entree item and should sell a lot of steaks.

Casa Conti

Glenside, Penna.

Virginia Room

Dining Room

Ballroom

Lorraine Room

MAY WE SUGGEST
THESE BEFORE DINNER
COCKTAILS . . .

* Martini

  * Manhattan

    * Old Fashioned

      * Daiquiri

        * Bacardi

Steaks & Chops

Appetizers

SHRIMP COCKTAIL	.75
MARINATED HERRING	.50
ASSORTED RELISH TRAY, Per Person	.25
HOMEMADE SOUP, du Jour	.35
CHILLED FRUIT COCKT	
GRAP JUICE	

CHOICE T-BONE STEAK	4.50
BROILED CHOICE FILET MIGNON, with Mushroom Caps	4.85
BROILED CHOICE BABY FILET MIGNON, with Mushroom Caps	3.75
BROILED CHOICE NEW YORK CUT SIRLOIN STEAK	4.50
BROILED CHOICE TOP SIRLOIN BUTT STEAK	4.
CHOPPED SIRLOIN S	

From Our Sandwich Board

Kosher Style Corned Beef
on Rye with Dill Pickle and Cole Slaw .80
Bacon, Lettuce, and Tomato on Toast .75
Combination Ham, Cheese, Lettuce, and Tomato on a Bun .80
Cream Cheese and Chopped Olives on Raisin Toast .55
Egg, Ham, Tuna, or Chicken Salad .60
Imported Boneless and Skinless Portuguese Sardines on
Rye Bread with Hard Boiled Egg, Onion, and Tomato Slice 1.15

Hot Sandwiches

Delicious All Beef Hamburger with
Lettuce, Tomato, and Onion .60   Cheeseburger .65
Grilled Open Faced Tenderloin Steak Sandwich
with French Fries and a Salad 1.55
Pickwick Delight: Open Faced Broiled Cheese,
Bacon, and Tomato with French Fries 1.15
Hot Roast Vermont Turkey, Gravy and Potatoes 1.25
Hot Roast Sirloin of Beef, Gravy and Potatoes 1.35
Swankie Frankie: A Frankfurter Stuffed with Cheese
wrapped in Bacon, and served on a Toasted Bun with Pickle .55
Grilled Cheese .50   Fried Egg .45   Western Sandwich .70

On The Light Side

Two Country Fresh Eggs with Toast and Jelly .60
Poached or Boiled Eggs .65
Light Fluffy Egg Omelette .70
Choice of: Western, Cheese, Jelly,
Chopped Ham, Bacon, or Mushroom Omelette .90
Golden Brown Waffle, Maple Syrup .55
Delicious Silver Dollar Pancakes, Maple Syrup .75

Side Orders

Ham, Bacon, or Sausage .50   Canadian Bacon .60
American or French Fried Potatoes .30   Hashed Brown .40
Golden Deep Fried Onion Rings .50   For Two .95

Desserts and Beverages

All the Pies, Cakes, and Pastries Served are Baked
Fresh Daily in Our Own Bake Shop
Homemade Pies and Cakes .35   a la Mode .45
Strawberry Shortcake, Whipped Cream .50
Cheese Cake .35   with Strawberries .55
Fresh Fruit Cocktail .40   Jello .25
Sodas .40   Sundaes .45   Banana Split .70
Ice Cream or Sherbet .25 and .40   Malted Milk .45
Coffee, Tea, Sanka, or Postum .15   Iced Tea .15
White or Chocolate Milk .15   Hot Chocolate .15
Soft Drinks .10 and .20

Cregar's Famous Club
A Giant Triple Decker
Sliced Turkey, Crisp Bacon,
Lettuce, Tomato and Dressing
1.30

Jumbo Hamburger Deluxe
An extra large Hamburger Patty
Served on a Toasted Bun
French Fried Onion Rings
French Fried Potatoes
Cole Slaw, Lettuce, and Tomato
1.40
Topped with Melted Cheese 1.50

Homemade Apple Pie
a la Mode
.45

Above: Quality color illustration plus the copy that "goes with" the picture right next to it, makes this use of color function effectively. Note the unusual layout of the other not illustrated items on this menu—a simple, balanced yet functional organization.

Opposite page, top: The Casa Conti uses color photography on the back cover of its menu to illustrate its eight different dining rooms plus the lobby and lounge.

Opposite page, bottom: This menu shows the use of both outline and square color photos.

cific steak—tenderloin, filet mignon, butt, N. Y. strip, etc. For this reason, the relevant copy—name of entree, what "goes with it" and the price should be next to the illustration.

The easiest way to make sure that the illustration and copy go together is to put them in a box or a panel. This can be a simple black line around the picture and type, a more complicated design border or a color panel.

At present, color illustrations on the menu are used mostly by chain operations that can spread the cost of color over a large run of menu printing to be used in a large number of outlets. But independent operators are using color more often, especially those restaurants that emphasize customer turnover. With the improvement of new color printing techniques and the accompanying reduction in cost, more and more color will be used on the menu.

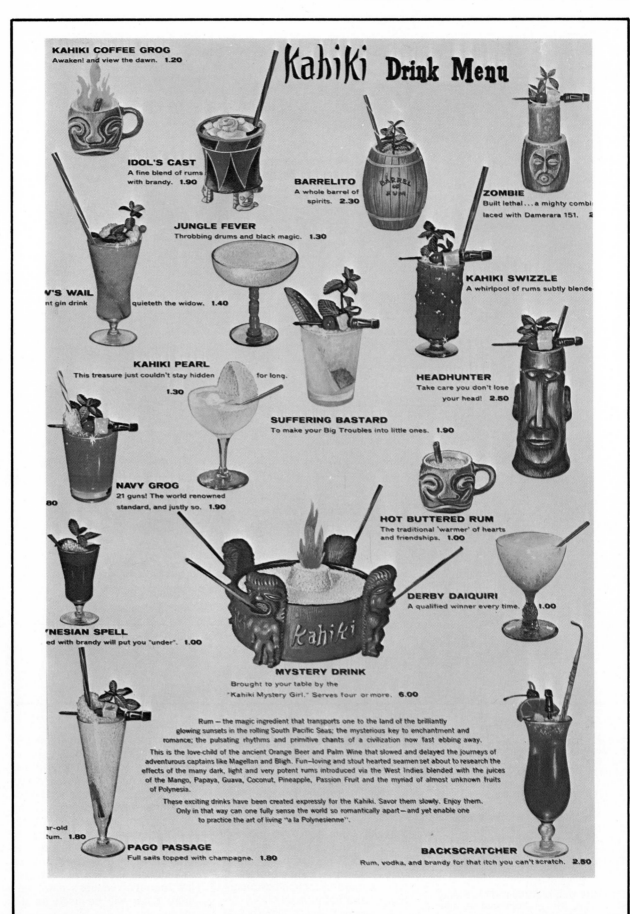

Kahiki Drink Menu

KAHIKI COFFEE GROG
Awaken! and view the dawn. **1.20**

IDOL'S CAST
A fine blend of rums with brandy. **1.90**

BARRELITO
A whole barrel of spirits. **2.30**

ZOMBIE
Built lethal...a mighty combi laced with Damerara 151. **2**

JUNGLE FEVER
Throbbing drums and black magic. **1.30**

V'S WAIL
nt gin drink quieteth the widow. **1.40**

KAHIKI SWIZZLE
A whirlpool of rums subtly blende

KAHIKI PEARL
This treasure just couldn't stay hidden for long. **1.30**

HEADHUNTER
Take care you don't lose your head! **2.50**

SUFFERING BASTARD
To make your Big Troubles into little ones. **1.90**

NAVY GROG
21 guns! The world renowned standard, and justly so. **1.90**

80

HOT BUTTERED RUM
The traditional 'warmer' of hearts and friendships. **1.00**

DERBY DAIQUIRI
A qualified winner every time. **1.00**

NESIAN SPELL
ed with brandy will put you "under". **1.00**

MYSTERY DRINK
Brought to your table by the "Kahiki Mystery Girl." Serves four or more. **6.00**

Rum — the magic ingredient that transports one to the land of the brilliantly glowing sunsets in the rolling South Pacific Seas; the mysterious key to enchantment and romance; the pulsating rhythms and primitive chants of a civilization now fast ebbing away.

This is the love-child of the ancient Orange Beer and Palm Wine that slowed and delayed the journeys of adventurous captains like Magellan and Bligh. Fun—loving and stout hearted seamen set about to research the effects of the many dark, light and very potent rums introduced via the West Indies blended with the juices of the Mango, Papaya, Guava, Coconut, Pineapple, Passion Fruit and the myriad of almost unknown fruits of Polynesia.

These exciting drinks have been created expressly for the Kahiki. Savor them slowly. Enjoy them. Only in that way can one fully sense the world so romantically apart—and yet enable one to practice the art of living "a la Polynesienne".

ar-old
um. **1.80**

PAGO PASSAGE
Full sails topped with champagne. **1.80**

BACKSCRATCHER
Rum, vodka, and brandy for that itch you can't scratch. **2.50**

SELLING OTHER THINGS
ON THE MENU

While food and drink are obviously the two primary items to be sold on the menu, "other" items, services, information and general promotion will vary from operation to operation. Not every establishment has decor, location or history to sell. Not every food service sells take-outs or has catering or banquet-party-meeting facilities. But even the operation with nothing special to sell can create some extras to add to its reputation, and often these extras can add extra income.

A list of "extra" or "other" items that appear most often on the menu:
a. History of food service operation
b. Story about management
c. Take-out or take-home service
d. Catering
e. Party-banquet-meeting facilities
f. Gift shop
g. Museum connected with establishment
h. Tourist attractions in the neighborhood, city or nearby area
i. City, state and national association affiliations
j. AAA, Mobile and other guide book recommendations
k. Credit cards honored
l. Map showing location

These are the more or less normal extras, but a surprising number of food service operations do not sell any of these merchandising possibilities on their menu. In fact, the average menu has a surprising number of blank pages—back cover, inside back and front cover, etc.—that could be used for some of this merchandising.

The following examples of extra or other merchandising on the menu are from restaurants across the country.

Rosoff's Restaurant at Times Square in New York City makes a big thing out of its proximity to the theater, movies and other places of entertainment. It has a map on the back cover of its menu showing the location of Rosoff's, 35 theaters, 18 movie theaters and six other auditoriums and meeting places. In addition, on the inside of the menu, the restaurant lists what is currently playing at the 35 theaters listed. This makes an excellent tie-in with people who eat out before going to the theater. Where do they eat out? Rosoff's, of course.

Not every restaurant has decor so unusual that it is worth writing about, but the Three Fountains Restaurant in St. Louis does. The following is just a portion of the descriptive copy:

"The decor of The Three Fountains was created through the use of materials and fictures salvaged from old St. Louis structures razed in the late 50's. The most striking example of the furnishings used in Victorian St. Louis is the back bar on the top level which originally served as a mantel in the old Gehner house at the Southeast corner of Taylor Avenue and Gehner Boulevard. The beautifully wrought staircase was disassembled from the Gehner house and handfit into the room by master cabinet makers. From this house came the wall panelling, the beautiful bevel cut front doors, and the colorful stained glass windows, depicting various foods, hanging on the North wall."

The Russ' Restaurants in Holland and Muskegon, Mich., get a lot of merchandising extras on a small menu. First, they feature a gift certificate as follows: "Give your friends a Russ Gift Certificate. Everyone likes to eat out. Certificate prices begin at 50¢. Inquire from our cashier."

Next, Russ' features copy on the preparation of their foods and take-home service:

"We prepare all the foods we serve right here on the premises. We make our own soups from plump tender chickens or juicy fresh beef and garden fresh vegetables. Try a bowl— pipin' hot! We grind our own steer beef daily, roast our own meats and turkeys. That's why our hamburgers and bar-b-que sandwiches are so tasty. We prepare our own salads and make our own dressings—to assure you a fresh crisp salad every time. We bake our own pastries— right here in our bake shop—M-m-m-m they're good! Try them here or take home some of those fresh strawberry tarts or a whole pie. We thank you for visiting us. We are happy to prepare for you the finest food in town and are gratified for this opportunity to demonstrate our service and hospitality. If you prefer, you can order by phone and take 'em home. Every item on our menu is available for carry-out service. For 31 years Russ' have taken every step possible to give you The Best of Foods, Cleanliness and Service."

Then they have a couple of paragraphs on Holland, Mich., and their growth since their founding.

"Holland is truly a 'favored city'! Dune-shored Lake Michigan and beautiful Lake Macatawa, rich fields, thriving industry, a most moving beginning with hardy Dutch pioneers seeking a haven for religious freedom. . .all have made Holland the wonderful community it is today. It's Tulip Time in Holland Every Year in May. Holland is famous for its internationally known Tulip Time Festival, held every year in mid-May; and for Windmill Island— an authentic bit of old Holland complete with working windmill, gardens and recreational attractions. As you travel through our town on the well-kept streets and through the rolling countryside and farmlands, you, too, will feel that indefinable something about the thrifty, clean, deeply religious and progressive Dutchman. . . .still carried on in the first and second generation.

"We here at Russ' Drive-In feel gratefully favored also. It is difficult to put into words our appreciation for your loyalty and friendship. . . .guaranteeing our success since our humble beginning in July of 1934. We, the management and personnel, are just as interested now, as we were in the growing up process, to merit your continued patronage through giving you the best food and service in the most pleasant and congenial surroundings. . .and, we invite your constructive suggestions and criticisms at any time."

And finally, they have two good maps showing their locations.

Mc Garvey's Restaurant sells some unusual other merchandising extras. To begin with, in the summer they serve the following Sip-Sup and Sail special:

"Every Wednesday, Sip-Sup-Sail. Enjoy a choice of Manhattan, Martini or Sip & Sail Cocktail, Dinner from the Captain's Table which includes:
Juicy Roast Sirloin of Beef
Fresh Lake Erie Perch
½ Tender Milk Fed Chicken
Fried Deep Sea Scallops
"And then—Relax on Lake Erie for an Hour's Moonlite Cruise—$4.85."

Another unusual aspect of McGarvey's Restaurant is a 12-month schedule showing different hours of business during the different seasons of the year, for this is a restaurant with a very seasonal business.

Hotel and motel restaurants, of course, have a great number of other things to sell—the motel's facilities, TV, room service, swimming pool, etc. The Yardarm Restaurant menu on p. 140 does a good job of selling all of its facilities.

This restaurant sells special catering service with full color photographs.

THE ORIGINAL WAVERLY INN

The Twentieth Century was four years distant when Waverly Inn first opened in 1896.

Walter Scott, a gentleman-scholar from Waterbury, purchased the white house with the square roof and cupola in the center from Judge Joel Hinman, chief justice of the Connecticut Supreme Court.

Scott converted what had been a historical homestead into an Inn he called Waverly, named from the epochal novels of his illustrious namesake, famed author Sir Walter Scott.

Located on the historically-significant College Highway, Waverly soon became a rendezvous for discriminating diners. Among its early and frequent visitors was William Taft, at the time a member of the Yale Law School faculty and, of course, later to become president.

In 1905, Scott purchased additional land and erected a building adjoining the Inn which became known as the Casino. No dinners were served here. Scott placed antiques in the Casino and diners browsed among them. Notable in the collection was a two-wheel shay which George Washington had imported from England and later used to tour New England. Scott established the tradition of providing attractive and artistic antiques at Waverly, a custom continued to the present.

At the turn of the century and in the decade that followed under Scott's ownership, the Inn specialized in serving fish and game dinners. The Waverly soon acquired a reputation for serving the finest "hot birds and cold bottles" in New England.

In 1952, the original Inn was destroyed by fire. The only object salvaged from the ashes was a black, cloisonne tole urn that still embellishes the Victorian table in the main lobby. Under the guiding genius of then owners, Rocco Diorio and Louis Ricciuti, a new Waverly rose on the same site, capturing in every detail the antiquity of the past and the charm of the present.

Many Nineteenth Century hallmarks lend an air of nostalgic enchantment to Waverly, most acquired from the famous Grand Union Hotel at Saratoga Springs, N. Y. Included are the Waterford cut glass chandelier hanging in the main dining room, subject of a Life magazine story several years ago; a Rosewood grand piano, upon which composer Victor Herbert created many of his musical scores, and an exquisite rolltop desk used by President U. S. Grant to write his memoirs.

In the lobby is a complete set of Waverly Novels which were purchased in London. Descending to the sumptuous Saratoga Room, one views 18 treasured old English wall prints.

Each of the facilities at Waverly has a blend of the old and the new to make dining more delightful. Present facilities, including the Crystal Room, Colonial Room, Saratoga Room, Tea Room, Directors Room, Blue Boy Room, Continental Room and the attractive cocktail lounge, can comfortably hold more than 1,000 diners.

Present Waverly proprietor Frank J. Nastri pledges to preserve the Inn's glorious traditions and enhance its future, not for a thousand persons, but only one . . . . you.

Chandelier estimated to be worth $70,000.

Piano - at which Victor Herbert composed many of his famous scores, including "Kiss Me Again", from Mmle. Modiste.

Unique mahogany clock, which houses one of the oldest self-winding mechanisms in the country.

History, tradition and decor can all be sold on the menu.

*T*here is a cherished tradition about the Stock Yard Inn. From the flaming gas torches at the entrance and on into the gleaming steak throne, a welcome warmth greets every visitor. During national political conventions the Inn has been home to presidents and political aspirants. In the century of the Yards' existence, the Stock Yard Inn has been the gathering place of ranchers, drovers, trail herders, barons of the meat industry and the crowned heads of Europe. We are happy that you have joined us in this tradition of conviviality and fine food. May your visit be a pleasant one, rewarding us with your return on many occasions.

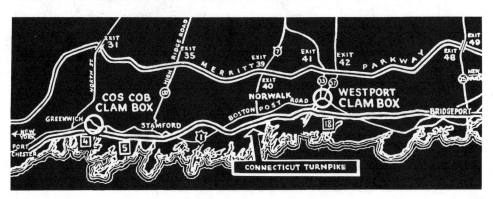

General copy helps sell your total restaurant and a map tells them where it is.

HORNE'S LOCATIONS
LOOK FOR THE YELLOW ROOFS

EXPANDING ALONG AMERICA'S HIGHWAYS

CIRCUS GRILLES
CARROUSEL RESTAURANTS
MOTOR LODGES
CROWN ROOM RESTAURANTS

EXECUTIVE OFFICES
DETROIT, MICHIGAN

A multiple operation should list its other locations on the menu.

Jack Tar Hotels

SERVING YOU — NORTH, SOUTH, EAST AND WEST

JACK TAR HOTEL — *Lansing, Michigan*
JACK TAR GROVE PARK INN & MOTOR LODGE — *Asheville, North Carolina*
JACK TAR DURHAM — *Durham, North Carolina*
JACK TAR FRANCIS MARION — *Charleston, South Carolina*
JACK TAR POINSETT — *Greenville, South Carolina*
JACK TAR GRAND BAHAMA HOTEL and COUNTRY CLUB — *West End, Grand Bahama Island*
JACK TAR KEYS MOTOR LODGE — *Marathon Shores, Florida*
JACK TAR HOTEL — *Clearwater, Florida*
JACK TAR BEACH HOUSE — *Destin, Florida*
JACK TAR CAPITOL HOUSE — *Baton Rouge, Louisiana*
JACK TAR HOTEL — *Orange, Texas*
JACK TAR HOTEL — *Galveston, Texas*
JACK TAR HOTEL — *San Francisco, California*

The customer can eat in only one room at a time, so if you have a multiple facility, sell the rest of the establishment on the menu.

Kolb's Famous Rooms

Smartest Meeting Place for Clubs, Civic Groups, Luncheons, Parties

Four fine rooms for banquets, dinners, luncheons. Varying in size from the immense to the intimately private.

Dresden Room

Bavarian Room

Tyrolean Room

Rose Room

Kolbs

★ ROSE ROOM, The Old European charm of crystal chandeliers and elegant carpeting make this room a favorite for the discriminating host. From 20 to 75 guests.

★ TYROLEAN ROOM, Banquet size, which will accommodate over 175 guests, also available in conjunction with the Rose Room for cocktail parties for larger groups.

★ DRESDEN ROOM, This exquisite room takes its name from the priceless collection of Dresden figurines on display therein. With its tapestry walls it is ideal for dignified dining for the small, select group, up to 12.

★ BAVARIAN ROOM, Lunch or dine in the atmosphere of an Old Bavarian Inn. Enjoy the ease of the roomy captain's chairs. Ideal for from 12 to 25.

TRY OUR FAMOUS SPECIALTY
THE COACHMAN'S INN WHISKEY SOUR
SERVED IN A LARGE GOBLET WITH ICE
80¢

Party and Banquet Facilities

For your next party, banquet or business conference . . . we offer

- **THE PUMP ROOM** . . . Elegant and Pleasant.

- **THE TALLY-HO ROOM** . . . Very charming with book shelves flanking the fireplace and a picture window overlooking the fountain in our formal garden.

- For larger groups or weddings . . . during the day . . . all rooms and lounges are at your disposal.

- For more details, call between 9:00 A.M. and 4:00 P.M. and ask for our Banquet Manager . . . 759-6852.

We Honor AMERICAN EXPRESS, DINERS CLUB,

CARTE BLANCHE and MARINE MIDLAND Credit Cards.

GIFT CERTIFICATE
Gift certificates, made out in any amount, good towards the purchase of dinners and cocktails of your choice.
Ask The Host For Further Information.

THE COACHMAN'S INN IS OPEN EVERY DAY

RECOMMENDED BY THE MOBILE TRAVEL GUIDE

THE COACHMAN'S INN
10350 MAIN STREET (Route 5)
4 Miles East of Transit Road (Route 78)
CLARENCE, NEW YORK 14031

A gracious welcome awaits you at the COACHMAN'S INN. After a stretch of daily routine, one appreciates its peacefulness and quietude. One also likes the INN for its attractive, cozy lounges and cheerful atmosphere of its three huge woodburning fireplaces. Forget the mad rush of the world outside while you partake of the leisurely atmosphere this friendly INN offers. The rich panelled walls of pecky cypress have mellowed and taken on a distinguished appearance, and as a result, are a feature of the dining-rooms. The lounges grouped around the merrily burning fireplaces are just the place to relax and visit with friends while sipping your favorite cocktail. The cuisine will impress you. The food is unusually good because quality is of the very best. You always dine by candlelight at the COACHMAN'S INN with soft soothing music lingering in the background. The Innkeepers courteous, congenial and efficient staff is always at hand ready to serve you. The COACHMAN'S INN represents a nostalgic era of the past where charm and old fashioned hospitality lingers again.

Write your message here

Address

PLACE 6¢ STAMP HERE

Besides being a self mailer, this memo sells a special drink, party-banquet facilities, special rooms and a gift certificate.

SPECIALS

Few, if any, food service operators consider every item on the menu—whether appetizers, soups, salads, entrees or desserts—as equal to every other item in the same category. There are always some items that deserve or should get "special" treatment. There are two basic types of specials from the operator's point of view. They are the items that the establishment is famous for (if it is famous at all) and, therefore, they deserve (and usually get) special treatment.

The second basic kind of "special" is the item that the operator would like to sell more of—high profit, easy to prepare items—entree, appetizer, salad, dessert or even side order items. The special, therefore, serves two purposes. It advertises the top selling items and it is a selling tool for making slow-moving items into faster-moving, profit items.

The important thing for the menu planner to do is to decide which items he wants to give special treatment, and then be sure that they are getting special treatment. The methods for giving "special" items special treatment are:

    1.   List specials in larger, bolder type than the rest of the menu.
    2.   Give specials more descriptive, merchandising, "sell" copy.
    3.   Place specials in boxes, panels or some kind of graphic device to make them stand out from the rest of the layout.
    4.   Use more color and illustrations for specials.

Like all other segments of the menu, some appetizers can be "specials" as listed here: hot saute shrimp; oysters Bienville covered with a spicy sauce of chopped mixed seafood; baked, baby western ribs; and, of course, the antipasto tray or relish tray (for two or more) is often a natural appetizer special.

The following are some "specials" which show imaginative and better than average treatment in the various menu categories from appetizer to dessert. The list of entree "specials," luncheon or dinner, could be endless, but those listed here are some unusual ones:

SPECIAL LUNCHEON—clam chowder, tossed green salad, grilled fillet of turbot, french fried potatoes, sour dough french bread, ice cream, coffee—$3.50.

DINNER SPECIAL—Relish platter, salami, martadella, clam chowder, ravioli, tossed green salad, veal scaloppine, lobster thermidor, filet of turbot, garden vegetables, sour dough french bread, ice cream, coffee.

DANISH DINNER—consomme a la Mermaid, flounder filet, roast Long Island duck, red cabbage (Danish style), cucumber salad, lingonberries, petite browned potatoes, Ris-a-l'Allemande with Cherry Heering sauce, coffee—$5.50.

SAINT AND SINNER—a combination of lobster and choice tenderloin of beef—a delightful treat—$4.95. This is a popular "special" combination of beef and seafood sometimes called SURF AND TURF. It is popular enough on many menus to indicate considerable public acceptance.

CONTINENTAL SPECIAL—steak Diane Flambee with wild rice—mignonettes of beef cooked at your table, sauted in sweet butter, bathed in their own sauce. Served with fresh mushrooms on a bed of wild rice and flavored with brandy. This is typical of flaming dish specials.

PLANKED STEAKS BOUQUETIERRE—sirloin planked steak for two—only U. S. prime steaks are used—"broiled to a turn," and planked with a generous selection of fresh garden vegetables and mushrooms. This is just one of the many "for two" specials which are becoming very popular on the menu.

EGGS BENEDICT on toasted English muffins. Specially selected broiled ham, poached fresh eggs covered with sauce hollandaise and topped with a truffle, a mark of distinction—$3.00. This entree shows that a "special" does not have to be beef or seafood.

CARPETBAG STEAK—tenderloin steak stuffed with Sydney rock oysters, served with french fries, field mushroom sauce and hearts of lettuce. This is certainly a different steak special.

OLD FASHIONED SHORE DINNER—the works, choice of Maine chowder or lobster stew, crackers and pickles, steamed clams, bouillon and drawn butter. Then, fried clams, hot boiled lobster, chef salad, french fried potatoes, rolls, old fashioned Indian pudding with whipped cream and coffee. An adventure in good eating (Amen).

CHATEAUBRIAND—the ultimate in superior steaks. Thick and generous this rich U. S. choice steak is recognized the world over as an epicurean masterpiece. Served for two or more, the chateaubriand is a king-sized cut of tenderloin broiled with the grain running horizontal, against the heat. This gives a succulent, crisp, tender crust with a pink warm center. This is an "occasion" steak which should be sliced cross-grain and served with a good wine and enjoyed by good company.

FROM THE BAR

The Hearthini, a masterful blend of imported gin, vodka and French vermouth. This is a change from the run of the mill martini; it was created by the Hearth restaurant and featured in a box at the top of its liquor listing. Another unusual way to sell and "specialize" manhattans and martinis is to sell them by the bucket. Patterson's Supper Club, for example, sells a bucket of Martinis and Manhattans (more than half a pint) for $2.15.

BREAKFAST

The breakfast menu can have "specials" just like any other part of the menu. Steak and eggs are a common breakfast special, but Norm's Restaurant goes one (or two) better. It lists and features three breakfast steak and egg combinations. They are: 1. Large porterhouse steak and eggs, $1.95; 2. Large New York cut steak and eggs, $1.95; 3. Large top sirloin steak and eggs, $1.85—served with hashed brown potatoes, toast and jelly.

SIDE DISHES

Even the lowly side dish or extra, a la carte, can be a "special" if you decide you want to give it special treatment. Some more common side dishes that have been given "special" treatment on the menu are: garlic rolls, cheese rolls, charcoal broiled mushrooms, charcoal broiled Bermuda onions.

DESSERTS

Some of the most popular "special" desserts, as noted on menus with big dessert listings, are: cherries jubilee, crepes suzette (for two, usually), peaches flambeau kirsch, and baked Alaska. But a simple dessert such as ice cream can get a "special" treatment. One restaurant, for example, sells an eight-inch-high super sundae for 75¢, a "haystack" (5 scoops high) for 69¢ and a super soda (4 scoops of ice cream—2 vanilla, 2 your choice) for 60¢. The number of specials on a menu, of course, is important. If everything is made a special, then nothing becomes special. The rule should be to keep specials down to 20 to 30% of the items listed on the menu. This means that, if you list ten entrees or appetizers, desserts, etc., two or three of them should or can be specials. To alternate and create variety in specials, they can be printed on tip-ons and changed daily, weekly or rotated in any other way you wish to experiment.

Specials Hot

Please ask your server for the Carved Meat Feature and Prepared Dishes of the day which includes potatoes, vegetable of the day, hot rolls and butter

OR

The carved Weight Watcher of the day consisting of the same Specials served with cottage cheese, freshly sliced tomatoes, ry-krisp, polyunsaturated margarine.

$1.60

Buffet

We invite you to serve yourself from Verdugo Oaks fine Luncheon Buffet . . . a wondrous variety of enticing salads, meats, cheeses, fruits and a choice of delicious hot dishes

(Includes coffee, tea or milk and oven-hot rolls)

$2.10

SOUP DU JOUR 35   SMALL DINNER SALAD . . 50

MICHELOB BEER 50c

Weight Watchers

The following entrees can also be served as Weight Watcher dishes, priced as below. We are proud to feature at your request, low fat milk, polyunsaturated margarine, ry-krisp, sanka and sucaryl.

Broiled and Grilled

CHOICE PETITE FILET MIGNON 3.25
BROILED LAMB CHOPS 2.75
BROILED GROUND SIRLOIN 1.65
LIVER AND ONIONS 1.65
GRILLED HALIBUT STEAK, Lemon and Tartar Sauce 1.60
FILET OF SOLE, Saute Meuniere 1.75
Served with Potatoes and Vegetable, Hot Rolls and Butter

THE GOLD MEDAL SANDWICH 2.35

(A Blue-Ribbon Open-Faced Sandwich on Thin Pumpernickel Bread, Paired with Choice Medallions of Beef Tenderloin and Paté de Maison. French Fries and Sliced Sweet Bermuda Onion Garni, Make this a Real Winner!)

NEW YORK STEAK SANDWICH, Garlic Bread,
French Fries, Garni 2.65
VERDUGO SPECIAL HAMBURGER 1.35
(Choice Ground Sirloin, Accented with a Slice of Cheese, on one of Our Famous Onion Rolls)
LONDON RAREBIT au Maison, Garnished with Crisp Bacon 1.50
TURKEY, HAM AND AVOCADO SUPREME en Casserole . 1.85

Eggs and Omelettes

EGGS BENEDICT 2.25
(Ham and Poached Eggs on Toasted English Muffin, topped with Hollandaise Sauce)
HAM OR BACON AND (3) EGGS 1.90
(Potatoes, Toast and Butter)
CREAM SCRAMBLED EGGS 1.50
(Tomatoes and Chives, Potatoes, Toast and Butter)
SPANISH OR MUSHROOM OR CHEESE OMELETTE 1.75
(Potatoes, Toast and Butter)
GAMBLER'S EGGS 1.75
(Cream Scrambled Eggs (3) and French Toast)
CORNED BEEF HASH AND POACHED EGGS 1.75
(with Toasted English Muffin)

We reserve the right to refuse service to anyone.
Not responsible for loss of personal property.
5% Sales Tax will be Added to the Price of All Food and Beverage Items Served at Tables in this Room

Salads

VERDUGO OAKS SALAD (Mixed at Your Table) 2.35
(Lobster, Shrimp and Crabmeat)
SHRIMP, CRAB OR LOBSTER LOUIE 2.25
OUR SUPREME FRUIT SALAD, Crowned with a
Fluff of Whipped Cream 1.95
SOUTHLAND CHEF'S SALAD 1.85
STUFFED RIPE TOMATO WITH SHRIMP 1.95
TRI-SALAD (interesting salad assortment) 1.75
HALF AVOCADO STUFFED WITH SHRIMP OR CRABMEAT 2.10
COLD PRIME RIB PLATE 2.60
(Potato Salad and Sliced Tomatoes)

CAESAR SALAD (mixed at your table) . . . . for one 1.45
Each additional person, $1.00

Specialties and Sandwiches

COLD PRIME RIB SANDWICH on French Bread 1.75
(with French Fries - Garni)
GRILLED HAM OR BACON AND CHEESE on White Bread 1.50
(Cole Slaw and French Fries)
BACON AND TOMATO 1.35
CLUB SANDWICH 1.85
(Towering Layers of Delectable Bacon, Tomato and Sliced Turkey)
SLICED TURKEY on White Bread 1.50
(Cole Slaw and French Fries)
FRIED SHRIMP SANDWICH (3) on Toast 1.50
(Cole Slaw and French Fries)
DODGER SPECIAL (This came from Brooklyn, too) 1.75
(Finely Sliced Turkey, Ham and Cheese on Country Rye Bread, Kosher Dill and Cole Slaw)
BLACK FOREST SANDWICH 1.60
(A Grilled Delicacy on Pumpernickel Bread, Thin-Carved Roast Beef and Swiss Cheese, with Cole Slaw)
THE MONTE CRISTO 1.95
(An Aristocratic French-Toasted Sandwich Combining Ham, Turkey and Cheese)

Sweet Talk

THE FINEST IN FRENCH PASTRIES FROM THE CART 60
FRESH FRUIT AND FRESH CREAM PIES 45
OAK RUM CAKE 65   ICE CREAM OR SHERBET 40
CHEESE CAKE 50   SMALL STRAWBERRY SUNDAE 50

Coffee 25   Tea 25   Sanka 25   Milk 25
Iced Tea or Coffee 25   Low Fat Milk 25

Graphics can help to make specials even more special. These are very good and blend with the type and general appearance of menu.

Our Special Flaming Dishes

Sword of Beef Tenderloin, Flamed with Cognac —
Served on a Bed of Saffron Rice
Vegetable or Chef's Salad
Rolls & Whipped Butter $3.95

Half Roast Boneless Native Duckling, Sliced Orange,
Sauce Bigarade, Flamed with Triple Sec
Baked Potato
Fresh Vegetable or Chef's Special Salad
Hot Rolls & Whipped Butter $4.25

POP SIZE -- one-half Chicken - $1.95

5 Pieces Tender, Golden Fried Chicken, Crisp Fries or Mashed Potatoes,
Country Gravy, Green Salad, Freshly cooked Vegetables, Hot Roll
and Honey

MOM SIZE $1.60

3 Pieces Golden Fried Chicken, Crisp Fries or Mashed Potatoes, Country
Gravy, Green Salad, Hot Roll and Honey

ALL WHITE -- 3 pcs. -- $1.75

ALL DRUMSTICKS -- 4 pcs. -- $1.75

ALL THIGHS -- 3 pcs. -- $1.80

ALL WINGS -- 6 pcs. -- $1.40

GIZZARDS -- 7 pcs. -- $1.15

Above served with soup or tossed green salad, choice of potatoes,
country gravy, freshly cooked vegetables, hot roll and honey

*Flaming dishes make a natural special and chicken can be "specialized" as shown
here on the menu directly above.*

OUR SPECIALTY
FOR OVER TEN YEARS
YOUNG DOMESTICATED RING-NECKED PHEASANT

Disjointed, Saute Sec with spiced crabapple. Delivered fresh to us from a Santa Cruz Mountain flock which is raised under the inspection of the California Department of Agriculture.

A COMPLETE DINNER 4.10

Broiled Live Maine Lobster

with Hot Drawn Butter, Vegetable, Fresh Garden Salad

Medium - 1¾ lbs. avg. $6.25
Large   - 2½ lbs. avg. $7.25

Prime Sirloin Steak

Our ultimate in fine steaks,
served with
mushroom caps, baked potato
tossed mixed green salad
with french dressing

$6.50

Filet Mignon

Well marbled and rich,
served with
mushroom caps, baked potato
tossed mixed green salad
with french dressing

$6.50

An unusual item such as pheasant makes a "special", and unusual graphics and type make lobster and steak "special".

MONDAY

No. 1 MEAT BALL & SPAGHETTI, Tossed Green Salad, Rolls, Butter, Coffee or Tea 1.00

No. 2 CHICKEN FRIED STEAK, Green Garden Peas, Carrot and Raisin Salad, Rolls, Butter, Coffee or Tea 1.00

No. 3 ITALIAN SAUSAGE & SPAGHETTI, Tossed Green Salad, Rolls, Butter, Coffee or Tea 1.00

TUESDAY

No. 1 SPAGHETTI & BRACIOLONI, Tossed Green Salad, Rolls, Butter, Coffee or Tea 1.00

No. 2 CHICKEN GIZZARDS, Rice and Gravy, Leon's Salad, Rolls, Butter, Coffee or Tea 1.00

No. 3 STUFFED BELL PEPPER with Tomato Sauce, French Fried Potatoes, Tossed Green Salad, Rolls, Butter, Coffee or Tea 1.25

WEDNESDAY

No. 1 IRISH STEW, Cole Slaw, Rolls, Butter, Coffee or Tea 1.00

No. 2 CHICKEN & SPAGHETTI, Tossed Green Salad, Rolls, Butter, Coffee or Tea 1.00

No. 3 POT ROAST OF BEEF, Jardiniere Sauce, Creamed Potatoes, Peas, Rolls, Butter, Coffee or Tea 1.25

THURSDAY

No. 1 VEAL MOZZARELLA & SPAGHETTI, Tossed Green Salad, Rolls, Butter, Coffee or Tea 1.00

No. 2 LASAGNE, Tossed Green Salad, Rolls, Butter, Coffee or Tea 1.00

No. 3 SALISBURY STEAK, French Fried Potatoes, Leon's Salad, Rolls, Butter, Coffee or Tea 1.00

FRIDAY

No. 1 FRIED CATFISH, French Fried Potatoes, Tossed Green Salad, Rolls, Butter, Coffee or Tea 1.00

No. 2 MEAT LOAF, Garden Green Peas, Potato Salad, Rolls, Butter, Coffee or Tea 1.00

No. 3 HALF DOZEN FRIED OYSTERS, French Fried Potatoes, Pickled Bean Salad, Rolls, Butter, Coffee or Tea 1.00

TUESDAY & WEDNESDAY '49er DAYS

ALL THE BUTTERMILK PANCAKES YOU CAN EAT!

49¢

A weekly menu that offers three specials every day is a special special. "All You Can Eat" always makes a special.

Specials in a Basket

CHICKEN-IN-THE-BASKET

Chicken Fried to a Crisp Golden Brown. Served with French Fries, Cole Slaw, Buttered Roll.

1.35

HAMBURGER BASKET

2 Patties of Freshly Ground Beef. French Fries and Cole Slaw.

.75

JUMBO HAMBURGER BASKET

¼ lb. of Freshly Ground Beef. French Fries, Cole Slaw

1.00

SHRIMP-IN-THE-BASKET

Ocean Fresh Shrimp Deep Fat Fried and Served with Cocktail Sauce, French Fries, Cole Slaw, Buttered Rolls.

1.55

FRIED PERCH BASKET

with Tartar Sauce, Grilled Bun. French Fries and Cole Slaw.

.95

SWARZBURGER BASKET

with French Fried Onion Rings, French Fries, Cole Slaw.

1.25

More than one item can be a "Special in a Basket."

Steaks are given special treatment with special art work, special copy and big, bold type at the Brass Rail Restaurant. In addition, a selection of wines is suggested to go with the steaks. The guest will not ignore this special menu listing.

from our charcoal broiler

All entrees are served with choice of baked potato or french fried potatoes, crisp green salad bowl.

KANSAS CITY SIRLOIN STRIP _____ 5.25
A full pound of boneless steak from premium steers

EXTRA CUT FILET MIGNON _____ 4.75
A ¾ pound tenderloin steak, cut extra thick for extra goodness

BRASS RAIL TOP SIRLOIN _____ 4.75
A ¾ pound choice lean steak full of rich flavor

BRASS RAIL FILET MIGNON _____ 3.75
The last word in fine steak of mouth melting goodness

CLUB STEAK _____ 3.50
A small choice top sirloin steak

SMALL BEEF TENDERLOIN STEAK _____ 2.65
A small steak for a delicate appetite

*Our steaks are broiled over a sharp hot flame that finishes the meat to a sear on the outside—juicy and tender within—seals in the rich juices that add to that tantalizing taste and aroma.

Sparkling Burgundy
or Crackling Rose'
Champagne
$3.00 - $6.00

OUR SPECIALTIES

WILLOW GROVE CRAB CAKE DINNER

French Fries, Cole Slaw

$2.00

CHESAPEAKE BAY ROCK FISH

Tartar Sauce, Lemon Wedge
French Fries, Cole Slaw

$1.75

BROILED TOP SIRLOIN STEAK

Baked Potato, Chef Salad

$4.00

ONE-HALF MARYLAND FRIED CHICKEN

French Fries, Green Peas

$1.75

Illustrations—in this case line drawings—can be used to highlight and feature specials.

Black Angusburger

A Whopping (5 oz.) Chopped Sirloin of Beef (U. S. Choice) prepared to your preference. Served on a Hot Buttered Toasted Sesame Bun, with our own Special Relish, Crisp Lettuce and Tomato, Sliced Bermuda Onion, and Humm-n-n . . . a generous wedge of Garlic Pickle, Curly Cue Potatoes.

.85

Black Angusburger, Sr.

Same as above with Melted Cheese.

.95

OLD FASHIONED BUTTERMILK PANCAKES .60

Just Like Mother's

BLUEBERRY PANCAKES .85

Full of Plump Juicy Blueberries

HAWAIIAN PANCAKES .90
Tribute to the 50th State. Full of Hawaiian Pineapple

BANANA PANCAKES .90
A Tropical Delight with Powdered Sugar

PECAN PANCAKES .70

Loaded with Crunchy Pecans

STRAWBERRY PANCAKES .95
Rolled Pancakes Filled with Fresh Strawberries

"devil 'n dan" **COCKTAIL**
Makes the simplest soul an expounding philosopher... .95

House Specialty! **RANCH CUT STEAK**
salad
Potato - Vegetable
$5.25

...Roast Stuffed **NATIVE DUCK** served flambe
our rice! $3.50

Petit **CHATEAUBRIAND**
the tenderest of beef served in a bed of our special rice!...
$4.25

Sauteed **CALVES LIVER** w/ bacon...
salad Potato
$4.25 vegetable

"a whale of a treat" one pound of genuine **WHALE STEAK**
salad
Potato vegetable
$3.75

Specials can fit into a variety of shapes and panels.

Foote Cafe's Special Dinners

Family Style Chicken Dinner ____$1.75
EVERY WEDNESDAY, 5:00 TO 10:00 P.M.

Pan fried chicken with all the trimmings. Children four to 10 years of age $1.00, under three free. With the chicken you will be served mashed potatoes, creamed chicken gravy, corn, cole slaw, cottage cheese, biscuits, ice cream and drink.

Family Style Dinner _____$1.75
EVERY FRIDAY NIGHT

We start your dinner with an appetizer of stuffed celery, radishes, onions, pickles, crackers, and a large combination salad with dressing. Next we serve you with all the fried shrimp, chicken, and fillet of deep sea cat fish you can eat. All of the French fried potatoes and hot garlic bread you can eat and you can have second or third helpings of anything on this dinner at no extra cost. The price for children, four to 10 years is $1.00, under four free. **These special dinners are served in the dining room only.**

Please Call FA 4-5674 For Reservations

BEEF N' BOTTLE
MR. & MRS. CHAMPAGNE DINNER
For That Special Festive Occasion

Aperitif—Two Glasses Rose Wine
For Mr. a Planked 12-Oz. New York Cut Sirloin
For Mrs. a Planked 8-Oz. New York Cut Sirloin
10th of Paul Masson Champagne
WOP Salad (a House Specialty) or Dinner
Salad and Choice of Dressing
Relish Dish
Rolls and Butter   Coffee, Tea or Milk
Baked Alaska for Two
Complimentary Cake for That Special Lady
14.75

Special deals for children on the Family Style Chicken Dinner, and two sizes of steak (one for the man, another for the woman) plus WOP salad and Complimentary Cake for that Special Lady—make for extra special specials.

VARIETY IS THE SPICE OF THE MENU

To get the "same old food," the customer can eat at home. Of course, the standard entree, appetizer, dessert, sandwich and salad items, perennial favorites, are necessary for a successful menu. But the unusual, exotic gourmet treat is the sign of a successful restaurant. And even if these unusual items do not get ordered as often as the old "standbys," since some people are afraid to venture into unknown cuisine territory, the "word of mouth" advertising from those who do try your exotic entrees makes them worthwhile.

The following examples show real creative menu building. Even if they do not sound like items that would fit into your menu, they should stimulate your creative thinking so that your menu will become more interesting, exciting and salesworthy.

Gordon's Rainbow Inn, for example, has a clever listing of "Combinations." These are entree items that are half one entree and half another. This is an easy method of extending the menu, without really adding any new entree to it, while creating unusual items. They are:

Combinations

THE SPECIAL (Patty Ground Sirloin, Half Order Chicken)	$2.95
THE TWIN (Patty Ground Sirloin, Half Order Giant Lobster Tail)	$5.25
THE DUET (Half Order Chicken, Half Order Giant Lobster Tail)	$5.25
THE GOURMET (Half Order Chicken, Half Order Filet Mignon)	$4.95
RAINBOW DELIGHT (Half Order Filet Mignon, Half Order Giant Lobster Tail)	$6.50
THE FAVORITE (Half Order King Crab Legs, Half Order Filet Mignon)	$5.75

Neither soup nor salad need be "ordinary." The two following examples from Herb Traub's Pirate House illustrate exciting menu ideas:

Soul Satisfying Soups

Served with mixed cracker basket or home baked bread and butter, Miss Edna's Seafood Bisque. Something to write home about! Nourishing nuggets of fresh, flavorful crabmeat and plump Savannah shrimp swimming in a skillful blend of cream of tomato and pea soup. . .delicately flavored with sherry.   . . . . .Bowl $1.60 Cup $1.10

Gems from Our Salad Galley

Served with hot home-baked bread and crisp crackers, Pineapple Dreamboat—so cooling, so delightfully refreshing is this sun-ripened Hawaiian pineapple that's been scooped out and filled with mixed fruit, then topped with coconut and orange ice, orange—cream cheese—pecan dressing; date-nut bread sandwiches too! . . .$2.75

Nearly everybody serves the ubiquitous hamburger in some shape or form, but The Governor's Tavern serves it nine different ways. Here they are:

Beefburgers

A luncheon specialty of the house, available in nine delicious variations, each one man-sized, solidly constructed of at least one-quarter pound of choice ground beef. Broiled over charcoal and served on a fresh roll.

Your Choice of Nine Varieties. . . .$.90

1. RELISH BURGER, our regular beefburger topped with old-fashioned red pepper relish.
2. CHEDDAR BURGER, a real favorite served with melted New York State cheddar cheese.
3. PEPPER BURGER, a beefburger served with sauteed Italian green peppers.
4. GOURMET BURGER, our famous beefburger garnished with imported Danish bleu cheese.
5. ONION BURGER, a breath taking beefburger topped with a raw or sauteed Bermuda onion.
6. MUSHROOM BURGER, if you like sauteed mushrooms, you'll enjoy this beefburger, it's smothered with 'em.
7. DIET BURGER, for the calorie conscious—no roll, but accompanied by some cottage cheese.
8. DANDY BURGER, a beefburger, all dressed up with a slice of tomato, lettuce and mayonnaise.
9. BRINY BURGER, breaded whitefish fillet served like a beefburger and garnished with tartar sauce.

If there is unusual wild life, fish or other edibles available in the area of your restaurant, consider serving it on your menu. The Holiday Inn of Thomasville, Georgia, for example, serves South Georgia Quail in its Orchid Room. It is served southern style with grits, salad, biscuits and honey, coffee or tea. One quail is $3.00, two quails are $5.50.

Many restaurants serve spaghetti and many restaurants serve chili, but few serve them together as Tops restaurant does. They call it Pasta Fiesta, and it is spaghetti covered with Top's own piping hot chili, melted cheese, cherry pepper and toast for $.90.

Many restaurants use imagination in naming their entrees. The Pickwick Room, a restaurant in Lancashire, England, shows imagination in the entree listing shown here:

Mr. Tupman's Treat
Half, barbecued English chicken served with old fashioned sage and onion stuffing, small tasty carrots, watercress and potatoes.
Sam Weller's Choice
Prime sirloin steak, garnished with mushrooms, tomato, tasty small carrots, watercress and your choice of potatoes.
Augustus Snodgrass Delight
Sliced Gammon ham with fresh farm egg, tomato, mushrooms, garden peas, watercress and potatoes.
Alfred Jingle "Putting On"
Three egg omelette, your choice of cheese, herbs or mushrooms, served with garden peas, tomato, watercress and potatoes.

Mrs. Bardell's Favorite
Choice fillet steak, garnished with mushrooms, tomato, watercress,
garden peas and potatoes.
Joe the Fat Boy's Snack
Juicy T-bone steak served with mushrooms, tomato, watercress, tasty
carrots and potatoes.
Mr. Pickwick's Specialty
Half Norfolk duckling, roasted to a crispy tenderness, served with
apple and cherry, old fashioned sage and onion stuffing, garden fresh
peas, watercress and your choice of potatoes.
Mr. Winkle's Choice
Selected deep fried scampi served with creamy tartar sauce and gar-
nished with lemon, watercress, tomato, garden peas and potatoes.

Occasionally, what the entree is served in can make the difference. The following is an
entree item served by the Chandelier restaurant at the Queen's Quarter Hotel in the Virgin
Islands.

"IN A COCONUT"
Lobster meat, shrimp and langostinos in a rich Newburg sauce,
baked in a pastry sealed coconut . .$6.50

And at the same restaurant, the following flaming dessert is unusual to say the least:

BAKED BANANAS AND ORANGE GRENADA
Bananas and orange slivers baked slowly in brown sugar, lime and
other delectables, served flaming at your table in a juice you will not
soon forget.

Finally, the answer to "assorted pies" on the menu, which never really sells pies, we
have again the Pirate's House menu—the dessert menu this time:

Pies: Like Mother wishes she could make!

BLACK BOTTOM PIE
Rich, mouth-melting chocolate fudge custard in a crunchy chocolate
wafer crust, topped with a triple-thick layer of tantalizing rum-flavored
chiffon filling, whipped cream and bitter-sweet chocolate shavings
. . . . . . .Merely Terrific! . . .$.75

GRASSHOPPER PIE
Totally Different! Totally Delightful! Absolutely Delicious!
Just imagine. . .A luscious light-as-a-cloud chiffon concoction made
with pure cream, pale green creme de menthe and mellow creme de cacao nestled atop a rich bittersweet chocolate fudge base. . .all this in a
crunchy chocolate wafer crust. . .then on top, a crown of thick whipped
cream and bitter-sweet chocolate shavings! Better save room for a
slice or two!   . . . . .$.75

FRESH GEORGIA PEACH ICE CREAM SUNDAE PIE
Double-rich peach ice cream piled high in a crunchy almond-flavored
crust. . .topped with thick whipped cream, loads of luscious sliced
peaches and a cherry impaled on a tiny plastic sword. Wotta way to
die! . . . .$.75

The "Delicatessen" type menu need not be ordinary. This one is 12 pages (includ-
ing cover) spiral bound and on high quality paper. The illustrations are excellent,
and each page offers a selection of sandwiches, burgers, steaks, platters, extras,
soups, side dishes, salads, breakfast specials and desserts.

THE BROTHERS

RESTAURANT   NINETEEN SOUTH SEVENTH STREET   MINNEAPOLIS

SANDWICHES from our Delicatessen Counter

The Brothers Famous			Grilled Cheese, Bacon and	
Corned Beef Sandwich			Tomato	1.00
Hot or Cold	.95		Roast Beef, Hot or Cold Beef	.95
Jumbo Size	1.35		Baked Ham	.95
SPECIAL: Hot or Cold Corned Beef			Kosher Salami	.75
Sandwich, With Potato Salad	1.20		Kosher Bologna	.75
THE RUBEN SANDWICH			Liverwurst	.70
Hot Corned Beef, Sauerkraut			Swiss Cheese	.60
and Grilled Swiss Cheese	1.35		Chopped Chicken Liver	.90
THE "PEPE" SANDWICH			Chicken Salad	.85
Hot Pastrami and Grilled			Tuna Salad	.75
Hot Pepper Cheese	1.25		Egg Salad	.50
Turkey 1.00 All White Meat	1.15		Bacon, Lettuce and Tomato	.85
Hot Roumanian Pastrami	.95		Grilled Cheese	.65
Cold Peppered Beef Sandwich	.95			

Sandwiches on Bagel, Onion Roll or Kaiser Rolls 5c Extra

COLD COMBINATION SANDWICHES

Hot or Cold Corned Beef			Hot Corned Beef, Cole Slaw and	
and Swiss Cheese	1.25		Russian Dressing	1.20
Baked Ham and Swiss Cheese	1.25		Turkey, Swiss Cheese, Cole Slaw	
Turkey, Cole Slaw			and Russian Dressing	1.45
and Russian Dressing	1.25			

First spread, The Brothers Delicatessen menu.

"COLOSSALS" on individual French Bread

1. "Dora's Favorite" Club — Turkey, Bacon, Lettuce and Tomato   1.50
2. "Brother Fred"—Open Face Sliced Turkey, Corned Beef, Swiss Cheese, Lettuce and Tomato with French or Thousand Island Dressing   1.65
3. "Brother Sam"—Turkey, Baked Ham and Swiss Cheese   1.50
4. "Brother Len"—Corned Beef, Pastrami and Swiss Cheese   1.50
5. "Little Brother"—Corned Beef, Salami and Grilled Cheddar Cheese   1.60

6. "Charlie Boone in the Afternoon" Treat — Hot Pastrami, Swiss Cheese, Cole Slaw Combination   1.45
7. Randy Merriman's "Honest To Goodness" Special — Turkey, Corned Beef, Cole Slaw, Swiss Cheese and Russian Dressing   1.60
8. Bill Carlson's Late Show Special — Turkey, Hot Pastrami, Swiss Cheese, Cole Slaw and Russian Dressing   1.60

HOT SANDWICHES

Roast Turkey,
Mashed Potato, Gravy   1.40
All White Meat   1.50

Roast Sirloin of Beef, Mashed Potato and Gravy   1.40

Bar B Q Beef Sandwich, French Fries, Cole Slaw   1.15

KOSHER HOT DOGS

1. Sauerkraut and Mustard   .60
2. Mustard, Relish and Onions   .60
3. Hickory Smoked Bar-B-Q Sauce   .60

4. Chili, Onions and Grated Cheese   .70
5. Zesty Cheddar Cheese, Bacon Strips and Bar-B-Q Sauce   .80

Second spread.

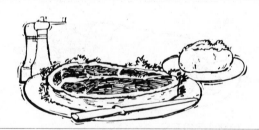

STEAKS & SAVOURIES

Only The Finest Top Quality Choice Steer Beef Especially Selected
To Meet The High Standards Of The Brothers Specifications

SPECIAL TEXAS SIRLOIN STEAK   3.35
(A Sensational Steak) Served with tossed green salad, choice of french, thousand island or blue cheese dressing, baked or french fried potatoes

U.S. CHOICE EIGHT OUNCE BROILER STEAK   2.65
Tossed green salad with choice of thousand island, french or bleu cheese dressing, french fries or baked potato.

BROILED HAMBURGER STEAK AND GRILLED ONIONS   1.95
(½ lb.) hearty favorite of hearty eaters . . . really wonderful with your choice of baked potato (at 5 p.m.), or french fries, mixed green salad with french, bleu cheese, or thousand island dressing, and oven fresh rolls.

SHRIMP DINNER   2.25
Jumbo shrimp from the blue waters of the Louisiana Gulf, deep fried to a golden brown, served with mixed greens, choice of dressing, french fries or baked potato—(after 5 p.m.).

FRIED CHICKEN   2.25
Half finest quality, milk fed, spring chicken; mixed greens, choice of dressing, and baked potato.

THE BROTHERS' BURGERS

well, medium or rare

1. RUSSIAN DRESSING	.65
2. HICKORY SMOKED BAR-B-Q SAUCE	.65
3. JUST PLAIN CATSUP	.65
4. CHILI, ONIONS & GRATED CHEESE	.85
5. OUR GREATEST HAMBURGER	.95

   served with zesty cheddar cheese, bacon strips and russian dressing

6. ON A DIET?
(135 CALORIES — NO BUN)
THE BURGER   .95
   served with sauerkraut or mixed green salad

7. MAYONNAISE, LETTUCE, TOMATO & CUCUMBERS	.85
8. BLUE CHEESE CHEESEBURGER	.90

   broiled and bubbled

BROTHERS' ONION
PATTY MELT   1.35
   An open face treat you will love! Our delicious hamburger, open face on pumpernickel all topped with zesty melted cheese and onions, grilled tomatoes and french fries

CHEESEBURGER	.80
SWISS CHEESE BURGER	.80

   Served with sliced cucumbers, add   .15

GOLDEN SOLE ON A ROLE   .95
   Golden fried fillet of sole served on a toasted bun with Russian Dressing, pickles, potato chips and our good Cole Slaw

with melted cheese	1.10
with melted cheese and bacon strips	1.25
CALIFORNIA HAMBURGER	.85

THE BROTHERS DELICATESSEN PLATTERS

Corned Beef Platter with Potato Salad and Sliced Tomato	1.65
Combination Corned Beef and Pastrami, Potato Salad and Sliced Tomato	1.65
Sliced Roast Beef Platter, with Potato Salad and Sliced Tomato	1.75
Chopped Chicken Liver Platter, with Potato Salad and Egg Wedges	1.50
Fresh Smoked White Fish with Potato Salad, Sliced Tomato	1.75

The Brothers Special:
ASSORTED COLD
CUTS PLATTER   1.95
   Corned Beef, Pastrami, Roast Beef, Chopped Liver, Salami, Breast of Turkey, and Cheese, Potato Salad, Sliced Tomato

Kosher Knockwurst Platter served with Potato Salad and Baked Beans	1.20
Kosher Frankfurter Platter with Potato Salad and Baked Beans	1.20

Oven Fresh Rolls and Butter Served with Above Orders

BAGELS ON PARADE

Plain or Toasted	.20	with Smoked Salmon	.85
with Cream Cheese	.40	with Smoked Salmon	
with Cream Cheese and Jelly	.50	and Cream Cheese	1.10

COUNTRY MATTERS — Carry Out Only

DRUMS OF FRIED CHICKEN

8 pieces serves 2 or 3	2.50	16 pieces serves 6 to 8	4.95
12 pieces serves 4 or 5	3.75	20 pieces serves 8 to 12	6.25

Third spread, The Brothers Delicatessen menu.

SOUPS

DAILY

Chicken Noodle or Rice Soup		Chicken Soup with Matzo Balls	
		Chicken Soup with Kreplach	
Bowl	.35	Bowl	.45
Cup	.20	Cup	.35

Daily Specials

Cup....20   Bowl.....35

Monday	*Green Split Pea Soup*	Thursday	*Cabbage Borscht*
Tuesday	*Navy Bean Soup*	Friday	*New England Style Clam Chowder*
Wednesday	*Soup of the Day*	Saturday	*Cabbage Borscht*

SIDE DISHES

MIXED GREEN SALAD	.55	COLE SLAW	.25
russian, french, or delicious bleu cheese, all delectable		HASH BROWN POTATOES	.40
		SIDE OF COTTAGE CHEESE	.25
FRENCH FRIED POTATOES	.35	POTATO SALAD	.35
FRENCH FRIED ONION RINGS	.50	BAKED POTATO (After 5 p.m.)	.40
BETTER THAN EVER BAKED BEANS	.25	*lots of butter, chopped onions and sour cream*	

Final page.

HOT CAKES, EGGS & OMELETTES

The Brothers Miniature Buttermilk Pancakes with Maple Syrup	.75	Eggs (2) Any Style	.65
		Eggs (2) with Ham or Bacon	1.25
Miniature Buttermilk Cakes with One Sure Fresh Egg	.95	Salami and Eggs, Pancake Style	1.15
		Corned Beef and Eggs, Pancake Style	1.25
Miniature Buttermilk Cakes with Two Sure Fresh Eggs	1.10	Cheese or Onion Omelette	1.10
Miniature Buttermilk Cakes, Full Order of Ham or Bacon	1.20	*Fresh Rolls or Toast and Butter Included with egg orders*	

THE BROTHERS FABULOUS FANCIES

Chocolate Whipped Cream Cake	.50	Pure Whipped Cream Cream Puff	.40
German Chocolate Cake	.40		
Rum Cake	.30	Hot or Cold Apple Pie	.30
Coconut Cream Pie	.45	With Cinnamon Ice Cream	.45
Banana Cream Pie	.45	Cheese Cake - Plain	.40
Pecan Pie with Whipped Cream	.45	Cheese Cake - Fruit Topped	.50
Chocolate Fudge Pie	.45	Chilled Grapefruit	.35
Fresh Strawberry Pie with Whipped Cream (in season)	.50	Cantaloupe	.40
		Hot Fudge Sundae	.50

Malts	.50	Iced Tea or Coffee	.15
Milk Shakes	.40	Sanka or Tea, per pot	.15
Root Beer Float	.40	Milk or Buttermilk	.15
Soft Drinks	.15	Orange Juice	.25 and .40
Chilled Tomato Juice	.25 and .40	Whipped Hot Chocolate	.20
Coffee	.15		

SALADS & DAIRY DISHES

For Your Salad, We Have Delicious Russian, French, Bleu
or Thousand Island Dressing. Served With Oven Fresh Rolls

FRUIT SALAD BOWL 1.50

*a mountain of peaches, prunes, kadota figs and banana chunks
with your choice of creamed cottage cheese, vanilla
ice cream or sherbet.*

COLD CANNED COLUMBIA RIVER SALMON 1.65

*served with potato salad, our fine beefsteak, tomatoes,
cucumbers, sliced raw onions, fresh rolls*

CHEF'S SALAD 1.65

*tossed greens, julienne of ham, turkey, swiss and american
cheeses, sliced egg, cucumbers, juicy red beefsteak tomato
wedges and asparagus spears . . . french, bleu cheese dressing.*

½ Chef's Salad Bowl .... .95	Jumbo Shrimp Cocktail, Brothers Special Cocktail Sauce 1.00
Peach and Cottage Cheese 1.15	
Chicken Salad, Lettuce, Tomato and Egg Wedges, Potato Chips 1.45	Hearts of Lettuce and Tomato .. .50 Tossed Salad, Mixed Greens, Tomato, Cucumber and Onion . 1.25
Tuna Fish Salad, Lettuce, Tomato and Egg Wedges, Potato Chips 1.35	Cheese Blintzes with Sour Cream and Strawberries Blintzes....(2) 1.10 ....(3) 1.45

Oven Fresh Rolls and Butter Served with Above Orders

An unusual "special" menu is this Sandwich menu which includes some side orders and desserts.

McGarvey's Famous Features...

(A) **filet mignon steak sandwich 1.85**
our house specialty

(B) **'mister five by five' super steakburger .80**
a meal in itself

(C) **hot roast beef sandwich 1.20**
with mushroom gravy, choice of potatoes

(D) **golden brown fried shrimp plate 1.55**
choice of potatoes, hot roll and butter

(E) **triple decker ham sandwich .95**
tastes as good as it looks

(F) **broiled tenderloin tips 1.95**
with fresh mushrooms, choice of potatoes

Sandwiches...

(G) **hot roast beef .60**

(H) **fresh lake erie perch .50**

(I) **cheeseburger .60**

(J) **steakburger .50**

for that something Special...

(K) **our delicious whipped baked potato .35**

(L) **french fries .35**

(M) **fresh garden salad .35**

(N) **french fried onion rings .50**

Sweet shop...

(O) **fresh strawberry pie,** made from luscious juicy berries flown in from California, and loaded with whipped cream **.60**

(P) **mom's old fashioned cheesecake .40**
topped with fresh strawberries or blueberries **.20** extra

(Q) **fresh baked apple pie .35**

(R) **sherbet .25**   **(S)** **ice cream .25**

WELCOME ABOARD

the "good ship" McGarvey.
We are happy you chose to
sail with us on a dining adventure.

Your Host **EDDIE SOLOMON**

*This Menu is Dedicated
to the Memory of the late
Charles Solomon.
1904--1963*

BEVERAGE PRICE LIST

CHAMPAGNES

gay, bubbly and delicious, the perfect complement to your meal or after   ½

	BOTTLE	BOTTLE
Great Western Extra Dry Champagne	6.00	3.50
Great Western Sparkling Burgundy	6.00	3.50

RED DINNER WINES

robust wine . . . a complement to any red meat or game   ½

	BOTTLE	BOTTLE
Great Western Burgundy	2.50	1.50
Great Western Rose	2.50	1.50
Chianti (Imp.)	3.50	2.00
Pommard St. Vincent (Imp.)	4.50	2.75
Lancers (Sparkling)	4.95	2.95

WHITE DINNER WINES

Delicate and delicious . . . goes well with seafood or fowl to give added pleasure to dining   ½

	BOTTLE	BOTTLE
Great Western Sauternes	2.50	1.50
Great Western Rhine	2.50	1.50
Widmer's Lake Niagara	2.50	1.50
Liebfraumilch (Imp.)	3.75	2.00

COCKTAILS (Per Gallon)

Mahattan	25.00	Daiquiri	25.00
Martini	25.00	Whiskey Sours	25.00
1 Gallon of Wine Punch			15.00
1 Gallon of Fruit Punch			7.00
1 Gallon of Champagne Punch			20.00

WHISKIES (Quarts)

Seagram's 7 Crown	12.50	Jim Beam Bourbon	15.00
Seagram's V.O.	15.00	DeWar's White Label Scotch	15.00
Canadian Club	15.00	J & B Scotch	15.00

Set-Ups Included

Local Beer	8.00 PER CASE
Premium Beer	9.50 PER CASE
Canadian	11.00 PER CASE

PLACE 6¢ STAMP HERE

THE COACHMAN'S INN

10350 MAIN STREET   CLARENCE, N. Y. 14031

TO

The Coachman's Inn

AN IDEAL SETTING FOR YOUR PARTY

RESTAURANT

10350 MAIN STREET   ::   CLARENCE, N.Y. 14031

Phone: 759-6852

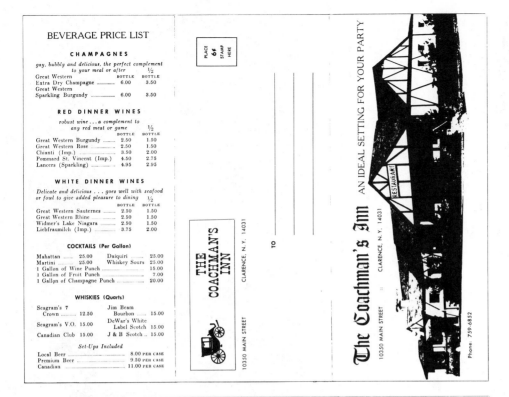

THE COACHMAN'S INN BANQUET MENU

BANQUET DINNER MENU
(FOR 15 OR MORE)

CHOICE OF:
Fruit Cup - Tomato Juice - Onion Soup or
Soup du Jour - Shrimp Cocktail .75 Extra

ASSORTED RELISH TRAY

PRIME RIBS OF BEEF au Jus "Our Specialty"	4.95

BROILED HALF SPRING CHICKEN "Excellent for Banquets"	3.50

Ham Steak, raisin sauce	3.50
Prime Ribs of Beef and Lobster	5.25
Broiled Tenderloin Steak with Garlic Toast	4.50
Filet Mignon	5.95
Lobster Tails Two	5.50
One	4.50
Lobster Newburg	3.95
New York Strip Steak	5.50
Broiled Country Inn Pork Chops	3.95
Roast Turkey, stuffing	3.50
Tavern Style Beef with Gravy	3.50

Choice of Potato: Baked, French Fries or Whipped
Coachman's Chef Salad - Choice of Dressings
Vegetable
Home Made Bread and Butter
Sundae — Chocolate, Mint, Rum
Sherbet

Coffee	Tea	Milk

(PLEASE LIMIT TO 2 ENTREES)

GRATUITY AND SALES TAX NOT INCLUDED IN ABOVE PRICES.

BUFFET (For 40 or More)

$3.25 Per Person

Assorted Relish Trays
Sliced Ham
Hot Swedish Meat Balls
Sliced Turkey
Cottage Cheese
Potato Salad
Cheese Platter
Macaroni Salad
Jello Mold with Fruit
Chef Salad
Home Made Sliced Bread
Choice of: Coffee, Tea or Milk
Choice of: Ice Cream or Sherbet

BUFFET (For 40 or More)

$4.25 Per Person

Assorted Relish Trays
Macaroni Salad
Chef Salad
Chicken a la King
Cottage Cheese
Sliced Roast Beef
Potato Salad
Sliced Turkey
Jello Mold with Fruit
Sliced Ham
Cheese Platter
Hot Swedish Meat Balls
Baked Beans
Home Made Sliced Bread

	Choice of:	
Coffee	Tea	Milk
	Choice of:	
Ice Cream	Sherbet	Sundae

BANQUET LUNCHEON MENU
(FOR 35 OR MORE)

Tomato Juice - Onion Soup - Soup du Jour

Chicken a la King	3.00
Roast Turkey, Dressing	3.00

Potato or Vegetable
Chef Salad
Home Made Rolls - Butter
Sundae or Sherbet
Coffee, Tea or Milk

Also . . .

Coachman's Plate: Slices of roast beef, ham, turkey, cheese, potato salad	3.00
Chicken Salad Plate: Garnish of tomato wedges and egg quarters, cottage cheese	3.00
Fruit Salad Plate: Sherbet, cottage cheese	3.00

Includes rolls, dessert and coffee.

A GRACIOUS WELCOME

awaits your party at the COACHMAN'S INN. Everyone likes the INN for its gaiety and cheerful atmosphere. The huge fireplaces and rich panelled walls provide an attractive setting for your party, just the place to relax and be with friends. The drinks are superb and the food is unusually good because quality is of the very best. You always dine by candlelight at the COACHMAN'S INN. Your party is sure to be a success because the innkeeper's courteous, congenial and efficient staff will be on hand to greet and serve your guests.

FOR MORE INFORMATION AND RESERVATIONS

May we suggest you contact our
Banquet Manager any Monday thru Friday
from 8:30 A.M. to 4:30 P.M.

PHONE 759-6852 And Ask For MRS. WEISSER

This banquet menu is excellent. In addition to an outstanding selection of banquet, buffet and luncheon items plus a wine and liquor list, this menu is also a mailer. Good merchandising.

Shown here are four special menus used by a motel—a Room Service menu, a Poolside menu, an After Theater menu and a special Breakfast menu.

Holiday Inn CONTINENTAL BREAKFAST – served all day

Choice of Chilled Orange, Tomato, Grapefruit or Pineapple Juice
Pot of Freshly Brewed Coffee, Cream and Sugar
Danish Sweet Roll – Butter
.75

S N A C K S

SANDWICHES SERVED WITH POTATO CHIPS AND PICKLE SLICES

Beefburger on Toasted Bun	.75	Club House Sandwich	1.65
with Melted Cheese	.85	Sliced Turkey, Bacon, Lettuce & Tomato	
with Lettuce and Tomato	.85	Bacon, Lettuce & Tomato	.95
Sliced Turkey with Lettuce	1.25	Grilled Cheese	.65
		Sliced Ham on Rye	.95
Grilled, Split Jumbo Frank		Bratwurst on Sesame Bun	
on Toasted Bun	.55	with potato salad	1.10

REUBEN SANDWICH – Kosher style, thinly Sliced Corned Beef,
Swiss Cheese, Sauerkraut on Rye Bread, grilled and served
with Potato Chips and Kosher Pickle chips **1.50**

DESSERTS		BEVERAGES	
Deep Dish Apple Pie	.45	Chilled Juice Small . . .25 Large	.40
Holiday Ice Cream or Sherbet	.35	Pot Freshly Brewed Coffee	.25
Cream Cheese Cake with Strawberries	.50	Tea, Hot or Iced	.20
Hot Fudge Sundae	.55	Milk	.20

ROOM SERVICE .25 PER PERSON   COFFEE ONLY .40

For Distinctive Dining Visit Our Main Dining Room – Serving Breakfast From 6:30 A.M. – Elegant Dinners From 5:00 P.M.

SANDWICHES

Club House
SANDWICH
Sliced Turkey, Bacon,
Lettuce, Tomato
$1.65
Served with
potato chips and garne

HAMBURGER with Potato Chips & Garne 75
HOT DOG on Bun with Potato Chips & Garne 35
BRATWURST on Sesame Seed Bun with Sauerkraut & Garne . . .95
SLICED HAM on Rye with Potato Chips & Garne 95
GRILLED CHEESE with Potato Chips & Garne 55
BACON, LETTUCE & TOMATO on Toast
with Potato Chips & Garne 95
CLUB HOUSE SANDWICH, Potato Chips & Garne 1.65
SLICED TURKEY, BACON, LETTUCE & TOMATO
with Potato Chips & Garne 1.65

All sandwiches served with potato chips and dill pickle stick

Reuben
SANDWICH
Kosher Style Corn Beef
Swiss Cheese
Sauerkraut on Rye Bread
Grilled and served with
Potato Chips and dill pickle stick
$1.50

PLATE LUNCHES

Golden Broasted Chicken (½ Chicken) 1.75
French Fries & Cole Slaw, Roll & Butter
French Fried Shrimps – 6 jumbo 1.75
French Fries and Cole Slaw, Roll and Butter
Fresh Fruit Plate with Cottage Cheese 1.50
and assorted crackers
Cold Cuts, Cheese, Potato Salad Plate 1.50
(Sliced Ham, Bologna, Corned Beef, American and
Swiss Cheese, assorted crackers)

Desserts
Deep Dish Apple Pie . . . . .45¢
Holiday Ice Cream
or Sherbet . . . . . . .35¢
Creme Cheese Cake
with Strawberries . . . .50¢
Hot Fudge Nut Sundae . . .55¢

Ala Carte
French Fries	35¢	Teem	25¢
French Fried		Diet Soda	25¢
Onion Rings	50¢	Ice Tea	25¢
Coke	25¢	Milk	25¢
Root Beer	25¢	Coffee	15¢

Holiday Inn DOWNTOWN

CACKLE BERRIES
SCRAMBLED EGGS, SLICE OF HAM & HASH BROWN POTATOES
TOAST, JELLY, COFFEE
1.15

S N A C K S

SANDWICHES SERVED WITH FRENCH FRIES AND PICKLE SLICES

Beefburger on Toasted Bun	.85	Club House Sandwich	1.75
with Melted Cheese	.95	Sliced Turkey, Bacon, Lettuce & Tomato	
with Lettuce and Tomato	.95	Bacon, Lettuce & Tomato	1.00
Sliced Turkey with Lettuce	1.50	Grilled Cheese	.65
LITTLE ABNER	1.65	Sliced Ham on Rye	.95
A combination sandwich with cooked salami,		Bratwurst on Sesame Bun	
corned beef, bologna, American cheese, Swiss		with potato salad	1.10
cheese and mozzarella cheese served on a huge			
French roll with lettuce and tomato			

RIVER ROOM SPECIAL – Sliced Turkey with Bacon – creamy cheddar cheese sauce
topped with special cheeses and broiled to a golden brown **1.75**

REUBEN SANDWICH – Kosher style, thinly Sliced Corned Beef,
Swiss Cheese, Sauerkraut on Rye Bread, grilled and served
with French Fries and Kosher Pickle chips **1.50**

DESSERTS
Deep Dish Apple Pie	.55		
Holiday Ice Cream or Sherbet	.35		
Cream Cheese Cake with Strawberries	.50		
Hot Fudge Sundae	.55		

Holiday Inn's WAFFLE
Made with Cream from our old-fashioned recipe.
They are crisp and tender with that "Melt in your
mouth goodness." Served with whipped Butter, hot
Maple Syrup, and pot of fresh hot coffee **75¢**
with strawberries and whipped cream **1.00**

Good Morning

Holiday Inn's WAFFLE
Made with Cream from our old-fashioned
recipe. They are crisp and tender with
that "Melt in your mouth goodness."
Served with whipped Butter, hot Maple
Syrup, and pot of fresh hot coffee.
75¢
with Strawberries and
whipped cream
1.00

Fresh Farm Eggs (2)	.75
Bacon 'n Egg (1)	.85
Sausage 'n Egg (1)	.90
Ham 'n Egg (1)	1.00
Bacon 'n Eggs (2)	1.05
Sausage 'n Eggs (2)	1.15
Ham 'n Eggs (2)	1.15
Egg Omelet with jelly or cheese	1.15
Egg Omelet with ham or bacon	1.25

*Above orders include buttered toast,
jelly and pot of fresh hot coffee.*

Side Orders
Bacon – 3 strips	.45
Sausage – pork – patties	.45
Ham	.60
One Farm Egg	.25
Two Farm Eggs	.45
Rasher Hash Browned Potatoes	.30
Sweet Roll and Butter	.25
Buttered Toast and Jelly	.25
English Muffin	.30
Cinnamon Toast	.25
Chilled Fruit Juice – small . . .20 large	.35
Milk . . . . .20 Tea	.15
Coffee. Hot – per pot	.25
Decaffeinated Coffee	.20
Hot or Cold Cereals with Milk .35 ½ & ½	.50
Stewed Prunes . . .35 Half Grapefruit	.35
Melon – in season	.35

HUNGRY JACK'S FAMOUS
Stack of three Pancakes	.75
Platter of two Pancakes 'n Egg	.95
Platter of two Pancakes 'n Eggs	1.15

*Above orders include whipped Butter, hot Maple Syrup
and pot of fresh hot coffee.*

Blueberry THREE *Pancakes*
Sprinkled through with Blueberries.
Served with whipped Butter, hot Blueberry Syrup
and pot of fresh hot coffee
95¢

Old Fashioned FRENCH TOAST
Made and served from an Old French
recipe. Thick golden brown – grilled in
special batter and served with whipped
Butter, powdered sugar and pot of fresh
Hot Coffee
75¢
with apples **90¢**

Room Service: 25¢ per person – Coffee only – 40¢ per pot.
Breakfast: Served until 11 A.M.

Notice that while there are four different menus, the items served are interchanged—sandwiches, desserts and even breakfast items can be served at different times and places.

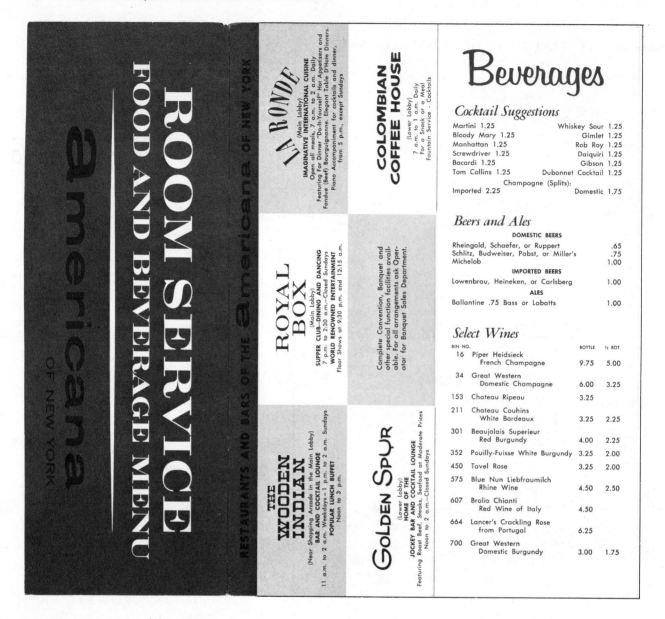

RESTAURANTS AND BARS OF THE **americana** OF NEW YORK

americana OF NEW YORK

ROOM SERVICE
FOOD AND BEVERAGE MENU

LA RONDE
(Main Lobby)
IMAGINATIVE INTERNATIONAL CUISINE
Open all meals, 7 a.m. to 2 a.m. Daily
Featuring For Dinner "Do-It-Yourself" Hot Appetizers and
Fondue (Beef) Bourguignonne. Elegant Table D'Hote Dinners.
Piano Accompaniment for cocktails and dinner,
from 5 p.m., except Sundays

COLOMBIAN COFFEE HOUSE
(Lower Lobby)
7 a.m. to 1 a.m. Daily
For a Snack or a Meal
Fountain Service - Cocktails

ROYAL BOX
(Main Lobby)
SUPPER CLUB—DINING AND DANCING
7 p.m. to 2:30 a.m.—Closed Sundays
WORLD RENOWNED ENTERTAINMENT
Floor Shows at 9:30 p.m. and 12:15 a.m.

Complete Convention, Banquet and
other special function facilities available. For all arrangements ask Operator for Banquet Sales Department.

THE WOODEN INDIAN
(Near Shopping Arcade in the Main Lobby)
BAR AND COCKTAIL LOUNGE
11 a.m. to 2 a.m. Weekdays—1 p.m. to 2 a.m. Sundays
POPULAR LUNCH BUFFET
Noon to 3 p.m.

Golden Spur
(Lower Lobby)
HOME OF THE
JOCKEY BAR AND COCKTAIL LOUNGE
Featuring Roast Beef, Steaks, Seafood at Moderate Prices
Noon to 2 a.m.—Closed Sundays

Beverages

Cocktail Suggestions

Martini 1.25	Whiskey Sour 1.25
Bloody Mary 1.25	Gimlet 1.25
Manhattan 1.25	Rob Roy 1.25
Screwdriver 1.25	Daiquiri 1.25
Bacardi 1.25	Gibson 1.25
Tom Collins 1.25	Dubonnet Cocktail 1.25

Champagne (Splits):
Imported 2.25   Domestic 1.75

Beers and Ales

DOMESTIC BEERS

Rheingold, Schaefer, or Ruppert	.65
Schlitz, Budweiser, Pabst, or Miller's	.75
Michelob	1.00

IMPORTED BEERS

Lowenbrau, Heineken, or Carlsberg	1.00

ALES

Ballantine .75 Bass or Labatts	1.00

Select Wines

BIN NO.		BOTTLE	½ BOT.
16	Piper Heidsieck French Champagne	9.75	5.00
34	Great Western Domestic Champagne	6.00	3.25
153	Chateau Ripeau	3.25	
211	Chateau Couhins White Bordeaux	3.25	2.25
301	Beaujolais Superieur Red Burgundy	4.00	2.25
352	Pouilly-Fuisse White Burgundy	3.25	2.00
450	Tavel Rose	3.25	2.00
575	Blue Nun Liebfraumilch Rhine Wine	4.50	2.50
607	Brolio Chianti Red Wine of Italy	4.50	
664	Lancer's Crackling Rose from Portugal	6.25	
700	Great Western Domestic Burgundy	3.00	1.75

Breakfast

The Continental 1.75
(Available Up to Noon)

CHOICE OF CHILLED FRUIT JUICES
TOAST, BREAKFAST ROLLS OR DANISH PASTRY
WITH BUTTER AND JAM
BEVERAGE

The Club Breakfast 2.75
(Available Up to Noon)

CHOICE OF FRUIT JUICE OR CEREAL
TWO EGGS ANY STYLE
WITH HAM, BACON OR SAUSAGE
TOAST OR BREAKFAST ROLLS
WITH BUTTER AND JAM
BEVERAGE

A LA CARTE BREAKFAST SELECTIONS

FRUITS and JUICES
FRESHLY SQUEEZED ORANGE JUICE .85   LARGE 1.15
CHILLED TOMATO, PRUNE, PINEAPPLE, GRAPEFRUIT OR
PAPAYA JUICE .75   LARGE 1.05
KADOTA FIGS .80   HALF GRAPEFRUIT .85
ICED MELON IN SEASON 1.15   STEWED PRUNES .80
SLICED BANANA WITH CREAM .95
CHILLED BERRIES IN SEASON WITH CREAM 1.30

CEREALS
CHOICE OF:
OATMEAL OR CREAM OF WHEAT, CORN FLAKES, RICE
KRISPIES AND OTHER DRY CEREALS WITH CREAM .90

CAKES and WAFFLES
CRISP WAFFLE, WHEAT CAKES OR FRENCH TOAST 1.10
WITH HAM, BACON OR SAUSAGE 1.70

EGGS
ONE EGG, ANY STYLE .65
WITH HAM, BACON OR SAUSAGE 1.25
TWO EGGS, ANY STYLE 1.10
WITH HAM, BACON OR SAUSAGE 1.70
PLAIN OMELETTE 1.40   CHEESE, MUSHROOM, SPANISH,
JELLY OR WESTERN OMELETTE 1.65

MAIN COURSE DISHES
GRILLED SUGAR CURED HAM (1 slice) .65   (2 slices) 1.10
LINK SAUSAGES (3) .85   (6) 1.45
ORDER OF BACON (6) 1.45   RASHER OF BACON (3) .85
CORNED BEEF HASH 2.10   CREAMED CHIPPED BEEF 2.35
BROILED KIPPERED HERRING 2.35
CREAM CHEESE AND LOX 2.45
BREAKFAST STEAK 4.50
HASHED BROWN, FRENCH FRIED OR
LYONNAISE POTATOES .80

FROM THE BAKERY
DANISH PASTRY .80   TOASTED ENGLISH MUFFIN .65
FRENCH CROISSANTS OR BRIOCHE .55   BAGELS .55
TOAST OR BREAKFAST ROLLS .40   DOUGHNUT .40
BLUEBERRY, BRAN OR CORN MUFFINS .55
CINNAMON TOAST .55   MILK TOAST .55

BEVERAGES
COFFEE, TEA OR COCOA .55   MILK .55
HOT CHOCOLATE .55   SANKA .55

ROOM SERVICE CHARGE 50c PER PERSON

Dining in your room

NOON TO MIDNIGHT
★STARRED ITEMS NOT AVAILABLE AFTER 10 P.M.

APPETIZERS AND SOUPS

CHILLED TOMATO JUICE .75   FRUIT CUP SUPREME 1.10   HALF GRAPEFRUIT .85
MELON IN SEASON 1.15   CHOPPED CHICKEN LIVERS 1.15   SHRIMP COCKTAIL 1.95
LOBSTER COCKTAIL 2.60   CRABMEAT COCKTAIL 2.60   BLUEPOINT OYSTERS 1.75
CHERRYSTONE OR LITTLE NECK CLAMS ON THE HALF SHELL 1.65
PROSCIUTTO WITH MELON 2.35   SMOKED NOVA SCOTIA SALMON 2.35
FRENCH ONION SOUP AU GRATIN 1.00   CHICKEN BROTH .90   JELLIED MADRILENE .95
HOT DOUBLE CONSOMME .90   SOUP DU JOUR .90   COLD VICHYSSOISE .95

FROM THE SEAS, RIVERS AND LAKES

Fresh Filet of Sole Saute aux Champignons 3.65   ★Curry of Shrimp Bengale 3.95
Cold Filet of Gaspe Salmon Parisienne 4.15   ★Long Island Scallops Amandine 3.35
★Broiled South African Lobster Tail, Drawn Butter 6.25

ENTREE SPECIALTIES SERVED WITH BAKED POTATO OR FRENCH FRIES

Roast Prime Ribs of Beef 5.50   Filet Mignon 7.25   Sirloin Steak 7.50
Chateaubriand (for 2) 15.00   Chicken a la King 3.60
Chopped Sirloin Steak 3.35   ★Two Prime Lamb Chops 5.25
★Sugar Cured Ham Steak 3.10   ★Breaded Veal Cutlet 3.45
★Broiled Calf's Liver and Bacon 3.75   ★Broiled Chicken 3.45
FOR LUNCHEON AND DINNER SPECIALTY ITEMS THAT CHANGE DAILY, DIAL 2.

FROM THE GARDEN

BAKED IDAHO, FRENCH FRIED, LYONNAISE OR MOUSSELINE POTATOES .80
BRAISED CELERY, CARROTS, FRENCH PEAS, STRING BEANS .80
WHITE CALIFORNIA ASPARAGUS .80 WITH HOLLANDAISE SAUCE 1.15
FRESH GREENS-OF-THE-SEASON AND TOMATO WEDGES 1.10
YOUR CHOICE OF VINAIGRETTE, FRENCH OR RUSSIAN DRESSING

COLD BUFFET -- SALADS

Sunset Salad 2.95
JULIENNE OF TURKEY AND BEEF TONGUE, QUARTERED EGG AND TOMATO
WITH FRESH GREENS-OF-THE-SEASON
★South Pacific 2.50
BOWL OF SLICED FRESH FRUITS ON A BED OF LETTUCE,
CENTERED WITH AMERICANA SHERBET OR COUNTRY COTTAGE CHEESE
★Monte Carlo 2.75
FRESH AVOCADO PEAR WITH DICED CHICKEN AND CELERY MIMOSA
YOUR CHOICE OF DRESSINGS

SANDWICH PLATES

THREE DECKER AMERICANA CLUB 2.65   SIRLOIN STEAK SANDWICH 6.95
BEEFBURGER ON A TOASTED BUN 2.10   CHOPPED CHICKEN LIVER 1.50
SUGAR CURED HAM 1.95 WITH IMPORTED SWISS CHEESE 2.25
GRILLED CHEESE, TOMATO AND NOVIA SCOTIA SALMON 2.50   SLICED TURKEY 2.45
OPEN FACE COLD ROAST BEEF 3.25   AMERICAN CHEESE 1.45
(CHOICE OF RYE, WHOLEWHEAT OR WHITE BREAD, PLAIN OR TOASTED)
AFTER MIDNIGHT TO 6 A.M.—A FINE SELECTION OF SANDWICHES ARE AVAILABLE

BREAD AND BUTTER 50c PER PERSON

Room service menus must do a special job of selling a great number of foods and beverages and also the services and facilities of the operation.

"COMPARE OUR QUALITY AND PRICE"

IVANHOE
GOURMET MASTERS
DINNER SERVICE
P. O. Box 52 - 395
MIAMI, FLORIDA 33127

633 - 0215
**FLORIDA'S OLDEST AND FINEST
CATERER FOR ANY OCCASION**
*"NO BOTHER OR FUSS . . .
LEAVE THE COOKING TO US"*

PRICE SCHEDULE
PAYABLE IN ADVANCE

	3 Day	4 Day	5 Day	6 Day
1 Person	5.00	6.25	7.50	8.50
2 Persons	8.45	10.50	12.35	14.00
3 Persons	11.85	15.00	17.95	20.00
4 Persons	14.65	18.75	22.45	25.75
5 Persons	17.75	22.85	27.35	31.75
6 Persons	20.70	26.80	32.45	37.25

For 7th Day Service (Delivered Sat.) 1.00 per Person. Add sales tax and 1.00 local delivery charges.
(Outlying Areas 1.50. Remote Areas 1.75)

DELIVERY TIME BEFORE 6 P.M.

MONDAY, FEBRUARY 13, 1967

SERVINGS_____ ACCT._____

SELECT ONE (1) PER FAMILY

1 ☐ GOLDEN BROWN FILET OF SOLE, TARTAR SAUCE
2 ☐ SOUTHERN FRIED CHICKEN
3 ☐ BAKED MEAT LOAF, MUSHROOM GRAVY
4 ☐ BREADED MILK-FED VEAL CUTLET, PARMAGAN
5 ☐ VIRGINIA HAM STEAK, RAISIN SAUCE
6 ☐ BROILED BABY BEEF LIVER, ONION SAUCE
7 ☐ POTTED SWISS STEAK, JARDINERE

SELECT THREE (3) PER FAMILY

8 ☐ CHINESE EGG DROP SOUP
9 ☐ OLD FASHIONED VEGETABLE SOUP
10 ☐ CALIFORNIA TOMATO JUICE
11 ☐ HOT GERMAN POTATO SALAD
12 ☐ OVEN BROWNED POTATO
13 ☐ GARDEN GREEN PEAS
14 ☐ CAULIFLOWER BUDS
15 ☐ HEARTS OF LETTUCE, THOUSAND ISLAND DRESSING
16 ☐ CHOCOLATE PUDDING

SUGGESTED HOT DINNER

17 ☐ POTTED SWISS STEAK, JARDINERE
HOT GERMAN POTATO SALAD
HEARTS OF LETTUCE, THOUSAND ISLAND DRESSING
CHOCOLATE PUDDING

(Incomplete Menus Will Receive Above Selections)

SUGGESTED COLD DINNER

18 ☐ TOMATO JUICE
COLD SLICED BAKED HAM
HEARTS OF LETTUCE, THOUSAND ISLAND DRESSING
CHOCOLATE PUDDING

LOW CALORIE DINNERS
CALORIES

19 ☐ Broiled Baby Beef Liver, Onion Sauce ... 350
20 ☐ Baked Meat Loaf, Mushroom Gravy ... 350

Served With

California Tomato Juice ... 55
Cauliflower Buds ... 30
Hearts of Lettuce, Thousand Island Dressing ... 25
Diet Rolls ... 55

TUESDAY, FEBRUARY 14, 1967

SERVINGS_____ ACCT._____

SELECT ONE (1) PER FAMILY

1 ☐ BROILED NATIVE SNAPPER, BUTTER SAUCE
2 ☐ YANKEE POT ROAST OF BEEF, JARDINERE
3 ☐ STUFFED CABBAGE ROLLS, HUNGARIAN STYLE
4 ☐ BRAISED LAMB STEAK, JARDINERE
5 ☐ ROAST LOIN OF PORK, SWEET & SOUR SAUCE
6 ☐ CUBED BEEF, CANTONESE (Tasty Choice Beef with Chinese Vegetables)
7 ☐ HALF BROILED CHICKEN, AU NATURAL

SELECT THREE (3) PER FAMILY

8 ☐ CONSOMME WITH NOODLES
9 ☐ GREEN SPLIT PEA SOUP
10 ☐ SWEET AND SOUR MEAT BALL APPETIZER
11 ☐ CREAMY WHIPPED POTATOES
12 ☐ CHINESE FRIED RICE
13 ☐ BUTTERED BROCCOLI
14 ☐ SLICED CARROTS, BUTTERED
15 ☐ PICKLED GREEN BEANS WITH ONIONS
16 ☐ PINEAPPLE CRUMB PIE

SUGGESTED HOT DINNER

17 ☐ HALF BROILED CHICKEN, AU NATURALE
SWEET AND SOUR MEAT BALL APPETIZER
CHINESE FRIED RICE
PINEAPPLE CRUMB PIE

(Incomplete Menus Will Receive Above Selections)

SUGGESTED COLD DINNER

18 ☐ APPLE SAUCE
ONE HALF COLD BROILED CHICKEN
PICKLED GREEN BEANS WITH ONIONS
PINEAPPLE CRUMB PIE

LOW CALORIE DINNERS
CALORIES

19 ☐ Broiled Native Snapper, Butter Sauce ... 150
20 ☐ Half Broiled Chicken, au Naturale 100

Served with

Buttered Broccoli ... 40
Sliced Carrots ... 30
Pickled Green Beans with Onions ... 25
Diet Rolls ... 55

WEDNESDAY, FEBRUARY 15, 1967

SERVINGS_____ ACCT._____

SELECT ONE (1) PER FAMILY

1 ☐ BAKED FILET OF WHITE FISH, CREOLE
2 ☐ CHICKEN A LA KIEV (Chicken Breast stuffed with Chopped Liver, Breaded and Fried)
3 ☐ OUR OWN CORNED BEEF HASH WITH POACHED EGG
4 ☐ VEAL PAPRIKASH, WIDE NOODLES
5 ☐ HAM HAWAIIAN (BONELESS HAM DIPPED IN EGG BATTER, DEEP FRIED)
6 ☐ BRAISED SHORTRIBS OF BEEF, BROWN GRAVY
7 ☐ ROAST YOUNG TURKEY, GIBLET GRAVY, DRESSING, CRANBERRY SAUCE

SELECT THREE (3) PER FAMILY

8 ☐ CREAM OF MUSHROOM SOUP
9 ☐ TURKEY GUMBO SOUP
10 ☐ STEWED PRUNES
11 ☐ CANDIED LOUISIANA YAMS
12 ☐ FLUFFY LONG GRAIN RICE
13 ☐ CUT GREEN BEANS
14 ☐ WHOLE KERNEL CORN
15 ☐ MIXED GREEN SALAD, FRENCH DRESSING
16 ☐ JELLY ROLL

SUGGESTED HOT DINNER

17 ☐ ROAST YOUNG TURKEY, GIBLET GRAVY, DRESSING, CRANBERRY SAUCE
STEWED PRUNES
CANDIED LOUISIANA YAMS
JELLY ROLLS

(Incomplete Menus Will Receive Above Selections)

SUGGESTED COLD DINNER

18 ☐ STEWED PRUNES
COLD TURKEY PLATTER, CRANBERRY SAUCE
MIXED GREEN SALAD, FRENCH DRESSING
JELLY ROLL

LOW CALORIE DINNERS
CALORIES

19 ☐ Roast Young Turkey, Gravy, Dressing, Cranberry Sauce ... 225
20 ☐ Braised Brisket of Beef, Gravy ... 250

Served with

Fruit Nectar Juice ... 60
Cut Green Beans ... 15
Mixed Green Salad, French Dressing ... 25
Diet Rolls ... 55

A catering service menu presents a special menu problem, but it can be solved as

Name _____ Acc't No._____

Address _____ Apt. No._____

No. of People _____ No. of Days_____

Phone _____

INSURE PROMPT SERVICE—RETURN COMPLETED MENU BY FRIDAY
INCOMPLETE MENUS WILL RECEIVE SELECTION No. 17
Families May Order 2 Different Dishes by Paying a 15¢ Charge per Item

Cancellation And Change Must
Be Received By 11 A.M.

THURSDAY, FEBRUARY 16, 1967

SERVINGS_____ ACCT._____

SELECT ONE (1) PER FAMILY

1 ☐ FILET OF FLOUNDER, MIRABEAU
2 ☐ CHICKEN SAUTE, CACCIATORE
3 ☐ BROILED CHOPPED STEAK, HOME FRIED ONIONS
4 ☐ IRISH LAMB STEW, DUBLIN STYLE
5 ☐ BRAISED PORK STEAK, SAUCE ROBERT
6 ☐ BREADED MILK-FED VEAL CUTLET, TOMATO SAUCE
7 ☐ SLICED BAR-B-QUE BEEF, IVANHOE SAUCE

SELECT THREE (3) PER FAMILY

8 ☐ FRENCH ONION SOUP, CHEESE CROUTONS
9 ☐ LENTIL SOUP WITH FRANKS
10 ☐ FLORIDA ORANGE JUICE
11 ☐ PARSLEY BOILED POTATO
12 ☐ BUTTERED WIDE NOODLES
13 ☐ LEAF SPINACH, AU BEURRE
14 ☐ STEWED TOMATOES
15 ☐ LETTUCE AND ASPARAGUS CLUB SALAD, MAYONAISE SAUCE
16 ☐ ORANGE LAYER CAKE

SUGGESTED HOT DINNER

17 ☐ SLICED BAR-B-QUE BEEF, IVANHOE SAUCE
FLORIDA ORANGE JUICE
PARSLEY BOILED POTATO
ORANGE LAYER CAKE

(Incomplete Menus Will Receive Above Selections)

SUGGESTED COLD DINNER

18 ☐ CHOPPED LIVER, APPETIZER
ASSORTED COLD CUTS, GARNI
POTATO SALAD
ORANGE LAYER CAKE

LOW CALORIE DINNERS

	CALORIES
19 ☐ Broiled Filet of Flounder	125
20 ☐ Broiled Chop Steak, Fried Onions	35(
Served with	
Buttered Wide Noodles	30
Stewed Tomatoes	40
Continental Salad (Diced Garden Vegetables, Italian Dressing)	25
Diet Rolls	55

FRIDAY, FEBRUARY 17, 1967

SERVINGS_____ ACCT._____

SELECT ONE (1) PER FAMILY

1 ☐ JUMBO SHRIMPS, SCAMPI (Baked Shrimp in a Garlic Butter Sauce with Fine Herbs)
2 ☐ CHICKEN-EN-POT (Simmered Chicken with Vegetables in its own broth)
3 ☐ BRAISED BRISKET OF BEEF, BROWN GRAVY
4 ☐ CRABMEAT CAKES IMPERIAL, TARTAR SAUCE
5 ☐ BAKED VIRGINIA HAM, CORN FRITTER
6 ☐ SAUTE CHICKEN LIVERS WITH ONIONS
7 ☐ BROILED FILET OF HADDOCK, PARSLEY BUTTER SAUCE

SELECT THREE (3) PER FAMILY

8 ☐ CHICKEN CONSOMME WITH MATZOH BALL
9 ☐ NEW ENGLAND CLAM CHOWDER
10 ☐ FRUIT COMPOTE
11 ☐ HOME FRIED POTATOES
12 ☐ BAKED MACARONI AND CHEESE
13 ☐ SLICED CARROTS AND PEAS
14 ☐ BABY LIMA BEANS
15 ☐ CREAMY COLE SLAW
16 ☐ BOBKA (Russian Coffee Cake)

SUGGESTED HOT DINNER

17 ☐ BROILED FILET OF HADDOCK, BUTTER SAUCE
BAKED MACARONI AND CHEESE
CARROTS AND PEAS
BOBKA (RUSSIAN COFFEE CAKE)

(Incomplete Menus Will Receive Above Selections)

SUGGESTED COLD DINNER

18 ☐ FRUIT COMPOTE
SALMON SALAD PLATTER
CREAMY COLE SLAW
RUSSIAN COFFEE CAKE

LOW CALORIE DINNERS

	CALORIES
19 ☐ Jumbo Shrimp, Scampi	150
20 ☐ Chicken-en-Pot (Simmered Chicken with Vegetables in its own Broth)	100
Served with	
Fruit Compote	75
Carrots and Peas	40
Creamy Cole Slaw	50
Diet Roll	55

SATURDAY, FEBRUARY 18, 1967

SERVINGS_____ ACCT._____

SELECT ONE (1) PER FAMILY

1 ☐ FRIED FINGER OF SNAPPER, TARTAR SAUCE
2 ☐ SLICED LONDON BROIL, MUSHROOM SAUCE
3 ☐ SPAGHETTI AND MEAT BALLS, ITALIENNE
4 ☐ BRAISED LAMB SHANK, JARDINERE
5 ☐ GOLDEN BROWN PORK CHOPS
6 ☐ COC AU VIN (Tasty Chicken in a Fine Wine Sauce)
7 ☐ ROAST TURKEY DRUMSTICK, SAGE DRESSING, GRAVY

SELECT THREE (3) PER FAMILY

8 ☐ CONSOMME VERMICELLI
9 ☐ ITALIAN MINESTRONE
10 ☐ GRAPEFRUIT SECTIONS
11 ☐ BAKED STUFFED POTATO
12 ☐ SPAGHETTI WITH TOMATO SAUCE
13 ☐ MIXED VEGETABLES
14 ☐ BOSTON BAKED BEANS
15 ☐ PINEAPPLE WALDORF SALAD
16 ☐ ENGLISH CHOCOLATE BROWNIE

SUGGESTED HOT DINNER

17 ☐ ROAST TURKEY DRUMSTICK, SAGE DRESSING GRAVY
ITALIAN MINESTRONE
MIXED VEGETABLE
ENGLISH CHOCOLATE BROWNIE

SUGGESTED COLD DINNER

18 ☐ GRAPEFRUIT SECTIONS
CHICKEN SALAD PLATTER
PINEAPPLE WALDORF SALAD
ENGLISH CHOCOLATE BROWNIE

LOW CALORIE DINNERS

	CALORIES
19 ☐ Sliced London Broil, Mushroom Sauce	200
20 ☐ Baked White Fish	100
Served With	
Grapefruit Sections	55
Mixed Vegetables	40
Pineapple Waldorf Salad	40
Diet Roll	55

SUNDAY (Delivery Saturday)
SELECT FOUR (4) DISHES
(1 ENTREE - 3 SIDE DISHES)
FROM SATURDAY'S MENU
Write Numbers Here

No. of People_____

Selection Numbers

____ ____ ____ ____

(1)

shown on these pages.

LITTLE EXTRAS
MAKE A MENU BIG

Michelangelo is supposed to have said, "Trifles make perfection, and perfection is no trifle." While perfection is probably unattainable in a menu, and trifles certainly will not make a menu perfect, there are ways of imaginatively treating or expanding nearly every department of the menu from appetizers to desserts in a manner that will sell more. Also, any unusual items, drink or food, will advertise your operation by word of mouth which is the best form of advertising there is (and the least expensive).

Furthermore, the public expects something extra when eating out. The ordinary, routine cuisine they can get at home, but when they dine out they prefer unusual gastronomic surprises. This is also good business because, besides attracting more customers, the public is willing to pay more for culinary concoctions that are different as well as delicious.

The following examples are taken from menus of successful restaurants showing creative menuship on a variety of food and drink items, large and small.

The Beef 'N Bottle restaurant lists the following special dinner which is a gourmet and a merchandising combination designed to build business as well as make happy, come-again customers:

MR. & MRS. CHAMPAGNE DINNER, For That Special Festive Occasion, Aperitif—Two Glasses Rosé Wine, For Mr., a Planked 12 oz. New York Cut Sirloin, 10th of Paul Masson Champagne, WOP Salad (a House Specialty) or Dinner Salad and Choice of Dressing, Relish Dish, Rolls and Butter, Coffee, Tea or Milk, Baked Alaska for Two, Complimentary Cake for That Special Lady, $14.75.

The specialty restaurant can also feature a "special" dinner. The following menu from the Venetian Inn is a special dinner for parties of four or more that shows gourmet imagination and sales imagination, too:

Dinner a Siciliano, served to parties of four or more, PESCHE AL-VINO COCKTAIL, ANTIPASTO, Four Assortments of Spaghetti, TAGLIATELLE A LA SICILIANO, RIGATONI, RAVIOLI, MOSTACCIOLA, SIX VARIETIES OF MEAT, prepared exclusively a Siciliano, VEGETABLE TOSSED SALAD, ITALIAN BREAD AND BUTTER, and for the finale, A PIATO OF SPUMONI, $6.00 per person.

The southern restaurant with a homey, country menu style may seem to have a country bumpkin approach, but the folksy style usually contains clever, solid, creative merchandising that makes the biggest "city slicker" restaurant look slow by comparison. The following example from Creighton's Restaurant is a good example of "Confederate" merchandising:

"Florida Cracker" Sampler Plate, $4.75. (an assortment of foods us natives like). Us Crackers always got a Chicken, and a pig or two. Nearly any place there's water, you can find some crabs. (How true!) And shrimp! We have as many as taxes. Avocados grow in most backyards (as well as 5 or 6 brats). So we decided, for our perspicacious Northern Cousins to let them try all our good easy eating at one sitting, by arranging in our best Florida Manner a selected piece of Fried Florida Chicken, One Florida Pork Chop, One Deviled Crab, and a Florida Avocado stuffed with Fresh Florida Shrimp Salad, French Fried Potatoes, Assorted Breads and Butter, Coffee.

The drink portion of your menu need not be dull. The usual Martini and Manhattan (and all their cousins) are necessary, of course, but drinks can be exotic, imaginative and exciting, too. The following examples from Paul Shank's Restaurant should point the way to better drink merchandising:

CHI-CHI, An intriguing, superbly smooth concoction of pineapple juice, coconut milk and vodka, mixed on the Waring blender and served in a tall cool glass, $1.25. MAI-TAI, this favorite of the South Seas Isles consists of blended tropical fruit juices generous-ly spiked with both light and dark rum. . .sheer delight! $1.50. ORGIE D'AMOUR, a 60-oz. loving cup of mellow, festive wonderment. Enough to gladden the hearts of four lucky people and guaranteed to send you spiraling into the misty blue yonder frivolous—but happy. $6.00 PER FOURSOME.

Sandwiches can be exciting and different, too. In addition to the standards, Hamburger, Steak, Ham, etc., that most operations serve, the following unusual sandwiches served by Tally's, the Prairie Room and the Town House, respectively, show sandwich selling at its best:

"DIP AND EAT" PRIME BEEF DIP, $1.00. Delicious Tender Prime Beef Sandwich made on an Individual Loaf of French Bread and a cup of Tasty Au Jus for your Dippin' Pleasure. French Fries.

AN OLD FASHIONED SOUTHERN KENTUCKY HOT BROWN. An open-faced sandwich with chicken, cheese, mushroom sauce, broiled with sliced tomatoes and bacon strips, served on a sizzling platter.

SUBMARINE SANDWICHES. Served in a quarter-pound freshly baked French Loaf with Sauerkraut and Dill. YOUR CHOICE. . .$1.10. (1) Barbecued Turkey or Beef, with dip of our Special Sauce, (2) Sliced Ham, Canadian Cheese, Breast of Turkey with Russian Dressing.

The lowly vegetable need not take a back seat, either, on any menu. The following a la carte vegetable listing by the Buon Gusto Restaurant (at buon gusto prices) shows how to give your vegetables that "extra" merchandising treatment:

Special Baked Eggplant Parmigiana, $1.50; Andy Boy Broccoli Saute in Garlic and Olive Oil, $1.00; Boiled Escarole, Olive Oil and Clove of Fresh Garlic, $1.00; Escarole Saute in Garlic, Olive Oil, $1.00; Fresh Mushroom Saute, $1.25; Stuffed Artichoke, $1.00.

The same restaurant (Buon Gusto) has an a la carte listing of sauces that is unusual—just another "extra" to make an extraordinary menu. The following is the sauce list, a la Buon Gusto:

White or Red Clam Sauce, 75¢; Mushroom Sauce, 75¢; Garlic & Oil Sauce, 50¢; Marinara Sauce, 65¢.

If you think you have served and sold every part of the chicken in every way possible, consider the following item served both as an entree and an appetizer by the Ozark Barbeque Restaurant: Hickory Smoked Gizzards, (Tender as Livers), Mashed Potatoes & Gravy, Hot Rolls and Butter, $1.50.

Even Take-Outs can get special treatment for "sellability." The following example from Crowe's Dinner House is not a fancy listing, but it wraps up the two items neatly and makes them salable:

Fisherman's Box Lunch, 2 Pieces Fried Chicken, Home-made Bread, Potato Chips, Piece of Fruit, Apple Sauce Cake, $1.15; Sack Lunch, Roast Beef Sandwich, Baked Ham Sandwich, Potato Chips, Piece of Fruit, Apple Sauce Cake, 2 sandwiches $1.35, 1 sandwich $1.00.

The fountain menu does not have to be a dull listing of ice cream flavors. It can have all the imagination and flair of the biggest gourmet items. The following examples, from the 2-K Restaurant in Houston, show real fountain flair:

DUSTY ROAD, 2 Scoops Vanilla Ice Cream, Hot Caramel Topping, Sprinkled with Malted Milk Powder, Sliced Peaches, Whipped Cream, Cherry, 65¢, Half Size 45¢. OLD TIMER, An Old Fashioned Treat Made with Peppermint Stick and Coffee Ice Cream, Fresh Frozen Strawberries, Pineapple, Whipped Cream, Cherry, 65¢. TOUCHDOWN, Chocolate Covered Brazil Nut, Toasted Almond and Coffee Ice Cream, Coffee Syrup, Whipped Cream, Cherry. When you find the football, Touchdown! 65¢.

To add a twist to the after dinner menu, Garzanelli's Restaurant adds ice cream to brandy (combining dessert and an after dinner drink) and lists it as follows:

DELICADO—after dinner you'll love this delicious dessert-drink; brandy or your favorite liqueur multi-mixed with ice cream, 85¢.

As a final, super example of what can be done with the ordinary, common, every day cup of coffee, we list the coffee menu from The Cloister Restaurant which should show how a little item can make a menu big:

EXPRESSO (lungo), finely roasted, dark Italian coffee, 50¢; ESPRESSO ROMANO, dark Italian coffee, with lemon peel, 55¢; CAFFELATTE, half caffe espresso, half foaming steamed milk, 75¢; GRANITA, caffe espresso, ice, with whipped cream, 75¢; AUTHENTIC CAPPUCCINO, caffe espresso with steamed milk, chocolate, 75¢.

Specialties: CIOCCOLATA, hot chocolate with foaming steamed milk, 65¢; CIOCCOLATA CON PANNA, hot chocolate with whipped cream, 80¢; BOGOTA COFFEE, highland Colombian coffee, 80¢; INDIAN COFFEE, coffee, sugar, fragrant spices, topped with floating cream, 80¢; MOCHA COFFEE, combination of Viennese coffee and hot chocolate, 50¢.

Mit etwas Besonderem (with "something special"): CAPPUCHINO, caffe espresso, steamed milk, Italian chocolate, brandy, 95¢; MISCHIEVOUS CHOCOLATE, chocolate, steamed milk, gold label rum, 95¢; IRISH COFFEE, coffee, Irish whiskey, cream float, $1.25; CAFE DIABLO, coffee with flaming brandy, kirsch, $1.25; CAFE ROYAL, coffee with brandy, 95¢; CAFE AU RHUM, coffee with rum, 95¢; CAFFE PONCINO, caffe espresso with whiskey or brandy, 95¢; CAFE CACAO, caffe espresso, creme de cacao, whipped cream, $1.00; CAFE COINTREAU, caffe espresso, Cointreau, lemon peel, $1.00; CAFFE VENEZIA, caffe espresso, dark chocolate, milk, brandy, $1.00; COFFEE GROG, large coffee, buttered rum, spices, cinnamon stick, $1.25; "SANKY-PANKY", any of the above may be made with Sanka, $1.00; KAHLUA COFFEE, Mexican Kahlua refreshingly iced, $1.25.

Other good menu copy describing "extras" comes from the Yardarm menu:

"Riverside Villas. A unique recreational complex. Riverside Villas offers relaxation and an outdoor pleasure potential unmatched on Florida's West Coast. Here you will find pleasure boating and cruising of every description. Offshore Gulf fishing where every species abound. . .combined salt and fresh water fishing in the springfed headwaters—preserve hunting for quail, chukkar and pheasant.

"Air-conditioned motel and efficiency units. . .all with TV and telephone. . . . .swimming pool. . .marina. . .boat ramps. . .bait store. . . .tackle shop. Complete convention and meeting facilities. Convention hall with capacity of 150. Facilities for private parties and banquets for 25 to 125 people. Three bars and lounges.

"Homosassa Springs. Nature's Fish Bowl. A visit to this popular tourist attraction is truly one of Florida's most unusual recreational adventures. Thousands of fresh and salt water fish intermingle in giant fish-bowl spring. Wild life in profusion along nature trail. Alligators and crocodiles. Feed the deer and squirrels. Walk among water-fowl from worldwide collection. Scenic ride on sightseeing boats along spectacular wilderness canal. On U. S. Highway 19-98, 75 miles north of Tampa-St. Petersburg."

In addition, the Yardarm menu reproduces the complete flag alphabet for the information of nautical buffs.

Mammy's Shanty Restaurant has a gift shop where it sells special Civil War glasses, but to help sell the glasses and to help sell a special cocktail called the "Surrender" (1½ oz. rum, pineapple juice, crushed ice, dash of grenadine, chunk of pineapple and red cherry), "You can keep the glass to remember the battle. Additional glasses available in our gift shop."

Think you're selling everything possible on your menu? Then consider this. Rod's Shadowbrook Restaurant in Shrewsbury, N. J., offers the following list of cigars along with its desserts and after dinner drinks listing:

Coronas No. 3 - 50¢	Cambridge Monarch - $1.00
Coronas Coronas - 40¢	Oxford Romeo - 50¢
Coronas Belvederes - 25¢	Command Performances - 3/50¢
Coronas Chicas - 35¢	Medalist Naturals No. 7 - 3/50¢

Manners Big Boy Restaurant chain offers a special selection of take-outs, not just the common "Everything on the menu available for take-out." They list the following:

"You Can Take it with You! Enjoy these specialties in your home.

Manners Famous Big Boy Sauce. . . .50¢
Manners Sweet Red Pepper Relish. . .50¢
Big Boy's Seasoning Salt . . . . .39¢"

The Idlewild Cafe in Buffalo, Wyo., gives the traveling customer a little extra help. Instead of a map, they give distances in miles from Buffalo to 17 cities and towns (from 17 to 406 miles away) on the four main highways going north, south, east and west. A welcome bit of information along with good food, we're sure.

Another big chain of restaurants and motels—Horne's has an excellent map on the back cover of its menu. It is keyed to show Candy Shoppe and Circus Grill restaurants, Crown Room Restaurants, Candy Shoppes and Motor Lodges with another symbol for projected locations.

These examples of other selling, promotion, and merchandising uses of the menu do not begin to exhaust the possibilities in use by many creative and selling-wise food service operations. But perhaps these examples will stimulate you to add a few extras to your menu.

Win Schuler's

Sunday Suggestions

Rhine Wine Martini	$1.00
Sherry Manhattan	1.00
Schuler Sunday Sour	1.00
Wine Collins	1.00
Port Wine Flip	1.00
Rhine Wine & Soda	1.00
Cold Duck (for two)	1.50
Champagne Cocktail	1.00

Signs of Welcome

Try our International Cheese Plate,

served with a special Rye Bread

for $ .90 —

JUST THE RIGHT EVENING SNACK

****

A La Carte

Cheeses

Camembert (France)	.30
Cream Cheese (USA)	.30
Swiss Cheese (Switzerland)	.30
Gouda (Holland)	.30
Blue Cheese (Denmark)	.35

Served with Bread & Butter

Special Sunday drinks, an unusual cheese listing, a listing of local fish, a colorful tip-on and a well described salad dressing are unusual menu extras.

ENJOY DELICIOUSLY DIFFERENT

Chick-fil-A

1 pc. 85¢
2 pcs. 1.30

LAZIO'S
RECOMMENDS THE FOLLOWING LOCAL
FISH AS A PERSONAL SUGGESTION:
Filet of Petrale Sole
Grilled California Rex Sole
Filet of Sea Bass
Broiled Fresh Caught Salmon—In Season

A WORD ABOUT OUR DRESSINGS FOR OUR GARDEN SALAD

All our dressings are made with 100% Safflower oil, the highest Poly-unsaturated oil known! Many Doctors feel that Poly-unsaturated Oil such as Safflower Oil, has a tendency to reduce Cholesterol in the Blood Stream. Not all Doctors agree to this. But to be safe we have added 100% SAFFLOWER OIL to all our Dressings.

Hours of Service

Breakfast Daily
    7:00 a.m. to 11:30 a.m.

Luncheon—Tue. thru Sat.
    11:30 a.m. to 4:00 p.m.

Dinner—Tue. thru Sat.
    11:30 a.m. to 10:00 p.m.

Sundays   12:00 noon to 8:00 p.m.

Holidays   12:00 noon to 7:00 p.m.

Late Snacks in Parlour Car Bar
Daily except Sundays
9:00 p.m. to 12:00 midnight.

Closed Mondays and Christmas

Private Parties

For those festive occasions or business meetings the Silversmith can provide private dining rooms to take care of a few or as many as 250.

SAUCES AND CONDIMENTS

Brand's A-1 Sauce

Escoffier Robert Sauce

Major Grey's Chutney

Escoffier Diable Sauce

Green Pepper Sauce

Bahamian Mustard

House of Parliament Sauce

Red Pepper Sauce

Epicure Steak Sauce

Harvey's Sauce

Dijon French Mustard

5

TREATS CREATED WITH BONELESS CHICKEN

Each one is created with 4 oz. of Boneless Breast of Spring Chicken.

FRENCH

Breast of Chicken Cordon Bleu. Saut'eed boneless chicken with juicy grilled imported ham topped with thick melted cheese and mushroom cap, green garden peas. $1.55

SPANISH

Breast of Fresh Chicken cubes on Skewer. Broiled boneless chicken, diced onion, green pepper, saut'eed in tangy barbecued sauce, whipped potatoes. $1.50

AMERICAN

Breast of Chicken Rancher. Fried boneless farm chicken on open toasted bun with crisp bacon strips, cranberry sauce, French Fried potatoes. $1.35

SWEDISH

Breast of Chicken Low Calorie. Boiléd boneless chicken, creamy cottage cheese, sliced egg and tomato on crisp lettuce leaves, Melba toast. $1.25

BAMBERGER'S

Breast of Chicken Ideal. Boneless chicken, fried to golden perfection, on toasted bun, served with delicious cranberry sauce and crisp cole slaw ....$.95

Whether basic information like hours and days open, special sauces and condiments or a special chicken offering, extras like these on the menu add to sales.

Hear Ye!   Hear Ye!

All Items are complemented with the
Hospitality Plate . . .
yours without asking.

SALAD a la IVANHOE

A delectable combination of crisp, fresh
greens, thoroughly chilled.
Served with your choice of
Salad Dressings,
French, Thousand Island, Roquefort,
Oil and Wine Vinegar, Garlic and
Ivanhoe's Dressing
We'll be flattered if you take extra helpings.
Your salad and choice of dressing will be
served from the salad cart.

(CHOICE OF ONE)
IDAHO BAKED POTATO

Wrapped in foil, served with butter, or
sour cream and chives.

RICE PILAFF

Cooked in beef stock with
tomatoes served in casserole.
Cup yogurt on the side.

IVANHOE'S OVEN BROWN
POTATOES
(A Dish from The Crusade)
GOLDEN FRENCH FRIED POTATOES
(A King's Portion)

Basket of Bread, Crackers and Butter

*A lot of "extras" with the meal, or an extra, unusual nationality
dish deserve extra copy attention.*

Introduccion
A Las Tortillas

The tortilla is one of the earliest Mexican
foods. It has passed through the cen-
turies unchanged. Long before the
Spanish conquistadors embarked for the
American continent, the Aztecs were not
only using the tortilla (Spanish for "little
cake") as the staple food of their diet,
they were also using it as an eating imple-
ment!

TIA MARIA proudly continues this long
Mexican tradition. We think you will
enjoy watching the tortillas being
pounded from the unleavened cornmeal
in the manner that has been the age-old
custom.

**Today many people are at first con-
fused about handling a tortilla. We
suggest you attack it in the traditional
Mexican fashion. Hold it flat in one
hand, butter it, add the red sauce—
sparingly at first—roll and eat! Your
basket of hot tortillas will be delivered
as soon as your order has been taken.
We particularly recommend you enjoy
them with an imported Mexican beer.**

From the tortilla come many other traditional Mexican dishes. An Enchilada is
a soft-rolled tortilla filled with meat or
cheese and covered with a special sauce.
A crisp fried tortilla containing meat and
shredded lettuce is a Taco.

The Tamale is made of tortilla dough
spread on corn-husks, then wrapped
around a meat filling. Even chips are
deep fried tortillas. As a matter of fact,
the only Mexican dish on the TIA MARIA
Menu which does not start with the
tortilla is a Chile Relleno, a mild chile
pepper filled with cheese and fried in egg
batter.

GRANSON'S SWIRLERS
SWIRL YOUR OWN
Extra Size - Extra Kick
Smooth and Deeply Satisfying

1—**Martini Swirler** 1.25

2—**Vodka Swirler** 1.35

3—**Whiskie Sour Swirler** ..1.25

GARLIC BREAD . . . Sprinkled with Parmesan Cheese, Made to order, and served Oven Hot! Per Slice....... 25

IF WE KNOW YOU'RE COMING WE'LL BAKE A CAKE

Given 24 hours notice we will be happy to furnish FREE of charge a cake for your birthday or anniversary party — for groups of 6 or more.

FOR RESERVATIONS

PRIVATE PARTIES AND BANQUETS CALL BA 3-7534

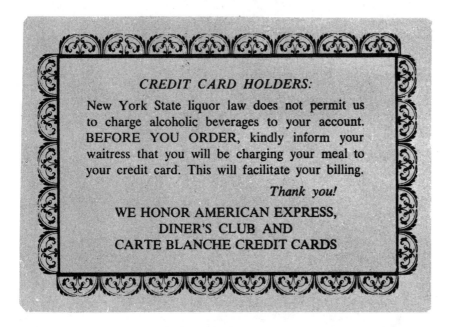

CREDIT CARD HOLDERS:

New York State liquor law does not permit us to charge alcoholic beverages to your account. BEFORE YOU ORDER, kindly inform your waitress that you will be charging your meal to your credit card. This will facilitate your billing.

Thank you!

WE HONOR AMERICAN EXPRESS,
DINER'S CLUB AND
CARTE BLANCHE CREDIT CARDS

A varied selection of little extras in information and food and drink offerings.

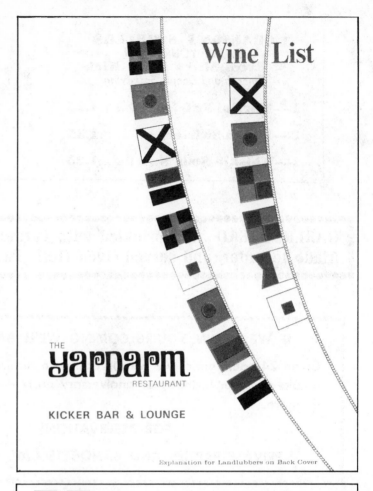

The front and back cover art and design of this wine list (as well as the menu itself) includes a flag and signal alphabet that compliments and underlines the nautical or seafood type of cuisine as well as supplying information and table conversation.

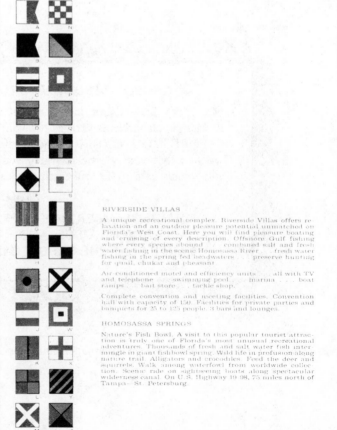

TAKE-OUTS ON THE MENU

There is no convenience food as convenient as take-out food; therefore, this part of the food service business is sure to continue to grow. And, the kinds of cuisine that are being sold in take-out packaging are increasing daily. Take-out business is a relatively easy way to increase food service business without increasing table and counter space, but this kind of new business will not sell itself. It must be advertised and promoted, and one of the most logical as well as inexpensive places to advertise take-out business is on the menu.

Point of sale displays and signs will sell take-out service, but they tend to spoil the decor and appearance of a fine dining room. The take-out story can be told more completely, effectively and in good taste right on the menu. Many operators do mention take-out service on their menus, but in a very inadequate manner. A line will very often appear at the bottom of a large menu listing that says, "Ask about our take-out service," or, ' All items listed on this menu are available for take-out." This is not good merchandising.

A more effective, creative advertising approach is to give the entire take-out story careful and complete treatment on the menu. The most logical place for this story is on the back cover. At present, over 50% of all the back covers of menus are blank—a complete waste of good advertising space. Considering the number of customers who look at a menu every day, month in and month out, the "advertising space" on the average menu is probably worth more than a large ad in most local newspapers. The food service operator who does not use this space is missing another promotional and merchandising opportunity.

Using the back cover, however, means using it effectively. Sell your take-out foods the way other advertisers sell in their space advertising. Start with a good heading—"Take-Outs, Tops in Convenience." Use a subhead—"Enjoy Gourmet Foods at Home—Pick Up or Delivery Service." Then use illustrations. The easiest way to illustrate take-outs is to photograph your most popular items (or the items you would like to make popular) in their take-out containers, or in the process of being packaged in the containers. This is important, because, while the customer may be sold on your good cooking, quality ingredients and varied and interesting cuisine, he does not know (if he is a new customer, and these are what you are looking for) how the take-out items are packed. By using packaging photographs, you overcome any consumer resistance concerning strength of packages, flavor loss, heat loss and carrying inconvenience.

Then, as in any good ad, use plenty of good copy. Describe each take-out item, list its price, tell how it is packed (paper box, tub, bucket—aluminum foil or returnable metal container). Also, list how many people each portion sold serves. Regardless of whether or not these same items are listed in the regular menu, it is good advertising to list them again. Even if the prices are the same as your regular menu, price repetition will not hurt.

If you have delivery service, sell this service also, and be sure to list your phone number prominently. If you treat your menu back cover as you would paid space, write good copy, use good illustrations and tell all the facts—you will have a "menu ad" that pulls. In addition, refer to your take-out story inside the menu so that the customer will not fail to read it on the back cover.

Obviously, your menu take-out story will sell only the customer who already patronizes your operation in a regular table or counter service capacity. To sell the public outside of your operation, you must use other advertising media. But for this, you can still use the menu. Print your back cover menu ad story on light paper suitable for mailing, either in an envelope or as a self mailer. This will save you money, since all of the preparation costs (copy, art, photos, typesetting) have been done for your menu. All you have to pay for is printing and paper.

In fact, if you want to use the entire menu—regular listing plus take-out story—as a promotion piece, you can use the same method and print it on lightweight paper to be used as a direct mail piece. Do not print "miniature" menus. In nearly all cases, the type becomes so small it is impossible to read, and the entire cost of printing becomes a total waste.

An almost separate category of take-outs is the party-banquet take-out or catering service. If you have room on your menu, tell this story there, also. Use photos to illustrate your party settings, center pieces, etc., and tell a detailed story in your copy. Some food service operations use a separate party-banquet catering menu to sell this feature of their food service which is good, but for the customer who will not ask (the average customer) about these services, the regular menu is still the place where this story can be told to the "mostest for the leastest."

Take Home Our Specialties

Oil Salad Dressing with Cheese, ½ Pint **1.50**	Full Pint **2.50**	
Creamed Roquefort, ½ Pint **1.50**	Full Pint **2.50**	
Our Own Cheese Crocks, 11 oz. . . . **2.00**	20 oz. . . . **3.75**	40 oz. . . . **4.95**
Chopped Chicken Liver Pate, ½ Pint **1.50**	Full Pint **2.50**	

We Will Deliver Any Entree On Our Menu, Complete With Relishes, Soup, Salad and Potato To Your Home or Motel. Another of the Charcoal Inn's Unique Services.

We Use Imported Roquefort In Our Dressing

Take-Outs should be specialties of the house or unusual items not readily available at the supermarket.

Verdile's
TAKE HOME CORNER

1 quart of Spaghetti Sauce	1.75
1 quart of Marinara Sauce	1.50
Meat Balls . . . . 2 for	.30
Fresh Sausage Links . . . . 4 for	.75

All Our Menu Items Are Available For
Take Home Consumption.

Just Call 235-9848
We Would Be Happy To Cook For You.

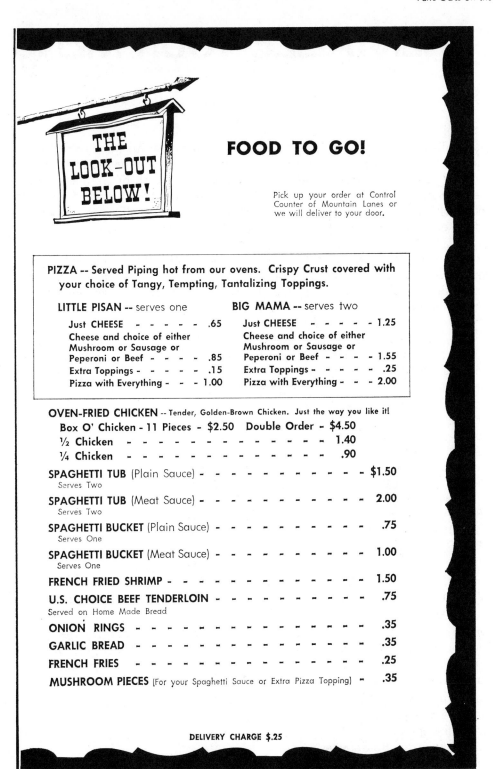

THE LOOK-OUT BELOW!

FOOD TO GO!

Pick up your order at Control Counter of Mountain Lanes or we will deliver to your door.

PIZZA -- Served Piping hot from our ovens. Crispy Crust covered with your choice of Tangy, Tempting, Tantalizing Toppings.

LITTLE PISAN -- serves one		**BIG MAMA** -- serves two	
Just CHEESE	.65	Just CHEESE	1.25
Cheese and choice of either Mushroom or Sausage or Peperoni or Beef	.85	Cheese and choice of either Mushroom or Sausage or Peperoni or Beef	1.55
Extra Toppings	.15	Extra Toppings	.25
Pizza with Everything	1.00	Pizza with Everything	2.00

OVEN-FRIED CHICKEN -- Tender, Golden-Brown Chicken. Just the way you like it!

Box O' Chicken - 11 Pieces - $2.50   Double Order - $4.50

½ Chicken	1.40
¼ Chicken	.90
SPAGHETTI TUB (Plain Sauce) Serves Two	$1.50
SPAGHETTI TUB (Meat Sauce) Serves Two	2.00
SPAGHETTI BUCKET (Plain Sauce) Serves One	.75
SPAGHETTI BUCKET (Meat Sauce) Serves One	1.00
FRENCH FRIED SHRIMP	1.50
U.S. CHOICE BEEF TENDERLOIN Served on Home Made Bread	.75
ONION RINGS	.35
GARLIC BREAD	.35
FRENCH FRIES	.25
MUSHROOM PIECES (For your Spaghetti Sauce or Extra Pizza Topping)	.35

DELIVERY CHARGE $.25

An example of good take-out merchandising that does an effective selling job.

CONTINENTALIZE YOUR MENU

Continental cuisine is becoming more popular on the menu. With the advent of new convenience food techniques, special continental type entrees are becoming easier to prepare and serve than they ever were before. Your chef need not be French or German to serve French and German foods, but the presentation on the menu of these foreign foods does present a menu problem. The two elements that seem to continentalize a menu are the sauce, either added or cooked in, and wine, either added or cooked in.

But we are not concerned here with the actual recipes for Continental cuisine, we are concerned about how these entrees are listed on the menu. As usual, we go to the source for menu information--menus of successful food service operators who are serving and merchandising continental cuisine on the menu.

To begin with, headings for types of entrees, appetizers, desserts, etc., can be in a foreign language, with an English translation, of course. The Trattoria Gatti, a restaurant specializing in Italian cuisine, does it like this:

ANTIPASTI	GRIGLIA
Hors D'Oeuvres	Grill
ZUPPE	LEGUMI
Soups	Vegetables
FARINACEI	INSALATE
Noodles	Salads
FARINACEI DELLA CASA	DOLCI
Home Made Pasta	Desserts
SPECIALITA DELLA CASA	FORMAGGI
Specialties of the House	Cheeses
PESCE	BEVANDE
Fish	beverages

As you can see, before he even begins to list his menu selections, this restaurant operator has raised his Italian food selection out of the ordinary, and out of the ordinary price category, too.

As one would expect, the Mews Dining Room, home of the Provincetown Mews Wine & Food Tasting Society, Inc., has a very Continental cuisine. To begin with, the Dinner is not just listed in plain fashion, but DINER TABLE D'HOTE (Full Course Dinners) and the Appetizers (Hors D'Oeuvres on the Menu) are out of the ordinary, as listed here:

Eggplant Maison
Demi Pamplemouse
Coquille Cape Cod
Les Escargots de Bourgognes
Sardines Portugaise
Assiette de Crudites

The following four entrees from the same restaurant give you an idea of the French approach with sauces and wines:

Sole Dieppoise
   Sole poached with mushrooms, shrimps, and mussels in a light cream sauce.
Shrimp per Bacco!
   Shrimp prepared with lobster sauce served with rice pilaf
Poulet Chasseur
   Chicken in the French style with tomatoes, mushrooms and spices.
Escallope de Veau au Madre
   Veal with Portugese wine sauce

You will note that in each case while a French name is given to the entree, the item is explained in English.

Your entire menu need not be continental. In fact, most restaurants will have a mainly American cuisine with a few continental items added. Hasenour's Restaurant, for example, has the two following German entrees included with its otherwise American menu:

WIENERSCHNITZEL ALA HOLSTEIN
   A tender cutlet of choice veal steak topped with a fried country egg
SAUERBRATEN MIT KARTOFFEL PFANNEKUCHEN
   U. S. choice beef roast marinated for seven days in vinegar and spice brine, roasted to a juicy goodness with spicy sweet-sour wine gravy
   Served with potato pancakes and wilted lettuce salad, typifying Old World eating at its best

For the ultimate in continental listing on the menu, the Old Swiss Village Restaurant in Tampa, Florida lists its appetizers, soups, entrees, desserts and beverages in three languages--French, German and English, as shown here:

Hors D'Oeuvres
   Pate de foie gras a la gêlee
   Gaensleberpastete mit gêlee
   The French goose liver classic with aspic

Escargots "Swiss House"
   Schnecken "Swiss House"
   Snails "Swiss House style"
Cocktail da crevettes frais
   Frischer krevetten cocktail
   Fresh shrimp cocktail
Filets de hereng Chantilly
   Hering mit schlagsahne
   Herring in sour cream
Huitres ou moules
   Austern oder muscheln
   Oysters or cherrystone clams
Potage - Suppen - Soups
   Consomme au sherry
   Klare fleischbruehe mit sherry
   Clear beef broth with sherry wine

Soupe de jour, chaude ou froide
Heisse oder kalte tasgesuppe
Today's hot or cold soup specialty

Soupe a l'oignon au gratin
Zwiebelsuppe au gratin, cup
French onion soup gratine, marmite

Frischer schwertfisch
Fresh Block Island swordfish tenderloin
    charcoal broiled

Pompano en court bouillon
Pompano in kraftbruehe
Fresh Florida pompano in herb
    broth with wine

Specialites de la Maison - Hausspezialitaeten - House Specialties

Escalopes de veau a la "Marsala," flambes
Kleine kalbsschnitzel a la "Marsala," flambiert
Veal cutlets coated in Romano cheese and sauteed with shallots, mushrooms and wine

Tournedoes Henri IV
Thin slices of filet mignon on artichoke hearts with Bearnaise sauce

Roti de boeuf au jus
Feinstes roastbeef in eignen saft
A generous slice of prime beef rib in nautral juices

Poulet tropical
Brathendl tropical
Pineapple filled with chicken breast in white wine sauce

Desserts

Peche Melba
Pfirsich Melba
Peach half on vanilla ice cream topped with red raspberry puree

Une selection de patisserie fine du wagon
Auswahl von feinem gebaech von dem wagon
Selection of fine pastries from the wagon

Glaces ou sorbets siverses
Auswahl von verschiedenen eissorten
Choice of ice cream or sherbet

Coupes: fraises, chocolat ou ananas
Sundaes: erdbeer, schokolade oder
    ananas
Sundaes: strawberry, chocolate or
    pineapple

Boissons - Getranke - Beverages

Creme cafe cognac
Eis kaffee mit kognac
Chilled coffee, chocolate, cream and brandy

Cafe irlandais
Irischer kaffee
Irish coffee

The, chaud ou froid
Tee, heiss oder kalt
Tea, hot or cold

Cafe a la maison
Haus kaffee
Swiss House blend coffee

Along with this continental selection, the Swiss House menu lists an excellent selection of wines as part of the menu. In fact, it is hard to visualize a real continental menu without a good wine selection. So if you plan to continentalize your menu, you'd better take a look at your wine cellar, or if you don't have one, call your wine merchant at once!

It's not often that a military installation menu, Officer's or N. C. O. Club has anything special to offer, but the menu of the International Grill at the Garmisch Recreation Area in Germany has an interesting feature. They list Grill Specialties from around the world. These are twelve entrees each from a different country—France, Yugoslavia, Russia, England,

Germany, Austria, Hungary, Italy, Spain, Turkey, Hawaii and the United States. The entrees for Yugoslavia, Hungary and Spain are listed here:

> From Yugoslavia:
> Rasnici
>> This specialty of a Balkan country features small pieces of tenderloin of beef, on a skewer, topped with fried onions and served on toast, salad.
>
> From Hungary:
> Fleica
>> From the smoky campfires of gypsies comes this exciting delicacy of two grilled pork chops topped with a tangy paprika sauce, and surrounded by French fries and cole slaw. Still wonderfully flavored even though there isn't a campfire.
>
> From Spain:
> Albondiguillas Creole
>> Talked about from Barcelona to Madrid and now in Garmisch, we bring you especially prepared meat balls grilled on a skewer, and served over rice with a spicy tomato-paprika sauce, salad.

The ultimate reason for adding French, German, Italian, Spanish or any other foreign names to the menu is, of course, not to make it harder to read. It is, let's face it, adding a certain snob appeal to your otherwise pedestrian listing, and thereby enabling you to charge more. Just adding foreign names, however, to a menu will not make the food, service and decor of a restaurant any better. But, if you are upgrading your food, service and decor, then adding foreign terminology is telling your customer that your entire restaurant package is getting better.

So get yourself a French, German or Italian dictionary and start up-grading your menu.

Continental Dishes

STEAK DIANE FLAMBÉE,
Wild Rice..................... **7.25**
Mignonettes of Beef cooked at
your Table, Sautéed in Sweet Butter, Bathed in our own Sauce.
Served with Fresh Mushrooms on
a Bed of Wild Rice and Flamed
in Brandy

STEAK AU POIVRE, FLAMBE
A L'ARMAGNAC, Wild Rice.. **8.00**

TOURNEDOS, ROSSINI,
Wild Rice..................... **7.50**

COQ AU VIN, Wild Rice............. **4.75**

Chicken Curry Calcutta

*Plump Cubes of Breast of Chicken cooked in an Exciting
Sauce of Apples, Fresh Ginger and Specially Blended
Spices. Served with Saffron Rice and
Assorted Condiments*...........*4.55*

Escalope de Veau Provencale

*Veal Cutlet stuffed with Ham and Gruyere Cheese,
Sautéed in Butter, then Topped with Mushrooms in
Provencale Sauce. Served with Artichoke Florentine
and Buttered Noodles*...........*4.65*

Emincé of Tenderloin Stroganoff

*A Delightful Combination of Choice Beef Strips, gently braised,
then simmered with Tomatoes and Seasonings, served with
Rice Pilaff and Tomato Parmesan*..........*4.65*

Breast of Chicken Romana

*Stuffed with Mushrooms, rolled in Parmesan Cheese,
sautéed in foaming butter, served with Rice Pilaff and
Artichoke Bottoms Florentine*..........*4.55*

Dining in the Grand Manner

CHATEAUBRIAND **9.75**
The ultimate in superior Steaks !
Thick and generous, this rich U. S.
Choice Steak is recognized the
world over as an epicurean masterpiece. A cup of delicious French
Onion Soup is served while this full
cut Steak is being prepared. When
ready, it is brought piping hot to
your table. (Cooking time 25 min.)
Serves two.

ROAST PRIME RIB
OF BEEF AU JUS **3.95**
A standing Rib Roast of the finest
aged Beef, roasted as succulently
rare or tenderly well done as may
please the most discriminate palate.
Medium rare at its best.

*Chicken or beef—dressed up and
served in continental style, it becomes dining instead of just eating,
with the price set accordingly.*

Specialita Della Casa

Grenadins of Beef Chasseur   7.00

Beef Tenderloin, Marsala Wine,
Mushrooms, Tomato, Tarragon, Risolé Potatoes

Breast of Chicken Jerusalem   5.00

Suprème Sauce, Madiera Wine,
Artichoke, Mushrooms, Turnips,
Rice Pilaf

Fritto Piccato   5.50

Medaillons of Veal, Zucchini Doré,
Mushrooms, Tomato, Gnocchi Romani

Escalope de Veau, Cordon Bleu   6.00

Imported Swiss Cheese, Ham, Mushrooms,
Asparagus, Broiled Tomato

Medaillon of Veal Normande   7.00

Tenderloin of Veal, Fresh Mushrooms,
Xères Wine, Sauce Normande,
Dauphine Potatoes, Cream of Spinach

Scampi Catalonia   6.00

Langostinas imported from Spain,
Sautéed in Olive Oil, Shallots,
Garlic, Wine, Spices, Rice

Tournedos Henry IV   7.95

Beef Tenderloin, Artichoke, Bearnaise,
French String Beans, Rissolées Potatoes

Steak Diane   7.95

Dauphine Potatoes, French String Beans

Steak Armagnac   8.50

New York Steak Sauté, Black Cracked
Pepper, Armagnac, Poivrade Sauce,
Dauphine Potatoes, French String Beans

*Italian, Spanish and French entrees
with unusual vegetables make this a
true continental listing.*

Exotic Specialties
from
Far Off Lands!

•

Mexican Iquana, Mole Sauce _____ 4.95

French Fried Grasshoppers (Japan) _____ 1.25

French Fried Butterflies (Japan) _____ 1.95

Chocolate Covered Giant Ants _____ 3.50
   (The genuine ants from South America which
   have been eaten there many years as the
   finest delicacy)

French Fried Ants _____ 3.50

Quail Eggs _____ 1.75

Sliced Smoked Octopus (Japan) _____ 1.50

Baby Bees in Soya Sauce (Japan) _____ 2.95

Chocolate Covered Baby Bees _____ 3.50

Roasted Caterpillars (Japan) _____ 1.50

Chocolate Covered Caterpillars _____ 3.50

Fried Agave Worms (Mexico) _____ 3.50

Diamondback Rattlesnake in Supreme Sauce ___ 3.75

Romanoff Beluga Caviar _____ 3.00

Rooster Comb in Jelly (France) _____ 2.95

Smoked Baby Clams (Japan) _____ 1.25

Kangaroo Steaks in Wine Sauce (Australia) ___10.00

Kangaroo Tail Soup (Australia) _____ 2.50

Smoked Quails (Japan) _____ 1.95

Alligator Soup _____ 3.50

Birds Nest Soup (England) _____ 2.25

Sharks Fin Soup (England) _____ 2.50

Cream of Snails Soup (Germany) _____ 2.25

Norwegian Reindeer Steak
   in Madeira Wine Gravy _____ 3.95

Smoked Petite Oysters (Japan) _____ 1.50

Smoked Frog Legs (Japan) _____ 1.50

Smoked Filet of Swordfish (Japan) _____ 1.75

Exotic and then some.

Les Poissons

WALLEYED PIKE SAUTEE 4.75
Wisconsin's favorite lake treasure sauteed in the traditional country manner

COLORADO MOUNTAIN TROUT "VERONIQUE" 4.95
From the crisp, clear creeks of Colorado, sauteed in butter and served with California grapes and toasted almonds

✳ **SOUTH AFRICAN LOBSTER TAILS** 7.50
Broiled to perfection and served with sizzling Wisconsin butter

FROG LEGS SAUTEE PROVENCALE 5.25
Sauteed in oil and garlic butter, served with grilled tomato

IMPORTED DOVER SOLE "MEUNIERE" 6.25
The delicacy of the North Sea sauteed in lemon butter sauce with a cover of finely chopped parsley

SCAMPI DANIELLE 5.50
This Danish Lobster Tail delicacy is a delicious addition for the friends of all sea foods. This shellfish is sauteed in butter and au gratin a la Cafe de Paris, with the famous special seasoned butter

Specialité de Pioneer

VEAL SCHNITZEL CORDON BLEU 4.95
The European specialty stuffed with Swiss Cheese and ham, breaded and sauteed, served with buttered noodles and broiled tomato

WISCONSIN SELECTED CALVES LIVER 4.75
Sauteed young liver, delicately prepared with smothered onions and apple rings

TENDERLOIN and SWEETBREADS "PARISIENNE" En Casserole . . . 5.50
Filets of beef and tender slices of sweetbreads, sauteed and served with white asparagus, peppers, and tomatoes

ORIGINAL RUSSIAN BEEF "STROGANOFF" 4.50
Prepared after the unique old St. Petersburg recipe that was a delicacy of the late Czar Nicholas

LONG ISLAND DUCKLING "NATURELLE" 6.25
This succulent Eastern bird is baked crisp in its own juice and served with fresh vegetables and croquette potatoes

SOFT OMELETTE WITH PFIFFERLINGE 3.50
For the gourmet with a light diet this fluffy egg dish is served with imported pfifferlinge, a special European mushroom. An interesting and excellent addition to our menu

PAN FRIED PORK CHOPS 4.50
Two Iowa cornfed pork chops pan fried in butter in the Early American manner, served with fresh apple sauce

DOUBLE CUT LAMB CHOPS DIABLO 5.95
Sauteed to perfection and glazed with English mustard and finished with fine herbs, garlic and bread crumbs

Les Legumes

SWISS PATTIE 50   FRESH VEGETABLE du jour . .50
SAUTEED MUSHROOMS . . . .1.25   WHITE ASPARAGUS 1.25
With sauce Hollandaise

Dining in high style.

This is a "Dutch Treat" that is completely out of the ordinary, with pea or potato soup, beef, fish, chicken and ham. And for dessert, Dutch Tarts, Mint Ice Cream and Hague Bluff.

The 12-page menu that is reproduced in its entirety on the next three pages lists all information and items in three languages—French, German and English. See inside front cover and pages 1, 2 and 3 of menu on facing page.

les Antiques d'Art

The priceless collection of rare antiques in the Old Swiss House was gathered for your enjoyment by Mrs. August A. Busch, Jr. and her brother, Willy J. Buholzer. Mr. Buholzer operates the original Old Swiss House in Lucerne.

Intricately hand-carved in oak, this German Baroque hutch was built in 1601. Grille Room, 2nd floor.

The KACHELOFEN, one of the oldest pieces in the collection (right) was used for heating and ornamentation in the 18th century. Delft blue and white tiles are of Swiss Baroque styling. 1st floor.

Bronze, brass and wood polished crystal Louis XV chandelier. "Views of Switzerland" wall murals, done from wood blocks carved a century ago, was the first wall-paper scenic ever printed. Only one other set exists. Banquet Room.

Swiss motto between antique French hand-carved grape columns, reads: "Time passes swiftly. Enjoy the hours as they come. If they're not good, let them pass. If they are good, enjoy them." Lounge, 2nd floor.

Hand-carved figures in poly-chrome and gold leaf, from a dismantled 18th century church. St. Catherina and St. Loedegar (far right), a Bishop born in 616, later beheaded. Foyer, 1st floor.

LEUCHTERWEIBCHEN or Light Lady, chandelier from the original Swiss House in Lucerne, has a woman's body and dolphin's tail, in the 17th century mermaid legend. Foyer, 1st floor.

Menu

Hors-d'oeuvres

Pâte de foie gras à la gelée Gaensleberpastete mit Gelee *The French goose liver classic with aspic*	1.50
Escargots "Swiss House" Schnecken "Swiss House" *Snails "Swiss House" style*	1.50
Cocktail de crevettes frais Frischer Krevetten Cocktail *Fresh shrimp cocktail*	1.50
Filets de hareng Chantilly Hering mit Schlagsahne *Herring in sour cream*	1.00
Huîtres ou moules Austern oder Muscheln *Oysters or cherrystone clams*	1.50

Carte Des Vins

Swiss:

Fine Selections from Cantons, Neuchâtel, Valais and Vaud—in the best vintages.

1 NEUCHÂTEL
Bouteille 4.25
Demi-Bouteille 2.50

2 OEIL DE PERDRIX
(Neuchâtel Rosé) Bouteille 6.00
Demi-Bouteille 3.25

3 FENDANT DE SION
Bouteille 5.50
Demi-Bouteille 3.00

4 JOHANNISBERGER
du VALAIS
Bouteille 5.50
Demi-Bouteille 3.00

5 DÔLE DE SION ROUGE
Bouteille 5.50
Demi-Bouteille 3.00

6 DEZALEY DE LAVAUX
Bouteille 4.75
Demi-Bouteille 2.50

7 AIGLE
Bouteille 5.50
Demi-Bouteille 3.00

8 LA COTE
Bouteille 3.75

Moselle:

19 BERNKASTELER
Bouteille 5.25
Demi-Bouteille 2.75

20 PIESPORTER
GOLDTROEPFCHEN
Bouteille 6.00
Demi-Bouteille 3.25

21 ZELLER SCHWARZE KATZ
Bouteille 5.25
Demi-Bouteille 2.75

Rhine:

10 LIEBFRAUMILCH:
MADONNA OR BLUE NUN
light, fruity and fresh, fleeting sweetness.
Bouteille 5.00
Demi-Bouteille 2.75

11 RUDESHEIMER
ROSENGARTEN,
fragrant, tangy.
Bouteille 5.00
Demi-Bouteille 2.75

12 RUDESHEIMER
BISCHOFSBERG SPATLESE,
Exceptional lustiness.
Bouteille 5.75
Demi-Bouteille 3.00

14 SPARKLING
LIEBFRAUMILCH,
Sumptuous liveliness.
Bouteille 7.00
Demi-Bouteille 3.75

15 NIERSTEINER
Bouteille 4.50
Demi-Bouteille 2.75

ANHEUSER FEHR
16 LAUBENHEIMER
Bouteille 4.50
Demi-Bouteille 2.75

17 LIEBFRAUMILCH
Bouteille 4.50
Demi-Bouteille 2.75

18 JOHANNISBERGER
Bouteille 4.75
Demi-Bouteille 3.00

White Bordeaux:

22 SAUTERNES GRANDE
TERRASSE,
moderately sweet.
Bouteille 5.00
Demi-Bouteille 2.75

23 CHATEAU d'YQUEM,
definitely the finest sweet full-bodied sauterne.
Bouteille 10.00
Demi-Bouteille 5.50

24 GRAVES, CHATEAU
DE LA BREDE,
more to dryness, full-bodied.
Bouteille 5.00
Demi-Bouteille 2.75

Red Bordeaux:

25 CHATEAU LAFITE
ROTHSCHILD,
tangy and light, having pronounced flavor.
Bouteille 7.50
Demi-Bouteille 4.00

26 SAINT JULIEN
Bouteille 5.00
Demi-Bouteille 2.75

27 MEDOC
Bouteille 5.25
Demi-Bouteille 3.00

28 PONTET CANET
Bouteille 6.00
Demi-Bouteille 3.25

BUDWEISER .60   BUSCH BAVARIAN .50

Carte Des Vins

White Burgundy:

29 CORTON CHARLEMAGNE,
Outstanding, medium full-bodied.
Bouteille 10.00
Demi-Bouteille 5.25

30 CHABLIS,
Very dry and flinty.
Bouteille 5.00
Demi-Bouteille 2.75

31 POUILLY FUISSE,
Pale, Light, Dry and "Clean" on the palate.
Bouteille 5.00
Demi-Bouteille 2.75

32 MEURSAULT,
Soft and full.
Bouteille 6.00
Demi-Bouteille 3.25

Rhone Valley:

33. CHATEAUNEUF DU PAPE
Bouteille 5.00
Demi-Bouteille 2.75

Rose:

34 ANJOU ROSE
Bouteille 4.00
Demi-Bouteille 2.25

Red Burgundy:

35 CLOS DE VOUGEOT,
full and rich, excellent bouquet.
Bouteille 10.50
Demi-Bouteille 6.50

36 POMMARD,
Well known, light and soft.
Bouteille 6.50
Demi-Bouteille 3.50

37 BEAUJOLAIS SUPERIOR,
light, gusty and fresh.
Bouteille 4.75
Demi-Bouteille 2.50

38 GEVREY CHAMBERTIN,
deep red, full-bodied.
Bouteille 6.50
Demi-Bouteille 3.50

39 CRUSE SPARKLING
BURGUNDY,
very popular and festive.
Bouteille 7.75
Demi-Bouteille 4.00

Champagnes:

Need no introduction, only an occasion.

40 DOM PERIGNON,
Distinct Masterpiece, absolutely the finest. Vintage
Bouteille 15.00

41 BOLLINGER, brut,
extra quality. Vintage
Bouteille 12.00

42 MUMM'S CORDON ROUGE,
brut.
Bouteille 12.00

43 PIPER HEIDSIECK,
extra dry.
Bouteille 11.00
Demi-Bouteille 6.00

Italian Wines:

44 BARDOLINO,
red, vivacious.
Bouteille 4.00
Demi-Bouteille 2.25

45 SOAVE BOLLA,
White, dry.
Bouteille 4.00
Demi-Bouteille 2.25

Spanish:

46 CEPA DE'ORO,
Dry, White, fine table wine.
Bouteille 3.50
Demi-Bouteille 2.00

47 MARQUES DE RISCAL,
Deep red, robust, rich and nutty on the palate.
Bouteille 4.50
Demi-Bouteille 2.50

Portuguese:

48 LANCER'S CRACKLING ROSE
Bouteille 6.50
Demi-Bouteille 3.50

America's Fine Wines:
from California

	Bottle	Half Glass
49 Pinot Noir	2.75	.50
50 Pinot Chardonnay	3.00	.50
51 Champagne Brut	6.25 3.25	.85
52 Sparkling Burgundy	7.00 3.75	
53 Dubonnet	4.50	.50

Other Imports:

54 Dry Sack	7.00	.85
55 La Ina	6.50	.65
56 Harvey's Bristol Cream	9.00	1.00
57 Double Century	5.00	.50
58 Harvey's Hunting Port	6.50	.65

MICHELOB - Bottle or Stein   .85

Potages · Suppen · Soups

Consomme au sherry
Klare Fleischbruehe mit sherry
Clear beef broth with sherry wine .40

Soupe du jour, chaude ou froide
Heisse oder kalte Taggessuppe
Today's hot or cold soup specialty .40

Soupe à l'oignon au gratin
Zwiebelsuppe au Gratin *cup* .40
French onion soup gratine *marmite* .75

Les Fruits de la Me · Fische · Seafood

Homards du Maine
Gedaempfter Hummer von Maine
Steamed Maine lobsters 6.25

Filet de sabre fraise
Frischer Schwertfisch
*Fresh Block Island swordfish tenderloin
charcoal broiled* 3.80

Sole meunière
Gebratene Dover Schollen
Imported Dover sole saute in lemon butter 3.90

Pompano en court bouillion
Pompano in Kraftbruehe
*Fresh Florida pompano in herb broth
with wine* 4.25

Spécialités de la Maison · Hausspezialitaeten · House Specialities

Escalopes de veau à la "Marsala," flambés
Kleine Kalbsschnitzel à la "Marsala" flambiert
*Veal cutlets coated in Romano cheese and
sauteed with shallots, mushrooms and wine* 4.40

Rôti de boeuf Au Jus
Feinstes Roastbeef im eigenen Saft
*A generous slice of prime beef rib in
natural juices* 4.75

Tournedoes Henrie IV
Tournedoes Henri IV
*Thin slices of filet mignon on artichoke
hearts with Bearnaise sauce* 5.90

Poulet Tropical
Brathendl Tropical
*Pineapple filled with chicken breast in
white wine sauce* 3.75

From the Charcoal Broiler

Choice sixteen-ounce sirloin 5.50
Planked Chateaubriand
(2 persons) 12.00
Small six-ounce tenderloin 3.70

Choice tenderloin steak (ten ounces) 5.20
Double rib French lamb chops 4.50

All entrees served with fresh French rolls, butter,
tossed Swiss House green salad, and Alpine potatoes or saffron risotto.

Desserts

Pêche Melba
Pfirsich Melba
*Peach half on vanilla ice cream topped
with red raspberry puree* .60

Glaces ou sorbets diverses
Auswahl von verschiedenen Eissorten
Choice of ice cream or sherbet .40

Banana Flambé 1.40

Une Séléction de Patisserie Fine du wagon
Auswahl von feinem Gebaech von dem wagen
Selection of fine pastries from the wagon .50

Coupes: fraises, chocolat ou ananas
Sundaes: Erdbeer, Schokolade oder Ananas
Sundaes: strawberry, chocolate or pineapple .50

Crêpes suzette 1.40

Boissons · Getranke · Beverages

Crème café cognac
Eis Kaffee mit Kognac
*Chilled coffee-chocolate,
cream and brandy* 1.25

Thé, chaud ou froid
Tee, heiss oder kalt
Tea, hot or cold .30

Café Irlandais
Irischer Kaffee
Irish coffee 1.15

Café à la maison
Haus Kaffee
Swiss House blend coffee .30

Liqueurs Importes

1.00

Williams Pear Brandy . . . Swiss Kirschwasser . . . Goldwasser
Crème de Cacao (Blanche ou Brune) . . . Cherry Heering . . . Crème de Menthe (Verte ou Blanche)
Curacao . . . Benedictine . . . Drambuie . . . Benedictine und Brandy
Chartreuse (Verte ou Jaune) . . . Grand Marnier . . . Cognacs
Galliano . . . Tia Maria

Fondue
THE NATIONAL DISH OF SWITZERLAND

The one whose morsel of Swissbread falls off the spear into the bubbling
kirschwassered cheese, by custom, buys the wine. (A round of drinks will do.)

1.75 per person
(Not less than two, please)

Lass' uns das gute Mahl geniessen und mit einem Glase Wein begiessen.

History of the Old Swiss House

The Old Swiss House is an enlarged replica of the famous restaurant of the same name in Lucerne, Switzerland, built in the early 18th century. The original Swiss House, one of Switzerland's outstanding restaurants, is operated by Willy and Kurt Buholzer, who took over its management from their late father. The Old Swiss House, like the original restaurant, contains an antique collection of rare beauty.

Colorful flags outside the Swiss House represent the 22 cantons, or provinces, of Switzerland. The wood-carved doors are massive replicas of those on the Swiss House in Lucerne. Notice the 17th century walnut hutch in the Grille Room and the magnificent 18th century walnut chest in the second floor Powder Room. The signed oil-on-wood still life by Swiss master Petrus Schotanus (Grille Room), and the solid copper holy water reservoir with its original hinged lid, are collectors' items. The original Jean Holbein hand-colored engravings are dated 1751.

Many of the smaller items have fascinating histories. The sand urns are solid copper cooking utensils used over 200 years ago. The canton shields, Buholzer crests, game trophies and the grape masher are hand-carved. In the Cocktail Lounge, the Chemine' Fence, the wine bottles, solid copper foot and bed warmers all were used in the 17th century, as were the Alpine cattle yokes and ancient Swiss weapons. Notice the tole coal scuttle at the fireplace, the warrior's shield above it and the ceramic beer stein from the year 1508.

All items of construction, decorating and furnishing are either an exact replica or an antique import. From this exacting completeness, plus the perfection of superb cuisine deftly served in an atmosphere of continental luxury, comes the Old World charm of the Old Swiss House.

A signed 19th century pastel on canvas by Swiss master Johann Rudolf Koller, entitled "Girl with Cow" is a collector's item. Grille Room, 2nd floor.

An early 18th century Armure in hand-worked iron was originally used as a candle cutter. Cocktail Lounge, 2nd floor.

A Louis XV PANETIERE of hand-carved walnut, with original lock and key. Bread was so precious in the 1700's it had to be locked up for safety. Less affluent families used bird cages or chicken coops in which to store the staff of life. Cafeteria, 1st floor.

An ornate parquetrie inlaid walnut spinning wheel of the early 18th century. Powder Room, 2nd floor.

An 18th century enamelled-faced walnut grandfather clock with brass mountings in the original finish. Cocktail Lounge, 2nd floor.

Hand-carved oak COSTUMER with the Caryatids and Empire Rose of the Napoleonic era; hand-carved strips borrowed from the German stylings. Foyer, 2nd floor.

An elegant antique with a romantic background, this hand-decorated DOWRY CHEST of Dutch styling bears the owner's name and date, 1768. Foyer, 1st floor.

An 18th century walnut chest with small carvings and applied wood panels, styled in the Palladian fashion. Powder room, 2nd floor.

Foreign menus can be studied for ideas usable by American food service operations.

SPÉCIALITÉS DU CHEF	OUR CHEF'S SPECIALITIES	SPEZIALITAETEN UNSERES CHEFS	
Brochette Stördebecker	Roasted meat on spit Stördebecker	Gebratenes Fleisch nach Stördebeckerart	12.—
Mignons de veau Sans Gêne	Small veal-fillets Sans Gene	Kleine Kalbsfilets Sans Gene	12.—
Caneton de Nantes vigneronne**** (4 personnes)	Duckling Nantes-style with raisins**** (4 persons)	Ente nach Nanteserart mit Trauben**** (4 Personen)	44.—
Poulet sauté Belle Othéro** (2 personnes)	Sauted chicken Belle Othero** (2 persons)	Sautiertes Hähnchen Schöne Othero** (2 Personen)	28.—
Emincé de volaille Idaho (2 personnes)	Flakes of chicken Idaho (2 persons)	Geschnetzeltes Geflügel- fleisch Idaho (2 Personen)	20.—

GRILLADES ET BROCHE	GRILLADES AND BARBECUES	GRILLADEN UND SPIESS	
Casserole vieux Berne	Mixed grill on Rösti	Mixed-Grill auf Rösti	12.—
Tranche de foie de veau	Sliced calf's liver	Kalbsleber	10.—
Rosette de Charollais Rachel	Tournedos Rachel	Tournedos Rachel	13.—
Rognon de veau aux herbettes de la Provence	Veal kidneys with spices	Kalbsniere mit Kräutern aus der Provence	10.—
Carré d'agneau de lait chatillonnaise* (2 personnes)	Lambchops Chatillonnaise* (2 persons)	Lammkarree Chatillonerart* (2 Personen)	26.—
Jeune coq grillé aux trois moutardes** (2 personnes)	Grilled young cock with mustards** (2 persons)	Junges grilliertes Hähnchen mit Senf** (2 Personen)	19.—
Châteaubriand périgourdine* (2 personnes)	Châteaubriand perigourdine* (2 persons)	Châteaubriand Perigordiner- art* (2 Personen)	26.—
T-Bonesteak grillé Montfort** (4 personnes)	T-Bonesteak grilled Montfort** (4 persons)	Grilliertes T-Bonesteak Montfort** (2 Personen)	50.—

This excellent menu lists everything in three languages—French, German and English.

MERCHANDISING LOW CALORIE ITEMS

It's hard to open a newspaper, read a magazine or watch TV these days without being aware of the weight problem, diets, calorie counting and related foods, pills and doctor's recommendations. Even for people without a weight problem, there is an awareness of the problem. As a result, there is evidence that the public is changing its eating habits. Certain types of foods, usually the high protein, low carbohydrate items, are favored. Also, the amount of food eaten at each meal is a subject for concern.

For the food service operator this may seem to be a problem. After all, if guests don't eat a lot, the operation will not sell as much and, therefore will not make as much money. But a problem can be an opportunity. The food service establishment can change its menu in many ways to meet this challenge and, in effect, serve less food for the same price.

The first way to adjust the menu to the changing, selective and calorie-aware public is to list more items a la carte. This gives the customer more choice. He may want an appetizer, but no potatoes. Or he may want just a salad to go with his steak. Or he may want an after dinner drink instead of a dessert. There is a definite trend toward more a la carte listing on the menu. And the menu that is more a la carte is usually a more expensive menu which means more profit to the restaurant.

The second way to adjust to the calorie-conscious customer is to deliberately list low calorie specials. There is a limited amount of this kind of listing on the menu at present. The following are some examples:

LOW CALORIE HI PROTEINS

Waist Watcher $1.15
　　For the diet conscious, broiled ground sirloin with melted nippy cheese, Melba peach, cottage cheese, and Ry-krisp. Try a low cal Tab—1 calorie per 8 oz. serving.

Tiger-High Protein $1.35
　　½ lb. of ground sirloin, cottage cheese and tomato wedges, roll and butter.

Lou Jones $1.45
　　Slices of rare roast beef—cottage cheese and fruit or cole slaw, roll and butter.

LOW CALORIE SPECIALS

Broiled Chopped Sirloin Patty $1.15
　　with creamy cottage cheese, peach half, sliced tomatoes and melba toast.

Cold Sliced Turkey $1.25
   with creamy cottage cheese, peach half, sliced tomatoes and melba toast.

DIET SPECIALS

½ Lb. GROUND ROUND STEAK $1.40
   (with cottage cheese, choice of two peach halves or
two pineapple rings).

THE BOYS' STEAK SANDWICH $2.45
   (½ lb. choice beef served on French roll with cottage
cheese and fruit. Choice of two peach halves or two
pineapple rings).

FILET OF SOLE $1.25
   (cottage cheese and choice of two peach halves or two
pineapple rings).

NIK'S LOW CALORIE SPECIAL

Choice of tomato or orange juice, freshly ground hamburger patty, cottage cheese or garden fresh lettuce,
sliced tomato, melba peach $1.10

CALORIE SPECIALS

New York Steak $1.40
Jumbo Sirloin Patty $1.20
Sirloin Patty . . . . $ .95
above served with mound of cottage cheese, hard boiled
egg and Ry-krisp.

THE SKINNY VIRGINNY BURGER

Minus the bun for weight-watchers, and served with a
bowl of sliced egg, a mountain of cottage cheese and
juicy tomato wedges on lettuce. Melba toast, of course.
                            . . . . $1.25

DIET BURGER for the calorie conscious—no roll, but
accompanied by some cottage cheese.

   The low-calorie item par excellence on the menu, of course, is the salad. And the
menu that lists no entree salads is taking a chance of losing customers. Salads do not have
to be listed as low-calorie items. The public generally is convinced of the diet value of
salads.   But some restaurants do list salads as low-calorie, diet entrees as shown in
examples here:

DIET PLATES

LOW CALORIE DIET PLATE
(approximately 224 calories)
Choice of chilled shrimp, chopped beef or sliced chick-
en, sliced tomato, half peach, cottage cheese, melba toast
and coffee or tea $1.55

CHICKEN SALAD BOWL
(approximately 320 calories)
A salad of tossed greens and vegetables. Your favorite
dressing. Rolls, butter and coffee or tea $1.45

SHRIMP SALAD BOWL
(approximately 285 calories)
A salad of tossed greens and vegetables. Rolls, butter
and coffee or tea $1.45

FRUIT SALAD PLATE
(approximately 305 calories)
Cottage cheese, fruit cocktail, peach half, orange and
pineapple slice. Rolls, butter and coffee or tea .. $1.45

Even the salad dressing can be sold from a diet angle as shown in the example below:

ON A DIET?

ASK YOUR WAITRESS FOR

"SAFFLOWER"
French dressing
Garlic dressing
Oil
Mayonnaise
with the highest ratio of polyunsaturated
fats of all edible oils

WONDERFUL FOR SALADS

Finally, a real calorie opportunity presents itself when the subject is desserts. The "Decline of the Desserts," if it is real, is probably due to the common comment, "Oh, I shouldn't, it's fattening." The easiest way to get around this dessert obstacle and still build the check is to sell after-dinner drinks—brandies, cordials, dessert wines, after-dinner cocktails, coffee royal, etc. They are easy to serve, come prepared to a large extent and present no storage problem. They may still have calories, but to the customer they "seem" to be less fattening.

So, from beginning to end, the menu that presents more gourmet excitement and less "bulk" may be the menu of tomorrow.

Salads and cold plates can be converted to "Diet Plates" by listing calories for each item.

Diet Plates

CHICKEN SALAD BOWL
(APPROXIMATELY 320 CALORIES)

A Salad of Tossed Greens and Vegetables, Your Favorite Dressing.   Rolls, Butter and Coffee or Tea.

1.45

SHRIMP SALAD BOWL
(APPROXIMATELY 285 CALORIES)

A Salad of Tossed Greens and Vegetables, Your Favorite Dressing.   Rolls, Butter and Coffee or Tea.

1.55

LOW CALORIE DIET PLATE
(APPROXIMATELY 225 CALORIES)

Choice of Chilled Shrimp, Chopped Beef or Sliced Chicken Sliced Tomato, Half Peach, Cottage Cheese, Melba Toast and Coffee or Tea.

1.55

FRUIT SALAD PLATE
(APPROXIMATELY 305 CALORIES)

Cottage Cheese, Fruit Cocktail, Peach Half, Orange and Pineapple Slice.   Rolls, Butter and Coffee or Tea.

1.45

Diet Plates

Hamburger Patty 1.25
With Cottage Cheese,
Sliced Tomatoes

Sliced Turkey, Ham and Tongue 1.50
with Cottage Cheese and
Sliced Tomatoes

Cold Rare Roast Beef 1.50
with Cottage Cheese and
Sliced Tomatoes

Half Avocado Julienne 1.85
Served Chilled on Hearts of
Romaine Lettuce with Orange
and Grapefruit Segments
and Crab Apples

YOUR CHOICE OF DRESSING

SERVED WITH MELBA TOAST OR
ROLLS AND BUTTER

The Red Roof Restaurant lists a selection of diet plates in a prominent place on the menu, plus a selection of sandwich, salad and cold cuts.

The breakfast menu can also feature a low-calorie, high protein special, as shown here.

Low Calorie — High Protein Breakfast

(LESS THAN 400 CALORIES!)
ORANGE JUICE
SPECIAL K
(PROTEIN CEREAL) WITH MILK
ONE POACHED EGG
WHITE TOAST (1 SLICE)
BLACK COFFEE

$1.00

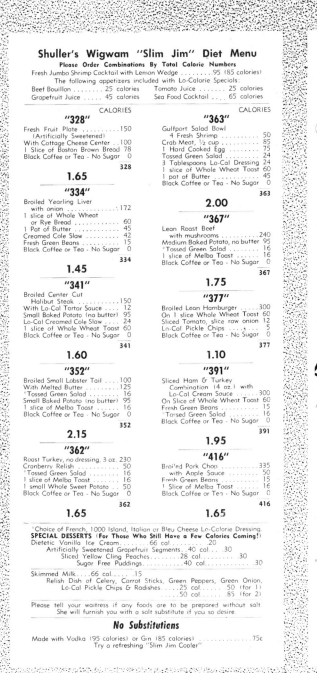

Shuller's Wigwam "Slim Jim" Diet Menu

Please Order Combinations By Total Calorie Numbers

Fresh Jumbo Shrimp Cocktail with Lemon Wedge . . . . .95 (85 calories)

The following appetizers included with Lo-Calorie Specials:

Beef Bouillon . . . . 25 calories	Tomato Juice . . . . 25 calories
Grapefruit Juice . . . . . 45 calories	Sea Food Cocktail . . . . 65 calories

CALORIES

"328"

Fresh Fruit Plate 150
(Artificially Sweetened)
With Cottage Cheese Center . .100
1 Slice of Boston Brown Bread 78
Black Coffee or Tea - No Sugar 0
328

1.65

"334"

Broiled Yearling Liver
    with onion 172
1 slice of Whole Wheat
    or Rye Bread 60
1 Pat of Butter 45
Creamed Cole Slaw 42
Fresh Green Beans 15
Black Coffee or Tea - No Sugar 0
334

1.45

"341"

Broiled Center Cut
    Halibut Steak 150
With Lo-Cal Tartar Sauce 12
Small Baked Potato (no butter) 95
Lo-Cal Creamed Cole Slaw 24
1 slice of Whole Wheat Toast 60
Black Coffee or Tea - No Sugar 0
341

1.60

"352"

Broiled Small Lobster Tail 100
With Melted Butter 125
°Tossed Green Salad 16
Small Baked Potato (no butter) 95
1 slice of Melba Toast 16
Black Coffee or Tea - No Sugar 0
352

2.15

"362"

Roast Turkey, no dressing, 3 oz. 230
Cranberry Relish 50
°Tossed Green Salad 16
1 slice of Melba Toast 16
1 small Whole Sweet Potato . . 50
Black Coffee or Tea - No Sugar 0
362

1.65

CALORIES

"363"

Gulfport Salad Bowl
    4 Fresh Shrimp 50
    Crab Meat, ½ cup 85
    1 Hard Cooked Egg 75
    Tossed Green Salad 24
    3 Tablespoons Lo-Cal Dressing 24
1 slice of Whole Wheat Toast 60
1 pat of Butter 45
Black Coffee or Tea - No Sugar 0
363

2.00

"367"

Lean Roast Beef
    with mushrooms 240
Medium Baked Potato, no butter 95
°Tossed Green Salad 16
1 slice of Melba Toast 16
Black Coffee or Tea - No Sugar 0
367

1.75

"377"

Broiled Lean Hamburger 300
On 1 slice Whole Wheat Toast 60
Sliced Tomato, slice raw onion 12
Lo-Cal Pickle Chips 5
Black Coffee or Tea - No Sugar 0
377

1.10

"391"

Sliced Ham & Turkey
    Combination (4 oz.) with
    Lo-Cal Cream Sauce 300
On Slice of Whole Wheat Toast 60
Fresh Green Beans 15
°Tossed Green Salad 16
Black Coffee or Tea - No Sugar 0
391

1.95

"416"

Broiled Pork Chop 335
    with Apple Sauce 50
Fresh Green Beans 15
1 Slice of Melba Toast 16
Black Coffee or Tea - No Sugar 0
416

1.65

°Choice of French, 1000 Island, Italian or Bleu Cheese Lo-Calorie Dressing.

SPECIAL DESSERTS (For Those Who Still Have a Few Calories Coming!)
Dietetic Vanilla Ice Cream . . . . .66 cal 20
    Artificially Sweetened Grapefruit Segments . .40 cal 30
        Sliced Yellow Cling Peaches . . . . .28 cal 30
            Sugar Free Puddings . . . . .40 cal 30

Skimmed Milk . . . .66 cal 15
    Relish Dish of Celery, Carrot Sticks, Green Peppers, Green Onion,
    Lo-Cal Pickle Chips & Radishes . . . . .25 cal . . . . .50 (for 1)
        . . . . .50 cal . . . . . .85 (for 2)

Please tell your waitress if any foods are to be prepared without salt.
She will furnish you with a salt substitute if you so desire.

No Substitutions

Made with Vodka (95 calories) or Gin (85 calories) 75c
    Try a refreshing "Slim Jim Cooler"

Here is a complete "Slim Jim" diet menu that lists the total calorie count for each entree as well as the price.

WHERE YOU LIST IT ON THE MENU MAKES A DIFFERENCE

Without changing any of the items on the menu or their price, you can improve your menu and your profit picture just by rearranging your listing. The secret is how does the customer's eye travel as he first looks at your menu? What does he see first? What catches his eye, holds his attention and makes him order one item over the other? The answer is not complete. There is no science of eye or mind attention. Advertising has been studying the problem for years. But there are some rules that you can follow that are the result of research and trial and error methods, especially in the case of menus.

The first two rules to remember are that we in the Western world read from left to right and top to bottom, just the opposite of the Chinese. The reader's eye to a large extent, therefore, will follow this route, but not entirely. To begin with, let us take a simple one-page menu as shown in Figure A.

FIGURE A

The one-page menu is arranged with the appetizers at the top, numbered 1, 2, 3 and 4.

The entrees are next, numbered 1, 2, 3, 4, 5 and 6. Through the method of trial and error of many food service operations and menu printers and designers, it has been found that the general rule is that appetizer number one, entree number one and dessert number one will be your best sellers simply because they are number one on this list. The reasons probably are two. First, the fact referred to before, that we read from top to bottom, makes the top number one item the one that hits the eye first and makes the first and probably most lasting impression. Second, we are psychologically conditioned to assume that number one is really "number 1," that is, it is the best, the tops, the winner in the category, no matter what kind of a list it is—food, beverage, class standing, athletes, etc.

The important thing for a menu planner to remember when arranging his items from top to bottom in any category—appetizers, salads, sandwiches, entrees, desserts, etc.—is to select item number one carefully and consciously. It should be the item he wants to sell the most of. This does not mean that it should necessarily be the most expensive item on the menu. In the case of steak and lobster versus chicken, for example, steak and lobster are big ticket items, while chicken is a lower priced item, but the profit to the food service operator from a chicken entree may be higher. The important thing is to list first what you want to sell the most. The number 2, 3, 4, 5, etc. order of listing is also important, but number one is the most important.

In addition to the order of item listing, there is the order of category of items. An example is shown in Figure B:

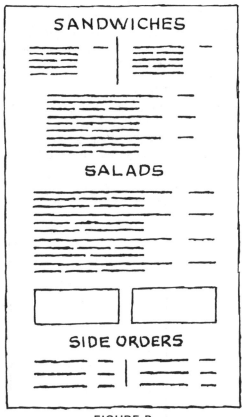

FIGURE B

Figure B could be a page or panel of a menu, but here again there is an order of importance. In this particular case, sandwiches are number 1, salads number 2 and side orders number 3. The important thing is that this is a conscious, deliberate selection. The desire in this particular case would be to sell more sandwiches than salads, more salads than side orders.

The next menu layout to consider is a two-page menu design as shown in Figure C:

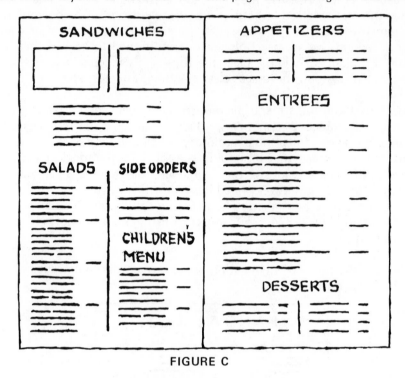

FIGURE C

Contrary to the reading rule of left to right, in this particular case, the eye of the reader-customer goes first to page 2, item number 1. The reason for this is not clear, but trial and error experiments have shown that this is the case. The answer probably is that this type of menu (in fact, most menus except the one-page card type) is held in a three dimensional fashion and should be considered three dimensional rather than just two dimensional.

FIGURE D

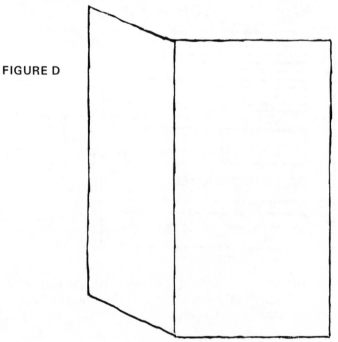

The drawing in Figure D shows what happens: panel or page one is held at an angle (usually) so that panel or page two gets number one attention. Carrying this analysis further and considering the three dimensional aspect of a folded piece of paper, let us look at a three-panel, two-fold layout, as shown in Figure E:

FIGURE E

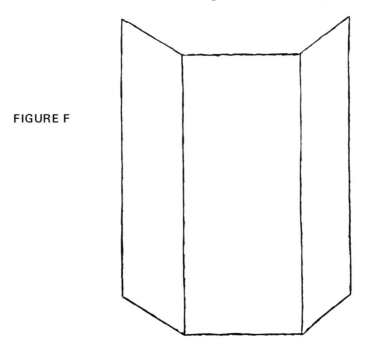

In the case of this type of menu layout, panel number two is the number one panel for attention. Therefore, those items that the food service operator wants to sell most of should be listed on panel two. The reason for panel two being number one in attention is again probably the three dimensional factor as shown in Figure F:

FIGURE F

As shown in Figure F, the eye goes to panel two naturally when the menu is held in Figure F position. When the menu is laid out flat, of course, this factor is less important, but when the customer picks up the menu, he tends to hold it first in the manner as shown in Figure F. A larger menu, the four page insert in a four page cover, for example, presents a particular problem. Figure G shows what can happen:

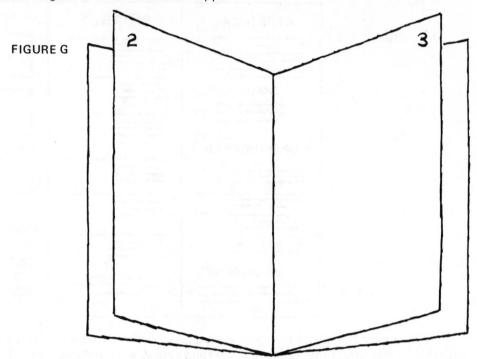

FIGURE G

The problem here is that while all eight pages of this kind of menu—cover, back cover and inside front cover and back cover, plus pages 1, 2, 3 and 4 of the insert, should be used, the result may be that if the menu opens up sort of naturally, as shown in Figure G, only pages 2 and 3 will get the customer's attention. This can be overcome in several ways. First,

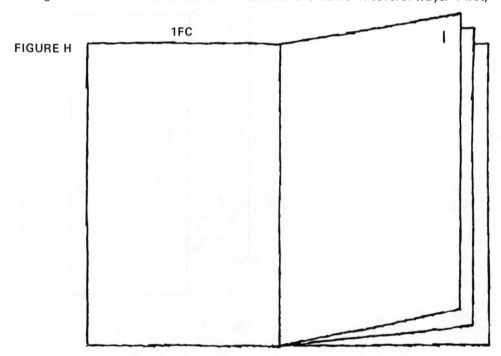

FIGURE H

have the waiter or waitress present the menu with page one and the inside front cover open, as shown in Figure H.

The result will then be that the customer is exposed to the copy on the inside front cover and page one (in this case the liquor listing and the appetizer-soup listing). The customer after looking at these two pages is going naturally to turn to the next two pages to look at the entree listing. He may not, however, look at page four and the inside back cover. But if the desserts are listed on page four and the after dinner drinks on the inside back cover, this presents no problem since the menu will be presented a second time to the customer and should be presented as shown in Figure I:

FIGURE I

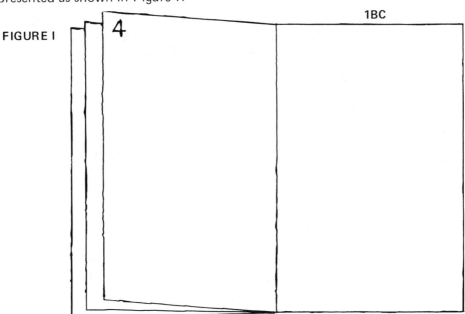

As you can see, if the waiter or waitress presents the menu a second time to the customer as shown in Figure I, page four and the inside back cover will be read. A separate after dinner dessert and drink menu will, of course, function in the same manner. Another

FIGURE J

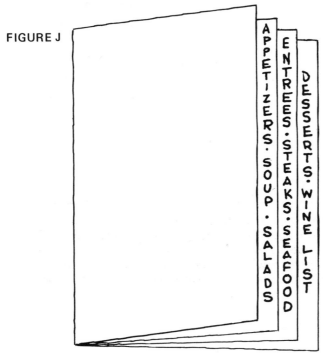

way of making sure that all eight pages of an eight-page menu get attention and readership is to provide an index. This can easily be done as shown in Figure J by folding each piece of paper off center.

The off center folds provide space for printing an index for the pages, listing particular items. The words Appetizers, Soups and Drinks can be printed on the page showing what is on page one and the inside front cover. The words Steaks, Seafoods, Chef's Specials, etc., can be listed on page three showing what is listed on pages two and three, and the projecting part of the inside back cover can be used to list the words Dessert, After Dinner Drinks, etc., to show what is listed on page four and the inside back cover.

It should be repeated that where you list items on the menu is important. It has been proven by experience that changing the order and the page where you list the menu items can improve the profit picture for any food service operation.

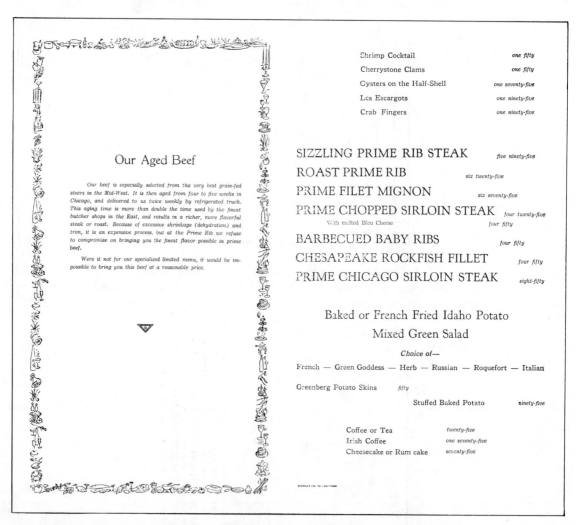

Shrimp Cocktail	one fifty
Cherrystone Clams	one fifty
Oysters on the Half-Shell	one seventy-five
Les Escargots	one ninety-five
Crab Fingers	one ninety-five

Our Aged Beef

Our beef is especially selected from the very best grain-fed steers in the Mid-West. It is then aged from four to five weeks in Chicago, and delivered to us twice weekly by refrigerated truck. This aging time is more than double the time used by the finest butcher shops in the East, and results in a richer, more flavorful steak or roast. Because of excessive shrinkage (dehydration) and trim, it is an expensive process, but at the Prime Rib we refuse to compromise on bringing you the finest flavor possible in prime beef.

Were it not for our specialized limited menu, it would be impossible to bring you this beef at a reasonable price.

SIZZLING PRIME RIB STEAK	five ninety-five
ROAST PRIME RIB	six twenty-five
PRIME FILET MIGNON	six seventy-five
PRIME CHOPPED SIRLOIN STEAK	four twenty-five
With melted Bleu Cheese	four fifty
BARBECUED BABY RIBS	four fifty
CHESAPEAKE ROCKFISH FILLET	four fifty
PRIME CHICAGO SIRLOIN STEAK	eight-fifty

Baked or French Fried Idaho Potato

Mixed Green Salad

Choice of—

French — Green Goddess — Herb — Russian — Roquefort — Italian

Greenberg Potato Skins	fifty
Stuffed Baked Potato	ninety-five

Coffee or Tea	twenty-five
Irish Coffee	one seventy-five
Cheesecake or Rum cake	seventy-five

This limited, all a la carte menu puts its entire listing on page 2. Less important general copy describing their "Our Aged Beef" is on page 1. The menu also explains that. . . . "Were it not for our specialized, limited menu, it would be impossible to bring you this beef at a reasonable price." Notice that each a la carte item (including coffee and tea) is listed with the price in words rather than figures—one fifty instead of $1.50.

WINE LIST

SATISFYING SELECTIONS FROM THE BAR TO SHARPEN YOUR
APPETITE AND MAKE YOUR DINNER EVEN MORE ENJOYABLE

APPETIZERS
Dubonnet .65   Martini & Rossi Vermouths .65
Harvey's Bristol Cream Sherry .80   Victoria Sherry .65
Findlater's Dry Fly Sherry .65   Bright's "74" Sherry .55

COCKTAILS
Daiquiri (light rum base) .90   Martini (gin base) .90
Manhattan (rye base) .90   Rob Roy (scotch base) .90
Old Fashioned (rye base) .90

HIGHBALLS
Scotch .85   Rye .80   Bourbon .85
Light Rum .85   Dark Rum .80
Gin .80   Vodka .80
including your choice of mix

BEERS & ALES
Newfoundland and Canadian Beers & Ales
Tuborg Danish Beer .60   Heineken's Dutch Lager .60
McEwan's Strong Scotch Ale .60   Guinness' Irish Stout .60

**DINNER &
SPARKLING
WINES**
Red Dinner Wines — Usually served with dark meats
St. Emilion – Bottle 3.80   St. Julien – Bottle 3.80
Chianti Bosca – Bottle 3.80   ½ Bottle 2.30
Beaujolais Red Burgundy – Bottle 4.80   ½ Bottle 2.30
Sorgrape Mateus, Rose – Bottle 4.20

White Dinner Wines — with light coloured meats, sea foods,
Guntrum's Liebfraumilch – bottle 4.70, Niersteiner – bottle 4.70
Bosca Orvieto – bottle 4.30, ½ bottle 2.30,
Chateau-Gai (Canadian) Sauternes 3.40

Dessert Wines — to conclude the meal
Newman's "A" Port .65,   Chateau-Gai Port .50

Champagne — a highlight for any festive meal
Mumm's Cordon Rouge – bottle 10.50, ½ bottle 5.50
Chateau-Gai (Canadian) – bottle 6.30

**LIQUEURS &
BRANDIES**
Drambuie .80   Cointreau .80   Creme de Menthe .80
Brandy & Benedictine .80   Hennessey's XXX Brandy .80
Bols Apricot Brandy .80   Bols Cherry Brandy .80

A Simple Guide to the Selection of Drinks

Appetizers – Before meals (sherries may also be taken with soup course or after meals)
Cocktails – Before meals   **Highballs** – Before or after meals
Beers, Ales or **Champagne** – Before, during or after meals
Red or White Wines – During dinner   **Liqueurs, Brandies** – After meals

---

BILL OF FARE

All of our luncheons and dinners include soup or juice, Woodstock dinner rolls and melba toast, potatoes, peas, carrots (or side salad), your choice of dessert and beverage. You will find both luncheon and dinner size orders in most selections, to suit your mood and appetite. Toward providing maximum dinner pleasure, we shall be offering special features every day. These will include seasonal delicacies such as salmon, lobster, flippers, strawberries and the like, when they are available.

WOODSTOCK SPECIALTIES

1 Country-style
GOLDEN CRISP CHICKEN PIECES
with glazed peaches
light luncheon   dinner   children's
size $2.00   size $2.50   orders $1.50

2 Woodstock
TENDER YOUNG ROAST TURKEY
with stuffing, partridgeberry jelly
light luncheon   dinner   children's
size $2.25   size $2.75   orders $1.75

3 Old English
ROAST PRIME RIBS OF BEEF
with Yorkshire pudding, horseradish sauce
light luncheon   dinner   children's
size $2.75   size $3.25   orders $2.25

4 Prime Western
FILET MIGNON STEAK
with mushroom gravy boat
light luncheon   dinner   children's
size $4.00   size $4.50   orders $3.25

5 Newfoundland
SEAFOOD SAMPLER
cod tongues, scallops, smoked salmon or cod, baked smoked herring, salt codfish, boiled potatoes, drawn butter, tartar sauce
order per   minimum of two orders
person $2.50   except on Fridays

6 Woodstock
COLD PLATE SPECIAL
two meats, two salads, lettuce, tomatoes
order per   children's
person $2.50   orders $1.50

ADDITIONAL TODAY

**YOUR CHOICES WITH THE
SPECIALTIES**
Juices — tomato, apple, orange
Soups — homemade turkey or split pea
Desserts — homemade pie, steamed pudding, trifle, ice cream and cookies, cheese and crackers
Beverages — coffee, tea, milk

A LA CARTE — A side salad may be ordered in place of a regular vegetable at no charge.
Side salad as an extra .30, mushrooms .30, onion rings .30, broccoli .30, cauliflower .30

Lighter luncheon selections are shown on the next page, subject to 25c additional per person ordering, for dining room service.

SPECIAL ORDERS

Given four hours' notice, we are delighted to prepare your special choice of dinners such as roast duck, squab, steak and kidney pie, rabbit stew and so on — for parties of two or more.

Woodstock Colonial Inn

Our Season
April 30th. to October 31st.
(subject to weather)

Cottages
10 comfortable cottages, in a park-like setting

Bookings
Private bookings for weddings dinners, except during the summer season.

Bill of Fare

The Lunch-INN-ette

. . . . . featuring many specialties renowned for their popularity throughout North America. The Lunch-INN-ette menu is designed so that you may make up many interesting and tasty combinations. The lighter lunches do for mid-day or evening meals or even for breakfasts. We are especially proud of our sandwich specialties which come with optional side orders and are extra delicious when chosen in company with one of the super soups. The most important of all ingredients is included in every item — Woodstock quality home cooking.

LIGHTER LUNCHES — Including Woodstock Dinner Rolls, Pie or Ice Cream, Beverage
Baked Beans and Weiners (Boston)   1.00
Pancakes and Sausages (Vermont)   1.00
Fish Cakes, Tomato Sauce, Peas, Carrots (Newfoundland)   1.00
Mushroom or Western Omelet, French Fries, Peas   1.25

SUPER SOUPS — Tasty large servings of Homemade Soup with crackers or rolls
Woodstock Turkey Vegetable   .40   Newfoundland Split Pea   .40

WOODSTOCK SANDWICH SPECIALTIES — Available with side orders
Baby **tenderloin steak** sandwich with chopped mushrooms or onions (Texas) — grilled Woodstock bun   .90
Baked orange-honey **ham steak** sandwich (from Virginia) — grilled Woodstock bun   .80
Chicken croquette sandwich, partridgeberry jam (from Maryland) garnished by Newfoundland) — grilled Woodstock bun   .70
Smoked meat on rye bread with mustard (the idea and ingredients all come from Montreal)   .65
Side Orders: French fries .25   Onion rings .30   Cole slaw .20

OUR OTHER SANDWICH SELECTIONS — on wonderful Woodstocks Buns
Turkey or Roast Beef   .60   Hamburgers   .45
Bacon, Tomato & Lettuce   .60   Cheeseburger   .55
Ham, Cheese & Lettuce   .50   Grilled Cheese   .45
Cheese, Tomato & Lettuce   .50   Hot Dogs   .25
Western   .50   Peanut Butter & Jam   .25
Chopped or Fried Egg   .40   Cheese   .25

Side Orders: French Fries .25   Onion Rings .30   Cole Slaw .20

SWEETS — Homemade Pie .30   Steamed Pudding .30   Trifle .30
Ice Cream & Wafers .30   Cheese & Crackers .30

BEVERAGES — Tea, Coffee or Milk .15   Soft Drinks .15

Our Breakfasts are shown on a separate menu. Please ask for it.

Here also the important BILL OF FARE items are listed on page 2— where the eye hits first—and the wine list is on page 1. Notice the numbering—1, 2, 3, 4, 5, 6 of the entrees for easy ordering. Also notice space for tip-on—ADDITIONAL TODAY. This menu solves the problem of where to put the luncheon menu by putting it on the back cover. A Simple Guide to the Selection of Drinks is included with the wine list.

★ THE ADMIRAL RISTY ★

Wines

THE ADMIRAL'S CHOICE

Bin No.		Litre	½ Litre
1	BURGUNDY	2.25	1.25
2	CHABLIS	2.25	1.25
3	ROSE'	2.25	1.25

CALIFORNIA WINES

Bin No:		Bottle	½ Bottle
	White		
4	GREEN HUNGARIAN	3.00	1.75
	Buena Vista		
5	GREY RIESLING	3.00	1.75
	Wente Bros.		
	Red		
6	PINOT NOIR	3.00	1.75
	Louis Martini		
7	CABERNET SAUVIGNON	3.25	1.85
	Buena Vista		

IMPORTED WINES

	White		
8	POUILLY-FUISSE	4.50	2.75
	A. Boux		
9	LIEBFRAUMILCH MADONNA	5.00	2.75
	Rosé		
10	NECTAROSE	4.00	2.25
	Anjou		
11	LANCER'S	6.50	3.50
	Crackling Rose		
	Red		
12	ST. EMILION,	4.00	2.25
	A. Boux		
13	CHATEAUNEUF-DU-PAPE	5.00	2.75
	Chateau de la Gardine		

CHAMPAGNES

14	KORBEL, Brut	7.00	3.75
15	MUMM'S, Cordon Rouge Brut	12.00	6.50

Entrees

SERVED WITH CHILLED GREEN SALAD, CHOICE OF DRESSING, HOT BREAD AND BEVERAGE

Top Sirloin Steak   **3.65**
"Admiral Perry's Cut"

New York Steak   **4.45**
"U. S. S. Texas Style"

Chopped Sirloin Steak   **2.25**
"Admiral Nelson's Choice"

Broiled Lobster   **4.55**
"From Ship to Shore to You"

Steak and Lobster Combination   **4.25**
"We have not yet begun to eat," John Paul Jones

Filet of Sea Bass   **2.50**
"A la Portuguese Bend"

FOUR PERCENT (4%) SALES TAX WILL BE ADDED TO THE ABOVE PRICES
OF ALL FOOD AND BEVERAGE ITEMS SERVED AT THE TABLES IN THIS ROOM

A la Carte

ROAST POTATO	50
"Done to a Turn" on a Spit,	
Hot Cheese Sauce and	
Bacon Chips or Butter	
ARTICHOKE (in Season)	65
with Butter or Mayonnaise	
or	
VEGETABLE DU JOUR	

Desserts

TRY OUR FAMOUS
"Banana Nut Torte"
*Direct From a
Mississippi River Boat*
65c

Fruited Sherbet	35

Beverages

Coffee	20
Tea, Hot or Iced	20
Milk	20

This interesting gate-fold menu is also die cut showing how paper can be cut into unusual shapes. The important big entree items—steaks and seafood—are listed in the center which is where the eye goes first. On the left hand small panel, a Wine List is printed. Since wine is a "with dinner" drink, this is a good place to list it. On the right hand small panel, a la carte vegetables, desserts and beverages are listed. Notice that when the side panels are closed, the name of the restaurant THE ADMIRAL RISTY, at the top of the menu, is still in evidence.

172

LIST IN FRENCH
BUT EXPLAIN IN ENGLISH

The 20th century is supposed to be the century of the "Common Man," but homage, fame and money still go to the uncommon man—and to the uncommon restaurant. Few outstanding restaurants try to serve an ordinary cuisine. In fact, the hallmark of a restaurant meal is usually its unusualness (best recipes often come from restaurants). To accent this different character of your menu, French words and phrases add a gourmet, "continental" flavor to menu copy. This is admittedly "snob" appeal. But, if it is good business, if it adds character and "class" to your cuisine and if it enables you to charge a little more—why not use it? It's the little "extras" in any restaurant operation that add up to the big profit. You don't need a French cuisine to use French terminology. For example, if you serve any kind of entree (American, Italian, or any other nationality) and serve or prepare it with almonds, the French word "Amandine" is appropriate.

But just using the word "Amandine" is not enough. In the descriptive copy, include a translation. To this, the restaurateur may say, "Why bother? Why not list it in English in the first place?" The answer again is "snob" appeal. Joe's Diner may serve just as good, nutritious and appetizing food as the Cafe d'Josephe, but the odds are that JOE gets less for his time and effort than JOSEPHE! There is also the reputation (well deserved) that French cooking has. Good restaurants take pride in engaging a French chef and serving French food, which has influenced both the language of the menu and the kitchen. Listed here is a glossary of basic French menu terms for use on your menu:

Agneau	Lamb	*Boeuf*	Beef
Aigre	Sour	*Boisson*	Drink, Beverage
Ail	Garlic	*Bouillabaisse*	Fish stew
Aileron	Wingbone	*Bouillon*	Broth
Allumette	Match stick potatoes	*Bouquetiére*	With mixed vegetables
Alsacienne	Alsatian style; usually served with sauerkraut	*Bourguignonne*	With onions and red Burgundy wine
Amandine	With almonds	*Bouteille*	Bottle
Américaine	American style	*Café*	Coffee
Ananas	Pineapple	*Canard*	Duck
Anchois	Anchovy	*Caneton*	Duckling
Andalouse	With tomatoes & peppers	*Carré*	Rack
		Cervelle	Brain
Auguille	Eel	*Champignon*	Mushroom
Argenteuil	With asparagus	*Chapon*	Capon
Artichaut	Artichoke	*Chateaubriand*	Thick Filet Mignon
Asperges	Asparagus	*Chaud*	Warm, Hot
Aspic	Decorated jellied piece	*Chevreuil*	Venison
Aubergines	Egg Plant	*Chou-Fleur*	Cauliflower
Béarnaise	In America, a sauce similar to hollandaise, fortified with meat glaze, and with tarragon flavor predominating	*Choux de Bruxelles*	Brussel sprouts
		Cochon	Suckling pig
		Coeur	Heart
		Compote	Stewed fruit
		Concombre	Cucumber
		Confiture	Jam, preserve
		Consommé	Clear soup
Bécasse	Woodcock	*Coquille*	Shell for baking
Béchamel	Cream sauce	*Cote*	Rib, Chop
Beignet	Fritter	*Créme*	Cream
Beurre	Butter	*Créme Fouettée*	Whipped cream
Bifteck	Beefsteak	*Crépe*	Pancake
Bisque	Thick, rich soup	*Crevette*	Shrimp
Blanc	White	*Croquette*	Patty of meat
Blanquette	Stew with white wine	*Déjeuner*	Breakfast, Lunch

Diable	Deviled	*Homard*	Lobster	*Pomme*	Apple
Dinde	Turkey	*Hors d'Oeuvres*	Pre-dinner Tid-bits	*Pomme de Terre*	Potato
Du Barry	With cauliflower	*Huitre*	Oyster	*Potage*	Soup
Eau	Water	*Jambon*	Ham	*Pot Au Feu*	Boiled beef with a variety of vegetables and broth served as a meal
Ecrevisse	Crayfish	*Jardiniére*	With vegetable		
Entrecote	Sirloin steak	*Julienne*	Thin strips		
Entremets	Sweet, Desserts	*Jus*	Juice, gravy		
Epinard	Spinach	*Lait*	Milk	*Poulet*	Chicken
Escargots	Snails	*Langouste*	Sea crayfish or rock lobster	*Purée*	Sieved food
Faisan	Pheasant			*Quenelle*	Dumpling
Farce	Ground meat	*Lapin*	Rabbit	*Ragout*	Stew
Farci	Stuffed	*Légume*	Vegetable	*Ris*	Sweetbread
Filet	Boneless ribbon	*Macédoine*	Mixed fruits	*Riz*	Rice
Flambé	Flamed	*Maître D'Hotel*	With spiced butter	*Rognon*	Kidney
Foie	Liver	*Marmite*	Beef Consomme	*Roti*	Roasted
Foie Gras	Goose liver	*Meringue*	Beaten egg white	*Roulade*	Rolled meat
Fondue	Melted cheese	*Meuniére*	Pan fried and served with brown butter	*Saumon*	Salmon
Forestiére	With mushroom			*Sauté*	Pan fried in butter
Four	Oven baked	*Mignon*	Dainty	*Sel*	Salt
Fricandeau	Braised veal morsels	*Mornay*	Cheese sauce	*Selle*	saddle
Fricassée	Chicken or veal stew	*Mousse*	Whipped foam	*Sorbet*	Sherbet
Frit	Deep fat fried	*Mouton*	Mutton	*Soufflé*	Whipped pudding
Froid	Cold	*Nantua*	Lobster sauce	*Tasse*	Cup
Frommage	Cheese	*Naturel*	Plain	*Tête*	Head
Fumé	Smoked	*Noir*	Black	*Tournedos*	Two small tenderloin steaks
Gateau	Cake	*Noisette*	Hazelnut		
Gelée	Jelly	*Nouille*	Noodle	*Tranche*	Slice
Gibier	Game	*Oeuf*	Egg	*Truite*	Trout
Gigot	Leg	*Oeufs Pochés*	Poached eggs	*Veau*	Veal
Glace	Ice, ice cream	*Oie*	Goose	*Veloute*	White sauce made from fish, chicken, or veal stock
Gratin	Brown, baked with cheese	*Oignon*	Onion		
		Pain	Bread		
Grenouille	Frog	*Paté*	Meat pie	*Vichyssoise*	Hot or cold potato and leek soup
Grillé	Broiled	*Patisserie*	Pastry		
Hereng	Herring	*Pêche*	Peach	*Viennoise*	Vienna style, breaded
Haricot Vert	String beans	*Petit*	Small	*Vinaigrette*	Dressing with oil, vinegar and herbs
Hollandaise	Sauce made with egg yoke, melted butter, and lemon	*Poire*	Pear		
		Pois	Peas	*Volaille*	Poultry
		Poisson	Fish	*Vol Au Vent*	Patty shell
		Poitrine	Breast		

Filet de Truite, Amandine   2.95

A generous Filet of Rainbow trout, delicately seasoned and covered with a browned butter sauce, fresh Lemon juice and toasted almond slices.

Suprême de Volaille, Le Ruth   3.50

A whole boneless chicken breast, stuffed with a real butter ball and lightly coated with toasted crumbs. Browned in butter and served over a mild wine sauce.

Emincé de Veau, René   3.75

Thin slices of milk-fed veal sauteed in butter and covered with a subtle wine sauce made with pure cream, chantrelle mushrooms and fresh seasonings.

Filet de Boeuf Aux Champignons   3.25

A petit tenderloin steak, selected for its rich, delicate flavor and pan broiled to your exact pleasure. Topped with sliced mushrooms in a natural sauce.

Entrecôte de Boeuf Au Poivre   4.50

A thick sirloin strip of choice beef, seasoned freely with fresh, coarse-ground peppercorns, broiled and served in a pungent sauce of burgundy and special herbs.

The descriptive copy tells what each of the French entrees is.

Diner

Hors-d'Oeuvres

Hors-d'Oeuvres Variées	2.50	Assorted Hors-d'Oeuvres
Pâté Strasbourg	2.00	Pâté Strasbourg
Caviar Malossol — Blinis	5.00	Malossol Caviar — Blinis
Escargots à la Bourguignonne	2.00	Vineyard Snails Bourguignonne
Crevettes a l'Ail au Four	2.00	Baked Shrimp with Garlic Sauce
Cocktail de Crevettes ou Crabe	1.50	Shrimp or King Crabmeat
Artichauts aux Sauces Diverses	1.25	Artichoke — Various Dressings
Champignons Farcis	1.25	Stuffed Mushrooms
Huitres Rockefeller	2.25	Oysters Rockefeller
Huitres	1.50	Oysters on the Half Shell
Coquille St. Jacques à la Parisienne	2.00	Scallops à la Parisienne

Potages

Soupe a l'Oignon Française	.50	French Onion Soup
Vichyssoise	.75	Vichyssoise
Soupe du Jour	.50	Soup of the Day
Avocado	.75	Avocado

Oeufs

Oeufs Pochés à la Benedict	2.50	Poached Eggs à la Benedict
Omelette au Gout	2.00	Omelette as Desired

Poissons

Sole à la Meunière, Pommes, Salade	4.95	Dover Sole à la Meunière, Potato, Salad
Cuisse de Grenouille à la Meunière, Garni	4.00	Frog Legs Meunière, Garni
Queue de Homard Danois, Salade	4.75	Danish Lobster Tails, Saffron Rice, Salad
Carrelet Farci, Brocolis, Tomate Grillée	4.75	Flounder Stuffed with Crab Meat, Broccoli, Grilled Tomato
Filet de Turbot Forestiere, Pommes, Salade	4.95	Filet of Turbot, Forestiere, Potatoes, Salad

Entrees

Poulet Sauté Trois Fontaines, Garni	3.95	Chicken à La Three Fountains, Garni
Escalope de Veau, Garni	4.00	Veal Scallopini, Garni
Coq à la Mode de Bourgogne	3.95	Chicken in Red Wine Sauce
Tournedos — Vieux Marché,	4.95	Beef Tenderloin — Old French Market Style
Filet de Boeuf à la Stroganoff	4.75	Beef Stroganoff
Riz de Veau Eugène	4.00	Sweetbreads Eugène
Foie de Veau au Bacon	4.00	Calf's Liver with Bacon
Daube de Boeuf à la Provençale	4.25	Braised Beef à La Provençale

Rotis

Caneton Rôti au Zeste d'Orange ou Cerise	4.75	Roast Long Island Duckling, Orange or Cherry Sauce
Côte de Boeuf Rôti, Garni	5.25	Prime Rib of Beef au Jus Idaho Baked Potato, Salad

This interesting type and layout arrangement lists everything on the left in French with the same item listed on the right in English. The price is listed in the middle. See next page for remainder of menu.

Grillades

Châteaubriand (Pour Deux), Bouquetière, Salade	12.95	Chateaubriand (For Two), Bouquetière, Salad
Aloyau de Boeuf, Pomme au Four, Salade	5.95	Prime Sirloin Steak, Baked Potato, Salad
Côte d'Agneau, Pomme au Four, Salade	5.00	Double French Lamb Chops, Baked Potato, Salad
Filet Mignon, Pommes, Salade	5.95	Filet Mignon, Potatoes, Salad
Petit Filet Mignon, Pommes, Salade	4.95	Petit Filet Mignon, Potatoes, Salad

Pommes de Terre

Pont-Neuf	.50	French Fried
Pommes au Gratin	.50	Au Gratin
Pommes Fondante	.50	Oven Browned
Pomme au Four	.50	Idaho Baked Potato
Pommes Noisette	.50	Hazel Nut Potatoes

Légumes

Brocolis	.75	Broccoli
Aubergines Meunière	.75	Egg Plant Meunière
Asperges	.75	Asparagus
Oignons Glacés	.75	Glazed Onions
Chou-Fleur	.75	Cauliflower
Champignons Sautés	.75	Sautéd Mushrooms

Salades

Salade à La Russe	1.80	Russian Salad Bowl
Poire Avocado	1.00	Avocado Pear with Fresh Fruit Slices
Endive Belge (En Saison)	1.00	Belgian Endive (In Season)
Salade Les Trois Fountaines	.75	The Three Fountains Salad
Salade César (Pour Deux)	3.00	Caesar Salad (For Two)

Sauces — Roquefort, Française, à la Russe, de la Maison, Vinaigrette, à l'Aille

Entremets

Patisserie Varíees	.65	Assorted Pastries
Cerise Jubilée (Pour Deux)	3.50	Cherries Jubiiee (For Two)
Gateaux au Fromage	1.00	Lemon Cheese Pie
Parfait Cognac	1.25	Cognac Parfait
Boule Noix de Coco au Rum	1.00	Coconut Snowball — Rum Sauce
Crêpes Suzette (Pour Deux)	4.00	Crêpes Suzette (For Two)
Pêche Flambée ou Pêche Melba	1.50	Peach Flambé or Peach Melba
Mousse au Chocolat	1.00	Chocolate Mousse

Fromages

Gruyère - Port Salut - Roquefort - Brie - Camembert   1.00

Café et Thé

American Coffee	. . . .	.35	Café Diable	2.00
Café à la Turque	. . . .	.50	Café Espresso	.75
Tea	. . . .	.35	Imported Tea	.75

See preceding page for first page of menu.

LISTING LIQUOR ON THE MENU

The first rule for your cocktail and wine menu list should be: "If you have it in your bar, service bar or wine cellar, list it on your menu." This sounds extremely elementary, but it is amazing how many establishments will have a wide bar and cellar selection and list only a few items on the menu. The result is "money in bottles" giving no return on the investment. No food service operation would prepare food items in the kitchen and not list them on the menu, but with liquor, wine and beer, the operator often seems to think that the customer "knows" what he wants. Yet a great number of liquor sales are of the "impulse" variety; so the sensible approach is to list it if you have it.

Next, where you list your beverages on the menu is important. Continuing the time sequence in the menu listing, let us examine the liquor time sequence. Which drinks are consumed when by most restaurant guests?

1. Before Dinner
   a. Cocktails
      (Martinis, Manhattans)
   b. Mixed Drinks
      (Scotch, Bourbon, etc.)
   c. Beer
   d. Wines
2. During Dinner
   a. Wines
   b. Beer
3. After Dinner
   a. Wines
   b. Cordials
   c. Brandies
   d. Liqueurs

To take advantage of this, the ideal would be three separate lists that are presented at the three appropriate times during the meal (a procedure, incidentally, which I think would pay the operator who trained his employees to use such lists.) In lieu of three lists, the location and order on the single menu is very important. If your menu has several pages, the beverage listing should be on the first page. If your menu is the standard two-page, self-cover type, the list should be on the left hand side.

The purpose is to expose the customer to the drink list first so that he will order a cocktail before he orders his meal. The standard question, "Do you care for a cocktail?" voiced by the waiter or waitress may do a partial job (if the question is asked). But a complete list, in large readable type with prices and brand names, if brought to the customer's attention at the right time, will do the complete merchandising job. Prices should be included with the beverage list. You would not think of listing your entrees or your a la carte appetizers, salads and desserts without prices; therefore, the customer expects to see prices on the liquor list. An elementary observation, yet many menus still list drinks without prices.

Also, list brand names on your liquor menu. The reasons are many. First, by listing brand names you are telling your customers that you serve quality liquor not just "bar liquor". And quality liquor is as important to a food service reputation as quality food. Next, your customer is used to brand names in scotch, bourbon, gin, wines and beer. He has his preferences and buys by the bottle at his store by brand name. So he is conditioned to buy the same way when he is in your establishment.

Listing brand names is also just good dollar sense for the food service operator. The public has been sold on brand name quality by million dollar ad campaigns. The public, therefore, knows that quality scotch and quality bourbon cost more and the public expects to pay more for a nationally advertised brand when they are drinking in your establishment. You, therefore, can charge more, and your percentage of profit or mark-up will be higher.

The two most popular cocktails are martinis and manhattans. Many menus, therefore, feature these two drinks in a box or panel, in larger type and with extra copy. They describe the size and quality of their martini and often refer to it as the "World's Finest Martini." This is good merchandising, but it does not have to be confined to martinis and manhattans. Just as you have many unusual and creative specials in the food portion of your menu, so you should create cocktails special to your operation. Give them a special name and feature them on your menu. Just a simple twist in serving or naming a cocktail will do the trick. Serving a "French 75" with an American flag transforms it into an "American 76."

If you have a large enough wine cellar, you will probably want a separate wine list. But, if you have just a few wines, list them with your other beverages. It is also good merchandising to recommend wines with entrees (in smaller type under the entree name and as part of the descriptive copy).

Finally, the customer has had a cocktail before his dinner, a bottle of wine or beer with his dinner and now is ready for dessert. To continue your menu liquor merchandising, list your desserts and after-dinner drinks together. You will probably make a greater profit on an after-dinner drink and you may even sell both the drink and dessert.

The ideal way to list the after-dinner drinks is in a separate dessert and after-dinner drink menu. The advantage of the separate menu is that the waiter or waitress (without asking) just presents to the customer this menu which has only after-dinner items on it. The chances of ordering with this kind of merchandising are much better than the standard, "Would you care for dessert?" and the very seldom heard, "Would you care for an after-dinner drink?" In lieu of a separate list of after-dinner drinks (brandy, cordial, liqueur, B & B, etc.), the next best method is to list them with your dessert listing on a separate page or at the bottom of the page after your entree listing.

MENU BEVERAGE CHECK LIST

1. If you serve a beverage, list it on your menu.
2. List beverages according to whether they are served before, with or after the meal.
3. List all prices on all beverages.
4. List brand names.
5. List some "special" drinks.
6. List after-dinner drinks with desserts.
7. List cocktails first so customer orders before meal.

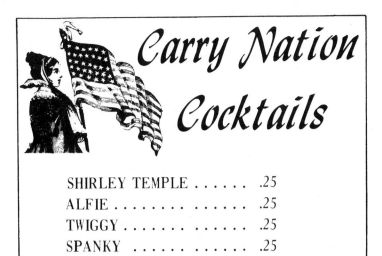

Carry Nation Cocktails

SHIRLEY TEMPLE 25
ALFIE 25
TWIGGY 25
SPANKY 25

For the kiddies!

TAKE HOME
A BUCKET
OF BEER

18 Cans Beer
. . . . . . Iced . . . . .
In Five Gallon Heavy
Duty Reusable
Picnic Bucket

$4.25

Liquor can be a "Take Home" too.

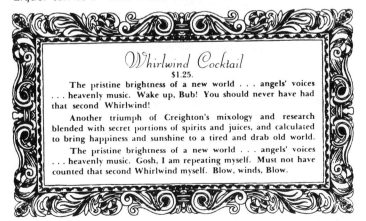

Whirlwind Cocktail
$1.25.

The pristine brightness of a new world . . . angels' voices
. . . heavenly music. Wake up, Bub! You should never have had
that second Whirlwind!

Another triumph of Creighton's mixology and research
blended with secret portions of spirits and juices, and calculated
to bring happiness and sunshine to a tired and drab old world.

The pristine brightness of a new world . . . angels' voices
. . . heavenly music. Gosh, I am repeating myself. Must not have
counted that second Whirlwind myself. Blow, winds, Blow.

Really way-out copy.

*Three drinks really merchandised like this
are better than a hundred just listed.*

THE THREE HOUSE DRINKS...
BEST...BAR NONE

Shoyer's Gay Nineties Cocktail .90

It's Velvety, Exciting and Refreshing.
Tell us, Mr. Bartender, tell us the secret
of your Shoyer's Gay Nineties Special.
The bartender smiles proudly. Why should
he reveal the secret that is his fortune
. . . the secret of the finest drink this side
of heaven. Truly, this is no ordinary cocktail. Men and women who know its taste,
proclaim it Shoyer's premier concoction.
We warn you in advance . . . neither
kind words nor harsh, fair means nor
foul, will pry loose the recipe. You will
not be able to duplicate it at home.
Once you taste it we have you . . . you
must become a regular visitor at Shoyer's.
It's a scurvy trick, but you'll bless us
for it.

1874 OLD FASHIONED

Like nowhere else is the distinctively
original Shoyer Old Fashioned. You'll
positively flip when this smoothie is
deftly delivered for your pleasure. It
comes in a beautiful and unique glass
that is a museum piece.
A true masterpiece priced at .90

THE SOUVENIR GLASS $1.25

The Gaslight .95

A sprightly refresher in Scotch, complemented by vermouth and orange curacao,
is a replenisher in the true spirit of the
fabulous gaslight era. This fabulous drink
is called Gaslight and is an inimitable
Shoyer creation. We prefer to call it a
gasser. The recipe: Scotch, Italian Vermouth, a dash of orange Curacao; shake
well and let glisten down the rocks in a
thin glass; garnished with a twist of
orange skin; and pour a thimbleful of
Drambuie over THE GASLIGHT.

Before Dinner Drinks

.60 MARTINI

Dry Vermouth or Taylor's Pale Dry
Cocktail Sherry, Dry Gin with Olive

.60 MANHATTAN

Sweet Vermouth, Blended Whiskey,
Angostura Bitters with Maraschino
Cherry

.60 GIBSON

Martini with Pickled Onion, Lemon
Peel

.65 OLD FASHIONED

Blended Whiskey, Angostura Bitters,
Sugar, Orange and Cherry

.60 DAIQUIRI

Light Puerto Rican Rum, Lime Juice
and Sugar

.65 WHISKEY SOUR

Blended Whiskey, Lemon, Sugar,
Cherry, Orange

.85 PINK LADY

Dry Gin, Grenadine, Egg White and
Cream

1.25 CHAMPAGNE COCKTAIL

One Cubette Green Creme de
Menthe, One Cubette Grenadine,
Bitters, Champagne

.60 TOM COLLINS

Dry Gin, Lemon Juice, Sugar, Club
Soda and Fruit

.60 CHERRY FIZZ

Cherry Liqueur, Lemon Juice

.60 BACARDI

Light Puerto Rican Rum, Lime Juice
and Grenadine

.85 SIDE CAR

Imported Brandy, Cointreau and
Lemon Juice

.85 ALEXANDER

Dry Gin or Brandy, Creme de Cacao
Cream and Nutmeg

.65 ORANGE BLOSSOM

Gin, Orange Juice, Sugar

.75 DUBONNET

Dry Gin, Dubonnet Wine and Fruit

.75 ROB ROY

Scotch Whiskey, Vermouth and Angostura Bitters, Lemon Peel

.80 WARD VIII

Bourbon, Lemon and Orange Juice
and Grenadine

.75 HORSE'S NECK

Brandy, Angostura Bitters, Ginger
Ale and Fruit

.60 SCREWDRIVER

Vodka and Orange Juice

.60 GIN AND TONIC

Dry Gin, Schweppes Quinine Water
with A Slice of Lime

.75 GIN RICKEY

Dry Gin, Lime Juice and Club Soda

.60 SLOE GIN FIZZ

Sloe Gin, Lemon Juice and Club
Soda

All Above Drinks Using Scotch, Bourbon, Canadian Whiskies,
Imported Gins and Brandies — 15c Extra

All Above Drinks on the Rocks or Extra Dry (Extra Portion)
15c Above Listed Price.

*A short descriptive listing of their ingredients helps to
sell these mixed drinks.*

IF THE *"Scotch"* DISTILL IT,
WE SERVE IT!

Ambassador 8 - 12 - 20 yrs.

B & L (Bulloch & Lades)

Ballantine's

Bell's Royal Vat 8 - 12 yrs.

Black & White, Extra Light

Buchanan's Deluxe

Catto's G. L. DeLuxe 12 yrs.

Chequers

Chivas Regal

Chivas Salute 21 yrs.

Clan McGregor

Cluny's 8 yrs.

Cutty Sark

Dewar's White Label

Gilbey's Spey-Royal

Glen Rossie

Grand Macnish

Grant's 8 - 12 yrs.

Haig & Haig 5 Star — Pinch

Highland Mist

House of Lords

House of Stuart

Hudson's Bay "Best Procurable"

Inver House

J & B Rare

John Begg "Blue Cap"

Johnnie Walker, Black Label & Red Label

J. W. Dant

King George IV

King William IV

Lauder's Royal Northern Cream

Long John

Macnish V.L.

Martin's V.V.O.

McCullough's

McMaster's

Muirhead

Old Mr. Boston

Old Rarity

Old Smuggler

Park & Tilford Special

Peter Dawson

Prince of Scots

Queen Anne

Robertson's Yellow Label

Robbie Burns

Royal Scott

Sandy McDonald

Scottish Majesty

Sir Malcolm

Something Special

Teacher's Highland Cream

Usher's "Green Stripe"

Vat 69

Wee Burn

White Heather DeLuxe

White Horse

Pride of the Bar
HAVE YOU TRIED . . .

KING SIZE ROB ROYS

MANHATTANS

MARTINIS

Served to you in swirlers.

An unusual liquor listing like this will make your bar selection "special."

WHET YOUR APPETITE WITH ONE OF THESE FAMOUS SOUTHERN "POTABLES"

PLANTERS PUNCH....
A SPECIAL RECIPE OF LIGHT AND DARK RUMS TOPPED BY A 151 PROOF RUM – WE SUGGEST ONLY ONE.   **1.50**

SAZARAC SPECIAL....
PREPARED AND MIXED FROM AN OLD RIVERBOAT RECIPE. A DRINK OF THE "OLD SOUTH" IN THE TRADITION OF REAL SOUTHERN HOSPITALITY.   **1.25**

RAMOS GIN FIZZ....
FOR THE LADIES, RICH AND CREAMY WITH JUST THE RIGHT AMOUNT OF SPIRITS . . . . AS SERVED BY CAPTAIN JOE SALON OF THE SHOWBOAT SARI-S IN CHICAGO.   **1.50**

SHOWBOAT SCARLET O'HARA....
EVERYBODY'S FUNTIME FAVORITE. YOU DON'T HAVE TO WAIT FOR DINNERTIME TO ENJOY THE FAMED SCARLET O'HARA . . . . ENCHANTING AS ITS NAMESAKE. HERE'S A DRINK THAT TASTES GREAT ANYWHERE . . . . AS SERVED AT ANTOINES RESTAURANT, NEW ORLEANS.   **1.15**

COTTON BLOSSOM....
A SECRET RECIPE PREPARED BY OUR OWN HEAD BARTENDER – FOR ALL "SHOWBOAT" DEVOTEES.   **1.25**

COCKTAILS

MANHATTAN
Calvert Reserve, imported sweet vermouth, maraschino cherry

DRY MARTINI
Dry gin, imported dry vermouth, olive

VODKA MARTINI
Vodka, imported dry vermouth, olive

ROB ROY
Scotch, imported sweet vermouth, maraschino cherry

ALEXANDER No. 1
Dry gin, creme de cacao, sweet cream

TOM COLLINS
Dry gin, lemon juice, sugar, soda water

BRANDY COLLINS
Brandy, lemon juice, sugar, soda water

JOHN COLLINS
Calvert Reserve, lemon juice, sugar, soda water

RUM COLLINS
Bacardi Gold rum, lemon juice, sugar, soda water

ALEXANDER No. 2
Brandy, creme de cacao, sweet cream

GRASSHOPPER
Creme de menthe, creme de cacao, sweet cream

GIMLET
Gin, lime juice, fine sugar

BACARDI
Bacardi Silver rum, lemon juice, sugar, grenadine

DAIQUIRI
Light rum, lemon juice, sugar

JACK ROSE
Applejack brandy, lemon juice, grenadine

OLD FASHIONED
Calvert Reserve, lump sugar, soda water, angostura bitters, fruit

LONG, TALL AND COOLING

PINK LADY
Dry gin, apple brandy, cream, grenadine

SIDE CAR
Cointreau, brandy, lemon juice

STINGER
Brandy, white creme de menthe

SCREW DRIVER
Vodka, orange juice

BLOODY MARY
Vodka, tomato juice

DUBONNET
Dubonnet wine, dry gin

WHISKEY SOUR
Calvert Reserve, lemon juice, sugar

SINGAPORE SLING
Dry gin, cherry brandy, bitters, sugar, lemon juice, soda water

BRANDY PUNCH
Brandy, Benedictine, lemon juice, sugar, soda water

McKINLEY PUNCH
Calvert Reserve, grenadine, lemon juice, soda water

PLANTERS PUNCH
Rum, lime juice, sugar, orange juice

WARD 8
Calvert Reserve, lemon juice, grenadine, slice of orange, maraschino cherry

BRANDY FLIP
Cognac, sugar, whole egg

CUBA LIBRE
Bacardi Gold rum, fresh lime, cola

GIN BUCK
Dry gin, ginger ale

GIN RICKEY
Dry gin, lime juice, soda water

SLOE GIN FIZZ
Sloe gin, lemon juice, sugar, soda water

IMPORTED GIN and TONIC
Imported gin, fresh lime, tonic

DOMESTIC GIN and TONIC
Domestic gin, fresh lime, tonic

RE-FRESHERS

VODKA and TONIC
Vodka, fresh lime, tonic

WINE, BEER AND ALE

PLEASE ASK YOUR SERVICE HOSTESS FOR THE SELECTION

Illustrations, good copy and a large listing make this a selling drink menu.

Five unusual drinks listed big and bold with good copy make this a good "before" drink listing.

WINE LISTS

"A beer is a beer" . . . goes part of a recent TV commercial, but nobody ever said "a wine is a wine," and this is part of both the problem and the opportunity of serving wine in your dining room. But even if the subject of wine is complex, every food service operation can serve some wine, even if it is only a glass of rosé, or a selection of one red and one white wine served by the glass. Some simple rules for listing and serving on the menu are in order.

The first rule is to list the wines you serve on the menu. A separate Wine List means the customer must ask for it and most people do not ask. As for where on the menu to print the Wine List, the answer is next to the entrees. Wine is a beverage to drink with the meal more than before (cocktails) or after (cordials). There are, of course, aperitif (appetizer) wines and dessert wines, but most wines are consumed with the entree.

Another good wine menu merchandising rule is to suggest food to go with types of wines—red, white, rosé, champagne, etc. This affinity of certain wines with certain foods can be merchandised on the menu by listing with the entree descriptive copy in a second color, red, for example.

Wine can also be merchandised on the menu by selling "packages", individual or for two. This means such combinations as a complete dinner with a glass of rosé wine thrown in or a Champagne Dinner—all the champagne you can drink for a fixed price or a combination special, Beef, Bay and Burgundy. The combinations are unlimited, and many are offered by wine-aware food service operators.

The wines available for your menu are numerous and they can be either inexpensive, moderately priced or expensive. American wines, for example, include New York, Ohio and Michigan; Eastern wines from the native American grape (Vitis Labrusca), and the wines of California from the vines transplanted from Europe (Vitis Vinifera).

From Europe there are the great wines of France and Germany plus those from Spain, Portugal and Italy, and there are good wines from South America, Chili and Argentina, for example. It is obvious, therefore, that you can tailor your wine selection to fit your menu. If you serve Italian food, you can match it with good Italian wines, and if you have a German cuisine, the delightful wines of Germany (as well as German beer) can make a good menu great.

A concern voiced by some operators is "If I offer wine they will not order cocktails." This need not be so because cocktails are a before dinner drink while wine is a with dinner beverage. The trick is to sell both—cocktails and wine. Also, unless you are a very exclusive, very expensive restaurant where only gourmets eat who order wine as a matter of routine, you should have a price range that allows the customer with a smaller budget to order a glass or bottle of wine. This usually means some American wines (often just as good or better than imported wine) that are less expensive. This means offering wine by the glass.

Every distinctive atmosphere restaurant should have a Wine List, preferably a separate list, but if not this, at least a separate section of the menu for wines. Some of the best cooking is French. Some of the best wines come from France. Therefore, if a restaurant has a wine list (no matter how small), there is an automatic "association" by the customer. The wine list becomes an inferred testimonial that the cuisine is better than average . . . and it usually is.

Wine is actually the drink par excellence to go with food. This fact has been testified to by gourmets for thousands of years. Cocktails may be good before the meal, and brandy, cordials and. liqueurs may be good after the meal; but the right wine is good before, with and after the meal. Thousands of years ago the Greeks appreciated this chemical affinity of wine to food so highly that they named one of the Gods on Mt. Olympus Bacchus, in honor of the juice of the grape. Ancient custom and modern usage have continued this happy association, and every Gourmet Dinner worthy of the name serves a different, appropriate wine with each course. Besides, if you are a practical American food service operator, there is profit in wine.

Before you can create a wine list, of course, you must have a wine cellar. We do not propose to suggest any such grave undertaking, but would suggest the following to any operator who is not a wine "expert" at present or cannot afford an expensive advisory service. First, collect the wine lists of some of the better restaurants and clubs in this country, and there are many. Next, consult a reputable wine merchant. The thing to avoid with a wine merchant, however, is his propensity to recommend only the wines he sells. Also, the wine list should include imported and American wines. For additional help, the Wine Advisory Board in San Francisco gives valuable service to the wine-interested food service operator.

As to the size of the wine list (and the cellar), from 8 to 10 good wines are enough to make an excellent wine list. And, a list with 20 good wines is a real gourmet selection which will enhance the reputation of any quality establishment. The wine list can be printed in the following forms:

1. Separate wine list—wines only.
2. Separate wine list with other drinks (cocktails, beer, etc.).
3. Separate section of the menu—wines only.
4. Separate section of menu—wines and other drinks (cocktails, beers, etc.).

We will consider the separate wine list first. The listing of wines in a wine list is usually broken down under the following categories:

1. Place of origin
   a. Imported—France, Germany, Italy, Portugal, etc.
   b. American—California, Eastern.
2. Type of wine
   a. Sparkling—Champagne, Sparkling Burgundy.
   b. Still wines—all others.
3. Style of wine
   a. Dry
   b. Medium
   c. Sweet
4. Color of wine
   a. Red
   b. White
   c. Rosé
5. Vintage (or Non Vintage)

In America especially, it is the custom to separate the imported and American wines, and it is generally considered better form to refer to American wines as American and not

"Domestic." The reason for separating California from Eastern (New York, Michigan, etc.) wines is that each is made from a different grape—the Eastern from the Concord grape, and the California from the vines transplanted from Europe.

The imported section of the wine list usually (and rightly so) begins with the great wines of France—Bordeaux, Burgundy, Champagne. This can be followed by the fine wines of Germany—Rhine, Moselle, Rhinegau, Rhinehesse. A listing of the "special" wines of Alsace, Rhone, Loire, Italy, Portugal, Spain, and South America can follow if a really "big" list is in the making.

The best California wines, which will stand comparison with most of the wines of Europe, are produced from an area of famous valleys around San Francisco Bay. These valleys and counties are Napa, Sonoma, Livermore and Santa Cruz. The best wines from these areas are the varietals—wines which take their name and their characteristic flavor and bouquet from the grape variety from which they were produced. Care must be used in selecting California wines for the wine list. For example, any red California wine can be labeled "Burgundy", but a varietal red wine such as Pinot Noir must be made from a minimum of 51% of Pinot Noir grapes, the same grape used exclusively to make the finest French red Burgundies.

In listing the wines on the wine list, each wine should be identified by a bin number. The bin number should be written on the label of each bottle in the bin for further identification. The names of wines are usually French or German, and are hard to pronounce, identify and remember. The average waiter or waitress who is not a trained sommelier needs the bin number system for easy identification and efficient service. The bin number system also provides for quick, easy inventory.

Prices for wine are usually broken down into three categories—per bottle, half-bottle and glass. A word of caution is offered here. Don't charge too much. The retail wine store is restricted by law to a 50 per cent mark-up. Therefore, a wine which a retailer buys for $1.00, he usually sells for $1.49. If the restaurant charges $3.00 for this same bottle, the customer is going to resent the difference. A 100 per cent mark-up is a good rule for restaurants.

The names of most wines are French, and, therefore, unless the customer is French or has studied French, the pronunciation presents a challenge if not an insurmountable obstacle. To overcome this problem on the wine list, a pronouncing glossary or phonetic spelling under the wine name is recommended. The following are some phonetic pronunciations for wines:

Beaujolais—BOW-ZHOW-LAY   Graves—GRAH-VE
Chablis—CHAH-BLEE   Haut Brion—O-BREE-ON
Chateau d'Yquem—SHAT-O-DEEKEM   St. Emilion—SANT-EH-MEE-YON

The rule for the wine list intended for the average customer, who knows little about wine, is to make it easy for him to order wine without showing his lack of wine knowledge.

The next question to be considered is which wines to order with which foods. For the guest who has sampled many wines and knows the wine-food combinations that he prefers, rules are not necessary. And besides it's a free country. But, there is a consensus of agreement among gourmets as to what wines are best with certain foods. For the non-expert, also, it is reassuring when the wine list recommends certain wines to go with certain entrees.

First, Champagne is the most versatile of all wines. It may be served with any food, or by itself, and it is an elegant aperitif, an ideal dinner and a perfect after-dinner wine. Pink wines (Rosé) are also intermediate and go with almost any food.

If more than one wine is being served, the rule is to start with the lighter (usually white) and proceed to the heavier, more pungent (usually red) and finish with a sweet dessert wine (Sauternes-Rhine or California).

The following simplified Wine-Food Chart is offered for reference:

CANAPES	
Cheese, crackers	*SHERRY*
Olives, etc.	*CHAMPAGNE*
SOUP	*SHERRY*
SEAFOOD	*CHABLIS*
	DRY SAUTERNE
	RHINE
	WHITE BURGUNDY
FOWL	
Cold chicken,	*CHAMPAGNE*
turkey, roast	*DRY SAUTERNE*
chicken, duck,	*RHINE*
turkey, pheasant	*WHITE OR RED BURGUNDY*
MEATS	*CLARET*
Steak, veal, lamb,	*BURGUNDY*
roast beef, stew	*ROSÉ*
ITALIAN DISHES	*CHIANTI*
	ZINFANDEL
	BARBERA
DESSERTS	*SWEET SAUTERNE*
	CHAMPAGNE

The next consideration on the wine list is vintage. Vintage means "gathering of the grapes," and vintage wine is one produced from grapes of a specified year. Weather plays an important part in the quality of French and German wines. In bright, sunny weather the grapes grow to full maturity, size and flavor while bad weather will result in a hard, green small-sized grape. A high rated vintage year indicates that the weather was so favorable that it resulted in top quality grapes from which the extra high quality wine was made. Because the weather and growing conditions in California are so constant from year to year, it is not customary to give vintage year labels to California wine.

On the wine list, vintage can be listed several ways. The best and biggest wine lists give the vintage year for each wine. Other equally good but less detailed wine lists just add the word vintage after the vintage wines on the list with no year. For a wine that is non-vintage, it is better usage not to list the fact that it is a non-vintage wine or even use the abbreviation N. V. One problem with listing vintage years is that the wine in a vintage year does get used up and cannot be replaced. The wine list then has to be reprinted, or "paste-ons" must be used to show the replacement.

Concerning descriptive copy on each wine served, it is not absolutely necessary, but it helps the guest who has had limited acquaintance with the many wines available. The following descriptions from the Standard Club wine list do the job very well with a few well chosen words:

CHATEAU LA DAME BLANCHE 1955
A very good vintage, medium dry with a pleasant bouquet.

CHATEAU LA GUARDÉ, ESCHENAUER
A fine dry Chateau bottle Claret, light and full flavored.

Copy describing the main categories of wine (Bordeaux, Burgundy, Rhine, etc.) is most helpful on any wine list. It indicates that the operator knows his wines and has stocked his cellar with skill and loving care.

As for listing other beverages on the wine list, it is the custom on Continental wine lists to list the other drinks at the end of the wine list after all the wines have been listed. The Central Hotel in Glasgow, Scotland, for example, lists the following beverages on the wine list after the wines, as follows: Cognac, Armagnac, Liqueurs, Aperitifs, Gin, Rum, Scotch Whiskey, Irish Whiskey, Canadian Whiskey, Beer, Stout and Lager, Cider and Mineral Waters. It's obvious that nobody leaves Scotland thirsty!

When the wine list is a section, page or panel of the food menu, be sure that it gets the proper billing and attention. If the wines get lost in the printed scramble of the menu, they will age forever in the wine cellar and never get sold. And it's not always true that the older the wine the better!

An effective method of selling wine is to list it right with the food it complements. For example, the following entree and wine could be listed together:

Rack and Loin of Spring Lamb served with
Baby Carrots, Pearl Onions
Garnished with Watercress

For a wine to accompany this entree, we recommend
Red Bordeaux
La Chateau Margaux
1953

In short, wine helps to sell the food, and the food helps to sell the wine, and both help to keep the operation solvent.

Brand names are important for wine listing. Also, if yours is a ➡
"national" restaurant—French, German, Italian, etc., feature the
wines of that country plus American wines.

DEUTSCHE ROTWEINE

60er Walporzheimer Steinkaul
     Spätburgunder   8.50

64er Affenthaler Rotwein Spätburgunder   10.—
     Affenflasche Beerwein

64er Ihringer Winklerberg Spätburgunder
     natur   12.50
     Kaiserstühler Winzergenossenschaft

SÜSS- UND DESSERTWEINE

Insel Samos   7.—

Malaga Hellgold Lagrimas Christi   7.50

Mavrodaphne   9.—

Original TERRY-Sherry pale, trocken   10.—
Reidemeister & Ulrichs, Bremen

Portwein, Old Tawny   ½ 6.50   12.—
Butler, Nephew & Co.

Fine Old Madeira Boal, Portugal   12.—
Reidemeister & Ulrichs, Bremen

Sandeman's Portwein, rot   13.50

Sandeman's Portwein, weiß   15.50

Sandeman's Sherry „Apitiv"   15.50

SCHAUMWEIN UND CHAMPAGNER

54 KUPFERBERG Gold, Zwerg Dry   4.—

55 Schloß Wachenheim Grün   9.—

56 HENKELL TROCKEN   14.—

57 KUPFERBERG Gold   ½ 7.50   14.—

58 Matheus Müller extra Auslese   14.—

59 BURGEFF Grün   14.—

60 Deinhard CABINET -TROCKEN-   14.—

61 Deinhard LILA -EXTRA DRY- ½ 9.—   17.—

62 SÖHNLEIN Fürst v. Metternichscher
     Schloß Johannisberg Sekt   17.—

63 SÖHNLEIN Assmannshäuser Spätburgunder 18.—

64 Mumm ELTVILLE, Dry   18.—

65 KUPFERBERG Schwarz-Gold
     Fürst von Bismarck, Extra Dry 20.—

66 Heidsieck Monopole, Red Top ½ 17.— 32.—

67 Champagner Heidsieck Monopole Dry 40.—

The wine list (reproduced on this and the next two pages) is designed to reflect the care which this food service operator used in assembling his wine offerings.

Sparkling Wines

Bin No.		CHAMPAGNE	Bottle	Half Bottle
1	BOLLINGER	Extra Dry, non-vintage. Madame Bollinger is a perfectionist. This wine is worth much more than she asks. Great drinking.	$6.00	
2	VEUVE CLICQUOT	Gold Label, Ponsardin, vintage, Brut. Magnificently dry, light and clean . . . one of the great champagnes.	9.80	$5.25
3	TAITTINGER	Blanc de Blanc, vintage, Brut. A superb champagne made solely from the Pinot Chardonnay variety . . . and each berry hand-selected (epluchage)!	13.50	
4	KORBEL BRUT	Sonoma Valley, California. Many say this jewel is equal to the French product.	6.00	3.35
5	GOLD SEAL	Brut, New York State. Produced by Charles Fournier, this country's most eminent champagne-maker. Light and truly fine.	5.25	2.80
6	ALMADEN	Blanc de Blanc, Paicines Vineyards, California. Like Taittinger, made only from the Chardonnay . . . and very good it is.	7.75	
7	RAMEY CHAMPAGNE	Brut. Monee, Illinois. The first champagne "produced and bottled" solely in the state of Illinois. A remarkable Cuveé made without variation by the true French method.	6.50	
8	SPARKLING CUVEÉ	(Non-alcoholic), Ramey & Allen Champagne Vineyards, Monee, Illinois. For everyone who enjoys fine, pure grape juice...and for the person who has to think the next day. A light, clean, medium sweet blend of the Delaware and Catawba varieties.	2.90	

SPARKLING BURGUNDY (and Rosé)

Bin No.			Bottle	Half Bottle
9	CHAUVENET RED CAP	France. The most popular sparkling Burgundy in the world . . . medium dry.	7.60	4.00
10	KORBEL PINK	Sonoma Valley. For our money (and palate) the best pink champagne made (amen).	5.80	
11	TAYLOR'S SPARKLING BURGUNDY	New York State. Fruity and pleasant—not too heavy . . . an American favorite.	5.70	3.15

Sherries and Aperitifs

		by the glass
LA INA	Pedro Domecq (dry).	.65
AMONTILLADO	Duff Gordon (quite dry).	.65
DRY SACK	Williams and Humbert (medium dry).	.80
BRISTOL DRY	Harvey's (medium dry).	.90
BRISTOL CREAM	Harvey's (rich, sweet).	1.10
DUBONNET		.65
LILLET	(apéritif de France).	.60
CAMPARI		.85
CINZANO VERMOUTH	(dry or sweet).	.60

White Wines

Bin No.	**RHINE and MOSELLE**		Bottle	Half Bottle
12	*LIEBFRAUMILCH*	Blue Nun, vintage, H. Sichel Soehne. Light and not too dry. Extremely popular.	$3.80	$2.00
13	*ZELLER SCHWARZE KATZ*	Means "black cat," but no bad luck here . . . a pleasant Moselle.	3.25	
14	*SCHLOSS VOLLRADS*	Vintage, Graf Matushka. Wonderful bouquet, fruity, light—one of the finest white wines produced anywhere!	2.95	
15	*SCHLOSS JOHANNISBERG*	Vintage, Feine Spaetlese. Rare flavor! and nicely, lightly sweet . . . another "great."	5.50	
16	*KREUZNACHER STEINBERG*	Anheuser and Fehrs. From the Nahe River Valley . . . a wonderfully light, rare, subtle bouquet . . . so very drinkable.	3.25	
17	*BERNKASTELLER DOKTOR SPAETLESE*	Dr. Thanisch, vintage. Only thirteen acres, three owners . . . Dr. Thanisch owns the sunny side, the best side! . . . probably the finest Moselle made.	8.40	
18	*GEWURTZTRA-MINER*	Almaden, Paicines Vineyard, California. Fragrant, delicate, like eating pretty flowers (only better)!	3.00	1.65
19	*JOHANNISBERG RIESLING*	Louis M. Martini. From the famed Napa Valley, California . . . depth and finesse. Produced from the true white Riesling.	3.45	
20	*DELAWARE*	Great Western, New York State. A crisp pleasure from the Finger Lakes region.	3.35	1.90
	WHITE BURGUNDY			
21	*POUILLY FUISSE*	Vintage, Frank Schoonmaker. Delicate . . . somewhat tart, a nice luncheon partner.	2.90	1.60
22	*CHABLIS*	Vintage, Jacques Prieur. Twice as much "Chablis" is sold as is produced, so the shipper's name is most important. Frederick Wildman, not a compromising man, is the shipper!	3.90	
23	*LE MONTRACHET*	Vintage, Baron Thenard. The most expensive dry, white wine of France . . . many experts say the finest white made anywhere. Your opinion?	12.95	
24	*PINOT CHARDONNAY*	Vintage, Frank Schoonmaker. True Chablis is made only from the Chardonnay variety. A Schoonmaker selection is always excellent!	2.00	
25	*CHABLIS*	Wente Brothers, Livermore, California. A small vineyard, and this country's finest producer of white wines.	2.45	1.25
	WHITE BORDEAUX			
26	*CHATEAU COUHINS*	Vintage, Graves. Medium-bodied, dry, white . . . an excellent buy.	3.10	1.60
27	*SEMILLON*	Haut Sauterne, Wente Brothers. The first American "varietal." Moderately sweet and of rare bouquet . . . a fine wine by any standard.	2.15	1.40
28	*CHATEAU d'YQUEM*	Vintage, Gran Cru. Luscious, sweet, so fragrant . . . the world's finest Sauternes!	11.40	
	LOIRE WINES			
29	*POUILLY-FUME*	Pouilly-sur-Loire, vintage. Chateau du Nozet, Ladoucette Freres. An extremely good white wine produced from the Sauvignon blanc variety. Light, fragrant, and young— as it should be!	3.75	2.10
30	*VOUVRAY*	Marc Bredif, Estate Bottled, vintage. From year to year Vouvrays vary in taste, color, degree of dryness and stillness. This beauty is moderately dry, crisp, and nicely aged—another perfect white wine.	3.95	

Red Wines

RED BORDEAUX (Claret)

Bin No.			Bottle	Half Bottle
31	HAUT-MEDOC	Vintage, Frank Schoonmaker Selection. An excellent "regional" claret . . . dry, fruity.	$2.35	
32	ST. EMILION	Vintage, Frank Schoonmaker Selection. The Cabernet vineyards surrounding St. Emilion are the finest in all Bordeaux. Rich in color and body.	2.35	$1.35
33	CHATEAU LAFITE-ROTHSCHILD	Vintage. The finest Claret in the world (en garde, Mouton partisans)!	7.35	
34	CHATEAU MOUTON-ROTHSCHILD	Vintage. Others say, "The finest Claret in the world." Bottled luxury.	6.80	
35	CABERNET SAUVIGNON	Almaden, Paicines Vineyards, California. A truly fine "American" Claret, made from the Bordeaux Cabernet variety . . . and brilliantly made.	3.00	1.70

RED BURGUNDY

Bin No.			Bottle	Half Bottle
36	POMMARD	Vintage, Clos de la Commaraine. Jaboulet-Vercherre. Full, soft, just right!	4.90	2.65
37	BEAUJOLAIS	Vintage, Louis Latour. Chosen by one of Burgundy's most reputable shippers . . . mellow and full of character.	3.50	1.85
38	CLOS de VOUGEOT	Vintage, Frank Schoonmaker. Classic quality and powering bouquet. Another "great."	5.75	
39	LE CHAMBERTIN	Vintage, Jaboulet-Vercherre. One of the greatest red wines of the world!	7.35	
40	PINOT NOIR	Louis M. Martini, Napa Valley, California. The American counterpart of France's Cote de Nuits Burgundy . . . the same variety but with its own lighter-bodied charm.	2.75	1.60

ROSE (Pink)

Bin No.			Bottle	Half Bottle
41	LANCER'S CRACKLING ROSÉ	A Portuguese sparkling pink . . . as good as it is colorful . . . slightly sweet.	4.00	2.30
42	MATEUS ROSÉ	Also from Portugal, but not sparkling . . . slightly sweet and flowery. Perfect with luncheon.	2.25	
43	TAVEL	Vintage, Frank Schoonmaker. The pink wines of France are called "Tavel" after the tiny Rhone village where these colorful creatures were born . . . young and refreshing!	2.90	1.60
44	GRENACHE ROSÉ	Almaden, Paicines Vineyard, California. Produced from the true "Tavel" variety, the Grenache . . . and perfectly produced!	2.45	1.40

In both selection and listing this is an excellent wine list, and it can be followed by any food service operator who wants to create a fine wine list. (See preceding pages for rest of list.)

Italian Wines

We tasted and chose, one hundred per cent, the selections of Frank Schoonmaker's amazing palate.

Bin No.			Bottle	Half Bottle
45	CHIANTI SANT ANDREA	(In straw fiaschi). Rich, red, full, brash, good!	2.35	1.30
46	VALPOLICELLA	Vintage. Made in Verona, this is probably northern Italy's finest red wine.	2.15	
47	SOAVE	Vintage. An excellent white wine—light, dry, fresh, well-balanced.	2.15	1.25

Wine List
JACQUES FRENCH RESTAURANT

Champagnes and Sparkling Wines

French Champagne is made from grapes that grow on the chalky hillsides south of the Cathedral City of Reims. The sparkle which is characteristic of champagne results from a second fermentation that occurs after the wine has been bottled. Champagne is appropriate throughout the entire meal and makes every dinner a festive occasion.

Bin No.		Vintage	Bottle	Half Bottle
2	Moet & Chandon, Dom Perignon	1952/53	15.00	
3	G. H. Mumm, Cordon Rouge	1952/53	12.50	6.50
4	Piper Heidsieck, Extra Dry	1952/53	12.50	6.50
21	Moet & Chandon Dry Imperial	1952/53	12.50	
5	Moet & Chandon White Seal	N. V.	10.50	
1	Pol Roger Dry Special	N. V.	10.50	
6	Pol Roger, Brut	1947/52	12.50	
11	Cook's Imperial Brut (American)		7.25	3.75
12	Korbel, Brut (American)		7.25	
16	Chauvenet, Red Cap (French Sparkling Burgundy)		8.50	4.50
17	Cook's (American Sparkling Burgundy)		7.25	3.75
18	Lacrima Christi (Italian)		8.50	
19	Piper Heidsieck Pink		11.50	
20	Oeil De Perdrix (Sichel)		10.50	5.50

Red Bordeaux

Near the ocean port of Bordeaux lie the vineyards that produce the pleasing and agreeable wines which bring out the very best in duck, steaks and chops. The best wines are sold under the name of the chateau or estate on which they are grown and at which they are bottled.

25	*Château Latour, Pauillac	1955	7.00	
26	*Château Lascombes, Margaux	1952/55	6.00	3.25
30	*Château Haut Brion, Pessac-Graves	1952/55	8.50	4.25
31	*Château Margaux, Margaux	1952/55	8.50	4.25
32	*Château Ducru Beaucaillou, St. Julien	1952/55	5.50	2.75
33	*Château Ripeau, St. Emilion	1955	5.25	2.75
34	*Château Prieuré Lichine, Contenac-Margaux	1952	5.50	2.75
35	*Château Mouton Rothschild	1952	9.50	
36	*Château Lafite Rothschild, Pauillac	1955	9.50	4.75
37	*Château Calon Segur, St. Estephe	1937	12.00	

The wine list of Jacques French restaurant features French wines and a wine map.

UN REPAS SANS VIN EST UN JOURNEE SANS SOLEIL

	BORDEAUX	BURGUNDY	RHONE	CHAMPAGNE	RHINE	MOSELLE
1947	EXCELLENT	EXCELLENT	EXCELLENT	OLD	VERY GOOD	VERY GOOD
1948	MEDIOCRE	POOR	POOR	NON-VINT.	POOR	POOR
1949	EXCELLENT	EXCELLENT	EXCELLENT	EXCELLENT	EXCELLENT	EXCELLENT
1950	VERY GOOD	GOOD	GOOD	NON-VINT.	GOOD	GOOD
1951	POOR	POOR	POOR	NON-VINT.	MEDIOCRE	MEDIOCRE
1952	EXCELLENT	EXCELLENT	EXCELLENT	EXCELLENT	GOOD	VERY GOOD
1953	EXCELLENT	EXCELLENT	EXCELLENT	EXCELLENT	EXCELLENT	EXCELLENT
1954	MEDIOCRE	MEDIOCRE	GOOD	NON-VINT.	POOR	POOR
1955	EXCELLENT	EXCELLENT	EXCELLENT	EXCELLENT	GOOD	VERY GOOD
1956	POOR	MEDIOCRE	POOR	NON-VINT.	POOR	POOR
1957	VERY GOOD	EXCELLENT	EXCELLENT	EXCELLENT	GOOD	VERY GOOD

A vintage rating chart is a good guide for the wine ordering customer.

NO.	BORDEAUX, RED	VINT.	BOT.	½ BOT.
185	CHÂTEAU LA TOUR CANON *Fronsac*	1950	27/6	
140	CHÂTEAU MARTINET *Grand Cru Saint-Emilion*	1950	27/6	
195	CHÂTEAU MEYNEY *Saint-Estèphe*	1950	29/-	
	CHÂTEAU COS D'ESTOURNEL *2me Cru Saint-Estèphe*	1953	29/-	15/-
194	CHÂTEAU CHEVAL-BLANC *1er Grand Cru Saint-Emilion*	1953	30/-	16/-
188	CHÂTEAU SMITH-HAUT-LAFITTE *Graves. Château Bottled*	1952	32/6	
114	CHÂTEAU LÉOVILLE-POYFERRÉ *2me Cru Saint-Julien*	1953	29/-	
183	CHÂTEAU RAUSAN-SÉGLA *2me Cru Margaux. Château Bottled*	1937	45/-	
138	CHÂTEAU MOUTON-ROTHSCHILD *2me Cru Pauillac. Château Bottled*	1952		
134	CHÂTEAU HAUT-BRION *1er Cru Pessac. Château Bottled*	1950	52/6	
122	CHÂTEAU LATOUR *1er Cru Pauillac. Château Bottled*	1950	52/6	
95	CHÂTEAU LAFITE-ROTHSCHILD *1er Cru Pauillac. Château Bottled*	1950	52/6	
86	CHÂTEAU MARGAUX *1er Cru Margaux. Château Bottled*	1934		

This wine list shows vintage years of wine served.

CANAPES
   Cheese, crackers
   Olives, etc.
	SHERRY
	CHAMPAGNE

SOUP	SHERRY
SEAFOOD	CHABLIS DRY SAUTERNE RHINE WHITE BURGUNDY

FOWL
   Cold chicken, turkey
   Roast chicken, duck,
   turkey, pheasant
	CHAMPAGNE
	DRY SAUTERNE
	RHINE
	WHITE OR RED BUGUNDY

MEATS
   Steak, veal, lamb
   roast beef, stew
	CLARET
	BURGUNDY
	ROSE

ITALIAN DISHES	CHIANTI ZINFANDEL BARBERA
DESSERTS	SWEET SAUTERNE CHAMPAGNE

A wine and food affinity chart helps the customer select the wine most suitable to the food he is eating.

Bohemian Grove Wine List is center piece for table. It fits into a wooden holder and is printed both sides.

"Wine is one of the most civilized things in the world, and one of the natural things that has been brought to greatest perfection. It offers a greater range for enjoyment and appreciation than possibly any other purely sensory thing that may be purchased."

ERNEST HEMINGWAY

FINE AMERICAN AND IMPORTED WINES

Fine foods deserve fine wines. The management has endeavored to offer our patrons a selection of excellent wines, appropriate to every occasion and menu, and suited to every individual taste. Particular care, too, is taken to serve the wine of your choice at precisely the correct temperature to produce its finest flavor and bouquet.

SPARKLING WINES

Before, During and After Meals	Bottle	½ Bottle	Glass
Great Western Extra Dry Champagne	6.50	3.50	
Great Western Sparkling Red Burgundy (sweet)	6.50	3.50	
Mumm's Cordon Rouge Brut (very dry)	10.75		
Lancers Vin Rosé (Portugal)	6.25	3.50	

APÉRITIF WINES

Before Dinner Wines

	Glass
Dubonnet	.75
Duff Gordon Amontillado Sherry (dry and pale)	.75
Martini & Rossi Sweet Italian Vermouth	.60
Noilly Prat French Dry Vermouth	.60
Taylor's Sherry (not sweet or dry)	.60

WHITE DINNER WINES

With Fish, Shellfish, Fowl and Lighter Meats

	Bottle	½ Bottle	Glass
Barsac — A. deLuze & Fils Bordeaux (sweet, full-bodied)	4.50	2.50	
Almadén Rhine (semi dry, fruity)	3.25	2.25	.60
Almadén Sauterne (dry, fruity Bordeaux)	3.25	2.25	.60
Almadén Chablis (light, delicate, dry)	3.25	2.25	.60
Liebfraumilch Guilden Krone (medium dry Rhine)	4.75	3.00	
Tavel Rosé (Rosé Rhone wine, delightful with any dish)	3.75	2.50	

RED DINNER WINES

With Steaks, Roasts, Chops, Ham and Heartier Foods

	Bottle	½ Bottle	Glass
Beaujolais — A. deLuze & Fils (light Burgundy)	4.50	2.50	
Almadén Claret (fresh, soft, delightful)	3.25	2.25	.60
Almadén Burgundy (full bodied)	3.25	2.25	.60
Melini Chianti Imported	4.50		
Tavel Rosé (Rosé Rhone wine, delightful with any dish)	3.75	2.50	
Tipo California Chianti	2.25		
Mogen David Concord	2.25		.60

DESSERT WINES

To Enhance the Flavor of Every Dessert

	Glass
Harvey's Bristol Cream Sherry (full pale)	.95
Molinet Ruby Port (Portugal)	.70
Sandeman Tawny Port (Portugal)	.75
Taylor's Port (sweet)	.60
Taylor's Muscatel	.60
Great Western White Port	.60
Mogen David Concord	.60

A good selection of before, with and after dinner wines in bottle, 1/2 bottle and glass.

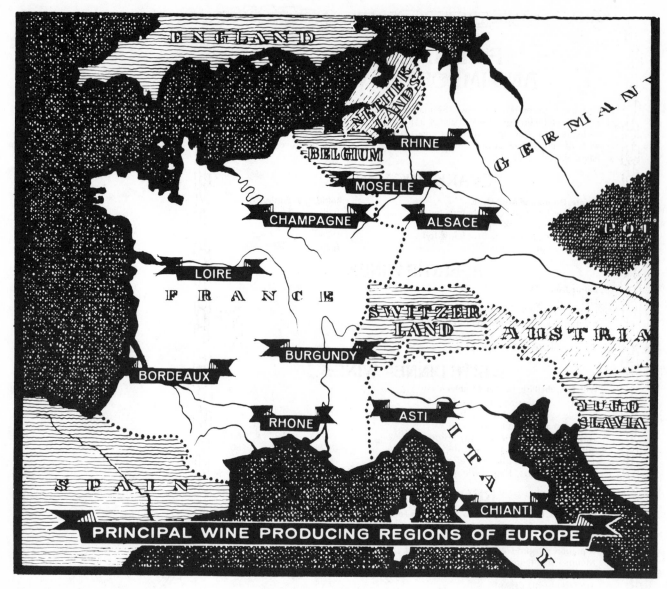

Maps help to identify, merchandise and sell wine.

Wines

The Proper and Perfect Partners to Fine Foods

For an Appetizer Wine

Amontillado Sherry from Spain
Harvey's Bristol Cream Sherry from England

For a Red Dinner Wine

To Accompany Roasts, Steaks, Prime Rib, Chops, etc.
Red Bordeaux or Burgundy from France
Red Chianti from Italy

For a White Dinner Wine

To Accompany Fowl, Fish or White Meat
White Bordeaux or Sauterne from France
Rhine — or Moselle — Wines from Germany

For a Rose Dinner Wine

A Vin Rose from France, a Complement to Any food,
On Any Occasion

For a Dessert Wine

Port Wine from Portugal
Muscatel Wine from Italy

At Last . . . . But By No Means Least

French and Domestic Champagnes
. . . Can Be "All Things to All Foods".

*Good information, attractively presented with good type
selection and a decorative border, add to the wine story.*

BORDEAUX CLASSIFICATIONS

MEDOC

Premiers Crus
(FIRST GROWTHS)

CHATEAU LAFITE
CHATEAU LATOUR
CHATEAU MARGAUX
CHATEAU HAUT-
  BRION (Graves)

Deuxiemes Crus
(SECOND GROWTHS)

Chateau Mouton-Rothschild
Chateau Rausan-Segla
Chateau Rauzan-Gassies ·
CHATEAU LEOVILLE-
  LAS CASES
Chateau Leoville-Poyferre
Chateau Leoville-Barton
Chateau Dufort-Vivens
CHATEAU LASCOMBES
Chateau Gruaud-Larose
Chateau Brane-Cantenac
Chateau Pichon-Longueville
Chateau Pichon-
  Longueville-(Lalande)
Chateau Ducru-Beaucaillou
CHATEAU COS-
  D'ESTOURNEL
Chateau Montrose

Troisiemes Crus
(THIRD GROWTHS)

Chateau Giscours
Chateau Kirwan
Chateau d'Issan
Chateau Lagrange
Chateau Langoa
Chateau Malescot-Saint-
  Exupery
Chateau Cantenac-Brown
Chateau Palmer
Chateau la Lagune
Chateau Desmirail
Chateau Calon-Segur
Chateau Ferriere
Chateau Marquis-d'Alesme-
  Becker
Chateau Boyd-Cantenac

Quatriemes Crus
(FOURTH GROWTHS)

Chateau Saint-Pierre-
  Bontemps
Chateau Saint-Pierre-
  Sevaistre
Chateau Branaire-Ducru
Chateau Talbot
Chateau Duhart-Milon
Chateau Poujet
Chateau la-Tour-Carnet
Chateau Rochet
Chateau Beychevelle
Chateau le Prieure
Chateau Marquis de Terme

Cinquiemes Crus
(FIFTH GROWTHS)

Chateau Pontet-Canet
CHateau Batailley
Chateau Haut-Batailley
Chateau Grand-Puy-Lacoste
Chateau Grand-Puy-Ducasse
Chateau Lynch-Bages
Chateau Lynch-Moussas
Chateau Dauzac
Chateau Mouton-
  d'Armailhacq
Chateau le Tertre
Chateau Haut-Bages
Chateau Pedesclaux
Chateau Belgrave
Chateau Camensac
Chateau Cos-Labory
Chateau Clerc-Milon
Chateau Croizet-Bages
Chateau Cantemerle

ST. EMILION

Premiers Grand Crus
(FIRST GREAT GROWTHS)

CHATEAU AUSONE
Chateau Cheval Blanc
Chateau Beausejour
Chateau Bel-Air
Chateau Canon
Chateau Clos Fourtet
Chateau Figeac
Chateau Magdelaine
CHATEAU PAVIE

POMEROL

Premier Grand Cru
(OUTSTANDING GROWTHS)
(Unofficial)

CHATEAU PETRUS
Chateau l'Evangile
Chateau La Conseillante
Chateau Vieux Certan
Chateau Trotanoy

SAUTERNES

Grand Premier Cru
(GREAT FIRST GROWTH)

CHATEAU D'YQUEM

Premiers Crus
(FIRST GROWTHS)

Chateau La Tour-Blanche
Chateau Peyraguey
Chateau Rayne Vigneau
Chateau Suduiraut
CHATEAU COUTET
Chateau Climens
Chateau Bayle (Guiraud)
Chateau Rieussec
Chateau Rabaud

GRAVES (Red)

(OUTSTANDING VINEYARDS)
(Unofficial)

CHATEAU HAUT BRION
Chateau La Mission Haut
  Brion
Chateau Pape Clement
Chateau Haut Bailly
Chateau Carbonnieux

GRAVES (White)

(OUTSTANDING GROWTHS)
(Unofficial)

CHATEAU HAUT BRION
  BLANC
Chateau Carbonnieux
Chateau La Ville Haut Brion
CHATEAU OLIVIER
Domaine de Chevalier

OUTSTANDING WINES of RHINE and MOSELLE

RHINEGAU

(From west to east)

RUDESHEIM—Rudesheimer
Berg, Schlossberg,
Roseneck

GEISENHEIM—Rotherberg.
Katzenloch, Lickerstein

JOHANNISBERG—
SCHLOSS JOHANNIS-
BERG, Erntebringer,
Holle, Klaus

WINKLER—SCHLOSS
VOLLRADS, Hasen-
sprung, Jesuitengarten,
Steinacker

MITTELHEIM—Bangert

OESTRICH—Lechnchen,
Eiserweg, Doosberg

HALLGARTEN—Schonhelt,
Deitelsberg

HATTENHEIM—Engel-
mannsberg, Willborn,
Nussbrunnen

ERBACH-ELTVILLE—
Schloss Reinhartshausen,
MARKOBRUNN,
Bruhl

KLOSTER EBERBACH—
Steinberg

KIEDRICH—Grafenberg,
Sandgrube

RAUENTHAL—Steinacher,
Burggraben

HOCHHEIM—Domde-
chaney, Daubhaus

RHINEHESSE

(North to south)

LAUBENHEIM—Burg,
Edelmann, Kalkofen

BODENHEIM—Kahlenberg,
Silberbergt, Burgweg

MACKENHEIM—
Rotenberg

NIERSTEIN—Domtal,
Glock, Hipping, Rehbach

OPPENHEIM—Sacktreger,
Zuckerberg, Schlossberg

WORMS—Liebfrauenkirche
(its wine is labeled Lieb-
frauen Stiftstein or Kirch-
ensteuck, but not Liebfraumilch).

BENSHEIM—Streichling

MIDDLE MOSELLE

(Trier to Traben,
south to north)

NEUMANN—Lasenberg

UHRON—Hofberg

PIESPORT—Goldtropfchen,
Falkenberg, Lay,
GRAFENBERG

WINTERICH—Geierslay

BRAUNENBERG—Juffer,
Falkenberg

LIESER—Niederberg,
Schlossberg

BERNCASTEL-CUES—
DOCTOR, Badstube

GRAACH—Domprobst,
Himmelrich, Abtei

JOSEPHSHOFER—
Josephshofer

WEHLEN—Sonnenuhr,
Nonnenlay, Rothlay

ZELTINGER—Himmelrich,
Rotlay, Schlossberg

UERZIG—Wurzgarten,
Kranklay

ERDEN—Treppchen, Pralat,
Herrenberg

CROV—Crover-Steffenberg

OUTSTANDING WINES OF BURGUNDY

GEVREY-CHAMBERTIN
Tetes de Cuvees
(OUTSTANDING VINEYARDS)

Le Chambertin
CHAMBERTIN CLOS
DE BEZE

Premiers Crus
(FIRST GROWTHS)

Latricieres
Mazoyeres
Charmes
MAZIS
Ruchottes
Griotte
Chapelle

MOREY-SAINT-DENIS
Tetes de Cuvees
(OUTSTANDING VINEYARDS)

Clos de Tart
Clos des Lambrays
Bonnes-Mares

CHAMBOLLE-MUSIGNY
Tetes de Cuvees
(OUTSTANDING VINEYARDS)

LES MUSIGNY
Les Bonnes-Mares

Premiers Crus
(FIRST GROWTHS)

Les Amoureuses

VOUGEOT
Tete de Cuvee
(OUTSTANDING VINEYARD)
CLOS DE VOUGEOT

FLAGEY-ECHEZEAUX
Tetes de Cuvees
(OUTSTANDING VINEYARDS)
Les Grands-Echezeaux
Les Echezeaux

VOSNE-ROMANEE
Tetes de Cuvees
(OUTSTANDING VINEYARDS)
Romanee-Conti
La Romanee
La Tache
Les Gaudichots
LES RICHEBOURG

Premiers Crus
(FIRST GROWTHS)
La Romanee Saint-Vivant
Les Malconsorts
Les Beaux-Monts
Les Suchots

NUITS-SAINT-GEORGES
Tetes de Cuvees
(OUTSTANDING VINEYARDS)
Les Saint Georges
Les Boudots
Les Cailles
Les Porrets
Les Pruliers
LES VAUCRAINS

ALOXE-CORTON
Tetes de Cuvees
(OUTSTANDING VINEYARDS)
Le Corton
LE CLOS DU ROI
CHARLEMAGNE
Les Bressandes
Les Renardes

BEAUNE
Tetes de Cuvees
(OUTSTANDING VINEYARDS)
LES FEVES
Les Greves
Les Marconnets
Les Bressandes
Les Clos de Mouches

POMMARD
Tetes de Cuvees
(OUTSTANDING VINEYARDS)

Les Epenots
LES RUGIENS

Premiers Crus
(FIRST GROWTHS)

La Platiere
Les Pezerolles
Les Petite Epenots
Clos de la Cammaraine
Les Jarollieres

VOLNAY
Tetes de Cuvees
(OUTSTANDING VINEYARDS)
Les Caillerets
Les Champans
Les Premiets
Santenots

MEURSAULT
Tetes de Cuvees
(OUTSTANDING VINEYARDS)
Clos de Perrieres
Les Perrieres

Premiers Crus
(FIRST GROWTHS)
LES GENEVRIERES
Les Charmes (Dessus)
Santenots
Sous Blagny

PULIGNY-MONTRACHET
Tetes de Cuvees
(OUTSTANDING VINEYARDS)
LE MONTRACHET
Premiers Crus
(FIRST GROWTHS)
Le Chevalier Montrachet
Le Batard Montrachet
Les Combettes
Blagny-Blanc
Champ-Canet
La Pucelle

CHASSAGNE-MONTRACHET
Tetes de Cuvees
(OUTSTANDING VINEYARDS)
LE MONTRACHET

Premiers Crus
(FIRST GROWTHS)

Le Batard Montrachet
Les Ruchottes
Cailleret

CHABLIS
Grand Crus
(OUTSTANDING GROWTHS)

Vaudesir
LES CLOS
Blanchots
Baugros
Valmur
Grenouilles
Les Preuses
La Moutonne

General information about wine gives your wine list a more authentic aspect.

Old World
AND New World WINES

◆—●●—◆

Since the dawn of civilization wine has held an important place in man's inventory of delights and necessities. It long ago became a basic medium in the art of dining.

When America was young, slips were cut from the vines of the great vineyards of Europe, tenderly wrapped and brought to these shores as part of the humble treasures of the early settlers. Many were brought by monks to serve the need for sacramental wines in the New World missions.

Here these cuttings found similar combinations of soil, climate, and sunlight on the hills overlooking New York's Finger Lakes and on the foothill slopes along the great valleys of California. From these slips out of century-old vineyards in Europe has developed a great American wine industry, producing today not only the traditional wines but many new varieties. Thus, the Hershey Motor Lodge wine cellar is international, too, providing a colorful assortment of the finest in imported and American wines.

PLANNING YOUR DINNER

To assist you in planning a completely delightful meal, this menu has been designed to offer appropriate wines for each course of your dinner. They appear on the page opposite our food course offerings: aperitif wines with appetizers, dinner wines with entrees. Your preference, however, may be one wine or possibly a champagne to complement your entire meal. We hope your dining adventure in the Hershey Motor Lodge will be complete in enjoyment and truly memorable.

As Ben Johnson once said, "Eat thy bread with joy and drink thy wine with a merry heart."

Copy like this creates a "Wine Atmosphere" on the menu.

STEAK MERCHANDISING

Don't just list your steaks, sell them with informative, descriptive, merchandising copy that motivates the guest. Expensive items deserve top billing on any restaurant menu. Most restaurants list steaks on their menu, but in too many cases it is only a listing. The supposition is probably that everybody knows what a steak is, so why talk about it. This, however, is not the case. In the first place, there are many kinds of steaks, and in the second place, there are many grades of steaks. These two factors alone call for copy, and when you combine them with size, weight, and type of preparation, you can see that there is plenty to talk about. The following is "steak copy" which can be used by any restaurant to increase "steak business," which, considering prices, is an important part of any restaurant.

STEAK DESCRIPTIONS

1. Porterhouse—this is considered by some to be the finest, greatest steak cut of all. It is a combination of two steaks in one divided by the bone, a filet and a strip steak. Aged and broiled on the bone to retain more juice, this is a steak to take the appetite by the horns!

2. Filet Mignon—this is the tenderest steak of all, cuts like butter, melts in your mouth! Specially selected from heavy U. S. choice tenderloins; selection, aging and trimming make this filet fabulously flavorful.

3. T-Bone—the steak that "Won the West", practically two steaks in one. You get a U. S. prime center-cut strip plus a small filet. Broiled "bone-in" for extra flavor to make appetites expand.

4. Tenderloin—a large cut of U. S. choice tenderloin with a slight trace of sweet fat for flavor makes this choice cut "tenderful and flavor fabulous," an all-time favorite.

5. Bone-in-Strip—sometimes called Kansas City sirloin, this is the same strip as the sirloin—tender, flavorful, succulent. The bone, however, is not trimmed away. Broiling with the bone helps broil in more flavor and juice. This is a great steak worthy of any gourmet prize.

6. Strip Sirloin—often called New York strip or New York sirloin, this is a tender, but not too tender, filet that is even more flavorful than the regular filet. The sweet, prime fat on the sides of this cut should be eaten with the meat to make it even tastier. A steak worthy of the name Sir Loin!

7. Butterfly Filet—this is the same piece of U. S. choice as Filet Mignon but sliced lengthwise before cooking. The chef suggests this steak for those who order steaks medium well to well done. All the tender, soft, juicy flavor will make you say—"well done!"

8. Tip Butt Sirloin—a solid, generous cut of top U. S. prime beef done to perfection. Easy on the budget, this steak will satisfy the biggest appetite ever. Called Club or Chef's Special some places, this steak has all the taste appeal of prime grade beef, an All American Favorite!

9. Chateaubriand—the royalty of steak, prepared and served for

two or more, the chateaubriand is a king size cut of tenderloin broiled, with the grain running horizontal, against the heat. This gives a succulent, crisp, tender crust with a pink, warm center. This is an "occasion" steak which should be sliced cross-grain and served with a good wine and enjoyed by good company.

10. Chopped Steak—a generous tasty serving using only U. S. choice and prime beef, and lifted out of the ordinary with whipped egg and good burgundy wine, a 'good eatin' item.

While steak descriptions are probably the most important words on your steak menu, the question of how the customer likes his steak is also important in keeping him happy. In order that everyone has the same definitions, it is well to print the descriptions in the adjoining column and also to tell your guests what grade you serve:

HOW DO YOU LIKE STEAK?

1. Rare—brown, seared crust with a cool red center.
2. Medium Rare—brown, seared crust, steak warmed through with a red warm center.
3. Medium—outside of steak well done, dark brown with a pink hot center.
4. Medium Well—outside dark brown, inside done through, steak has little juice left.
5. Well Done—outside black-brown, inside dried out, restaurant not responsible for well done steaks.

What kind of meat (in the form of steak) does your restaurant serve? If you serve good meat, say so. The following is a list of U. S. Beef Grades:

BEEF GRADES

1. Prime—highest possible quality beef, flavorful, juicy and tender. From young, well-fed beef cattle, this lean meat is well "marbled" with fat.
2. Choice—this is high quality beef with less fat than prime. Highly acceptable and palatable, this is juicy and tender meat.
3. Good—this meat has little fat, therefore lacks juiciness of higher quality beef, but with acceptable quality.
4. Standard—thin fat covering, meat is mild, unflavorful and lacking in juice.

The final thing to remember about your steak menu listing is that we are talking about important, expensive items on your menu that deserve "Top Billing." This means that they should get the best possible position on the menu, be set in the largest type that you use for listing and they should get the most descriptive, merchandising, sell copy.

Know Your Steaks

• A steak by any other name is still a steak, but when it's called a Delmonico or a shell steak you may have trouble identifying the exact cut. Here is a list of common steaks, giving, first, the name used by the U.S. Department of Agriculture and the National Live Stock and Meat Board, then other names by which the cut is known in various sections of the country. To make sure of getting the cut you want, check the sketches.

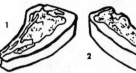

1. Club steak: Delmonico steak, T-bone steak, porterhouse steak, sirloin strip steak.

2. Top loin steak or New York Cut: Kansas City steak, boneless hip steak, shell steak, boneless

hotel steak, minute sirloin steak, loin strip steak, Delmonico steak, club steak, boneless sirloin steak.

3. Porterhouse and T-Bone steaks: Tenderloin steak, club steak.

4. Tenderloin or Filet mignon: (Chateaubriand steak), filet.

5. Sirloin steak: Hip steak, short hip steak, sirloin butt steak, rump steak.

The more you tell, the more you sell applies to steaks as well as the rest of the menu.

Steak House Special . . .
STEAKS

To help stamp out home cooking

THE FIESTA PORTERHOUSE: Best we got, an extra thick
4.75   so thick you won't want it cooked no more than medium, with salad, taters and coffee.

THE FLYING T-BONE: A man-sized slab of meat that sprawls
3.85   all over the platter, so that it don't hardly leave no room for the taters.   You get salad and coffee, too.

RANCHERS STRIP STEAK: A thick hunk of extra fine flavored
3.50   steak for when you aint hongrey enough to tackle the Fiesta, with all the handsome fringe beneyfits, too.

THE ROUGH-HOUSE: Also knowed as the poremans T-bone,
3.40   cut from where the reglar T-bone plays out, with salad, taters, and a heaping glass of ice water.

DELMONICO STEAK: Enough to please anyone.
3.15

RANCHERS RIB STEAK: Purt 'n' near the same as the rough-
2.95   house, an you git salad, taters and coffee, too.

SIRLOIN TIP: Delicious, juicy sirloin smothered with mush-
2.35   rooms or onions,   Salad, taters and coffee.

LADIES SPECIAL: A tremendous minaturee filly clobbered with
2.60   mushrooms.   And you get salad, taters and coffee, too.

THE CHARKY: Sirloin, cooked with charcoal seasoning to give
1.80   it that cooked out-of-doors flavor.   For folks who dont have their own Bar-B-Qpit. Salad and taters, too.

STEERBURGER STEAK: Half a pound of steerburger meat
1.35   cooked the way you like it, steak style, salad and taters, too.

FRENCHMAN'S STEAK: Served with Roquefort Salad,
2.70   Potatoes and Beverage.

An interesting selection of steaks very well described with creative selling copy.
The type is large and easy to read also.

OMAHA STEAKS FROM OUR AGEING ROOM

CHARCOAL BROILED OMAHA FILET MIGNON (Hi-Protein and Lean) . . . . .

Here you will find a tasty, juicy, tender . . . real delicious Steak that is also very **lean.** Those eating just for pleasure or folks on a "Lean Meat" and Hi-Protein Diet, can find great enjoyment with this fine steak. This tender piece of steak is a favorite with many. (With Idaho Baked Potato)

PRIME RIB ROAST OF BEEF, WITH AU JUS (June thru Oct.) . . . .

This beautiful Beef from Steers that have been kept over an extra year on CORN, is well floured and marbled. Roasted under a Blanket of Rock Salt to insure full flavor and juiciness. This is Roast Beef at its BEST (With Idaho Baked Potato) PLEASE DO NOT ASK FOR MEDIUM OR WELL-DONE PRIME RIB. It only comes PINK RARE accomplished by roasting in a slow oven under the heavy cover of Rock Salt. We do have two "outside cuts" on each loin which gives us a very few outside cuts. BUT WE ONLY SERVE THE PRIME RIB . . .PINK RARE: Which Beef lovers demand and we cater to them.

CHARCOAL BROILED "SHORT LOIN" STEAK (11-oz.) . . . .

These delicious and tasty "short loins of beef" are selected especially for us. These Steaks, in the Loin, are carefully "aged" in our modern Beef Ageing Room (Customers are welcome to see). For those who are interested in "cuts" of meat . . . the "Short Loin" is that section of beef, found only between the "hipbone and the rib". This Steak is our favorite recommendation. Tender, full of delicious juice and flavor . . . A REAL HEALTH BUILDER. (With Idaho Baked Potato)

DOUBLE "XX" SHORT LOIN STEAK. (Full 1-lb.) . . . .

Double "XX" Steak is named after a Beef Ranch in Nebraska. This Double "XX" Steak is from steers . . . carried over an extra year on corn. **Our Favorite** when you **are real hungry.** A REAL CELEBRA-TING MEAL! (With Idaho Baked Potato)

Each year, we have Swift and Co. of Omaha, Neb., buy just over 700 head of **Half White Faced Here-fords** and **Half Black Angus.** See if you can tell the difference! (This is Prime Beef) After they have been fattened on CORN. **(Corn is low in unsaturated fat)** This gives us a flowing supply of 1,400 Short-Loins for our Steaks. **Our Steaks** are **babied** and **pampered** ALL THE WAY.
Then into our Special "Ageing Room" and then to the Charcoal Broiler and then to you . . .m . . .m . .mm BUT THEY ARE GOOD!
The **Secret** is in **the Corn** and **The Ageing!**

This very good steak listing not only describes the steak individually, it indicates how it is prepared, size by weight and where the quality beef served comes from, and also describes the aging process.

U. S. PRIME N. Y. STRIP SIRLOIN   5.00

*A steak of Royal Flavor ! It's cut thick and juicy from the top of a
beef short loin, then boned and trimmed. We cook it to the
tenderest turn, so the meat just sizzles with juicy flavor.
Served with Potatoes and Salad.*

U. S. PRIME PORTERHOUSE   5.00

*A treat for hearty steak eaters ! By cutting the heavy end from the
T-Bone cut, we create our tender and tempting Porterhouse steaks.
Each one is a beauty that rewards your every bite with delite.
Served with Salad and Potatoes.*

U. S. PRIME FILET MIGNON (For those who want the best)   6.00

*A tenderness unexcelled ! Prime tenderloin meat with all
surface fat and outside membrane material removed.
Served with Potatoes and Salad.*

*If you serve top grade U. S. prime,
say so!*

Old Time Western Cattle

Ranchers Who Should Know,

Prefer Their Steaks 'Charred'.

These Are Seared and Charred

On The Outside and Remain

Rare Or Very Rare On The

Inside. Accomplished With

Tenderloin Or 'Sir-Loin' Steaks

Only.

Treat Yourself To It . . .

No Extra Charge.

A bit of "extra" steak copy.

*Dressed up beef for two or beef
prepared in a special manner with
wine suggestions add up to steak
specials that make dining an occasion and help pay the overhead.*

ENTRECOTE DOUBLE (For Two)

An Extra Thick Cut of Charcoal Broiled
Blue Ribbon Prime Strip Sirloin Flamed
and Carved at Your Table. A Beautiful
Array of Fresh Vegetables en Bordure.
Your Selection of Salad and Potato. Hot
Rolls and Butter.

13.00 (for 2)
We Suggest Champagne or Burgundy

**CHATEAUBRIAND BOUQUETIERE
(For Two)**

A Double Special Center Cut from a
Selected Prime Beef Tenderloin. Garden
Fresh Vegetables en Bordure. Potato and
Salad Selections of Your Choice. Flamed
at Table-side for Added Flavor. Hot Rolls
and Butter.

13.00 (for 2)
We Recommend Beaujolais or Pommard

TOURNEDOS ROSSINI

Two Delicate Tenderloin Steaks Broiled
to a Turn. Served with a Broiled Tomato
and an Intriguing Deviled Butter Sauce
Prepared and Flamed at Table-side. Tossed
Salad and Your Choice of Vegetable or
Potato. Hot Rolls and Butter.

5.75
We Suggest Rosé or Burgundy

All steaks are U.S.D.A. Graded Choice or Better Western Beef

Carefully Selected and Aged
Grilled, or Broiled
All Steaks are Served with Relish Tray
A Large Scrubbed and Rubbed Baked Idaho or French Fries
Green Salad, Choice of Dressing or Cole Slaw
Bread and Beverage

$1.00 Extra will be Charged Persons Sharing a Steak

Our Varieties of Steaks only Requires You to Pay What Your Appetite Calls for

New York Sirloin Strip

10 oz.	$3.75
12 oz.	4.25
16 oz.	5.50
24 oz. Steak for 2	8.50

Filet Mignon Steak

6 oz.	$3.25
8 oz.	4.25
10 oz.	5.25

T Bone Steaks

16 oz. T Bone	$4.25
20 oz. T Bone	5.25

Boneless Club Steak

6 oz.	$2.75
8 oz.	3.50

Fried Sweet Crispy Bermuda Onion Rings 35c

All he-man appetites can be appeased in grand style if the variety of steaks we have listed on our menu does not suit that big hungry man appetite. We will have our Chef roll out the butcher-block and scales, cut and weigh before your eyes any size boneless sirloin steak that your appetite might suggest. This succulent steak is sized and priced at 40c an ounce and, presto, the noblest prime sirloin anyone could command goes back to our broilers to be cooked just the way the KING OF THE ROAD wants it, and all the goodies listed above go with it.

Listing steaks by size with a different price for each size makes sense for both the customer and the food service operator.

STEAK CLUB DINNERS
You are invited to select and brand
your steak at our Steak Throne

THE SIRLOIN SALAD
Crisp Tender Salad Greens Flavored with Chopped Chives,
Garnished with Tomato, Anchovy and Grated Egg Yolks
Blended with your Choice of Dressing

*HEREFORD SIRLOIN ROOM SPECIAL
Our Most Popular Bone-in Sirloin Steak $5.75

*BLACK ANGUS SADDLE & SIRLOIN
A Hefty, Hearty Boneless Sirloin
as Served in the Club $6.75

*SHORTHORN TENDERLOIN STEAK
Beautifully Finished Filet Mignon
Cut from Heavy Beef $6.25

SIRLOIN ROOM À LA MINUTE
Aged Boneless Sirloin, Branded and Fired
as a Saddle & Sirloin Jr. $5.25

TENDERLOIN STEAK À LA MINUTE
A Minute Filet Mignon of Beef
for the Smaller Appetite $5.25

SPECIAL STEAK PREPARATION FOR TWO

SADDLE & SIRLOIN ENTRÉCOTE STEAK
Bone-in Double Sirloin Steak Thick and
Juicy, Sliced at Your Table $12.00

POSTILLION DOUBLE TENDERLOIN
Beautifully Finished Chateaubriand Style
Gourmet's Dream . . . Sliced at Your Table $13.00

CLASSICAL WINE SAUCE **WITH STEAKS** IF DESIRED

Above entrees include

French Fried Potatoes	Crispy and Crunchy
or	French Fried
Baked Potato	Onion Rings

Sour Dough Bread or French Hard Roll

*NOTE: The names of our steaks do not necessarily reflect the fact that these steak cuts come
from the breeds named. It is just our way of paying tribute to our nation's traditional breed lines.

The listing of the Stockyard's Inn with its steak selection from a "Steak Throne" is a good model for any food service operation to use.

DESCRIBE YOUR SEAFOOD

Seafood is an important entree on most food service menus, and its importance should be enhanced by good descriptive, merchandising copy. Many seafood items and methods of preparation are unknown to many guests, so just plain facts are needed in many cases.

A one or two-sentence line under the seafood listing is usually enough to set the word picture. Some of the points that should be covered in the copy are: where the fish or seafood comes from, how it is prepared, special sauces, flavoring, etc., with a few adjectives like flavorful, epicurean, enticing, mouth-watering, succulent, tender, etc.

When printing the descriptive copy, be sure it is set in a smaller and different type face from the entree listing, but not so small that it is hard to read. A good rule is to set the entree listing in caps—bold face, and the descriptive copy in a lighter, lower case type face. The descriptive copy for seafood entrees reproduced here can be used as examples and guides for your menu:

LOBSTER THERMIDOR (in shell)
Chunks of lobster meat sauteed in butter, blended in our own sherry 'n egg sauce, placed in the original shell, sprinkled with parmesan cheese and baked to an epicurean turn . . . . .

LOBSTER SALAD
A large epicurean delight. Enticing flavor with just the right spice 'n herb combination. Cole slaw and crisp lettuce served with this gourmet treat . . . . . .

BROILED SWORDFISH STEAK
Something to write home about. The tender fillet of this exotic fish—found only in the waters of James Michener's South Pacific, served with drawn butter . . . . .

COLUMBIA RIVER SALMON
Only hours ago flashing silver through the cascading Columbia. Fresh, firm, delicate pink, broiled to your taste. Only in the Pacific Northwest do you find this world-famous fish. Find out why salmon is king . . . . .

SHRIMP
They're pink perfection. Straight out of the "Gourmet's Almanack," smacking of that special shrimp flavor—spice too. In essence, nobody prepares shrimp the way we prepare shrimp . . . let us introduce you herewith . . . . .

DEEP SEA SCALLOPS
These small bivalves we bring in from the coast. They are good enough to import if need be. Tiny, succulent balls of white meat, these scallops are like abalone, only more tender . . . . .

CRAB AU GRATIN
A mystic blend of mushrooms, delicate crab meat and satiny cheddar cheese sauce that becomes ambrosia in the deft hands of our chef. It's simmered 'til there's mouth-watering flavor in every cranny of this bubbling casserole . . . . .

SEAFOOD PLATTER
If you'd like a little of everything listed under seafood, this is it! Shrimp, oysters, scallops and crab legs. A potpourri of succulence meriting the gastronomic Pulitzer Prize! . . . . .

JUMBO CRAB LEGS

All of our crab legs are large, but a select few are even larger than that! These we save. Hoard is a better word—to deep fry for you, sealing-in that distinctive flavor . , . . .

SHRIMP POLYNESIAN

Fresh, succulent shrimp marinated with exotic South Pacific spices and sauces. Broiled on a skewer with pineapple and bacon . . . . . flavors from Paradise . . . . . .

WHOLE ATLANTIC FLOUNDER

We flounder to find the right words to describe this fish feast. Perfectly seasoned and gently pampered and broiled in pure creamery butter . . .

OLD-FASHIONED SHORE DINNER

The works. . . like grandpa used to eat. . .choice of Maine chowder or lobster stew, crackers and pickles, steamed clams, bouillon and drawn butter. Then. . .fried clams, hot boiled lobster, chef salad, french fried potatoes, rolls, old-fashioned Indian Pudding with whipped cream and coffee. An adventure in good eating . . . . .

SWORDFISH STEAK

A flavored, flavorful treat from the sea. A boneless fish steak skillfully broiled to the peak of perfection and served with drawn butter and tartar sauce . . . . .

JUMBO LOBSTER LUMPS

Tender, tasty lumps of lobster meat prepared en casserole with pure creamery butter. A delectable, palate-pleasing treat for those who like lobster but dislike the mess . . . . .

FILLET OF PERCH

From off the shores of New England, from the deep sea. Breaded, broiled and seasoned with tender loving care by our chefs, this is a real fish delicacy . . . . .

FROG LEGS

This delicacy is marinated lightly in Chablis, sauteed in butter (garlic if you want it). This specialty has attracted gourmets to this restaurant from all over the country . . . . .

FRESH CATFISH

From the mighty waters of the Missouri River, fresh catfish fried the Dixie way—smothered with Southern flavor—and served with "taters", cole slaw and hot hush puppies . . . . .

RAINBOW TROUT

Shipped to us daily from the cold, clear waters of our nearby Ozark streams and cooked Ozark style. This is the golden taste treat in your pot at the end of the rainbow . . . . .

LOBSTER NEWBURG

Our chef delights in cooking this delicacy to your taste, choice pieces of lobster sauteed in butter with cognac and madeira wine and cream. Served on a bed of rice . . . . .

BOUILLABAISSE

Neptune's harvest in the form of a special fish soup consisting of fresh lobster meat, scallops, filet of sole, shrimp (and any other good seafood that's handy) baked en casserole with brandy (a real gourmet specialty). . .

Combination seafood plates, whether hot or cold, should be unusual and creative without causing impractical problems for the chef in the kitchen.

Assorted Seafood Platters

SEAFOOD SPECIALTY No. 1, (KING OF THE SEA) **5.00**
Half Maine Lobster, Florida Frog Legs, Louisiana Shrimp, Maryland Crab Cake, French Fried Potatoes, Sliced Tomatoes

SEAFOOD SPECIALTY No. 3 .... **4.50**
Half Broiled Lobster, Jumbo Shrimp, Imperial Crab, Deep Sea Scallops, Creamy Slaw, French Fried Potatoes

SEAFOOD SPECIALTY No. 4, (FRANK ROBERTS) **4.75**
Shrimp Imperial, Crab Lumps Imperial, Sun-Ripe Tomato stuffed with buttered Lobster Chunks, Jumbo Shrimp, Deep Sea Scallops, Creamy Slaw, French Fried Potatoes

COLD SEAFOOD SPECIALTY No. 5 .... **5.00**
Half Cold Lobster, Crab Lumps, Jumbo Shrimp, Cherrystone Clams on Half Shell, Creamy Slaw, Sliced Tomatoes

FRESH LOBSTER A La Newburg $4.95

Chunks of Fresh Steamed Lobster Meat Blended with Tasty Newburg Sauce, Served in Casserole, Potato, Mixed Green Salad with Choice of Dressing

FRESH LOBSTER THERMIDOR $4.85

Lobster Meat Sauted with Shallots, Sliced Mushrooms, Sherry Wine, then placed in ½ Lobster Shell, Topped with Grated Parmesan Cheese and Browned Under the Broiler, Served with Potato, Mixed Green Salad with Choice of Dressing

FRESH LOBSTER CHUNKS Saute $5.25

Large Chunks of Fresh Steamed Lobster Sauted in Fresh Creamery Butter, Served on Toast, on Hot Skillet, Hot Melted Butter Pan, Potato Mixed Green Salad with Choice of Dressing

FRESH MARYLAND LUMP CRAB $3.45
MEAT - A La Newburg

Choice Lumps Selected Fresh Crab Meat (pride of the house), Blended with Newburg Sauce, made with Pure Light Cream, Sherry Wine Seasoned to Perfection, Served in Casserole, Potato, Mixed Green Salad with Choice of Dressing

ALASKAN KING CRAB MEAT $3.35
Au Gratin

Chunks of King Crab Meat Sauted in Creamery Butter, Selected Seasoning Herbs

COLD SEA FOOD PLATTER $5.25

Half Cold Boiled Lobster, Shrimp with Mayonnaise, Crab Meat with Russian Dressing, Clams on Half Shell, Cocktail Sauce

COMBINATION FRY $3.50

Clams, Filet of Sole, or Oysters (in season) Scallops, Shrimp, Soft Shell Crab (in season) Breaded and Cooked to Individual Order, served with Potato, Chilled Cole Slaw, Home Made Tartar Sauce, and Lemon Wedge

FRESH SHELLED SEA FOOD $3.50
Au Gratin

Freshly Opened Clams, Fresh Deep Sea Scallops, Lobster, Crab Meat, Sauted in Creamery Butter, Selected Seasoning Herbs, Blended with Pure Sweet Cream, Sherry Wine, Served in Casserole, Topped with Grated Parmesan Cheese and Browned Under the Broilers, Potato, Mixed Green Salad with Choice of Dressing.

CLAMS CASINO $2.60

Freshly Opened Cherrystone Clams, Crispy Bacon, Diced Pimentos, Diced Green Peppers

FROM OUR SKILLET

Fresh Catfish and Hushpuppies

From the mighty waters of the Missouri River fresh catfish fried the Little Dixie way and served with fried potatoes, southern cole slaw and hot hush puppies.

2.25

Ozark Mountain Rainbow Trout

Shipped to us daily from the cold clear waters of our nearby Ozark streams, cooked Ozark style and served with a hot baked potato, our famous tossed salad, and plenty of hot corn muffins and fresh butter.

3.00

Whether fresh from the ocean or the local rivers, streams and lakes, good selling in words moves the product.

CRAB IMPERIAL
Large Lumps of Seasoned Backfin Crabmeat
Baked in a Scallop Shell
Try It — You'll Love It
4.25

CONTINENTAL SEAFOOD PLATTER
Crab or Oyster Bisque (in season) — Main Lobster
Tail — Stuffed Shrimp — Filet of Trout Almondine
Crab Imperial — Shrimp Rockefeller — Hearts of
Romaine — Susie Q Potatoes
5.50

FILET OF GULF TROUT ALMONDINE
Fresh Gulf Trout Sauteed in Butter and Covered
with Toasted Almonds
4.25

BONELESS STUFFED FLOUNDER
Stuffed with the Rich Meat of Crab and Shrimp
and Deftly Seasoned by Our Happy Chef
4.25

STUFFED SHRIMP
Fresh Jumbo Shrimp Stuffed with Deviled Crabmeat
Rolled in Fresh Bread Crumbs and Deep Fat Fried
Tartar Sauce
3.50

STUFFED CRAB
Only the Finest Backfin Lump Crabmeat Sauteed in
Sweet Cream Butter and Prepared with
that Special Touch of Our Happy Chef
3.50

MAINE LOBSTER TAILS
Three (3) Broiled — Drawn Butter
7.95

FRESH SPRING CHICKEN LIVERS
Sauteed in Sweet Cream Butter — Almond Rice
3.15

GIANT MUSHROOM CAPS
Filled with Seasoned Gulf Shrimp Stuffing and
Fine Herb Sauce — Spiced Crabapple
3.25

FRESH ICED WHITE LUMP CRABMEAT
Red or Remoulade Sauce — This Crabmeat Is
Picked Daily Just 80 Miles from Houston
3.50

CRABMEAT AU GRATIN EN CASSEROLE
Lumps of White Crabmeat Topped with
Toasted Cheese
3.75

RED SNAPPER STEAK PONTCHARTRAIN
One of Our True Seafood Delicacies Is This Fine
Preparation — Filet of Red Snapper Sauteed in
Brown Butter and Topped with Fresh Crabmeat,
Shrimp and Lobster
4.95

CRABMEAT SAUTE ROYALE
No Rich Sauce, No Abundance of Seasoning to
Overpower the Delicate Flavor of the Crabmeat —
We Saute in Butter Only the Backfin Lump and
Added Just Enough Zest to Make This a
Gourmet's Delight — Served with Seafood Pilaff Rice
4.25

CRAB LORENZO
Delicately Seasoned Lump Crabmeat on Holland
Rusk, Tópped wih Sauce Hollandaise
3.50

FLORIDA LOBSTER
One-half Florida Lobster Broiled in Butter Sauce.
A Real Seafood Delight
4.25

STUFFED RED SNAPPER STEAK
Stuffed with Delicately Seasoned Crabmeat, Topped
with Boiled Shrimp, Baked in Lemon Butter
4.50

This is not just adequate seafood copy, but complete descriptive explanations.

DINNER   A LA CARTE

*Baked Filet of Sole 4.25   3.50

Baby filets stuffed and served with Lobster Sauce.

#5 Pouilly-Fuissé—$4.50   Almaden Chenin Blanc—$2.25

*Broiled Swordfish or Halibut Steak 4.75   4.00

Thick center cuts broiled and served with hot butter sauce.

#7 Macon Superior—$4.00   Paul Masson Chablis—$2.50

*Baked Stuffed Jumbo Shrimp . 5.25   4.50

Large chunky shrimps stuffed with scallops and fresh bread crumbs, seasoned with cheddar cheese and laced with sherry wine.

#10 Liebfraumilch—$4.00   Paul Masson Emerald Dry—$2.50

*Broiled or Fried Baby Sea Scallops 4.85   4.10

These scallops come to us from down the Atlantic Coast and are fried or broiled as desired.

#9 Traminer—$4.50   Almaden Gewurtztraminer—$3.00

*Broiled Boston Schrod . . . 3.65   2.90

A tender filet of the traditional New England baby Cod served with lemon butter.

#5 Pouilly-Fuissé—$4.50   Almaden Chenin Blanc—$2.25

Crabmeat Remick 5.25   4.50

Alaskan King Crabmeat in casserole topped with a tangy sauce and bacon browned under broiler.

#7 Macon Superior—$4.00   Paul Masson Pinot Blanc—$3.00

Alaskan King Crabmeat . . . 5.50   4.75

Boiled Crabmeat Chunks served in hot creamery butter on toast points.

#8 Chablis Vaillon—$6.50   Almaden Pinot Chardonnay—$3.00

*Baked Stuffed Lobster in Casserole 6.50   5.75

Lobster meat baked with fresh bread dressing, butter and cheddar cheese.

#12 Soave Bolla—$3.00   Paul Masson Emerald Dry—$2.50

Lobster Newburg in Casserole . 6.50   5.75

Chunks of lobster meat served on toast in a sauce of sherry, cream and egg yolks in casserole.

#8 Chablis Vaillon—$6.50   Paul Masson Pinot Blanc—$3.00

*Broiled Large Maine Lobster . on request

Ocean fresh lobster from the cold waters of Maine, stuffed with our own dressing and drawn butter, approx. 1½ lb.

#8 Chablis Vallion—$6.50   Almaden Pinot Chardonnay—$3.00

In addition to good descriptive copy, this seafood listing suggests an imported and an American wine to go with each entree.

Seafood

South African Lobster Tail **$4.25**
Broiled or perhaps for something different "Maine Style", breaded and then fried to the correct doneness

Fresh Fillet of Flounder, Lemon Butter **$3.25**
A delicacy of the sea, broiled or deep fried as you may desire

Sauteed Shrimp in Garlic Butter **$3.50**
The zesty garlic butter brings out the best in this epicurean treat from the sea

Crabmeat Casserole **$3.00**
Fresh lump backfin crabmeat served either hot in brown butter or cold with cocktail sauce

Benetz Inn Stuffed Shrimp **$3.00**
Jumbo shrimp stuffed with our famous deviled crab stuffing

Deviled Crab **$2.50**
Our own recipe prepared with skill and care

Fillet of Haddock **$2.50**
Broiled or fried and served with tartar sauce and lemon wedge

Fried Jumbo Shrimp **$2.50**
Served with tartar or cocktail sauce

Rocky Mountain Brook Trout, Meuniere Butter . . . **$3.75**
Meuniere butter is a delicious mixture of brown butter, lemon juice, and parsley. A worthy complement to the delicious trout

Seafood Combination **$4.00**
For the seafood enthusiast, Lobster Tail, Jumbo Shrimp, Fillet of Haddock, Scallops, and our Deviled Crab

Deep Sea Scallops **$2.75**
Tender scallops broiled or deep fried to suit your fancy

Appropriate graphics help to distinguish this appetizing seafood listing.

THE BREAKFAST MENU

Whether it is a part of your regular menu or a separate menu, plan your breakfast menu with care and imagination. Not every food service operation serves breakfast, but those who do should give more time and attention to the breakfast menu. It can influence sales just as effectively as a Luncehon or Dinner Menu. If the Breakfast Menu is a separate menu, make it large, set the type large and bold. If your Breakfast Menu is part of your regular Luncheon or Dinner Menu, do not crowd it in with other items so that it becomes hard to find and hard to read. Generally, a completely separate panel of the menu is required for an average breakfast listing.

One of the best solutions for the Breakfast Menu as part of the general menu is to print it on the back cover. This usually provides enough room for listing the average size Breakfast Menu (25 to 35 line items, including beverages), and, in addition, the extra colors used in printing the cover design can be carried over to the back cover at no additional cost since it is part of the same press run.

Most of the time, however, a complete, separate Breakfast Menu is the best solution for a good, effective, selling menu. It is an extra cost, but, like most things done right, it pays off. The exception is when the Breakfast Menu listing is served 24 hours or all of the hours the restaurant is open. Then, obviously, the Breakfast Menu must be part of the general menu. In connection with this hours of service question, be sure to always list the hours (and days, if you are not open every day of the week) that breakfast is served.

The average breakfast menu breaks down into the following subheadings or classifications:

1. Fruits and Juices
2. Cereals
    a. Dry cereals
    b. Hot cereals
3. Toast, Rolls, French Toast
4. Eggs
5. Egg Combinations or Specials
6. Omelettes
7. Side Orders
8. Pancakes
9. Waffles
10. Children's Breakfast
11. Beverages

Using these headings and setting them in a different, bolder or unusual type face (script, for example) will make the breakfast menu easy to read and easy to use in ordering. Do not run different types of breakfast items together (Eggs, Pancakes and Rolls, for example). Specials or Egg Combinations that come under the heading or category of Complete Breakfasts should get special treatment on the menu. They should get top billing because they are the biggest profit items and are what you want to sell the most.

Give the Special Complete Breakfast Combinations the best position on the menu; set them in the largest, boldest type and give them the most descriptive, merchandising, sell copy. Setting these listings in a panel or giving them large numbers—No. 1, No. 2, No. 3—is a common way of making them stand out and catch the customer's eye. After all, when a breakfast entree includes a small steak and costs $2.00 or more, it deserves better treatment than a 20¢ glass of orange juice.

A couple of Breakfast Menu listings that are not often included, but that should be because they are good merchandising, are the Children's Breakfast and the Low Calorie-High Protein Breakfast. If you have a Children's Menu or Kiddie Korner on your regular menu, it stands to reason that this listing should be on your Breakfast Menu. And a Low Calorie-High Protein Breakfast listing will sell a meal to the adult customer who otherwise would just order a cup of coffee.

When creating your Breakfast Menu, be sure to list everything you serve. Do not list "Juices," list each variety. Also, do not just list "Cereals," dry or hot, list the individual cereals, and, in the case of omelettes, do likewise. The rule should be if you make it in your kitchen or have it in your refrigerator or store room, list it on your Breakfast Menu.

A study of the number of items listed on the Breakfast Menu shows that the most popular number is in the 25 to 35 bracket (including beverages). However, the size of the Breakfast Menu varies enormously from a low of only five items to a high of over 60 items. So it is obvious that breakfast business can be large or small. But large or small, a careful, readable, imaginative listing will help to make it more profitable.

HOW BIG — THE BREAKFAST MENU?

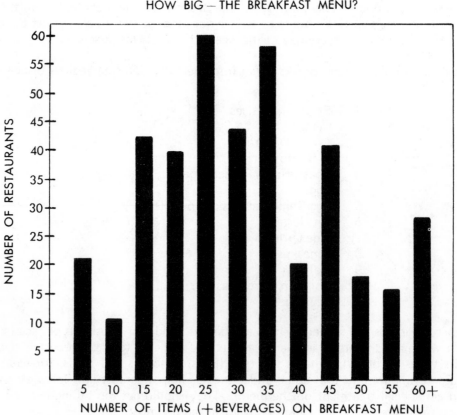

Eggs Hussarde 1.75
    Marchand de Vin Sauce over grilled ham and tomato on toast. Poached eggs and Hollandaise sauce.

Eggs Benedict 1.50
    Broiled ham and poached eggs on crisp toast. Hollandaise sauce.

Eggs Sardou 1.75
    Artichoke bottoms, poached eggs, creamed spinach and Hollandaise sauce.

Eggs St. Denis 1.50
    Souffled eggs and chopped ham served on croutons. Marchand de Vin sauce.

Eggs a la Turk 1.75
    Shirred eggs with chicken livers, fresh mushrooms and red wine.

Eggs Bourguignonne 2.00
    Omelette with escargots and vegetables. Red wine sauce.

Eggs aux Fines Herbes 1.00
    Omelette with finely chopped onions and parsley.

Eggs aux Champignons 1.00
    Omelette with fresh mushrooms.

There are eggs and there are eggs. This listing is distinctive copy—out of the ordinary.

"A TRADITIONAL
BRENNAN BREAKFAST

This is the way it was done in leisured antebellum days: first an absinthe *Suissesse* to get the eyes open, then a fresh Creole cream cheese. Now an egg Benedict, followed by a hearty sirloin with fresh mushrooms. Hot French bread and marmalade, and a chilled Rose wine. For the finale, *crepes Suzette, cafe au lait,* and a Cognac snifter. Important:

DON'T HURRY!"

A real gourmet breakfast.

Ready-to-Serve Breakfast

Orange Juice
Scrambled Eggs
Crisp Bacon
Hash Browned Potatoes
Toast or Sweet Roll
Beverage

$1.75

FAMILY PLATTER

SERVES FOUR

FRUIT JUICES
SCRAMBLED EGGS
BACON AND SAUSAGE
GOLDEN BROWN PANCAKES
BUCKWHEAT CAKES
BUTTERMILK PANCAKES
IOWA CORN CAKES
BEVERAGE

4.95

Each Additional Person 1.20
No Substitutions

Chuck Wagon Breakfast

Fruit Juice or
Hot or Cold Cereal
Ham and Eggs,
Hominy Grits or
Hash Browned Potatoes
Toast or Sweet Roll
Beverage

$1.95

Specials can be featured on the breakfast also.

Americana Special

No. 1 ONE TENDER HOT CAKE JOINED WITH AN EGG SURROUNDED BY A STRIP OF BACON AND A SAUSAGE LINK. CAPPED WITH A HOMEMADE BISCUIT WITH BUTTER. ALL THE COFFEE YOU WANT. .$1.25

New England Hearty

No. 2 CITRUS FRUIT FROM THE SOUTH, TENDER HAM SLICE, TWO EGGS, COOKED ANY STYLE, HOT BISCUITS WITH BUTTER, HOT COFFEE. $1.60

Traditional Favorite

No. 3 A TALL WELL CHILLED GLASS OF TOMATO JUICE, BOWL OF HOT OR COLD CEREAL, A TASTY SWEET ROLL AND HOT COFFEE. . .$1.00

From Grandmother's Kitchen

No. 4 A COMBINATION OF TENDER HOT CAKES WITH HAM OR SAUSAGE LINKS, TOPPED WITH MELTED BUTTER AND WARM MAPLE SYRUP. A CUP OF FRESHLY BREWED COFFEE. $1.35

OUR
QUICK SERVICE
SPECIAL

CHILLED ORANGE JUICE
CHOICE OF FRESH, CRISP CEREAL
BUTTERED TOAST OR SWEET ROLL
FRESH HOT COFFEE

85c

GR-R-REAT! FOR KIDS
(of all ages)

CHILLED JUICE
SUGAR FROSTED FLAKES
ONE SLICE OF TOAST
WITH JELLY
HOT CHOCOLATE OR MILK

70c

**LOW CALORIE—
HIGH PROTEIN BREAKFAST**
(LESS THAN 450 CALORIES!)
ORANGE JUICE
SPECIAL K
(PROTEIN CEREAL) WITH MILK
ONE EGG, ANY STYLE
WHITE TOAST (1 SLICE)
BLACK COFFEE

90c

Special combinations, color photos, low calorie and children's items plus quick service help to sell extras on the breakfast menu.

This breakfast menu includes combinations, an Old-Fashioned Southern Breakfast plus a complete a la carte listing that features fish and meats—not an ordinary breakfast listing.

THE RICHMOND SPECIAL

No. 1   **.95**

Fruit or Juice
Griddle Cakes or Waffles
with
Hot Maple Syrup, Marmalade or Honey
Coffee   Tea   Milk

No 2   **1.10**

Fruit, Cereal or Juice
Choice of
Two Eggs (Any Style)
or
One Egg with Ham, Bacon or Sausage
Assorted Rolls or Buttered Toast
Coffee   Tea   Milk

No. 3   **1.30**

Fresh Fruit in Season or Juice
Hot or Cold Cereal
Choice of
Two Eggs (Any Style)
with
Broiled Ham, Bacon or Sausage Cakes
or
Buckwheat Cakes with Sausage
Assorted Rolls or Buttered Toast
Coffee   Tea   Milk

OLD FASHION SOUTHERN BREAKFAST

No. 4   **1.50**

Fresh Fruit in Season or Juice
Hot or Cold Cereal
Choice of
Hominy Grits and Smoked Ham
with Two Eggs (Any Style)
or
Smithfield Ham and Eggs
Assorted Rolls or Buttered Toast
Coffee   Tea   Milk

BREAKFAST

SERVED FROM 7:00 UNTIL NOON

FRUITS

Sliced Oranges .35
Half Grapefruit .35
Fruit Compote .40
Stewed Prunes .35
Sliced Bananas .40
Berries or Melons
in Season

CONTINENTAL BREAKFAST

Fruit Juice
Assorted Rolls, Toast or
Sweet Rolls
Marmalade
Coffee   Tea   Milk
70¢

JUICES

Grapefruit .30
Orange .30
(double) .55
V-8 Juice .30
Prune .30
Pineapple .30
Tomato .30

CEREALS AND CAKES

Hot or Cold Cereal (Served with Cream) .35
Old Dominion Buckwheat Cakes .55   French Toast .50
Griddle Cakes .50   Waffles with Hot Maple Syrup .50

EGGS

Boiled (2) .45   Scrambled .55   Fried (2) .55
Poached on Toast .50   Plain Omelette .75
Bacon and Eggs .95   Spanish Omelette .75
Smithfield Ham Omelette 1.00
Garniture of Chicken Livers, Sausage, Bacon or Ham .40

FISH

Kippered Herring .70   Boiled Salt Mackerel .70
Fried Cod Fish Cakes with Bacon .75
Salt Roe Herring .65   Broiled Filet of Flounder .60

MEATS

Broiled Smithfield Ham 1.40   Hickory Smoked Bacon .75
Sausage Cakes or Links .85   Broiled Ham 1.20
Chipped Beef in Cream .95   Lamb Chop 1.30
Calves Liver with Bacon or Onions 1.50
Pork Chop 1.25   Breakfast Steak 1.75

POTATOES

Fried Hash Brown or Saute .35
Hashed in Cream, Au Gratin or Lyonnaise .35

BREADS

Dry or Buttered Toast .20   Cinnamon Toast .30
Danish Pastry .25   Hard or Soft Rolls .20

PRESERVES

Orange Marmalade .20   Currant Jelly .20
Apricot Jam .20   Strawberry Preserves .20
Apple Butter .20

BEVERAGES

Coffee .20   Hot Chocolate .30

Sanka .25   Buttermilk .20   Tea .20   Milk .20

A truly Gourmet Breakfast awaits you!

ONE GUN SALUTE
One egg, bacon or sausage and hashed brown potatoes .... .95

TWO GUN SALUTE
Two eggs, bacon or sausage, hashed brown potatoes 1.25

SOUTHERN GENTLEMAN
Steak and two eggs, hashed brown potatoes 2.25

LEXINGTON
Baked corn beef hash
w/poached egg, hashed brown potatoes 1.25

THE VIRGINIAN
Ham and eggs w/hashed brown potatoes 1.35

DIXIE FAVORITE
Center cut pork chop, two eggs, hashed brown potatoes 1.45

THE ILLINOIAN
Shirred eggs and little
pork sausage, hashed brown potatoes 1.25

THE KENTUCKIAN
Shirred eggs
w/ham or bacon, hashed brown potatoes 1.35

All the above orders served w/biscuits or toast and butter
Coffee til the Pot runs Dry

Glorious Pancakes

RAMADA WHEAT CAKES
Golden fluffy and light, begging for butter
and luscious maple syrup .... .60

GEORGIA PECAN CAKES
with the pecans baked right in the dough—
Country butter and maple syrup .... .75

LAND OF COTTON
Old time buckwheat cakes—The South's famous
buckwheat, whipped butter and maple syrup .... .60

DIXIE BACON CAKES
Golden, fluffy and light—Served with two strips of
bacon Dixie Style—Country butter, maple syrup .... .85

TENNESSEE MOUNTAIN STRAWBERRY CAKES
Wheat cakes topped with strawberries—'nuff said .... .95

SOUTH PACIFIC CAKES
Golden fluffy and light, topped with a grilled pineapple ring
begging for butter and luscious maple syrup .... .95

PIGLETS IN A BLANKET
Spicy little link sausages wrapped in a pancake coverlet .... .95

There's more than one way to serve eggs and pancakes.

CHILDREN'S MENU

Census figures show that the present median age of the country is 28 and going down. This means that 50 per cent of the population is 28 years or younger. A younger population is one that has had a narrower range of experience in time. The National Industrial Conference Board drew up a chart of the percentages of the American people, as of April 1, 1970, that had had no adult experience with the major events of the 20th Century. Here are some examples:

	%
World War I	93.0
Stock Market Crash	84.3
Mass Unemployment	70.9
World War II	66.0
Korean War	56.6
Pre-Space Age	52.0

In terms of the food service industry and your menu, what does this "youth explosion" mean? It means, first of all, that you will be having a great many new customers. They will probably never have had the experience of ordering a bottle of wine. And, most likely, they have never ordered a Chateaubriand. They might not be sure of the various cuts of steak—Sirloin, Porterhouse, Filet Mignon or the significance of the words U. S. Prime or U. S. Choice.

They will also probably never have ordered Capon or Lobster Thermidor, Long Island Duckling a la Orange or Grenadine of Beef Chasseur, etc., etc. The point is, for the customer whose experience does not include your cuisine, explanation is not just necessary, it is vital. You will be getting more and more customers who are gastronomic amateurs. And the menu, of course, is the logical place for this type of information. In fact, in most service restaurants, it is the only place.

If you are depending upon your waiters or waitresses to supply this information, you are leaning on a broken reed. Many of them are hard to educate. Your staff is constantly changing. And very often, a busy waiter or waitress does not have the time to explain the items on the menu. The answer is descriptive, merchandising, "how prepared," sell copy on the menu.

This does not mean long, flowery copy that takes a customer five minutes to wade through; but it does mean at least the facts as to what the entree, salad, dessert or drink is. It means taking as much time, thought and energy to describe your menu as your chef takes in preparing it. If you serve only hot dogs, hamburgers and malted milks, you have no problem. The big, new young generation was weaned on these items. But if you serve Cabernet Sauvignon, Tournedos a la Bernaise and Baba au Rhum, you have a language barrier that is confronting more of your customers than ever before.

Perhaps you think that your particular operation is not affected by "those who eat and drink young," because members of the barefoot, long-haired, guitar-playing set not only do not come to your restaurant, but are actively discouraged. But we are not just talking about "teen-agers." The population explosion in the balance of this decade will not be among babies or the elderly or even among teenagers. It will be in the 20-24 group which has soared

26.3 per cent from 13,700,000 in 1965 to 17,300,000 in 1970. The implication of this for the food service business is enormous.

If yours is a service restaurant serving liquor—cocktails, beer, wine, etc.—you know that you have a very large market that has few—and those few not very strong—drinking habits. This means that your drink listing and your wine list must do an extra job of informing and selling. It is either that or cutting down your bar service to beer, martinis and manhattans.

In a recent small survey made of steak listings on menus, it was discovered that 48 restaurants described their steaks with some copy (usually not very adequate), while 176 restaurants said nothing at all other than listing the name and price of the steak. And this is a situation existing for what are usually the most expensive entrees on the menu. Add this to the new factor of an enormous increase in new, young customers, and you can see that this is a critical area for menu improvement.

The nationality restaurant featuring a foreign cuisine—Italian, Greek, French, German, Chinese, etc.—has a built-in problem which needs even more explanation on the menu. Perhaps 20 or 50 years ago there were enough immigrants from these countries to read, understand and explain all the items on these specialized menus. But with the present All-American, TV educated, a Go-Go, young group, your menu may really be printed in a dead language. In fact, many adults with sophisticated eating and drinking habits have trouble with these menus. They list but they don't communicate.

In addition to the teen-age and young adult market and the problem of talking, writing and merchandising to them, there is the child market. If you operate a supper club type of restaurant where there are no children served, this does not concern you. But if you are a "family type" operation, this is a big concern.

Merchandising on the menu to this group (and their parents who pay the check) can be and is being done in three ways. First, you can say, "all items on this menu served in children's portions at a specified reduced price." Second, you can have a "Kiddie Korner" or children's menu printed as part of your regular menu. This is usually a short listing of special items, dinners or lunches of special appeal to children, at reduced prices. Or, finally, you can have a separate children's menu with only children's items listed on it.

This separate children's menu usually includes extra material besides the actual listing of food and prices, such as: a story, a puzzle or puzzles, games, or there is a secondary use for the menu, such as for a mask. Operations merchandising completely to children will include special children's desserts and favors or birthday presents.

Of the three methods of selling to children (and their parents), the separate children's menu is best. Next, the children's menu or "Kiddie Korner" listing as part of the regular menu can be very adequate and good merchandising if done well. The least satisfactory method is to suggest that all items on the menu can be served in children's portions. This is just not practical because a 14 oz. T-Bone steak cannot be cut down to 6 oz. and the average child will turn up his nose at Lobster Newburg regardless of the size of the portion.

Selling the youth market, whether children, teen-agers or young adults, will pay off for any food service operator, regardless of his cuisine. If a national soft drink merchandiser thinks it worth while to spend millions of dollars in advertising with the slogan, "for those who think young," it should certainly be worth the time and effort of the food service operator to take a look at his menu with "young eyes."

Daniel Boone and the Indians make a good child's menu theme.

KIDDIE KORNER

For Children Under 12 Years

SMALL SWISS STEAK	.90
CHICKEN SOUP	.40
BEEF STEW	.40
SMALL FILLET FISH	.70
FRIED CHICKEN	.90
FRENCH FRIED SHRIMP	1.00

Kiddie Korral

(For Children Under Twelve)

EENY — Two Savage Style Chicken Drumsticks
with French Fried Potatoes, Vegetable ...... .85

MEENY — Sliced White Meat of Turkey,
French Fried Potatoes, Vegetable .... .90

MINEY — Ground Beef Pattie, French Fried
Potatoes, Vegetable .... .75

MO — Three Fried Jumbo Shrimp, French Fried
Potatoes, Tartar Sauce 1.25
Served with Roll and Butter

JANS "JOE" "JO" — Ground Beef Pattie,
Served on Toasted Bun with Mustard
or Mayonnaise and Lettuce, and Tomato .... .50

Using Kiddie Korner, Kiddie Korral or some other name and combining it with a special selection of food items at a special price makes part of the menu sell children—and their parents.

For the Children...

"Hansel"

Fruit Cocktail, Royal
GOLDEN FRIED CHICKEN DRUMETTE
with Cranberry Sauce
Whipped Potatoes   Vegetable
Ice Cream   —   Milk

1.95

"Gretel"

Soup or Tomato Juice
BROILED CHOPPED BEEF STEAK
French Fries   Vegetable
Ice Cream   —   Milk

1.95

Masks and games make good children's menus.

Appetizers

Melon Balls in Cascades Syrup   .50

V-8 or Tomato Juice   .35   Soup du Jour   .40

Entrees

Half Breast of Chicken, Pennsylvania German
   Style, with Local Ham, Served with Choice
   of Two Vegetables, Salad, and a Flute of
   Bread 2.50

Chopped Beef Steak on Toasted English Muffin,
   Served with French Fried Potatoes, Sliced
   Onion and Tomato 1.75

Duck Pilaf with Hot Curried Fruit, Served with
   One Vegetable and a Salad 2.00

Children's Portion of Roast Rib of Beef, Served
   with a Baked Potato, One Vegetable, Salad,
   and a Flute of Bread 3.00

Desserts

Please Refer to the Regular Menu

Beverages

Coca Cola, Fresca,   Lime or Lemonade . .30
Grapeade, or Fanta   Milk or Skim Milk . .20
Root Beer 15   Buttermilk 20
          Iced Tea 25

*The children's menu can be a la carte and include appe-
tizers, desserts and beverages as well as entrees that do
not have to be the usual hamburgers.*

THE HOSPITAL MENU

The hospital menu presents a special communications problem. Unlike the regular menu which must sell as well as tell and try to merchandise the food and drink list, the hospital menu must be (1) functional, (2) economical, (3) act as a public relations media, and (4) operate within special diet requirements.

The menus of the New York University Medical Center shown here meet all of these requirements, and, in addition, attractive and appropriate artwork helps to brighten up an otherwise rather plain menu. It is a three-fold, three-panel menu with one panel for each meal—breakfast, lunch and dinner. The folds are perforated so that the panel for each meal can be torn off and used separately. And different colored stock is used for each day for easy identification.

One side of the menu, the side with the illustrations of various hospital food service personnel "doing their thing", is pre-printed in quantities on a light weight (60 lb.) inexpensive paper. On the other side the captions Breakfast, Lunch and Dinner are printed with a line of instruction copy which reads, "THIS IS YOUR MENU FOR TOMORROW. Please CIRCLE all food items you desire for each meal. Only the foods circled will be served on your tray. Please complete by 10:30 A. M." This results (within dietary restrictions) in the patient ordering only what he feels he can and will eat and cuts down on food waste.

Across the bottom the words DIET, BED NO. and NAME with appropriate spaces are left for the patient to fill out. The words "NO SUBSTITUTIONS CAN BE MADE WITHOUT SPECIFIC ARRANGEMENTS WITH THE DIETITIAN," plus "Menu subject to change without notice," are printed. This is the entire pre-printed portion of the menu.

The daily listing can then be done by electric typewriter and printed within the hospital. Considering the complicated and extensive food service requirements of even a modest size hospital (a hospital must serve three meals a day, 365 days a year, with no days off), the selection offered is generous. Two juices, one fruit, three cereals and two types of eggs plus beverages and pastry are offered for breakfast. And for lunch and dinner, soup or appetizer, two entrees, two and three vegetables, salad plus three or four desserts are offered.

With a generous selection of breads, rolls and beverages, the patient selects the food and drink he likes and the monotony plus "institutional" flavor of the meals is avoided. With wine even being offered in some hospitals, the food service in today's modern hospital has kept up with the developments in contemporary medicine.

DRAWING BY RICHARD TOMLINSON

New York University Medical Center

THIS IS YOUR MENU FOR TOMORROW. Please CIRCLE all food items you desire for each meal. Only the foods circled will be served on your tray.   Please complete by 10:30 A.M.

Breakfast M-3
THURSDAY, APRIL 24, 1969

Lunch M-3
THURSDAY, APRIL 24, 1969

Dinner M-3
THURSDAY, APRIL 24, 1969

Breakfast	Lunch	Dinner
ORANGE JUICE PEAR NECTAR	CREAM OF ASPARAGUS CHICKEN BROTH SF/FF SOUP, SF	CREAM OF MUSHROOM BEEF BROTH SOUP, SF SF/FF
UNSWEETENED SLICED PEACHES		TOMATO JUICE, SF
MALTEX, SF FARINA, SF	ROAST LEG OF LAMB SF/FF UNSWEETENED JELLY	ROAST SIRLOIN OF BEEF AU JUS SF/FF
SPECIAL K PUFFED RICE	BRAISED BEEF CUBES SF/FF	BROILED CHOPPED
	PARSLIED POTATOES SF/FF	BAKED IDAHO POTATO
	PIMIENTO WAX BEANS SF/FF	WHIPPED POTATOES SF/FF
	SLICED BEETS SF/FF	BROCCOLI SPEARS SF/FF
SCRAMBLED EGGS, SF		MASHED SQUASH SF/FF
EGGS, SOFT OR HARD COOKED (ONE OR TWO)	ESCAROLE AND ROMAINE SALAD FRENCH DRESSING SF/FF	MOLDED PINEAPPLE SALAD MAYONNAISE, SF
	SPICED CUP CAKE, SF	WHOLE PEELED APRICOTS
HARD ROLL	UNSWEETENED WHOLE PEELED APRICOTS	UNSWEETENED APPLESAUCE
	FRESH FRUIT IN SEASON	FRESH FRUIT IN SEASON

TOAST	COFFEE	MILK		COTTAGE CHEESE SF FF		MILK		COFFEE	COTTAGE CHEESE SF FF		MILK		COFFEE
WHITE SF	SANKA	SKIM MILK	TEA	WHITE SF	SOUR CREAM	SKIM MILK	TEA	SANKA	WHITE SF	SOUR CREAM	SKIM MILK	TEA	SANKA
RYE	BUTTER	BUTTERMILK	LEMON SUGAR	RYE	BUTTER	BUTTERMILK	LEMON SUGAR	JELLO SF	RYE	BUTTER	BUTTERMILK	LEMON SUGAR	JELLO SF
WHOLE WHEAT	SWEET BUTTER	LOW SODIUM MILK	SUGAR SUBSTITUTE	WHOLE WHEAT	SWEET BUTTER	LOW SODIUM MILK	SUGAR SUBSTITUTE	JUNKET	WHOLE WHEAT	SWEET BUTTER	LOW SODIUM MILK	SUGAR SUBSTITUTE	JUNKET
SOFT ROLL	DIETETIC JELLY	CREAM		SOFT ROLL	DIETETIC JELLY	CREAM		CUSTARD	SOFT ROLL	DIETETIC JELLY	CREAM		CUSTARD

NO SUBSTITUTION CAN BE MADE WITHOUT SPECIFIC ARRANGEMENTS WITH THE DIETITIAN.

Menu subject to change without notice.   Menu subject to change without notice.   Menu subject to change without notice.

DIET _____   DIET _____   DIET _____

BED NO. _____ NAME _____   BED NO. _____ NAME _____   BED NO. _____ NAME _____

This menu meets the four stated requirements of a hospital listing and in an attractive format as well.

DRAWING BY RICHARD TOMLINSON

New York University Medical Center

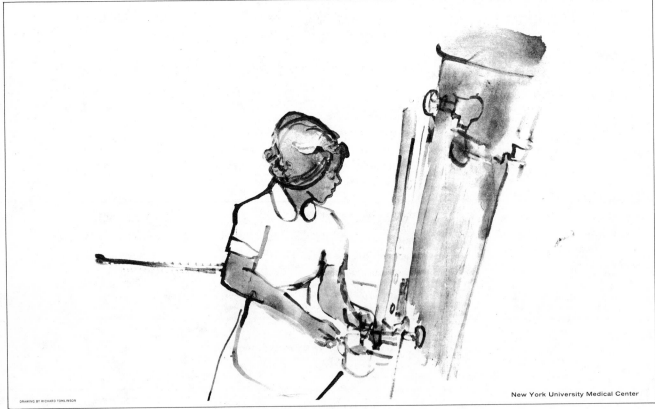

DRAWING BY RICHARD TOMLINSON

New York University Medical Center

THIS IS YOUR MENU FOR TOMORROW. Please CIRCLE all food items you desire for each meal. Only the foods circled will be served on your tray.   Please complete by 10:30 A.M.

Breakfast M-3
SATURDAY,   APRIL 26, 1969

Lunch M-3
SATURDAY,   APRIL 26, 1969

Dinner M-3
SATURDAY,   APRIL 26, 1969

Breakfast	Lunch	Dinner
ORANGE JUICE GRAPE JUICE	CREAM OF PEA BEEF BROTH SOUP, STRAINED	CREAM OF CELERY CHICKEN BROTH SOUP, STRAINED
PRUNE JUICE	BOILED BEEF, CUT	GRAPEFRUIT JUICE BOILED CHICKEN, CUT
FARINA	BROILED LAMB PATTY STRAINED OR MINCED BEEF	BROILED CHOPPED STEAK STRAINED OR MINCED CHICKEN
RICE KRISPIES	BOILED POTATO WHIPPED POTATOES GREEN PEAS PUREED GREEN PEAS MASHED SQUASH	BAKED IDAHO POTATO FLUFFY RICE ASPARAGUS TIPS PUREED ASPARAGUS WAX BEANS PUREED WAX BEANS
SCRAMBLED EGGS CRISP BACON EGGS, SOFT OR HARD COOKED (ONE OR TWO) HARD ROLL (NO SEEDS)	CINNAMON COOKIES BAKED VANILLA CUSTARD BUTTERSCOTCH PUDDING	POUND CAKE ORANGE ICE LEMON SNOW WITH CUSTARD SAUCE

Breakfast				Lunch					Dinner				
	COFFEE	MILK	TEA		COFFEE			COFFEE					COFFEE
HARD ROLL	SANKA	SKIM MILK	LEMON	COTTAGE CHEESE	MILK	TEA		SANKA	COTTAGE CHEESE	MILK		TEA	SANKA
WHITE	BUTTER	BUTTERMILK	SUGAR		SOUR CREAM	SKIM MILK	LEMON	JELLO		SOUR CREAM	SKIM MILK	LEMON	JELLO
SOFT ROLL	JELLY	CREAM	SUGAR SUBSTITUTE	WHITE	BUTTER	BUTTERMILK	SUGAR	JUNKET	WHITE	BUTTER	BUTTERMILK	SUGAR	JUNKET
				SOFT ROLL	JELLY	CREAM	SUGAR SUBSTITUTE	CUSTARD	SOFT ROLL	JELLY	CREAM	SUGAR SUBSTITUTE	CUSTARD

NO SUBSTITUTION CAN BE MADE WITHOUT SPECIFIC ARRANGEMENTS WITH THE DIETITIAN.

Menu subject to change without notice.   Menu subject to change without notice.   Menu subject to change without notice.

DIET ____ Low Residue   Bland   Soft ____   DIET ____ Low Residue   Bland   Soft ____   DIET ____ Low Residue   Bland   Soft ____

BED NO. _____ NAME _____   BED NO. _____ NAME _____   BED NO. _____ NAME _____

THIS IS YOUR MENU FOR TOMORROW. Please CIRCLE all food items you desire for each meal. Only the foods circled will be served on your tray.   Please complete by 10:30 A.M.

Breakfast M-3
SATURDAY,   APRIL 26, 1969

Lunch M-3
SATURDAY,   APRIL 26, 1969

Dinner M-3
SATURDAY,   APRIL 26, 1969

Breakfast	Lunch	Dinner
ORANGE JUICE GRAPE JUICE	FRENCH ONION SOUP	GRAPEFRUIT JUICE
KADOTA FIGS	BOILED BEEF WITH MUSTARD SAUCE SPICED HAM WITH RAISIN SAUCE	CHICKEN FRICASSEE STUFFED PEPPER WITH TOMATO SAUCE
PETTIJOHN FARINA	PARSLIED POTATOES	PARSLIED RICE
RICE KRISPIES· PUFFED WHEAT	WHIPPED POTATOES GREEN PEAS BUTTERED YELLOW SQUASH	BAKED IDAHO POTATO BUTTERED ASPARAGUS SPEARS CAULIFLOWER
SCRAMBLED EGGS CRISP BACON EGGS, SOFT OR HARD COOKED (ONE OR TWO)	PICKLED BEETS	CHEF'S SALAD BLEU CHEESE DRESSING
DANISH PASTRY	WALNUT BROWNIE BARTLETT PEAR HALVES IN SYRUP FRESH FRUIT IN SEASON	DEEP DISH CHERRY PIE ORANGE ICE GRAPEFRUIT SECTIONS FRESH FRUIT IN SEASON

Breakfast				Lunch				Dinner			
HARD ROLL			COFFEE				COFFEE				COFFEE
WHITE		MILK	SANKA	WHITE		MILK	SANKA	WHITE		MILK	SANKA
RYE	BUTTER	SKIM MILK	TEA	RYE	BUTTER	SKIM MILK	TEA	RYE	BUTTER	SKIM MILK	TEA
WHOLE WHEAT	SWEET BUTTER	BUTTERMILK	LEMON	WHOLE WHEAT	SWEET BUTTER	BUTTERMILK	LEMON	WHOLE WHEAT	SWEET BUTTER	BUTTERMILK	LEMON
SOFT ROLL	JELLY	CREAM	SUGAR	SOFT ROLL	JELLY	CREAM	SUGAR	SOFT ROLL	JELLY	CREAM	SUGAR

NO SUBSTITUTION CAN BE MADE WITHOUT SPECIFIC ARRANGEMENTS WITH THE DIETITIAN.

Menu subject to change without notice.   Menu subject to change without notice.   Menu subject to change without notice.

DIET _____   DIET _____   DIET _____

BED NO. _____ NAME _____   BED NO. _____ NAME _____   BED NO. _____ NAME _____

DRAWING BY RICHARD TOMLINSON   NEW YORK UNIVERSITY MEDICAL CENTER

THIS IS YOUR MENU FOR TOMORROW. Please CIRCLE all food items you desire for each meal. Only the foods circled will be served on your tray.   Please complete by 10:30 A.M.

Breakfast M-3
FRIDAY,   APRIL 25, 1969

ORANGE JUICE   BLENDED JUICE

UNSWEETENED STEWED MIXED FRUIT

FARINA, SF

CORNFLAKES   SF   PEP

EGGS, SOFT OR HARD COOKED
(ONE OR TWO)

HARD ROLL

TOAST	COFFEE	MILK	
WHITE SF	SANKA	SKIM MILK	TEA
RYE	BUTTER	BUTTERMILK	LEMON
			SUGAR
WHOLE WHEAT	SWEET BUTTER	LOW SODIUM MILK	SUGAR
SOFT ROLL	DIETETIC JELLY	CREAM	SUBSTITUTE

Menu subject to change without notice.

DIET _____

BED NO. _____ NAME _____

Lunch M-3
FRIDAY,   APRIL 25, 1969

CREAM OF TOMATO   CHICKEN CONSOMME
SOUP, SF   SF/FF

BAKED HALIBUT STEAK   SF/FF
LEMON WEDGE
ROAST LEG OF VEAL   SF/FF

WHIPPED POTATOES   SF/FF

CHOPPED SPINACH   SF/FF

BABY LIMA BEANS   SF/FF

MARINATED CUCUMBER SALAD

RASPBERRY ICE

UNSWEETENED FRUIT COCKTAIL

FRESH FRUIT IN SEASON

COTTAGE CHEESE SF FF		MILK		COFFEE
			TEA	
WHITE SF	SOUR CREAM	SKIM MILK	LEMON	SANKA
RYE	BUTTER	BUTTERMILK	SUGAR	JELLO SF
WHOLE WHEAT	SWEET BUTTER	LOW SODIUM MILK	SUGAR	JUNKET
SOFT ROLL	DIETETIC JELLY	CREAM	SUBSTITUTE	CUSTARD

NO SUBSTITUTION CAN BE MADE WITHOUT SPECIFIC ARRANGEMENTS WITH THE DIETITIAN.

Menu subject to change without notice.

DIET _____

BED NO. _____ NAME _____

Dinner M-3
FRIDAY,   APRIL 25, 1969

CREAM OF VEGETABLE   BEEF BOUILLON
SOUP, SF   SF/FF

APPLE JUICE

POACHED FILET OF SOLE   SF/FF
LEMON WEDGE

BROILED MINUTE STEAK   SF/FF

BAKED IDAHO POTATO

JULIENNE GREEN BEANS   SF/FF

DICED CARROTS   SF/FF

LETTUCE AND TOMATO SALAD
FRENCH DRESSING   SF/FF

FRUIT COCKTAIL

UNSWEETENED SLICED PEACHES

FRESH FRUIT IN SEASON

COTTAGE CHEESE SF FF		MILK		COFFEE
			TEA	
WHITE SF	SOUR CREAM	SKIM MILK	LEMON	SANKA
RYE	BUTTER	BUTTERMILK	SUGAR	JELLO SF
WHOLE WHEAT	SWEET BUTTER	LOW SODIUM MILK	SUGAR	JUNKET
SOFT ROLL	DIETETIC JELLY	CREAM	SUBSTITUTE	CUSTARD

Menu subject to change without notice.

DIET _____

BED NO. _____ NAME _____

SANDWICHES

Most menus list some sandwiches and some list a great number. How you list your sandwiches depends upon what portion of your business they constitute or how important they are. For a menu that features big entree items almost exclusively, sandwiches are almost a nuisance item and should be listed accordingly. They should be listed in smaller type on a separate page or panel away from the entree listing. On this kind of a menu, a good place for the sandwich listing is the back page, panel or cover with Late Evening Snacks.

If sandwiches are not big on your menu (on purpose), be sure they are listed in smaller type with less copy than your entrees. Basically you want the customer to order an expensive entree, not a moderately priced sandwich. If, however, sandwiches constitute an important part of your menu as money-makers and traffic builders, your listing should be of a different character.

You should then give sandwiches comparable billing to your entrees—good position, large, bold type and good descriptive copy. Even in this kind of sandwich listing, however, you should not give all of your sandwiches the same treatment. Some should get special listing, usually in a box or panel with even larger, bolder type and more descriptive copy. The selection of which sandwiches to feature should be on the basis of: (1) which are the favorites with the public and (2) which are the bigger profit sandwiches.

Prices on sandwiches can vary from a $2.00—$3.00 steak sandwich that is really an entree item, to a 15¢—20¢ hamburger that is basically a snack item. The hamburger is usually featured because it is a popular item, while the steak sandwich is both popular and a good profit item. It is obvious, however, that the sandwich listing on many a menu is guess listing made on the basis of what the food service operator thinks is a good list. The only good list for any operation is a list that "works"; that is, gets ordered by the public. A "dead" sandwich should not be on any menu. A main division in listing sandwiches, other than Specials, is between Hot Sandwiches and Cold Sandwiches, the usual difference being that more expensive (entree type) items should get bigger billing, again, larger, bolder type and more descriptive copy.

Of the 278 restaurant menus studied (see Charts 1 and 2), 208 had some sandwiches listed. Only 70 had no sandwiches listed at all, showing that sandwiches are popular on the menu (perhaps too popular in relation to their profit value) on a basis of 3 to 1 when compared to the menu with no sandwiches at all. The number of different sandwiches listed on the menu varies from only one to 35 (15 restaurants listed 35 different sandwiches).

The wide range in the number of sandwiches listed on the menu, from 70 with no sandwiches at all listed to 35 with 20 or more listed, indicates that how many sandwiches you list in your operation is a highly individual problem. The size of your sandwich list should obviously be tailored to your particular market.

As for sandwich popularity, as indicated by how often they are listed on the menu (see Chart 2), there are no real surprises. The 27 sandwiches listed are evidently "America's Favorites", and while you can list sandwiches other than these 27, you will have to promote them harder on the menu to sell them.

The ubiquitous hamburger and cheeseburger combined are tops in popularity, but the ham, cheese and ham and cheese sandwiches are close behind. The steak sandwich is naturally very high up in the popularity rating and the club, bacon-lettuce-tomato, lettuce-tomato and bacon-tomato (basically the same sandwich), if combined, reach a popularity that begins to challenge the hamburger and cheeseburger.

While this sandwich popularity rating chart is not the last word in what should be on the sandwich menu it is an indication against which you can check your menu. The rules for sandwich listing on the menu are:
1.   List only sandwiches that sell in your operation.
2.   Feature popular and big profit sandwiches.
3.   Separate hot sandwich and cold sandwich listings.
4.   Do not list your sandwiches so that they compete with your entree listing, unless you want to sell more sandwiches than entrees.

An Italian menu can feature Italian sandwiches, as shown here.

Giant Italian Sandwiches
A meal in a Loaf of Bread — Your Choice of Six Combinations

No. 1 .... **1.00**

"CASA'S" SANDWICH

A Loaf of Our Special
Italian Bread
filled with Salami, Capicola,
Provolone Cheese, Lettuce,
Tomatoes, Pickles, Onions and
Salad Dressing

No. 2 .... **.95**

**GIANT
"MEATBALL" SANDWICH**

A Loaf of Our Special
Italian Bread
filled with
Baked Italian Meatballs and
Casa Nova's Spaghetti Sauce

No. 3 .... **1.00**

**GIANT
"HAM" SANDWICH**

A Loaf of Our Special
Italian Bread
filled with
Ham and Salad Dressing,
Lettuce

No. 4 .... **1.00**

**GIANT
"HOT SAUSAGE" SANDWICH**

A Loaf of Our Special
Italian Bread
filled with
Baked Hot Italian Sausage and
Casa Nova's Spaghetti Sauce

No. 5 .... **.95**

**GIANT CHOPPED "SIRLOIN
TIP" SANDWICH**

A Loaf of Our Special
Italian Bread
filled with Sirloin Tip
cooked in Tomatoes and
Mushroom Sauce

No. 6 .... **1.00**

**A LOAF OF OUR SPECIAL
ITALIAN BREAD**

filled with
Ground Beef, Tomato, Lettuce,
and Salad Dressing

Sandwiches creatively presented can make good "specials."

Try Our

LITTLE GIANT

CORNED BEEF, delicious slices of fresh Kosher Corned Beef stacked sky-high on **OLD FASHIONED RYE** bread with plenty of **KOSHER DILLS** and a heaping plate of the finest **SAUERKRAUT.**

-·- A Man Sized Lunch ... and a Real Value 1.10

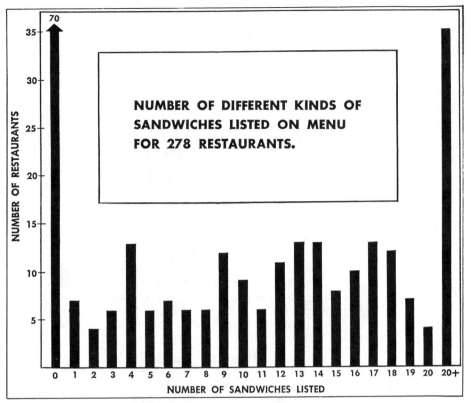

NUMBER OF DIFFERENT KINDS OF SANDWICHES LISTED ON MENU FOR 278 RESTAURANTS.

NUMBER OF RESTAURANTS

NUMBER OF SANDWICHES LISTED

CHART 1

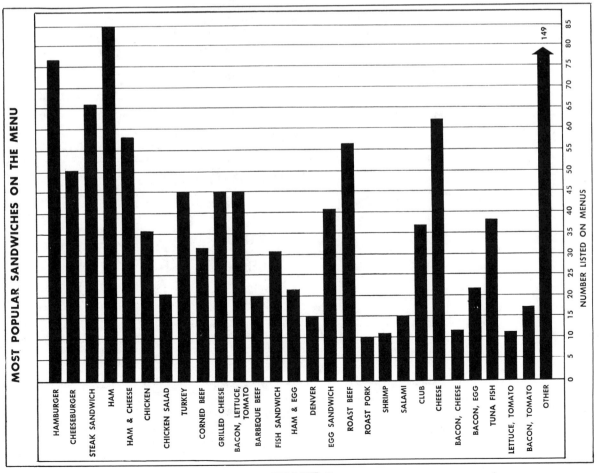

MOST POPULAR SANDWICHES ON THE MENU

NUMBER LISTED ON MENUS

CHART 2

From The Sandwich Board
Hot Sandwiches

BARBEQUE BEEF SANDWICH
Tender slices of beef in a sharp sauce on a toasted Bun
with French Fried Potatoes, Cole Slaw, Pickle   1.35

SLICED TURKEY ON TOAST WITH CREAM GRAVY
and Parmesan Cheese au Gratin, Spiced Peach,
French Fried Potatoes   1.85

MELTED OLDE ENGLISH CHEESE DELIGHT
Olde Cheddar Cheese over toast, crisp bacon and tomato,
Long Branch Potato, Cole Slaw   1.35

HOT ROAST BEEF SANDWICH,
Brown Gravy, Cream Whipped Potato, Peas in Butter, Cole Slaw   1.75

THE STEAK SANDWICH
Selected top sirloin steak on toast, bermuda onion grilled,
French Fried Potato, Cole Slaw, Tomato   2.95

JUMBO HAMBURGER ON TOASTED BUN
with Grilled Onion, Pickle, French Fried Potatoes   1.25
topped with Cheddar or Roquefort Cheese   1.50

Regular Sandwiches

THREE DECKER CLUB
Sliced Chicken, Bacon, Lettuce, Tomato, Mayonnaise
Garni, Cole Slaw, Olives, Saratoga Chips   1.60

SOONER OPEN FACE
Sliced Turkey, Crisp Bacon, Hard Boiled Egg, Tomato Slice on
Rye Bread, topped with Russian Dressing, Cole Slaw, Pickle Rings   1.50

SLICED TURKEY AND SWISS CHEESE, TOMATO
served on choice of bread, 1000 Island Dressing,
Saratoga Chips, Cole Slaw, Pickle   1.35

Baked Ham and Tomato 1.00   Sliced Chicken 1.00   Chicken Salad .90

Ham and Cheese 1.00   Denver .90   Fried Ham and Egg 1.00

French Fried Potatoes .25

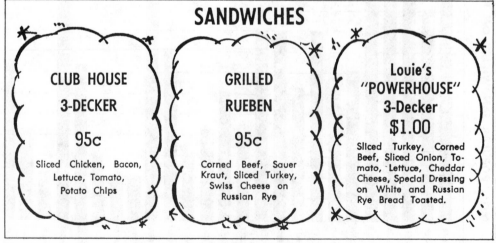

*Hot or cold, open face or triple deck, a good sandwich
listing should cover all types and shapes.*

Combination Sandwiches

(PLEASE ORDER BY NUMBER)

No. 1 "MARRON'S SUPREME" (Triple Decker) 1.55
Corned Beef, Salami, Roast Beef, Pastrami and Tongue
wtih Cole Slaw

No. 2 "LIDO SPECIAL" (Triple Decker) 1.65
Sliced Turkey, Roast Beef, Tongue with Russian Dressing
and Cole Slaw

No. 3 "MY HERO" on Club 1.75
Sliced Roast Turkey and Hot Pastrami, Sweet Red Pepper
and Cole Slaw

No. 4 "EAST END DELUXE" 1.35
Corned Beef with Chopped Liver and Cole Slaw

No. 5 "ATLANTIC BEACH DREAMBOAT" 1.20
Roast Beef, Sliced Onion, Lettuce and Tomato with
Russian Dressing and Cole Slaw

No. 6 "THE OCEAN FRONT" 1.45
Hot Pastrami and Corned Beef with Cole Slaw

No. 7 "WEST END GOURMET" (Triple Decker) 1.45
Tongue, Rolled Beef, Corned Beef, Russian Dressing
and Cole Slaw

No. 8 "PARK ST. SPECIAL" 95
Salami and Bologna with Cole Slaw

No. 9 "PT. LOOKOUT TREAT" 1.20
Tongue and Salami with Cole Slaw

Campbell House Favorites

THE KEFTABURGER . . . A RED LION CREATION	1.25
A tangy spiced Whopper Burger broiled over the flame, topped with Creamed Imported Roquefort Cheese and served on Sesame Roll	
REUBEN	1.35
Baked Corned Beef with Marinated Bavarian Sauerkraut on Rye Bread	
NEW YORKER	1.35
Kosher styled Corned Beef, spicy German Potato Salad with real Kosher Style Dill Pickle, Choice of Roll or Bread	
SIR-LOIN "SA" LOT	1.35
Thinly sliced brisket of Beef Au Jus, kingly portioned, tangy Horseradish, hot German Potato Salad, choice of Bread or Roll	
HOAGY ITALIANO	1.50
Hot Italian Pastramy stacked on choice of Bread, with our own German Potato Salad or tangy Sauerkraut	
KNIGHT'S SPECIAL	1.25
A bountiful portion of thin sliced Danish Ham on sliced Sesame Bun with our own Potato Salad	
RED LION EYE	2.65
Choice Rib-Eye selected from the heart of the rib, served open face with Potato Salad and Horseradish	

*Sandwiches do not have to be presented under the same
old names, as the examples shown here demonstrate.*

ROOM SERVICE MENUS

Of all menus, the Room Service Menu must work the hardest and sell the best because it stands alone. There is no waiter or waitress to answer questions or make suggestions and there are no appetizing looking dishes with tantalizing aromas being served at the next table. Yet this menu can describe and sell a great variety of foods, beverages and services of the hotel or motel—breakfast, lunch, dinner, hors d'oeuvres, wines and cocktails. In addition, it can list the hotel services—auto rental, airline reservations, banquet and catering service, dry cleaning and laundry service, stenographer service, wake-up calls, and restaurants and shops within the hotel.

Good design, good printing, the right paper and good copy are the answer here as in any good menu. And many hotels and motels create excellent room service menus that sell. For innovative copy, the following is from the Hollenden House menu.

ALL OF A SUDDEN IT'S FIVE O'CLOCK

And if you're the type who likes some liquid refreshment at the end of the day, head for the lobby and the Gazette Lounge or our very special Superior Bond Street Bar. But be prepared for a trip back to the Gay 90's, complete with live entertainment. The only thing modern about the Gazette is the service and the man-sized cocktails. You also will enjoy the different Superior Bond Bar with the old "Cleveland Look."

BUT DON'T STOP NOW
Ready for dinner? Good. Because here in the Hollenden, and right next to the Gazette Lounge is Cleveland's best-known, gracious dining, Marie Schrieber's Tavern. If you've spent any time in Cleveland, we don't need to say more. The specialty? Lots of things. But mostly steaks, chops and seafoods. Ask our captains for a sample of their epicurean talents. Also another small restaurant is open right in the lobby for a lighter or speedier meal.

A different item for a Room Service Menu is box lunches offered by Holly's Holiday Inn, as described on the next page.

BOX LUNCH

For your convenience, you may arrange to have box lunches packed for pick up at our front desk at time of departure. Call room service and place the order by 7:00 P. M. of the day before.

COMBINATION SANDWICH

Two freshly made sandwiches! Baked ham on rye and Swiss cream cheese on homemade white bread. Hard boiled egg, pickles, fruit and cookies.

GOLDEN FRIED CHICKEN

Tender, plump chicken pieces for easy finger-eating plus buttered homemade bread. Hard boiled egg, fruit and cookies.

This same motel, besides listing such unusual services as babysitters, photostats, irons and ironing boards, bottle warmers, bed boards, card tables and a golf driving range, does a good job of selling its restaurant, Ristorante Holly's with the following copy:

Visit the Ristorante Holly's and join in with the spirit of warmth and friendliness that abounds in the Mediterranean. We offer a menu that is not truly Spanish, French or Italian, yet our dishes do suggest in their appeal and flavor a universal love of good food and wine. In this atmosphere of camaraderie, food is prepared at the open hearth and served to meet your schedule.

When your interest in TV, paperbacks or roadmaps fades, there's always good fun in the Ristorante Lounge. No need for worry beads here, for our drinks are continental, the music lively, and our sing-alongs memorable events. In these surroundings friendliness is contagious, and it all adds up to an evening of fun in Grand Rapid's favorite meeting place.

The food offered on the Room Service Menu need not be dull or ordinary either. Consider the following offerings all taken from Room Service Menus:

BOOJUM WINE PIE

A frozen blend of wine, raisins and walnuts

AVOCADO DELIGHT

Sun ripened avocado filled with fresh crabmeat, accompanied with cold curried rice, sliced tomato and hardboiled eggs.

TAHITIAN PUPUS (Hors d'oeuvres)

Crab rangoons, egg rolls, fried shrimps, spareribs, rumakis.

THE CZAR'S FAVORITE
Fresh Beluga Caviar specially selected for us, served with all its entourage: chopped eggs (yolks and whites), chopped onions, parsley, sour cream and lemon. Toast sous serviette.

THE CONQUISTADORES BREAKFAST
One dozen real farm eggs on platter. Platter of smoked sausages or bacon. A real hoe cake. Homemade sorghum molasses. Tasty grits. A nip of whisky (8 year old), for four or six.

A listing of beverages—wine, spirits, beer and soft drinks—is also important, with the basic information, cost (if not included in price of food or beverage), hours of service and phone numbers.

(Serving Time 11:00 a.m.-10:00 p.m.)

SANDWICHES—COLD

BAKED HAM	1.25	THE CAPTAIN'S CLUB	1.75
HAM SALAD	1.15	White meat of turkey, crisp	
TUNA SALAD	1.15	bacon, lettuce and tomato	
CHICKEN SALAD	1.15	THE SHIP'S ROUND	1.50
SLICED CHICKEN	1.25	Tender sliced sirloin of	
HAM AND SWISS CHEESE	1.25	beef piled high on your	
AMERICAN OR SWISS CHEESE	.85	choice of bread	
PEANUT BUTTER AND JELLY	.85	THE DECKHAND'S CHOICE	1.75
BACON, LETTUCE AND TOMATO	1.25	Tartare steak on your choice	
		of bread	

Above Sandwiches Served with Lettuce, Pickle and Potato Chips
FRENCH FRIED POTATOES .50 • **FRENCH FRIED ONION RINGS** .50

SANDWICHES—HOT

BEEFBURGER	.95	STEAK SANDWICH	3.25
CHEESEBURGER	1.10	Served with french fried potatoes	
FILET OF WHITE FISH	1.10	and choice of salad	
FRIED COUNTRY HAM	1.95	THE STERNWHEELER	2.75
FRIED SUGAR CURED HAM	1.55	Sliced tenderloin of beef grilled	
GRILLED BACON AND CHEESE	1.25	with onions and smothered with swiss	

Above Sandwiches Served with
Lettuce, Pickle and Potato Chips

cheese. Served on a french roll, with
french fried potatoes and your
choice of salad

HOT BROWN 2.75
Sliced chicken on toast covered with
cheese sauce and topped with bacon
and a tomato slice. Served with your
choice of salad

THE RIVER GENTLEMAN 2.25
Melted swiss cheese over grilled
ham on your choice of bread.
Served with french fried potatoes
and your choice of salad

REUBEN SANDWICH 2.75
Corned beef, swiss cheese, sauerkraut, grilled on rye bread. Served
with french fried potatoes or german
potato salad

**THE PILOT'S JUMBO
CHOPPED BEEF SANDWICH** 2.25
8 oz. of choice chopped beef prepared
to taste. Served with french fried
potatoes and choice of salad

RAMADA INN

2220 First Street
Fort Myers, Florida

Notice that "Serving Time—11:00 a.m. to 10:00 p.m." is printed on this Room Service menu.

Off center binding allows for tab indexing on this Hilton Room Service menu.

The menu of the Houston Oaks Hotel is printed front to back in English and back to front in Spanish —a combination that is practical and adds sophistication to the room service listing.

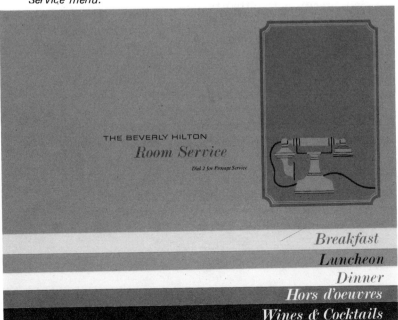

THE BEVERLY HILTON
Room Service
Dial 2 for Prompt Service

Breakfast
Luncheon
Dinner
Hors d'oeuvres
Wines & Cocktails

SPECIAL OCCASION MENUS

There are several kinds of menus that can be classified under the category of "Special Occasion." The first of these are menus printed for holidays—Christmas, Thanksgiving, New Year's, Mother's Day, etc. The second are special "Gourmet" dinners which may be given by a gourmet society at the restaurant or be sponsored by the restaurant as a means of increasing business, publicity and enhancing reputation. The third is the banquet or catering menu where a group, society or club is being sold a "package" of food and drink for a large number of people.

In each case, the menu serves as a selling tool and care should be taken in its preparation. The holiday menu may seem to be an excessive expense if it is used only for that one day. And if it is only used that one day it can be, although it adds style and class to any restaurant. The key to getting sales mileage out of this kind of menu is to expose it to the public before the holiday. This can be done in several ways. The menu can be a table tent and be on the table a week or so before the holiday. It can be a clip-on attached to the regular menu; it can be used as a direct mail piece, the basis for an ad, or it can be mounted and used as a poster placed in strategic locations. In the case of hotels or motels, copies can be left in each room.

The "Gourmet Dinner" involves a great deal more than a special menu if the restaurant is sponsoring the event. The following copy created by the Willoway Manor restaurant and published in a direct mail piece called Manor News indicates one approach to this type of promotion and the amount of careful preparation needed to make it successful:

WILLOWAY'S HERITAGE DINNER III TO BE HELD
NOVEMBER 30, 1971

Before the date had even been set for Heritage Dinner III, some of the Manor's friends had already committed themselves to reservations for it. This is a good indication of how well received the first two dinners were by those who were able to participate in them.

Heritage Dinner III is one that you really won't want to miss. We suggest you reserve right away so you will be assured of a table. It will feature an all American Menu as the first two dinners have. This one will be patterned after the sumptuous and bountiful Holiday dinners of our early original colonies. The recipes come from those used during our Revolutionary War period. Some are actually favorites of our founding fathers.

Our early settlers had left many comforts behind them in the Old World but they weren't afraid to compensate for what they lacked with what was at hand. America was a land of plenty. The fields, streams and forests produced for man abundantly.

Our settlers used their products abundantly, especially when entertaining. Heritage Dinner III portrays this. Our menu comes from authentic early American menus as reproduced by the American Heritage Publishing Company in the American Heritage Cookbook.

If you have someone special that you would like to give a special holiday treat to, November 30th is the time to do it. For one evening the air of the Manor will be filled with festive fragrances of banquets of yesteryear. We'll start serving promptly at 7:00 P. M. Join us for a relaxed gourmet dinner from the past. Allow a good two hours and be sure to bring a huge appetite.

After dinner you'll want to go to the Burgundy Room. There Naperville's own historian, Les Schrader, will share some more of his paintings with us. Les' memories, research and interest in Naperville's past, combined with his natural wit, make for a most interesting and informative nightcap on a perfect evening.

The third type of "occasion" menu, which is a listing of appetizers, entrees, desserts and beverages in combinations and with quantity prices, is a "talking piece" for the food manager and the customer to work from. It is also an advertising tool in that it can be mailed to potential customers who may be interested in the service. The Disneyland Hotel in Anaheim, California, does an especially good job with their Banquet Menu Suggestions. The graphics are very fine (all pick-ups from old engravings) and their "General Information" copy, listed here, covers in advance, nearly every question that the customer may ask:

GENERAL INFORMATION

BEVERAGES: Charges for a sponsored or cash bar and bartender: $25.00 per bartender until $150.00 worth in beverages has been consumed, in which case the Hotel will absorb the cost for the bartender.

With a sponsored bar, we can serve at:

$1.00 per drink: Manhattans, Martinis, CALL BRAND Scotch and Bourbon Highballs, Gin and Vodka.

$1.20 per drink: Manhattans, Martinis, PREMIUM BRAND Scotch and Bourbon Highballs, Gin and Vodka (J & B, Jack Daniels, V. O., Beefeater, Smirnoff).

With a cash bar: regular prices will apply.

SEATING: Rooms can be set with any size head tables on platforms; remainder of rooms to be set with either round tables of 10 guests each or special shaped tables such as "U" shaped tables, "T" shaped tables, etc.

DECORATIONS: Hotel will be happy to help you make arrangements with a local florist. Tall vases or centerpieces of freshly cut seasonal flowers for the head table from $15.00 and up, and centerpieces for individual tables of 10 guests from $5.00 and up.

AMPLIFICATION: We will provide 2 microphones free-of-charge for each food function for over 100 guests. Each additional microphone, charge $7.50.

MUSIC & ENTER-   We will be happy to assist and make arrangements.
TAINMENT:

LIGHTING: Hotel can provide baby spotlights at $7.50 each, and spotlight and operator at $50.00 per 3 hour minimum. $9.50 each additional hour. $20.00 per hour overtime after midnight.

CONTROL: Waitresses can collect tickets at the tables. We will provide committee tables at the door of rooms for food functions.

GRATUITIES: On all food and beverages consumed, local sales tax and gratuities are not included and will be added to the account.

GUARANTEE: Please notify this office two days before each food function of the exact number of guests attending. On food functions taking place on Sunday and/or Monday, we will require a guarantee by Friday. This figure will be considered as a guarantee for which you will be charged even if fewer guests attend. We will, however, set up and prepare food for 10% above this number for parties up to 500 guests. For parties above 500, we will set up and prepare food for 5% above the guarantee.

CATERING DEPARTMENT
Disneyland Hotel
ANAHEIM, CALIFORNIA
(714) 535—8171

HORS D'OEUVRES

HOT HORS D'OEUVRES

RUMAKIS *(Water Chestnuts, Pineapple, Chicken Livers wrapped in Bacon)*	@ $3.75 per dozen
FRIED LOBSTER & SHRIMP WITH SAUCE	@ $4.75 per dozen
COCKTAIL FRANKS	@ $2.50 per dozen
CHESTNUTS WRAPPED WITH BACON	@ $4.00 per dozen
LOBSTER IN BUTTER	@ $4.75 per dozen
SMALL HAMBURGERS ITALIENNE	@ $3.75 per dozen
CREPES *(Pancakes, rolled and cut)*, Stuffed A La Mornay or with Cheese, Creamed Chicken or Fish	@ $4.50 per dozen

COLD ASSORTED FANCY CANAPES

@ $3.00 per dozen

DEVILED HAM CANAPES
ANCHOVY CANAPES
LOBSTER CANAPES
SHRIMP CANAPES
AVOCADO & CHICKEN LIVER CANAPES
CHOPPED CHICKEN & HAM CANAPES
CHOPPED EGG CANAPES
ROQUEFORT CHEESE CANAPES
CHEESE & HAM CANAPES
CREAMED CHEESE & CHOPPED MUSHROOM CANAPES

ASSORTED COLD HORS D'OEUVRES

DEVILED EGGS	@ $3.00 per dozen
COLD SHRIMP WITH COCKTAIL SAUCE OR OTHER SAUCE	@ $4.75 per dozen
CURRIED CHEESE BALLS (Chutney & Butter, Curry Powder, Cream Cheese)	@ $3.00 per dozen
STUFFED CELERY WITH ROQUEFORT CHEESE	@ $3.00 per dozen
CORNETS OF AMERICAN CHEESE STUFFED WITH CHOPPED NUTS	@ $3.00 per dozen

Clever, creative use of old prints adds charm to this catering menu.

Thanksgiving Dinner

Grapefruit Basket of Fresh Fruit
Sweet Cider
Chilled California Tomato Juice
Beef and Chicken Broth
with Fresh Vegetables
Celery and Olives
Radish Rosettes

*Hot Popovers and Assorted
Breads with Creamery Butter*

ROAST STUFFED
YOUNG TOM TURKEY
Giblet Gravy
Cranberry Sauce
Creamy Whipped Potato
Candied Yams
Blue Hubbard Squash
Sweet Garden Peas
Tiny White Onions

Thanksgiving Salad

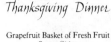

Royal's HEARTHSIDE RESTAURANT
RUTLAND, VERMONT

Hot Mince Pie – Rum Sauce
Orange Sherbet
English Plum Pudding – Hard Sauce
Fresh Apple Pie
Old-fashioned Pumpkin Square
with Whipped Cream

Special Blend of Coffee or Tea

Mixed Nuts
Bowl of Fresh Fruit
Mints

COMPLETE DINNER – 5.25
CHILDREN'S DINNER – 3.95

(Vermont Tax 5%)

*Fresh Opened Oyster, Shrimp or
Seafood Cocktail   1.75
Roast Prime Ribs of Beef
Steaks, Chops and Lobsters
Available on Request*

Royal's HEARTHSIDE RESTAURANT
RUTLAND, VERMONT

The two sides of the Thanksgiving menu shown here form a table tent that advertises the meal in advance of the holiday.

This simple, yet attractive "Holiday Feast" menu can be used for Thanksgiving, Christmas and New Years.

Golden Lantern

Holiday Feast

Appetizers

Shrimp Cocktail 1.75
Little Necks on Half Shell 1.25

Entrees

ALL ENTREES INCLUDE:
*Celery and Olives, Fresh Garden Salad,
Assorted Rolls and Butter
Our Famous Thanksgiving Vegetables
Served Family Style*
Choice of One:
Tomato Juice, Fresh Fruit Cup or Soup du Jour
ROAST STUFFED TURKEY 4.95
*with Dressing, Giblet Gravy and Cranberry Sauce
(Drumsticks and Wings - available on request)*
ROAST PRIME RIBS OF BEEF AU JUS 6.95
BONELESS NEW YORK SIRLOIN STEAK 7.50
BAKED STUFFED JUMBO SHRIMP 4.75
CRAB A LA GOLDEN LANTERN 4.50
BAKED LOBSTER - FISHERMAN STYLE
Priced according to size

Homemade Pies: Squash, Mince Meat, Apple

Desserts - A la Carte

Strawberry or Chocolate Parfait   .75

© AD ART LITHO, CLEVELAND, OHIO

THE GERMAN MENU

German food and German restaurants are a permanent fixture of the American gastronomic landscape, and the "Oktoberfest" is rapidly becoming another national holiday even though the date, in either September or October, is not fixed by Act of Congress. Combined with German wines and beers, the German, Austrian, Bavarian, etc. restaurant has a special "flavor." A most common design approach is to use gothic script on the menu, at least for headings. Too much of this type can become hard to read for most Americans not schooled in old German texts.

For artwork, there is a wide selection of "old" German artprints, woodcuts, emblems, steins, castles, wine labels, kegs and barrels as well as bottles of beer and maps of the famous German wine-growing areas. The important design factor to keep in mind is to have a menu that looks German as well as listing and selling the offerings of the house.

A listing of menu section headings is given here with English translations:

Vorspeisen	Appetizers
Abendbrot	Dinner
Fleischspeisen	Steaks
Spezialitaten	Specials
Krustentiere	Shellfish
Kuchen und Torten	Desserts
Getränke	Beverages

Some typical German entree items are listed here with appropriate English descriptive copy:

SAUERBRATEN
Choice beef steeped in savory marinade for one week, then roasted to fork-tenderness and served in a sweet-sour wine gravy with potato pancakes.

WIENER SCHNITZEL
A cutlet of tender veal dipped in egg batter and cracker crumbs, then richly sauteed to a golden brown and served with a lemon slice.

SCHNITZEL A LA HOLSTEIN
A Wiener Schnitzel topped with a bright fried egg, anchovies and capers, served in a spicy tomato sauce and garnished with sweet-sour pickled beets.

THUERINGER BRATWURST
A traditional German sausage of veal and pork, tastily seasoned, sauteed and served with burgundy red cabbage.

JUNGE BRATENTE A LA SALZBURG
Roast duckling, once reserved for nobility, partially boned and crisply roasted to tempt the palate of our royal guests. Served with orange sauce and red cabbage.

KASSLER RIPPCHEN
Kassler style smoked pork loin served with sauerkraut and Bavarian bread dumpling.

ROULADEN
Two generous slices of prime beef basted with Duesseldorf Loewensenf (imported mustard from the Rhineland), filled with hickory smoked bacon and onion strips are baked to butterknife tenderness, covered with a delicious mushroom sauce and served with potato pancakes and applesauce.

HASENPFEFFER
Sweet-sour wild rabbit, marinated in wine sauce and served with kartoffel kloessen (potato dumplings) garnished with crabapple.

HIRSCHBRATEN
Sliced venison in rich gravy, served with spaetzle (homemade noodles) mandarin orange garni.

Dining in a German or Austrian restaurant is also a "drinking experience". because both the wines and the beers of Germany/Austria are world renowned and deserving of their reputation. There are three main categories of German wines. They are: Rhein Weine—served with meat courses, Mosel Weine—served with fish courses and, for those who prefer a dry wine, Rot Weine—(yes, there is a red German wine) often the choice of connoisseurs.

RHEIN (white)
LIEBFRAUMILCH (spätlese)
A full-bodied wine with outspoken bouquet attributed to the late harvest grapes out of which it is made.

NIERSTEINER DOMTAL
A mild wine, fragrant and well balanced.

OPPENHEIMER KRÖTENBRUNNEN
A piquant, full-bodied wine.

RÜDESHEIMER
From Rüdesheim on the Rhine comes this light, crisp wine, suitable with meat courses.

JOHANNISBERGER
A world renowned wine just a bit sweeter than dry wines; mild and palatable.

MOSEL (white)
MOSELBLÜMCHEN
Light and dry from the Moselle River region; delightful with fish and fowl.

BERNKASTLER RIESLING
A dry wine from the Bernkastler region; excellent taste.

PIESPORTER GOLDTRÖPFCHEN
A full-bodied, piquant, golden wine.

ZELLER SCHWARZE KATZ
A popular wine, crackling in the taste attributed to the famous vineyards of the Zell; delightfully crisp.

ZELTINGER HIMMELREICH
A classic; has the heavy, dry bouquet of a fine wine.

ERDENER TREPPCHEN
A well-balanced Moselle, a bit on the dry side.

CRÖVER NACKTARSCH
A world famous wine, extra dry, known for its outstanding label.

WEHLENER SONNENUHR AUSLESE
One of the highest quality of elite wines; full-bodied with a golden sunshine bouquet.

RED

AFFENTALER SPÄTBURUNDER
In the original monkey bottle; full-bodied, with superb quality; a magnificent Palatinate wine—a true spaetlese.

KALTERER SEE AUSLESE
A red Austrian wine of fine fragrance; not too dry, but light.

For a German restaurant to be outstanding, it should serve genuine, imported German beers and feature them on the menu. Eberhard's restaurant in Columbia, Ill. does just this, offering fifteen of them. Here they are:

HERRENHÄUSER (from Hannover)
The most popular beer of the house; a light and malty lager.

DRESSLEL
Light lager.

DORTMUNDER AKTIEN (from Dortmund)
Sparkling and mellow.

WÜRZBURGER HOFBRAÜ (from Wuerzburg)
Mild and dark.

KULMBACHER SANDLER BRÄU (from
Kulmbach)
Light and sweet.

KULMBACHER SANDLER BRÄU
Dark and sweet

LÖWENBRAU (from Munich)
Light special.

LÖWENBRAU
Dark heavy.

MÜNCHNER HOFBRÄU (from Munich)
Light.

MÜNCHNER HOFBRÄU
Dark.

SPATEN-BRÄU (from Munich)
Light and mild.

PSCHORR BRÄU (from Munich)
Light.

PSCHORR ANIMATOR
Bock.

BERLINER WEISSE (from West Berlin)
Mit Himbeersaft (with raspberry syrup).

The Red Coach Grill introduces its customers to its "Oktoberfest" with the following interesting copy which describes the origin of the celebration and some of its history::

The Legend of Oktoberfest

Oktoberfest is the largest fair in Europe. Although its name in German means October Festival, the fair is usually held in September to take advantage of the fine weather.

It began in 1810, when Max Joseph of Bavaria gave a huge party to celebrate his son's marriage to Theresia of Sachsen-Hildburghausen. The party was so successful that the meadow where it was held was renamed "Theresia's Meadow," and the Meadow is still the site of Oktoberfest today.

The Bürgermeister of Munich opens the fair every year, leading a procession of beer wagons drawn by horses, decorated carriages driven by brewers, and huge floats carrying strong-armed waitresses. The parade ends at the first barrel of beer for the fair, a barrel which traditionally belongs to the Bürgermeister. He downs the first mug at noon, and the fair is officially begun. Thousands of revellers invade the hundreds of acres of the fair. Tented stalls line the long avenues. Oxen are roasted whole, chickens are roasted on spits, lakefish are grilled over wood fires. Hundreds of kinds of sausages are consumed. And the beer, of course, flows heartily.

We hope you'll share this spirit of revelry and good fellowship with us here at Red Coach, during our own recreation of Oktoberfest.

WELCOME TO THE
Oktoberfest
at Red Coach

Join our celebration of Europe's greatest festival. Bring your family to Oktoberfest. Enjoy its dining, its music, its drinks, and all its festivity now at Red Coach. For an Oktoberfest Night you won't forget!

The Oktoberfest Feast

Baked Spareribs or cup of hot Bean or Potato Soup

Broiled Chicken,
Bavarian style
Westphalian Ham
German Pot Roast

Potato Pancakes with Sour Cream or Apple Sauce

Bavarian Red Cabbage
Dark Bread & Butter • Pretzel Sticks

Apple Strudel • Beverage

all for only
$5⁹⁵

One special is featured on an entire page of this menu along with its "Oktoberfest."
Good art and type make for pleasant appearance and hard sell!

For die,
die garnet
haam wolle,
odder die,
die speeter komme,
gibts aach
nach 11 Uhr
noch was
zu Esse.

Awwer
um halb aans
misse mer
zumache.

A German emblem plus gothic type establish the "character" of this menu.

A wine map helps to merchandise your German wine list.

Gulpin Der Whole Keger Bier

If yur thirsten und vanten bier for vier er sechs, get der kegger to putten on yur table.

6.95
Serves 4-6

A little humor sells a lot of beer.

THE ITALIAN-AMERICAN MENU

The Italian restaurant is one of Italy's contributions to the American scene and to a more cosmopolitan cuisine. But, generally, the food is better than the menu that should sell, merchandise and explain the many unusual dishes served. In addition, the Italian-American menu is usually a large menu because, besides a listing of Italian specialties (entrees, appetizers, soups, salads, sandwiches and desserts), there is usually a complete American menu (steaks, seafood, fowl, chef's specials, etc.). And to make the menu even more complicated, there is often a large and varied Pizza listing.

The first consideration in building an Italian menu is to be sure that the menu is physically large enough to accommodate this large number of items. The next consideration is to separate the various categories on separate pages or panels of the menu. Separate the menu into the following three categories, (1) Italian foods, (2) American foods, and (3) Pizza. This gives the customer a clear, easy choice without confusion.

The Italian foods section of the menu can be broken down into subheads such as: Pasta, Veal, Fowl, Seafood, etc. The American foods section can be listed under the usual subheads of Steak, Seafood, Fowl, and any other Specials listed. The Pizza section can be small or so large as to be a complete menu by itself with all the possible combinations of cheese, meat and fish.

The Pizza listing is often broken down into large, medium and small Pizzas with three different prices. If the Pizza listing is broken down by size, indicate what the actual difference is, in terms of actual size (inches in diameter) or number of people the portion will serve.

A very important point to remember about the Italian portion of the Italian-American menu is that it contains many Italian words that are unknown to the average American customer. The Italian restaurateur tends to think that all of his customers know his cuisine, but except for the gourmet or "old" customer, much of his menu is foreign, unknown territory. The customer, therefore, in many Italian-American restaurants, must either "ask the waiter," order and take a chance, or order the old standbys such as spaghetti or ravioli.

Also, the Italian-American restaurant operator should consider the large young adult sector of the population (the largest sector by far). These young adults, especially, need informative, descriptive copy to help them order intelligently.

The following is a list of Italian menu terms that need descriptive, merchandising, sell copy when included on the menu:

Minestrone	Veal Marsala	Manicotti
Antipasto	Veal Pizzaiolo	Cannelloni
Peperoncini	Lasagne	Liquini Vongole
Veal Scaloppini	Marinara	Rigatino
Veal Veneziana	Chicken Cacciatore	Mostaccioli

Veal Marinara
Veal Zingara
Veal Parmigiana
Veal Dore
Scongigli Marinara
Calamaro Affogati
Castellana
Piccata di Vitello
Spumone
Tortoni

Chicken Vesuvio
Chicken Fiorentina
Gnocchi
Tortellini
Cannoli Siciliana
Zabaione
Saltimbocca alla Romana
Cavatelli
Calamaro
Scungilli

Vermicelli
Braciola
Saltimbocca Romana
Scampi
Brasciole
Soffritto
Ziti
Aglio Olio

Another common feature of the Italian restaurant is the Antipasto Tray or Appetizer. This is usually an attractive traffic builder offered as part of the entree or sold a la carte as a before dinner treat or appetizer. But, whichever the case, describe in detail what your antipasto consists of.

Even the Wine list can reflect the Italian part of the Italian-American menu. The following is a good example:

ITALIAN RED WINES

Ideal accompaniment with steak, spaghetti and highly seasoned foods
RUFFINO RED CHIANTI
FOLONARI VAL POLICELLA
BARDOLINO

ITALIAN ROSÉ WINES

A very delightful wine to complement all types of food, an all purpose wine
RUFFINO ROSATELLO

ITALIAN SPARKLING WINES

GANCIA BEBBIOLO (red)

ITALIAN WHITE WINES

Perfect companionship with chicken and seafood
RUFFINO WHITE CHIANTI
FOLONARI LUGANA
FOLONARI SOAVE

Sandwiches, desserts, salads and side dishes can also be broken down into the two main categories of Italian and American, but, in all cases, descriptive copy will help to sell more of the Italian menu.

Known Internationale **PRESUTTI'S VILLA**

PRANZO! (Good Dinner)   LA CUCINA ITALIANA (Italian Kitchen)

Antipastos

Italian Antipasto (For One)	1.50
Imported Provolone Cheese, bleu cheese, salami, melon wrapped prosciutto, garnish, celery, olives, spiced hot peppers, garbanzos and garlic bread	
Chilled Melon Slice	.75
Wrapped with imported prosciutto	
Fillets of Anchovies in Oil	.50
Minestrone Soup .60 Soup Du Jour	.50

Wafers or Melba Toast and Butter with Above Orders

Appetizers

Blue Points on Half Shell	1.50
(In season)	
Jumbo Shrimp Cocktail	1.00
Villa hot sauce supreme	
Chopped Chicken Livers	.85
Celery and Olives per order	.60
Chilled Fruit Cup Supreme	.35
Fresh Chilled Orange Juice	.30
Chilled Tomato Juice or Grapefruit Juice	.30

Pastas Home Made Spaghetti and Ravioli

All of our Pastas, Spaghetti — Ravioli — Lasagna — Manicotti are the genuine home-made Mamma and Pop Presutti original recipe

Fettuccini Alfredo 2.50
Suggest: White Frascati Wine No. 303

Spaghetti — served with

"Mamma and Pop" Presutti's original tomato sauce, Romano Cheese, large fresh garden Italian tossed Salad   2.20

Home Made Gnocchi Potato Dumpling with 2.20

Meatless Sauce	2.20	Heavy Meat Sauce	2.80
Polpetti (2)	2.90	Fresh Mushrooms	2.80
Clam Sauce (red or white)	2.90	Caruso Sauce — fresh mushrooms, chicken	
Fresh Chicken Livers	2.85	livers and green	
Italian Sausage	3.00	peppers	3.25

Suggest: Chianti Wine No. 500

Ravioli

served with Mamma and Pop Presutti's original tomato sauce, Romano cheese, large fresh garden Italian tossed salad   2.60 with

Spaghetti & Ravioli	2.60	Fresh Mushrooms	3.10
Fresh Chicken Livers	3.20	Heavy Meat Sauce	3.10

Suggest: Chianti Wine No. 500

Pastas Imbottiti (Baked Dishes and Casseroles)

Suggest: Chianti Wine No. 500

Cannelonni Imbottiti, a Forno Carne o ricotta, salsa pomodoro e parmagiano — Stuffed Macaroni with meat or Italian cottage cheese, tomato sauce, parmigiano cheese en casserole   3.35

Lasagna a Forno, carne o Mozzarella, salsa pomodoro y parmagiana. — Wide noodle baked in layers with tomato and meat sauce, pear shaped cheese, grated parmigiano cheese   3.45

Pollo Tetrazzini salsa bianche, pepe verde, funghi parmagiano Spaghetti bianche che Petto de Pollo al forno. — Tetrazzini, white sauce with Julienne green peppers, mushrooms, sherry wine, white spaghetti and breast of chicken, parmigiana cheese en casserole   3.45
Suggest: Soave Wine No. 302

INSALATA (Salads   Choice of)
Italian Tossed, Heart of Lettuce (choice of dressing) Italian Style Cole Slaw
Roquefort Dressing   .30

Piatti di Carni & Polo=Alla Italiano

(Dishes of Meats and Chicken, Italian Style)

Filetto Bistecca Fritti con Funghi e Pepe Verde — Filet of beef tenderloin sauteed in olive oil, smothered in mushrooms, green peppers, touch of garlic   4.75
Suggest: Bardolino Wine No. 501

Filetto Bistecca Pizziola — Filet of beef tenderloin sauteed in olive oil, touch of garlic, tomato sauce and mozzarella cheese   4.00
Suggest: Valpolicella Wine No. 502

Filletto di Pollo alla Cacciatora — All Breast Filet Chicken alla Cacciatora (hunter's style) with fresh mushrooms, green peppers, tomatoes, olive oil, touch of garlic, seasonings 3.60
Suggest: Nectarose or White Frascati No. 303 and 400

Vitella Scalloppine con Funghi Pepe Verde — Veal pieces sauteed in pure butter, touch of garlic, mushrooms and green pepper en casserole   4.00
Suggest: Chianti or Burgundy No. 500 and 503

Vitella Scalloppine alla Marsalla — Veal pieces sauteed in pure butter, touch of garlic, cooked in Marsalla wine en casserole 3.75
Suggest: Chianti or Burgundy No. 500 and 503

Vitella alla Parmigiana e Forno — Veal steak sauteed in olive oil, baked with tomato sauce and parmigiano cheese 3.85
Suggest: Frascati Wine No. 504

Frog Legs Provencale — sauteed in garlic butter and dry white wine, served en casserole au garni 4.50
Suggest: Orvietto No. 301

ZUPPE E SUCCHI de FRUITTI
(Appetizers — Soups and Juices) — Minestrone Soup, Soup du jour, Chilled Tomato or Grapefruit Juice

INSALATA (Salads — Choice of)
Italian Tossed, Heart of Lettuce (choice of dressing) Italian Style Cole Slaw
Roquefort Dressing   .30

PIATTI VARIETA   Side dishes (choice of one with above orders)
Spaghetti, vegetable of the day, potato

INDIVIDUAL GARLIC LOAVES .... .35

Facilities For Business Men's Luncheons, Wedding Breakfasts, Receptions, Buffets, Parties of all Types.   Also Carry Out Orders
(Call) HU 8-6440 HU 8-2488   Open 11 A.M. – Close 1 A.M.
Closed Sunday

Besides listing and describing in detail a wide variety of Appetizers, Soups, Pasta, Italian and American entrees plus Desserts, this menu has a map of Italy.

SPAGHETTI BRAVISSIMO

WITH MEAT SAUCE 1.45

WITH MEAT BALLS 1.65

(Served with soup, salad
and french bread.)

LASAGNE

WITH MEAT SAUCE $1.85

(Served with soup, salad
and french bread.)

Desserts

Ice Cream	.25	Apple Pie	.30
Fruit Cocktail	.25	(A La Mode)	.55
Spumoni	.25	Sundaes	.25
(Creme de Menthe Ice Cream)		Shakes	.35

Yes PIZZA

IS ALWAYS
EATEN WITH
THE FINGERS

THANK YOU FOR YOUR CUSTOM – CALL AGAIN SOON!

Pizza Legend

Once upon a time, during the 18th century, there lived an Italian chef named Monzu Testa. Monzu labored happily for a Spanish king, Ferdinand of Bourbon. Ferdinand was a real gourmet, and, consequently, his chefs experimented diligently in hopes of finding a novel palate-pleasure for him.

One day, Monzu presented his new creation, which he called pizza, to the king. The king was so delighted with it that he installed Monzu as the chief royal chef. And pizza was born.

"Not so," say the Italians, "it all started in Naples." One day a peasant woman was baking bread. The children were standing around, and, like all children everywhere, they were hungry. They couldn't wait until the bread was baked. Mama took some leftover bread dough, put some meat or cheese on it, and slid it into the oven, for a few minutes. Bang! La pizza!!

Pizza is that wondrously flavorful, smoky-crusted, crisp, and crunchy pie, bubbling with hot melted cheese and spicy tomato sauce, dotted with bits of sizzling, succulent sausage or laced with soft, salty anchovies. It is the joy of peasants and the delight of monarchs.

Giuseppi's is very happy that you dropped in for a visit and we hope you will return very soon. Till then, we wish you, Salute!

WHY NOT PICK UP A GUISEPPI'S
FROZEN PIZZA ON YOUR WAY OUT?

welcome ... ... enjoy

Giuseppi's PIZZA

FIRST IN
EDMONTON

● Pizza Cellar 8223 - 109 Street 439-1967 433-8161
● Capilano Mall 98 Street and 57 Avenue 469-0664
● North End 8017 - 118 Avenue 474-3636

Pizza ... buon appetito

Starters & Appetizers

Tomato Juice	Medium	.20
	Large	.30
Chef's Salad		.25
Minestrone Soup		.25
PIZZA SNACK		
1 Ingredient		.50
Garlic Bread (6 slices)		.35

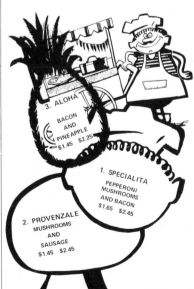

3. ALOHA
BACON
AND
PINEAPPLE
$1.45 $2.25

1. SPECIALITA
PEPPERONI
MUSHROOMS
AND BACON
$1.65 $2.45

2. PROVENZALE
MUSHROOMS
AND
SAUSAGE
$1.45 $2.45

4. HUSKIE
MUSHROOM, BACON,
SAUSAGE, SALAMI
AND PEPPERONI
$1.95 $2.85

5. COLOSSEUM
"FOR THE
PIZZA-EATER
WHO HAS
EVERYTHING"
$2.35 $3.45

			9" serves 1-2	12" serves 2-3
6.	MADAME BORGIA	Green Pepper and Ham	$1.45	$2.25
7.	MOMA ROSA	Pepperoni and Green Pepper	$1.45	$2.25
8.	GAMBERETTINO	Shrimp	$1.35	$1.95
9.	GLADIATOR	Beef and Onion	$1.45	$2.25
10.	CARUSO	Ham	$1.35	$1.95
11.	PALERMO	Pepperoni, Salami, Red Peppers	$1.65	$2.25
12.	ALICE	Anchovies	$1.35	$1.95
13.	HUMBLE PIE	Cheese	$1.05	$1.55
14.	MUKLUK	Mushrooms	$1.35	$1.95
15.	VESUVIUS	Pepperoni	$1.35	$1.95
16	CAESAR	Oysters	$1.35	$1.95
17.	MILANESE	Bacon Morsels	$1.35	$1.95
18.	ROMANESE	Salami	$1.35	$1.95
19.	PAISANO	Sausage	$1.35	$1.95
20.	GINA	Pepperoni and Olives	$1.45	$2.25
21.	SOPHIA	Bacon and Mushrooms	$1.45	$2.25
22.	RAQUEL	Ham and Tomato	$1.45	$2.25
23.	KLONDIKE	Any Two Ingredients	$1.45	$2.25
24.	SAN MARCO	Shrimp, Mushroom and Green Peppers	$1.65	$2.55
25.	WILDCAT	Any Three Ingredients	$1.95	$2.95

TO ORDER AHEAD OR TO MAKE
RESERVATIONS, 433-8161 AND 439-1967

When we offer live entertainment there will be a minimum food charge of
$1.25 per person from 9:00 p.m. till 1:00 a.m.

Giuseppi's Sandwiches

CHILDREN, WE HAVE A SPECIAL MENU FOR YOU !

26. GOLDEN BEAR $1.45
A loaf of French bread loaded with vast quantities of salami, bologna, sauce-piccante, mozzarella cheese, pepperoni and . . . that's all.

27. FRENCH DIP $1.35
Juicy roast beef generously stacked on one half loaf of French bread and served with a clear beef dip. (and a mini-salad!)

28. THE LEO LE CLERC ... $1.15
A rye bread double-decker delight loaded with spicy corned beef, sauerkraut, mild cheese slices and grilled by the chef...its flavor as distinctive as its namesake! (mini-salad included).

29. STROMBOLI .... .95
Discriminating diners will enjoy a taste of sunny Italy in this "dainty", fortified with bologna, salami, mozzarella cheese, diced pepperoni, and sauce-piccante.

30. POOR BOY $1.15
You'll love this combination of ham, salami, lettuce, tomato and a dash of green pepper. . . . real italian flavor.

PANINO IMBOTTITO
(Little Sandwiches)
31. HOT CORN BEEF .... .85
32. HAM AND CHEESE ...... .75
33. HAM .... .65
34. CHEESE .... .60
35. GARLIC BREAD .... .35

36. ROAST BEEF SANDWICH .85
Succulent slices of hot roast beef served on a sesame bun . . . delicious!

BEVANDA
Coffee .... .15
Hot Chocolate .... .15
Milk (medium) .... .15
(large) .... .20
Lemonade, Coke, Orange, Sprite
(medium) .... .15
(large) .... .20

TRY A BOTTLE OF OUR DELICIOUS CIDER

ONLY $2.00 PER BOTTLE

YES, WE HAVE SPAGHETTI TO GO !

Seven Course Italian
DINNER FOR TWO

**With a Bottle of
Imported Chianti Wine For Two**

......

Antipasto

......

Baked Lasagna

......

Chicken or Veal a la Cacciatore

CHOICE OF

Potato and Vegetable

or

Spaghetti with Tomato Sauce

Dessert

Beverage

A Pony of the Following Cordials
May Be Substituted for the Dessert
Anisette — Creme De Menthe — Creme De Cacao

5.95

A super Italian special for two!

Chicken Louigi ....
  Boneless Breast of Chicken, Mushrooms, Meat Sauce, Mozzarella Cheese, baked in oven

Boneless Breast of Chicken ....
  Served with sauted Peppers, Mushrooms, Onions, Meat Sauce, baked in oven, Mozzarella Cheese

Veal Scallopini ....
  Veal, Sauted in Olive Oil, Mushrooms, Meat Sauce, Onions and peppers

Veal Sicilian ....
  Breaded Veal, Mushrooms, Sauted in Olive Oil, Sauterne, Lemon Slices. **NO SAUCE.**

Veal Louigi ....
  Veal covered with Mushrooms, Meat Sauce, Mozzarella Cheese, Italian Herbs, Baked in Oven. **(HOUSE FAVORITE)**

Peppered Veal Cutlet ....
  Smothered with Green Peppers, Mushrooms, Onions, Italian Herbs, topped with Mozzarella Cheese

---

Descriptive copy tells what each Italian dish is.

Trip Around Italy

(FOR THE VENTURESOME)

A serving composed of each of our four popular "Goodies" which include home-made sausage, breaded veal, meat ball, and boneless breast of chicken, fortified with tomato sauce, mushrooms, onions, green peppers, mozzarella cheese and Italian herbs. Served with an iced salad, bread & butter. Side of Spaghetti.

SENSATIONAL!

4.50

"Chef's Suggestion"

BRASCIOLE

Fine Cut of Sirloin Steak

Rolled and filled with Ground Beef, Bread Crumbs, **Cheese**, Grated Hard Boiled Eggs and Pine Nuts. Cooked in Tomato Sauce. Served with Bread and Butter, Salad, Side of Spaghetti.

TRULY DELICIOUS!

4.95

Italian specials can be creative and interesting.

Chianti .... 8 oz. 1.00   16 oz. 1.75
32 oz. 3.50   64 oz. 7.00
Italy's Favorite Table Wine. Fresh, Fruity and full of Flavor

Riserva Ducale — 24 oz. 5.00
A choice, aged Red selected Chianti Wine. Notable for its suberbly clean taste, softness and full bouquet.

Rosatello .... 16 oz. 1.75   32 oz. 3.25
Light and Fruity — Pink in Color

Lancers Vin Rose — 25 oz. 4.50
Light-bondied Rose Wine. Slightly effvesent, delightfully different in taste

Bardolino .... 16 oz. 2.00   32 oz. 3.50
A clear, light, ruddy Wine, a pleasing dry taste.

Valpolicella .... 16 oz. 2.25   32 oz. 3.75
An excellent, deep ruby colored wine, with a delicate bouquet and mellow taste.

Valpantena — 25 oz. 7.00
Natural Sparkling Red Wine

Soave .... 16 oz. 2.25   32 oz. 3.75
Dry, "Suave" velvety white wine, with a soft, light yellow tone, distinguished white Italian wine.

An Italian wine listing complements the Italian cuisine.

VINO

Giovanni offers you his own selection of a dry but substantial Burgundy. This wine, carefully chosen by him, is drawn from his own casks and served decanted, Italian style.

Individual Caraffa	.95
Half Caraffa .... 1.45 Full Caraffa 2.55	

BEVERAGES

Schlitz on tap, light or dark.

Mug .... .35	Pitcher 1.80		

Lowenbrau on tap

Mug .... .55	Pitcher 2.25		

Bottled Beer

Schlitz or Coors	.50

COFFEE Served freshly ground	.20		
Tea .... .20	Buttermilk	.20	
Sanka .... .20	Coke	.20	
Iced Tea ...... .20	Root Beer	.20	
Milk .... .20	Sprite	.20	

DOLCES

Giovanni's Cheese Cake	.45
Fresh Fruit In Season	.20
Spumone	.35
Sherbet	.35

caffé giovanni

FOOD TO GO

Giovanni is delighted to prepare any item on our take-out menu for you to serve in your own home. Dial the letters "THE MOST" for prompt attention to your phone orders.

One Silver Dollar Will Buy Any Pizza.

Giovanni and his family, have been operating restaurants in the Bay Area for many years. They built the present Caffe Giovanni to provide the public with the highest quality of food and service in a warm, inviting, yet sophisticated atmosphere.

The construction and decor is suggestive of an old world caffe in the Bay of Naples area. Each of the three dining areas, different, yet complementary, is reminiscent of a Western Italian coastal town.

The Sidewalk Caffe contains elements of coarse-troweled stucco, terra cotta quarry tile, wrought iron partitions and fences, rusted iron chandeliers, and butted plank oak flooring. Its walls bear a collage of opera and theater posters from famous Italian teatros.

The Main Dining Room is built around an overscaled, hooded fireplace. Its walls are covered with murals painted in subdued earth colors accented with blues. They were designed and executed to accentuate the impression of a cruise along the Italian coast with its quaint ports and houses lining the harbors. The main pillars are Victorian porch posts stripped to the natural wood.

The Boat House, or party room, features intimate dining and is walled with a double row of weathered hatch covers. One wall is dominated by two huge sailfish caught in Mexico by Giovanni and his head chef.

Caffe Giovanni's superb cuisine by head chef Andy Fallas is prepared in an exposition kitchen, completely custom-designed so that the combining of fine ingredients and expert culinary skills in a unique facility, is in itself, a significant and appealing part of the decor and atmosphere.

Thank you! You have helped us succeed and grow. We have always tried to give you our best, both in quality and that extra care in preparing your food. Serving you shall continue to be our pleasure.

Your Host, GIOVANNI

CAFFÉ GIOVANNI
2420 Shattuck Avenue   Berkeley   843-6678

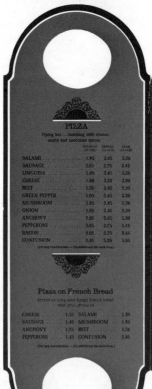

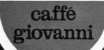

PIZZA

Piping hot ...bubbling with cheese, sauce and succulent spices.

	Individual (10 inch)	Medium (12 inch)	Large (14 inch)
SALAMI	1.95	2.45	3.20
SAUSAGE	2.05	2.75	3.45
LINGUISA	1.95	2.45	3.20
CHEESE	1.80	2.20	2.90
BEEF	1.95	2.45	3.20
GREEN PEPPER	1.95	2.45	3.20
MUSHROOM	1.95	2.45	3.20
ONION	1.95	2.45	3.20
ANCHOVY	1.95	2.45	3.20
PEPPERONI	2.05	2.75	3.45
BACON	2.05	2.75	3.45
CONFUSION	2.45	5.20	5.05

(for any combination — 20¢ additional for each item.)

Pizza on French Bread

Served on crisp sour dough French bread with your choice of

CHEESE	1.35	SALAMI	1.35
SAUSAGE	1.45	MUSHROOM	1.35
ANCHOVY	1.35	BEEF	1.35
PEPPERONI	1.45	CONFUSION	1.95

(for any combination — 20¢ additional for each item.)

BUON APPETITO!

The magic touch of Mama Savaria transforms dinner to pure delight.

From her collection of treasured recipes may we suggest:

BAKED LASAGNA	2.35
The traditional wide noodle with a rich sauce of meat and cheese.	
VEAL SCALLOPINI	3.65
Thinly sliced veal sauteed in a robust Italian Sauce.	
CANELLONI ALLA TOSCANA	2.35
Pipes of pasta filled with seasoned meat in a glorious tomato sauce.	
BROCHETTES OF BEEF	4.35
Choice Filet, green peppers, bacon, tomatoes, mushrooms on a skewer, with rigatoni.	
PASTA-A-PLENTY	2.45
Lasagna, ravioli and rigatoni, served in a savory sauce.	
STEAK ALLA GIOVANNI	4.85
The choicest New York cut, broiled to tender perfection, served with French Bread and Butter.	

All above served with French Bread and Butter.

Pasta

SPAGHETTI with meat sauce	1.55
SPAGHETTI with meat ball	1.90
RAVIOLI	1.65
RAVIOLI with meat ball	2.00
HALF SPAGHETTI — HALF RAVIOLI	1.85
HALF SPAGHETTI — HALF RAVIOLI with meat ball	2.20
RIGATONI	1.55
RIGATONI with meat ball	1.90
A delicious wide flat noodle in our own meat sauce.	
Spaghetti, Ravioli or Rigatoni .... ½ order	1.10
Mushrooms with Pasta	.80

All above served with French Bread and Butter.

On the Side

French Bread and Butter	.35
Oven Hot Garlic Bread	.45
Polpette (Two meat balls)	.70
Grilled Mushrooms with Butter	.80
Italian Style	.90

caffé giovanni

SANDWICHES

Steak Sandwich	French Dip Sandwich
Bianca butterati sliced on French roll with sauteed mushrooms, bossil salad and fresh greens.	Choice beef on French roll dipped in our special juices and served with potato or tossed salad.
2.15	1.65

American Cheese (Grilled)	.70
Roast Beef, Italian Style	1.10
Served hot on French roll with sauteed bell peppers.	
Polpette (Meatballs on French bread)	.95
Italian Sausage, Mama Savaria Style	.95
Grilled with our special sauce on French roll.	

IL HAMBURGO

Hamburger	.85
The finest fresh ground beef done to perfection.	
Cheese Burger	1.05
Topped with tangy cheese melted to mouth-watering goodness.	
Mushroom Burger	1.45
Smothered in delicate Italian mushrooms—Delicious!	
Mozzarella Burger	1.15
Light, golden Italian cheese—melts in your mouth!	
Onion Burger	1.15
Smothered in onions, sauteed to golden goodness.	
Pizza Burger	1.35
Covered with Giovanni's own secret sauce — Magnifico!	

MAMA SAVARIA'S SPECIALTY
Homemade Minestrone Soup — .45
A Specialty of the House, rich, hot and filling!

SALADS

CRISP, TOSSED GREENS — .45 (With Anchovies) —	.85
GIOVANNI'S POTATO SALAD	.40
Made with sour cream	
COTTAGE CHEESE	.40
COMBINATION SALAD	.95
Crisp greens mixed with fresh cherry tomatoes, salami, tangy pepperoncini and black olives.	

Choice of our dressings:
Italian, French, Thousand Island, Bleu Cheese, Garlic.

Please Pay Cashier

LUNCHEON

Served daily from 11:00 a.m. to 4:30 p.m.

LINGUISA SANDWICH	1.55
A smoked sausage smothered in green peppers and melted cheese. Served with fresh green salad.	
POLPETTE SPECIAL	1.15
Meatballs perfectly seasoned and sauced for a man with French bread and butter. Served with fresh green salad.	
ITALIAN SAUSAGE SANDWICH	1.35
Served open-face—Mama Savaria Style in Giovanni's special sauce. Served with fresh green salad.	
GROUND ROUND STEAK	1.95
Covered with our Special Sauce, sauteed mushrooms, and served with spaghetti, garnish, bread and butter.	
RIB EYE STEAK	2.35
Served with spaghetti, garnish, bread and butter.	
VEAL ALLA POMODORO	2.95
Thinly sliced veal sauteed with cherry tomatoes, mushrooms and green peppers. Served on a bed of Rigatoni with bread and butter.	
SLIMLINE	1.35
Broiled ground beef served with cottage cheese and fruit.	
ARROSTO FREDDO	1.15
Cold roast beef sandwich served with hot, hot soup or crisp salad.	
POOR BOY SANDWICH .... (For One)	.95
(For Two)	1.65
Made with cappacola, salami, cheese, tomato, shredded lettuce, and our Italian dressing on French bread — garnished with cherry tomato, black olive and tangy pepperoncini.	

All Luncheon Items above served until 4:30 p.m. daily.

GIOVANNI'S CHAMPAGNE BRUNCH
11:00 a.m. to 3:00 p.m.—Sunday
Giovanni invites you to a complimentary glass of champagne served with any food on our menu for your enjoyment during a Sunday Brunch — Italian Style.

Additional Glass of Champagne .65

Sunday Brunch Special
THREE EGG OMELETTE
Cheese, Salami, or Mushroom 1.50
Served with garnish and toasted French roll

caffé giovanni

This Italian menu is extremely well designed, well written and it sells. The die cut adds to the appearance with everything merchandised effectively.

THE CHINESE-ORIENTAL MENU

The story is told that once upon a time an embarrassed Chinese ambassador ran out of food during a banquet for his Western friends, and created Chop Suey to fill the small void still left in his guests. Since that day, the American dining public has progressed both in sophistication and appreciation of fine Chinese and other Oriental foods until today Peking Duck, Melon Cup Soup, and Lobsters with Black Bean Sauce occupy definite niches in the esteem of the gourmet.

But many people have only a superficial knowledge of Chinese-Oriental foods, and if they are to fully enjoy the epicurean delights open to the discriminating diner, the menu must inform and instruct accordingly. All of the requirements for a good menu, as set forth for American menus such as quality artwork and design, good paper selection, quality printing, good type selection, layout and listing that follows a logical ordering sequence, apply equally to the Chinese menu. But, in addition, some special requirements are necessary to merchandise this type of cuisine effectively.

Basically, it can be summed up in two words—more information. This means more descriptive copy about each item served as well as more information about Chinese or Oriental foods generally. The following copy from The Golden Pavillion restaurant illustrates what can be told about the subject:

HOW TO DINE WELL IN CHINESE

The secret of a good Chinese dinner lies in the variety of dishes which make it up.

There must be a sufficient number of persons to justify the number of dishes required for a good dinner. A good Chinese dinner requires six to ten persons at a table.

The best way to assure a good dinner is to order in advance, and permit our chef to suggest a menu. Even if you are very experienced with Chinese food, our chef will probably have many dishes unknown to you. Make use of the chef's many years of creative experience, and you will heighten your enjoyment of Chinese food.

Our dinners are composed to provide variety and to minimize the problems of selection. However, if you wish to exercise your own judgment and select from this menu, order a soup and one dish for each person at the table. Never order more than one dish from each basic category of food, (i.e.: pork, beef, chicken, duck, etc.). Please rest assured that your coming experience with items from our six Classic Chinese Cuisines will be a pleasant one.

General headings such as Appetizers, Soups, Special Dinners, Meats and Vegetables, Eggs, Seafood, Fowl, Bean Curd Dishes, Rice and Desserts are helpful. And if Chop Suey and Chow Mein (not strictly Chinese dishes) are served, these headings should be used. Most items on a Chinese menu are listed and sold a la carte. But special dinners, family dinners, seafood dinners and "for two" or more are also common. The following CHINESE BAN-QUET illustrates the "group" entree type listing which is required in many cases if the many types of foods are to be eaten at one meal:

> The Chinese Banquet or "Wine-Spread," as we call it, is truly an unusual experience in gourmet dining. The Traditional Chinese Banquet of the old days consisted of sixteen or thirty-two main courses. The most elaborate of all dinners, of course, was the "Manchu-Chinese Feast," consisting of 108 dishes.

> Harmony, contrast and accent are the three principles of the Chinese culinary art. Each dish must harmonize and contrast with the one before and after it. . .each dinner must have a point of focus in a principal dish.

> Here are a few banquet dishes around which an unusual dinner-party may be planned. When the occasion arises, let Mrs. Augusta Lee give you her version of a Chinese "Wine-Spread" that will please and intrigue your guests and have them talking about it for months.

> Our Hong Kong Banquet consists of ten to sixteen courses and is served for a minimum party of eight. The price is $9.50 to $15.00 per person.

After the opening copy about Chinese-Oriental foods in general, and after describing and featuring "specials" or "package" dinners, the specific copy relative to each entree, appetizer, dessert, etc., should be examined. The following examples:

APPETIZERS
PARCHMENT BEEF
Cubes of choice beef tenderloin, marinated, wrapped in edible parchment. A delight to taste.
$2.50

SOUP
SEAWEED SOUP (Gee Choy Tong)
Flaky imported Seaweed with Chopped Water Chestnuts and Egg Flower in a full bodied soup.
$1.25

POULTRY
SWEET-SOUR PRESSED DUCK
Boneless braised duck sauteed in our piquant sweet-sour sauce and garnished with imported sweet pickled vegetables for an unusual taste treat.
$4.25

LOBSTER
LOBSTER KEW
Chunks of fresh lobster meat blended with snow pea pods, water chestnuts bamboo shoots, mushrooms and succulent Chinese vegetables.
$4.50

SEAFOOD
HUNG SHEW FISH
Braised fresh fish smothered with shredded
pork, scallions, and Chinese vegetables,
accented with ginger and a dash of Chinese
liqueur.

$4.25

PORK
PORK SOONG
Minced fresh pork tastily blended with
snow pea pods, bamboo shoots, and
water chestnuts in a delicious sauce,
then topped with snow white rice
noodles.

$3.25

VEGETARIAN
CHOW SAN TONG
Delicious Chinese mushrooms, crunchy
bamboo shoots and crispy snow pea pods
blend harmoniously together in a dish fit
for a Buddha.

$3.50

GOURMET
WINTER MELON BALL
A gourmet's delight, famed for its unique
flavor and elaborate ingredients, this richly
flavored soup contains diced lobster, chicken,
Virginia ham, Chinese mushrooms, lotus seeds,
ginko nuts, water chestnuts, peas and bamboo
shoots. The whole winter melon is steamed
slowly and carefully, for a minimum of 24
hours.

$14.00

RICE
VANG CHOW FRIED RICE
A superb combination of fresh garden
peas, diced prawns, barbecued pork,
green onions and lettuce.

$1.75

EGGS
SHARK'S FIN OMELETTE
A favorite Chinese gourmet item seldom
found in America. Shark's fin in a fluffy
omelette, seasoned and garnished with
tidbits of mixed meats.

$4.50

MEATS AND VEGETABLES
VEGETABLES UNDER SNOW
Shredded garden vegetables, imported
mushrooms, and marinated beef, topped
with crisp Chinese vermicelli.

$2.25

DESSERT
ALMOND CURDS WITH LICHEES
Traditional Chinese pudding garnished
with tropical lichees.

$.50

Even the beverage portion of the Oriental menu can be interesting. The South Seas type of restaurant makes the best merchandising presentation of unusual drinks, but any Chinese restaurant can (and usually should) feature its alcoholic beverages better, if it serves them. There are oriental liqueurs—Mei Kwei lu, Ng Ka Py, Nomi Rice Liqueur, and Rice Wine, Saki, etc.

There is no excuse (except neglect and lack of concern) for any standard less than excellence in the artwork on any Chinese-Oriental menu, from cover to internal listing. The calligraphy of the written Chinese or Japanese word is beautiful enough by itself to constitute a design element, and other drawings, paintings and prints are available for use on the menu.

fowls

F 1 柱候燒乳鴿
BARBECUED SQUAB
Squab marinated in soya and spices, cooked to a golden brown.
Chinese spiced salt   **3.50**

F 2 金亭炸童鷄
CANTONESE SPICED HEN
Young hens, marinated in fragrant Chinese spices, and cooked with a crispened skin   **3.25**

F 3 窩燒鴨
MANDARIN DUCK
Boneless duck, steam cooked — then blend with spices, battered with waterchestnut flour. Fried to a golden brown. Served with a fruit sauce   **2.50**

F 4 北平掛爐鴨
PEKING DUCK
Whole duck marinated with honey and spices—then barbecued to a crackling brown. Served with individual steamed buns. A gourmet's "must"! Serves Six   **9.75**

F 5 杏仁鷄丁
ALMOND CHICKEN
Tender diced chicken, bamboo shoots, mushrooms, waterchestnuts and almonds. Toss-cooked   **2.25**

F 6 鴛鴦鷄
DRAGON AND PHOENIX CHICKEN
Layers of ham, spiced chicken and pork, barbecued together to achieve a blend of flavors   **8.50**

F 7 桃蓉焗鷄塊
CHICKEN IN WALNUT PASTE
Roast chicken prepared in chopped walnut spice sauce then roasted to a golden brown   **3.50**

F 8 毛菇鷄球
BUTTON MUSHROOM CHICKEN
Chicken chunks, button mushrooms, bamboo shoots, waterchestnuts, vegetables toss-cooked for flavor   **2.50**

F 9 豉汁鷄球
CHICKEN CANTONESE
Chicken cubes, toss-cooked in a black bean and garlic mash sauce with distinctive flavor   **2.75**

F 10 菠蘿鷄
PINEAPPLE CHICKEN
Chunks of boned chicken, diced pineapple, green peppers, onions sauted in a sweet and sour sauce   **3.00**

F 11 碎炸子鷄
SOUTH CHINA CHICKEN
Chicken cubes, marinated in mixture of Southern spices and fried in the Chinese manner   **3.00**

F 12 手撕鷄
SHREDDED CHICKEN
Salad-like dish of shredded chicken tossed with Chinese parsley, green onions, sesame seeds, chopped nuts and imported spices Half   **3.50**
Whole   **7.00**

Chinese characters, good copy, good type and layout, plus numbers for quick and easy ordering make this a good listing.

JADE PAGODA RESTAURANT

SPECIAL FAMILY STYLE DINNERS

PAGODA DINNER FOR TWO PERSONS $5.00
(EACH ADDITIONAL PERSON $2.50)

SOUP ALA PAGODA
BARBECUED PORK, MUSTARD, SESAME SEEDS
PAGODA EGG ROLLS
ALMOND FRIED CHICKEN
PORK CHOW MEIN
SWEET and SOUR SPARERIBS
PORK FRIED RICE
CHINESE TEA   FORTUNE COOKIES
Fried Shrimp added to above Dinner for Party of Four or More

Individual Chinese Combination Dinners

NO. 1 $1.35

PORK CHOW MEIN
PORK EGG FOO YOUNG
SWEET & SOUR SPARERIBS
BOILED RICE
TEA   FORTUNE COOKIES
(WITH FRIED RICE 35¢ ADDITIONAL)

NO. 2 $1.65

CHICKEN NOODLE SOUP
CHICKEN CHOW MEIN
SWEET & SOUR SPARERIBS
PORK FRIED RICE
TEA   FORTUNE COOKIES

NO. 3 $1.95

CHICKEN NOODLE SOUP
ALMOND CHICKEN CHOW MEIN
PINEAPPLE SWEET & SOUR SPARERIBS
FRIED LOUISIANA PRAWNS
BOILED RICE
TEA   FORTUNE COOKIES
(WITH FRIED RICE 35¢ ADDITIONAL)

NO. 4 $1.65

DELUXE VEGETABLE CHOW MEIN
SHRIMP FRIED RICE
FRIED LOUISIANA PRAWNS
TEA   FORTUNE COOKIES

Inexpensive daily specials can be part of the oriental menu also.

CHINESE COCKTAILS

New Import from Hong Kong

Temple Bells - - - 1.50
Mute and mellow, like the
temple bells,
This concoction is smooth
as velvet, strong as religion.

China Rose - - - 1.50
The China Rose blooms the whole
year round, may help summer
sing in you awhile longer.

Pink Jade - - - 1.50
Say love with Jade.

Lotus Blossom - - - 1.50
Lotus Blossom, all pink and white
will make a tiger of you tonight.

Precious Lantern - - 1.25
Festive fruits and non-alcholic
juices, colorful and inviting.

The Hong Kong Express - 2.20
Will give you a quick smooth ride
to wherever you want to go.

The drink menu or listing can be original and creative as well as oriental.

GOURMET SOUPS

(Minimum two persons)

CHINESE FAMILY SOUP.......... 1.95

A hearty delicious soup containing diced pork or chicken with Chinese vegetables.

BA BO SOUP 2.30

Ba Bo in Chinese means Eight Precious Ingredients. One of the highly honored soup courses in Chinese Banquet festivals. Everyone who eats Chinese food must be acquainted with it.

HONG KONG SPECIAL
WONTON SOUP 2.75

Made famous by us. Besides your favorite Wonton, it is served with finely cut shrimp, Imported ham, tender bamboo shoots, Chinese mushrooms, water chestnuts and many others.

WINTER MELON SOUP........... 2.75

One of the highly honored soup courses in Chinese Banquet festivals; Winter Melon, a special Chinese melon that is a vegetable and not a fruit. The soup is slowly simmered with fine oriental herbs, spices, seafood, chicken meat, imported ham and many others.

SUAN LA PUNGENT SOUP 2.75

A famous "Szechuen Province" contribution which is beloved and renowned in the whole of China. We have the pleasure to have it on our menu.
This is an art of blending which creates an exotic taste pungent and hot with imported Chinese special vegetables, bean cards, shredded bamboo shoots and Formosan mushrooms. A very recommended soup.

CHICKEN SUMI SOUP............. 2.50

A traditional Autumn Festival soup in Thanksgiving spirit for a rich harvest.
A warm thick soup made of finely minced boneless chicken and pork together with tender sugar-sweet corn egg creamed sprinkled with special Chinese greens.

YANGCHOW WOR WONTON . 4.95

AN EXCITING EXTRAVAGANT SOUP FOR Wonton lovers. "Yangchow, China" originated this special treat.

Besides "oodles" of Wonton, there are chunk size lobster meat, fresh shrimp, roast pork and chicken, simmered with assorted Chinese vegetables. Beware! It almost composes a meal by itself.

BIRD'S NEST SOUP
(Advance Order)   6.00

Bird's Nest is a direct translation from Chinese. It is actually the food for the young as honey is for the bee's young.
Besides the difficulties of obtaining them, its is also a challenge to the chef's culinary art to prepare it. According to Chinese lore, it is considered a "Fountain of Youth" rejuvenating both to spirit and body, truly for occasions as a Birthday Banquet.

The riches of ingredients such as minced chicken, lobster, imported ham mushrooms, waterchestnuts and others with the secret receipe of assorted oriental spices makes this soup both expensive and artistic.

SHARK'S FIN SOUP
(Advance order)   8.50

Shark's fin comes from a special breed of shark found in the Pacific Ocean around the China sea. This is the most expensive Chinese soup in banquet dinners. It takes days of preparation. Whole Chicken, Duck, Yung-nan Ham and Pork loin chops simmered over ten hours until all meats disintergrates, whereby a pair of chopsticks can separate them. Then choice selected Shark's Fin Chinese vegetables, mushrooms, bamboo hearts and others together with a secret recipe of the Chef's makes it delicious and exotic. This special soup is served on special occasions as Weddings and other important banquets.

Soup is not just soup if it is a special Chinese gourmet soup and merchandised accordingly.

Peking Duck.............................. 24.00

The world famous Peking Duck is prepared from an ancient and treasured recipe. It was created and developed in the Imperial Palace of Peking at the time when the Northern Capital was the center of China's cultural and epicurean arts. The Peking Duck is served in two courses: first, the luscious golden-brown crispy skin is served with a special sauce and Chinese steamed bread; then, the succulent meat is "quick-stirred" with either pineapple or choice Chinese vegetables into an entirely different tasting dish.

Winter Melon Bowl 18.00

A gourmet's delight, famed for its unique flavor and elaborate ingredients, this richly flavored soup contains diced-cut lobster, chicken, Virginia ham, Chinese mushrooms, lotus seeds, gingko nuts, waterchestnuts, peas and bamboo hoots. The whole winter melon is steamed, slowly and carefully, for a minimum of 24 hours.

Hung Shew Shark's Fins 38.00

The finest imported shark's fins simmered for hours in a sauce made from tender young chicken, Virginia ham, Chinese spices, imported wine, rock sugar and soy sauce. This dish is considered a superb delicacy fit for an emperor.

Ho Go (minimum for two) per person 8.50

Ho Go means Chafing Dish in English and Fire Pot in Chinese. A charcoal-burning Ho Go brazier, with a pot of merrily bubbling chicken broth, is placed before you, and you dip (or lose) the following delicacies in the broiling broth. Served with a tantalizing dip-sauce, this dish is perfect for a cold winter's eve and delightful fun for you and your friends to try.

Fresh chicken	Chicken liver
Fresh lobster	Chinese mushrooms
Filet mignon	Bean curd
Fresh shrimp	Waterchestnuts
Filet of fish	Chinese greens
Rice noodles	

Imperial Squab 24.00

Fried young squabs marinated with Chinese liqueur, spice and Yo Yu Sauce that almost melts in one's mouth, served with toasted salt and wedged lemon.

West Lake Duck 20.00

This renowned dish originated amid the unsurpassed beauty of the West Lake region of Hangchow. Stuffed with ten exotic ingredients, this boneless whole duckling is simmered over a low fire until it is so thoroughly tender that it literally melts in your mouth.

Squab Soong 15.00

Minced squab meat blended with waterchestnuts, snow pea pods, bamboo shoots, and Virginia ham. Served wrapped in crispy lettuce.

Roast Whole Pigling 45.00

If Charles Lamb spoke so highly of an accidentally roasted pig, he would have been overjoyed with our meticulously prepared pigling fragrant with Chinese herbs and spices. The tender crispy skin and fragrant juicy meat are served with a special sauce and Chinese steamed bread.

Hong Kong Roast Chicken 12.00

Tender young chicken roasted with special Chinese spices, wine and sauces. The skin is crisp and golden-brown and the meat is juicy and tender.

WHOLE FISH(Individual Portion) 4.95

Hung Shew
Prepared to your pleasure. Braised and smothered with shredded pork, scallions and Chinese vegetables, accented with ginger and a dash of Chinese liqueur.

Sweet and Sour
In our original sweet and pungent sauce topped with colorful imported Chinese condiments.

Steamed
With assorted condiments, fresh ginger and Chinese liqueur and imported spices.

Gourmet items get special, extra detailed copy treatment. The bigger the item—the more copy is a good rule.

How to Dine Well – in Chinese

The secret of a good Chinese dinner lies in the variety of dishes which make it up.

There must be a sufficient number of persons to justify the number of dishes required for a good dinner. A good Chinese dinner requires six to ten persons at a table.

The best way to assure a good dinner is to order in advance, and permit our chef to suggest a menu. Even if you are very experienced with Chinese food, our chef will probably have many dishes unknown to you. Make use of the chef's many years of creative experience, and you will heighten your enjoyment of Chinese food.

Our dinners are composed to provide variety and to minimize the problems of selection.

However, if you wish to exercise your own judgment and select from this menu, order a soup and one dish for each person at the table. Never order more than one dish from each basic category of food, (i.e.: pork, beef, chicken, duck, etc.). Please rest assured that your coming experience with items from our six Classic Chinese Cuisines will be a pleasant one.

"How to order" instructions are a valuable asset for any Chinese menu.

Ming's Chinese restaurant in Palo Alto, Calif. does an excellent job of merchandising their special type food and service.   In the descriptive material reproduced below, both "The Chinese dinner table" and the use of chopsticks are emphasized.   On a good menu, the facts are not enough. . .they must be presented in an interesting and exciting manner.   Seasoned with imagination and creativity any menu will tell more—and sell more.

The Chinese dinner table —

As an aid to your full enjoyment of this occasion we present to you our table setting and its functions:

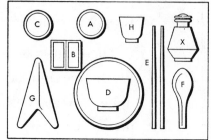

A—Soy Sauce (Se Yow) corresponds to salt at your table. Use accordingly. More is available in bottle **(X)** with the free-flow top. Do **NOT** remove top when pouring.

B—Mustard and Plum Sauce (Gai Lot, Mui Jeung). Mustard provides the "hot" quality of pepper. Plum sauce is a tangy condiment used usually with ducks and squabs.

C—Spiced Salt (Wah Yim) is used with fried or barbecued poultry. Note the delicate flavoring. Commercial seasoned salts are developed from this Chinese condiment.

D—Rice bowl (Fon Woon) is used for soup and rice. When eating rice the bowl is held to mouth and the rice is "brushed" into mouth with chopsticks. Rice is the staple course of a Cantonese meal. It takes the place of noodles used in North China and bread of the Occidental world.

E—Chopsticks (Fai Tze) are your "forks," and sometimes your "spoons"—used to convey food.

F—Porcelain Spoon (Chee Gung). Chinese soups are served piping hot! Where a metal spoon would burn, the porcelain spoon remains cool for comfort.

G—Napkins (Chon Gun) certain Chinese foods require the use of fingers. Instead of finger bowls, Chinese custom prescribes the use of a specially scented hot napkin.

H—Tea (Cha) is taken throughout the meal. Chinese tea is mild, and sometimes scented, and taken as an unflavored beverage to clear the palate. Different flavors can thus be savored without confusion of taste.

Using the chopsticks —

Hold first chopstick as shown in (Figure 1). This chopstick is held firm and stationary in fixed position. Take second chopstick as you would a pencil. With the tips of thumb, index and second fingers manipulate this stick to meet the first chopstick (Figure 2). This action forms a "clamp" to convey your food (Figure 3). Very easy—with a little practice! Otherwise, ask your waiter for a "Chaa" (translation—fork or spear.)

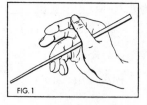

FIG. 1

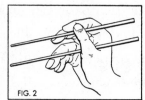

FIG. 2

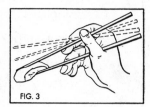

FIG. 3

DINNER MENU

SALAD A LA ORIENTALE
O-SUIMONO SOUP
PICKLED VEGETABLES
RICE · TEA · DESSERT

TEMPURA **$3.85**
  Delicately deep-fried prawns, fresh fish and assorted vegetables
  served with the traditional Tempura sauce.

YOSENABE (Cooked at your table — 2 persons minimum) **$3.85**
  Fish cake, fried bean cake, somen and assorted   per person
  fresh vegetables broiled in a delicious soup with chicken,
  beef and seafood.

MIZUTAKI **$4.50**
  Chicken, fresh vegetables, tofu (bean cake), bamboo shoots,
  mushrooms, and long rice cooked with our special FURUSATO
  STOCK and served in traditional mashiko ware.

SUKIYAKI (Cooked at your table — 2 or more persons) **$4.80**
  (Cooked in kitchen — 1 person)   per person
  Prime choice sliced beef, fresh vegetables, tofu (bean cake), bamboo
  shoots, mushrooms and yam noodles cooked with our special soy
  sauce and prepared before you by our hostesses.

YOSHITSUNE NABE **$5.00**
  (Cooked at your table on a traditional stove —   per person
  3 or more persons)
  Furusato's special Genghis Khan Yaki consisting of
  prime choice beef with assorted vegetables and enhanced
  by complimentary sauces.

FURUSATO SPECIAL OKONOMI AGE **$4.50**
  (Cooked at your table — 2 or more persons)   per person
  Fresh prawns, fresh fish, fish cake, choice beef, chicken and fresh
  assorted vegetables on bamboo skewers to be cooked by you in oil
  and prepared with a special sauce.

FURUSATO SUPREME SHABU-SHABU **$7.00**
  (Cooked at your table — 2 or more persons)   per person
  Prime choice of beef and assorted vegetables cooked to your own
  liking in a specially prepared FURUSATO STOCK.

A Japanese menu with good descriptive copy and large clear readable type.

MEXICAN-SPANISH MENUS

Americans have an almost unlimited appetite for ethnic foods, and two types of "foreign food" restaurants that have enjoyed increasing popularity in the last few years are Mexican and Spanish restaurants. The cuisine of these two types of foodservice operations is basically different. Mexican food—tacos, enchiladas, taquitos, chili, etc.—tends to be on the high-flavor, spicy side, while the foods of continental Spain are more acceptable in taste to the American palate, although gazpacho (cold vegetable soup of Andalusia) is a "hot" item.

The factor that connects the two types of restaurants is the use of the Spanish language, which means that while everything can and should be listed in Spanish to add verbal "color," the translation into English should follow immediately as shown in the following examples:

PAELLA VALENCIANA
National culinary delight of Spain contains shrimp, clams, crabmeat and other seasonal seafood, chicken, Spanish sausages, onions, Spanish red peppers, vegetables, saffron, seasoned with Spanish wine.

ARROS AMARILLO CON CAMERONES
Pacific coast shrimp baked with yellow rice, saffron, tomatoes, onions, Spanish red peppers and peas.

ARROS AMARILLO CON POLLO
One half spring chicken baked with rice, saffron, tomatoes, peas, onions and red peppers.

BISTEC SEGOVIA
Prime rib eye steak marinated in Spanish wine, charcoal broiled and topped with sauce Espagnole and sliced black olives.

CHILE RELLENO
Mexican Poblano pepper stuffed with spiced beef or cheese, rolled and fried in an egg batter and topped with a special tomato sauce.

PESCADO ALA VERACRUZANA
Sauteed filet of red snapper, simmered with capers, garlic, green olives, peeled tomato, pimento, parsley and garnished with large Mexican peppers.

CARNE ASADA TAMPIQUENA
Tenderloin of beef sauteed in butter accompanied by pink beans.

TERNERA CON LENTEJAS
Tender scallops of milkfed veal served with a Spanish sauce and accompanied by lentils.

BANDERILLA MEXICANA
Hearty cubes of beef broiled with mushroom caps, green peppers and tomatoes served on a flaming sword accompanied by Mexican rice.

ENCHILADAS—CARNE
Mild beef stuffing fills this rolled pancake-like Tortilla, baked with creamy red sauce and cheese.

TACOS—CARNE
Crisp envelope-like tortillas filled with meat topped off with shredded lettuce, tomatoes and cheese.

TOSTADOS CARNE
Large tortillas stacked high with layers of beef, frijoles refritos (refried Mexican beans) shredded lettuce, tomatoes and cheese.

The special drinks (bebidas) of a Mexican-Spanish menu are usually the Margarita cocktail (a blend of tequila, lime juice and triple sec), tequila desi cocktail (tequila, grenadine and lemon juice), or the increasingly popular sangria or Sant' Gria as it is sometimes called. A special recipe for Orange Sangria from the Senor Alfredo Mexican Restaurant is listed as follows:

ORANGE SANGRIA
A traditional Mexican-Spanish wine drink. Red wine base, orange juice, orange oil, sugar. Served in a chilled wine glass with crushed ice.

And here is another interesting Mexican wine cocktail:

SENORITA MARA WINE COCKTAIL
White wine base, sparkling cider, lemon. Served in a chilled wine glass with crushed ice and garnished with a slice of lemon and salt on the glass rim.

There are some very interesting Mexican after dinner drinks also. Some examples are:

CAFE MEXICANA
Flamed Spanish coffee, brandy and kahlua topped with whipped cream.

BANDERA MEXICANA
A pousse cafe of grenadine, cointreau and green creme de menthe.

AZTEC de ORO
Tequila and Strega on the rocks.

A listing of section headings for the Spanish-Mexican menu is given here. There are two ways of handling the language problem on the Mexican-Spanish menu (as with German, Italian, etc., menus). You can list in Spanish and then describe in English, or you can have two complete menus side-by-side with prices in pesos and dollars. The double menu adds a bit of cosmopolitan sophistication and also makes your listing look larger. A listing of section headings is given here with English translations:

Bebidas	Drinks
Antes de su Comida	Before your Meal
Vinos	Wines
Bebidas Compuestas	Mixed Drinks
Entremeses	Appetizers
Potajes	Soups and Consomme
Ensaladas	Salads
Carnes a la Parrilla	Charcoal Broiled
Pescados y Mariscos	Seafood
Platillos Mexicano	Mexican Dishes
Platillos Especiales	Specials
Aves	Poultry
Emparedados	Sandwiches
Postres	Desserts
Durante su Comida	During your Meal

The most famous of Spanish-Mexican salads (ensaladas) is the Guacamole, made from avocado, chili, onion, garlic, lemon, salt, pepper and tomato. And to give you an idea of how words can help the menu and stimulate the palate, consider this listing of just ordinary tomato juice:

Nectar from the Apple of Love
The tomato, introduced to Spain by the Conquistadores, was at first known as the Apple of Love!

Pescados y Mariscos

	PESOS
PESCADO BLACK BASS MAITRE'D	25.00
FILETE DE PESCADO AZUL SALSA TARTARA ...	18.75
PESCADO CABRILLA FRITO SALSA DE LIMON .	22.00
HUACHINANGO VERACRUZANA O SALSA DE VINO	22.00
CALLO DE HACHA A LA FRANCESA	18.75
ANCAS DE RANA AL GUSTO	28.00
COMBINACION DE MARISCOS	37.50
OSTIONES A LA FRANCESA	25.00
OSTIONES A LA DIABLA	25.00
OSTIONES EN SU CONCHA	25.00
CAMARON A LA FRANCESA	25.00
CAMARON A LA MEXICANA	25.00
CAMARON AL ALAMBRE	25.00
CAMARON AL MOJO DE AJO	37,50
LANGOSTA A LA PARRILLA, THERMIDOR, WILSON	37.50

Ocean Delights

	DOLARES
BOQUILLA BLACK BASS MAITRE'D	2.00
FILET OF BLUE FISH TARTAR SAUCE	1.50
CABRILLA BASS LEMON SAUCE	1.75
RED SNAPPER WINE SAUCE OR VERACRUZ...	1.75
FRENCH FRIED SCALLOPS	1.50
FROG LEGS, CHOICE	2.25
SEA FOOD COMBINATION	3.00
FRENCH FRIED OYSTERS	2.00
OYSTERS A LA DIABLA	2.00
OYSTERS ON THEIR SHELL	2.00
FRENCH FRIED SHRIMP	2.00
MEXICAN STYLE SHRIMP	2.00
SHRIMP EN BROCHETTE	2.00
SHRIMP WITH SPECIAL GARLIC SAUCE	3.00
LOBSTER THERMIDOR, WILSON NEWBURG OR BROILED	3.00

Seafood selection is listed twice, in Spanish and English, with prices in pesos and dollars.

Dolores in Continental Spain

(served from 8:30 p.m. to closing)

entremeses variados
(assorted appetizers) 2.50

guacamole in the manner Espagnole
(half avocado stuffed with avocado) 1.50

entremes de camarones
(gulf shrimp cocktail of Seville)
1.75

gaspacho andaluz
famous cold vegetable soup of Andalusia .90

sopa de Ajo con Huevo
(garlic soup for the strong in heart) 1.50

PAELLA VALENCIANA
National culinary delight of Spain contains shrimp, clams, crabmeat and other seasonal seafood, chicken, Spanish sausages, onions, Spanish red peppers, vegetables, saffron, seasoned with Spanish wine.
individual casserole	4.75
casserole for two	8.50

ARROS AMARILLO CON CAMERONES
Pacific coast shrimp baked with yellow rice, saffron, tomatoes, onions, Spanish red peppers and peas
individual casserole	4.25
casserole for two	8.00

ARROS AMARILLO CON POLLO
One half spring chicken baked with rice, saffron, tomatoes, peas, onions and red peppers
individual casserole	3.75
casserole for two	7.00

PESCADO
Fresh fish of the day — as prepared on the Costa Brava in Spain 4.50

BISTEC SEGOVIA
Prime rib eye steak marinated in Spanish wine, charcoal broiled and topped with sauce Espagnole and sliced black olives 6.75

all above entrees are served with ENSALADA MIXTA
in a true olive oil and lemon dressing

This Spanish menu has an attractive illustration, a good type selection and informative descriptive copy.

COMIDA MEXICANA DE VERDAD TRULY MEXICAN FOOD EN EL RESTAURANTE EL RIB ROOM DEL ROYAL ORLEANS

This attractive Mexican menu cover uses native motifs plus Spanish copy to give a colorful latin flavor.

THE FAST FOOD-MULTIPLE OPERATION MENU

Most chain or multiple operation restaurants can be classed under the fast food heading or category. Most, but not all, have a limited or smaller menu. And most are designed with the idea of getting the customer to make up his mind quickly as to what he wants so that the turnover is high and the number of customers is large to compensate for the smaller check. To achieve this purpose, and food service operations who may not consider themselves strictly within this category may want to get the same result, a special type of menu is required.

First, it must be a colorful menu that matches the bright, clean decor that is usually associated with this type of operation. This means bright yellows, blues, reds, greens, oranges, usually on a white background. A panel arrangement with squares, boxes, circles, etc., also in the same bright colors, where the type is printed big and bold is another common feature. Along with bright colors, 4-color food illustrations are another must for this type of menu. The items usually illustrated are:

> Appetizers—shrimp cocktail
> Sandwiches—hamburgers, steak sandwich
> Entrees—chicken, steak, seafood plate, shrimp
> Salads—chef's salad
> Dessert—apple pie, cheesecake
> Fountain—soda, sundae

The color illustrations are designed to encourage a quick decision from the customer to order these items. They should be both popular items and high profit items. The illustrations are generally color photography showing the food in an appetizing manner and as served in the operation on its china or in its glassware. Used less, but sometimes as effectively are color drawings of the food. This is not quite as true to life as a photo, but from the point of view of design and creating attention for the food items the restaurateur wants to sell, this type of illustration can work very well.

The next characteristic of this kind of menu is large, bold type, usually of the modern sans serif type. The type is often large enough for people who wear glasses to read without glasses. Headings can be script or a different type style, caps if the listing is in caps and lower case, and often in a different color, red or blue.

The paper this type of menu is printed on is usually a heavy, white enamel cover stock that is coated with a clear plastic or varnish after printing for longer life. Because of the use of 4 colors plus color illustrations and the heavy durable paper stock, the cost of this type of menu is usually high. For a multiple or chain operation where a big printing run is justified, the cost per menu can be a reasonable one. But for a single establishment with a short printing run, the cost per menu can be extremely high.

The other feature of this type of menu, if it is a standard uniform menu for all outlets, is a listing of addresses of all the locations of the restaurants in the chain. This is simple, basic but yet good merchandising. A problem with the one standard menu for a large chain operation is that of regional variation. This variation can appear in several forms. They are: a. Regional price variations; b. Regional food preferences.

To accommodate regional price variations as well as price changes is a relatively simple matter. All of the original run of menus can be printed without prices and prices printed later as they are used or for individual regional printing runs. Regional food preferences present a more complicated problem for the chain operation menu. For example, if 200,000 menus are printed with French fried shrimp as one of the color illustration features and in one area this item does not sell at all, a considerable portion of the selling space on the menu is wasted, but the item cannot be dropped from the menu in that area because all of the menus are printed identically.

To overcome this problem, color illustrations can be printed on tip-ons or paste-ons (on kleen-stick) for flexibility to accommodate regional preferences. Seasonal preferences are another variation that can be allowed for through this type of color illustration interchange. The layout in the drawing that follows shows how flexibility and color illustration (as well as easy price changing) can be achieved in menu design that allows for daily, weekly, seasonal and regional changes—all that can possibly be anticipated.

This is an 8-page menu—a 4-page cover with a 4-page insert. The 4-page insert is bound to the cover by means of an elastic cord with metal or plastic ends (like a shoe lace) that holds the four center pages to the cover but which can easily be removed, allowing for a different four pages to be inserted when desired. On page 1 (inside front cover), space is allowed for three (or more) sandwich specials. These would be color illustration pictures plus short identification copy, but no price. They would be held to the menu by plastic clip-on holders. On page 2, the regular sandwich and salad listing would be printed. (Note—one of the color illustrations could be a salad). On page 3, the ENTREE listing, Luncheon or Dinner, would be listed, and on page 4, three (or more depending on the size of the menu) Luncheon or Dinner SPECIALS, illustrated in full color and identified with short copy would be placed. Prices would not be printed on these color specials either. Page 5 would be used for a DESSERT, FOUNTAIN and BEVERAGE listing, and page 6 (inside back cover) could accommodate three dessert or fountain SPECIALS. The back cover of this menu could have a listing of the various locations of the restaurants in the chain. Or if it is a one-location restaurant, or two or three within a relatively small geographic area, a map would be a good merchandising device. If Take-Outs are a feature of the restaurant, they also could be merchandised here.

To accommodate price on the color illustrations, a changing factor in all menus, round kleen-stick tip-ons would be the answer. They can be attached to the color illustration and the price written on in ink. By making this menu longer, a total of twelve or fifteen (four or five per page) color illustrated specials can be allowed for. The color specials could be printed all at once on one sheet. The menu shown in the layout which allows for nine color specials could have twenty-seven color specials printed on one sheet. This would mean that three completely different menus could each have a special illustrated in color. This is just one example of how color food illustrations that sell menu specials can be worked into a menu in a manner that allows for change and seasonal-daily-weekly-regional variation.

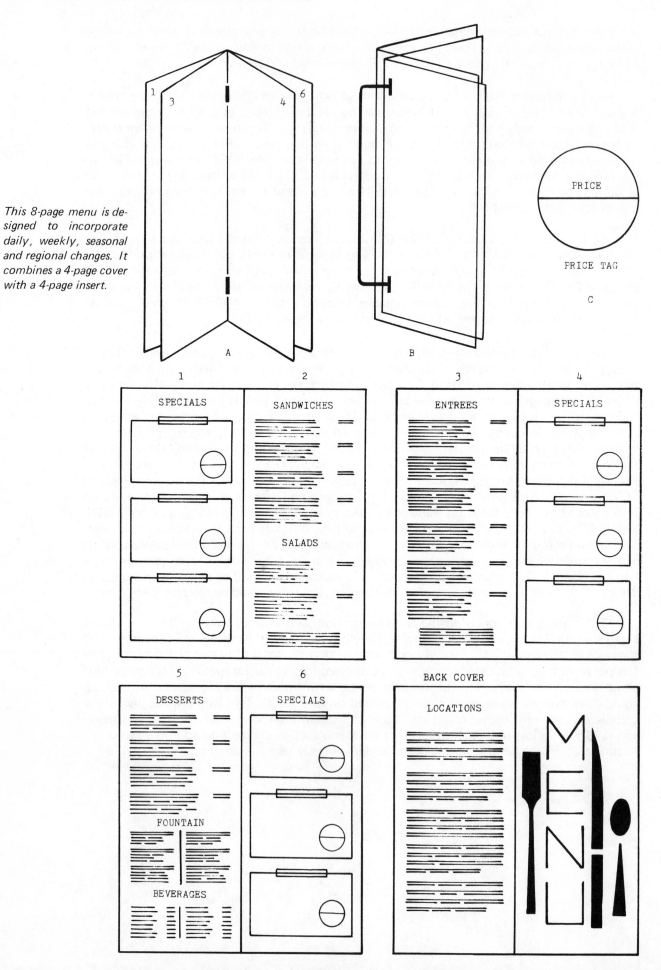

This 8-page menu is designed to incorporate daily, weekly, seasonal and regional changes. It combines a 4-page cover with a 4-page insert.

PRICE

PRICE TAG

C

A

B

1   2   3   4

1
SPECIALS

2
SANDWICHES

SALADS

3
ENTREES

4
SPECIALS

5
DESSERTS

FOUNTAIN

BEVERAGES

6
SPECIALS

BACK COVER

LOCATIONS

MENU

Effective use of color panels makes this menu effective. Notice also list of other locations on back cover.

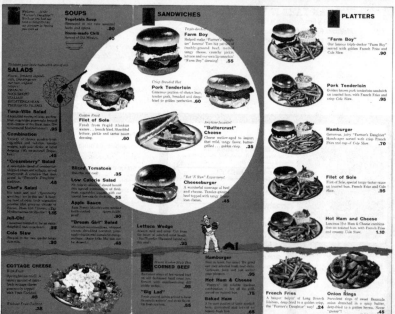

Good color food photography, clever design that sells when the menu is in half-open position (see right) plus a wide selection in every department make this an effective "fast-food" menu.

APPETIZERS

Most service restaurants serve and list appetizers on the menu. But many of these operations do not merchandise and, therefore, do not sell their appetizers. First, the place on the menu for appetizers is important. They are a before-dinner item and should be listed before the entree listing. When entrees are listed on one page or on two facing pages, the appetizer listing should be on the top. And, if the menu has many pages, appetizers should be listed on a page previous to the entree listing.

Next, on the average menu, more attention should be given to the appetizer listing. This means they should be listed in a readable type face, although not necessarily as large as the entree listing type face. Also, to give appetizers the merchandising attention they deserve, copy is sometimes called for. A good rule of thumb is if the appetizer costs $1.00 or more, it should have some descriptive, merchandising, sell copy.

From the customer's point of view, you're asking him to spend $1.00 or more he probably didn't plan on spending. To increase the total check, by selling what is basically an impulse food service item, requires sell copy. If your appetizer sales are not big, the fault probably is poor or no copy at all.

The charts included with this appetizer menu study show the results of a statistical study from current service restaurant menus. While the total number of menus studied was not great, the trends were established early and continued as more menus were studied.

The first question was what items are served most as appetizers? The number one favorite is shrimp cocktail; fruit is second, tomato juice is third and seafood, other than shrimp, is fourth. A study of the chart will show the popularity (in restaurants) of a variety of other appetizers. And since we can assume most restaurants list only appetizers that move, there should be correlation between the listings and sales.

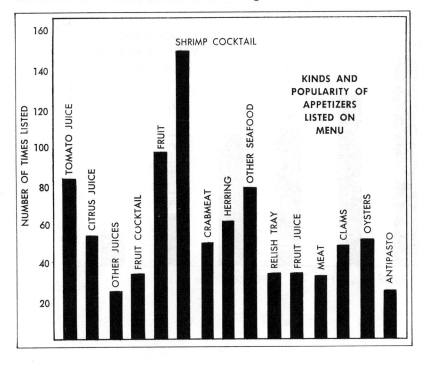

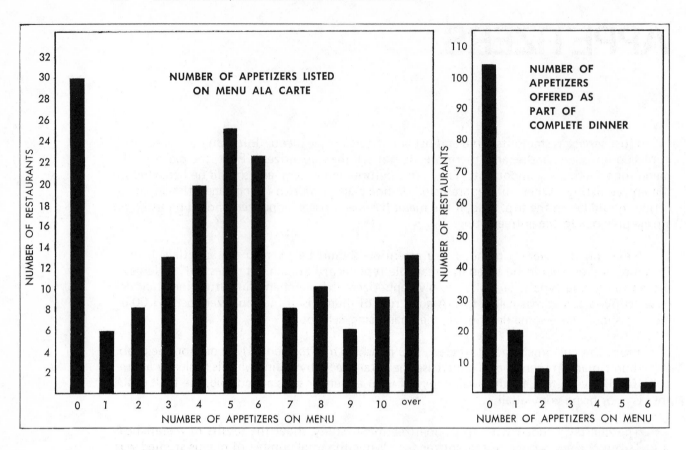

The next question studied was how many appetizers do restaurants list, both with dinner and a la carte? The first observation is that most service restaurants list appetizers a la carte, while the number listing appetizers as included in the price of the dinner is much smaller. On the a la carte appetizer chart, it would seem that five is the magic number. If you list five, you are average. If you list more, you are strong in the appetizer department, and if you list less, you are weak or below average.

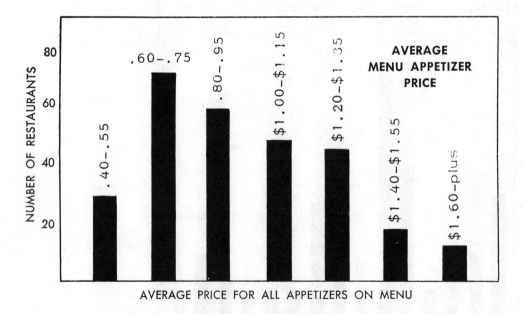

The final question studied (and probably most important to food service operators) was appetizer prices. The method was to compare total average appetizer price of each menu (to get your average appetizer price, add all your appetizer prices and divide by the number of appetizers). Here also, a curve was quickly established with the peak in the 60¢ to 75¢ range. But a considerable number of restaurants charged more than this mean price. For example, more restaurants charged an average price of $1.00 to $1.15 than charged 40¢ to 55¢.

Obviously, the number, variety and price of appetizers on a menu will be determined by many factors—costs, type of operation, location of operation, type of customers, etc. But comparison with other operations can show an individual operator where he stands in relation to the total picture.

The rules to remember are:

1. List appetizers before entrees.
2. List in readable type.
3. If the appetizer costs $1.00 or more, describe it.
4. List at least five appetizers.
5. The five most popular appetizers are (in order of preference) shrimp cocktail, fruit, tomato juice, seafood (general) and herring.

Appetizers

STEAMED CLAMS		EGGPLANT or ARTICHOKE		TOASTED RAVIOLI	
(for two)		*Hearts Fried in Olive Oil*		*with sauce*	
1.35		**.75**		**4 for .80**	

Anti-pasto	.85	Shrimp Cocktail	.50	Sliced Tomato & Onions	.40
Anti-pasto *(dinner)*	.50	Minestrone Soup	.35	Stuffed Anchovies	.55
Marinated Herring	.50	Olives Assorted	.35	Pepperoncini	.35

The above served with dinners only and when in season

The bigger appetizers get bigger treatment—bolder type and more copy—as they should.

the OVERTURE

GULF OF GEORGIA SMOKED SALMON

British Columbia Spring Salmon cured and smoked especially
for the Grouse Nest, served with capers, onion and Melba Toast
1.85

ESCARGOTS PROVENCALE

Imported French Snails broiled in Fine Herbs Butter with
just a hint of Garlic. One Half Dozen
2.00

DUNGENESS CRAB LEGS

Unique to the Pacific Northwest
Cocktail Grouse Nest
1.85

PACIFIC SHRIMP SUPREME

Tiny, delectable shrimps from cool Northern waters
with our own cocktail sauce
1.85

from the tureens

French Onion Soup au Gratin
1.00

Bongo Bongo Soup
1.25

Jellied Consomme Nikolai
Seasoned with dry sherry and topped with sour cream and caviar
1.45

Only four appetizers and three soups but not a dull one in the list.

"Appeteasers"

(Includes Rolls and Butter, Except * Items)

*Jumbo Shrimp Cocktail (5)	1.65	Marinated Herring in Sour Cream	.85
*Cherrystone Clams (6)	.85	Nova Scotia Lox	1.25
Filet of Matzes Herring	.85	Chopped Chicken Livers	.85
Gefilte Fish, Horseradish	.85	Stuffed Kishka	.85
*Soup Du Jour (Saltines)	.35	*Iced Beet Borscht	.35

*CHICKEN-NOODLE SOUP WITH MATZO BALL, Individual Crock .... .45

A photo or illustration will help sell the appetizer you want to sell the most!

cocktails from the sea around us . . .

the icy blue Pacific Ocean yields these delicacies . . .
from just 80 miles away, native Northwest seafoods are rushed to Poor Richard's daily . . .

(but first—cocktail sauce? Spicy red or creamy Thousand Island?)

Chilled Dungeness Crab as fresh as today's surf   I.IO

Oregon Shrimp au Crystal pink, plump, piquant   .95

Petite Oysters   tiny gourmet gems   2.25

if you knew louies like we know louies . . .

Meaty Dungeness Louie

or   —crisp heart-of-crab or juicy shrimp nested on a mountain
of iced lettuce, with that certain (secret) sauce!   2.25

Pink Oregon Shrimp Louie

a tart-sweet salad?

Traditional   The Northwest's orchards (with an assist from Hawaii and California)
yield nippy apples, luscious pineapple, prize-winning peaches, toothsome
Fruit and Cheese grapes — a colorful cornucopia of *today's* cottage cheese, freshly-churned.   I.25
(Note to dressing devotees: Choose from spicy red French or creamy Thousand Island or our delightful Fruit Dressing.)

from the colonial copper cauldron . . .

Clam Chowder   .35
Extraordinaire   —Blend herbs, ranch cream, succulent razor clams, and
broth, and . . . wow!   .65

Oyster Stew Willapas or Olympias line-up to volunteer for ours!   Willapa I.25   Petite   2.25

There's not one dull word in this combined appetizer, salad and soup listing.

APPETIZERS and SOUPS

Tuck your napkin under your chin, start with a delicious appetizer or soup and make all the noise you want.

Herring in Sour Cream ..... .60	Jumbo Shrimp Cocktail 1.25	
Marinated Wine Herring .... .50	Dinner-Size Shrimp Cocktail .... .75	
	Tomato Juice .... .25	

Minestrone .... .35

The portrait of the Italian Chef who created this masterpiece is enshrined reverently in our kitchen. The vitalizing products of the vegetable garden are blended with rich beef stock and seasonings.

Soup du Jour .... .35

The description of Minestrone shown here is one to paste in your hat and memorize, if you're in the business of selling soup.

Devilish Good Appetizers

OYSTERS OR CHERRYSTONE CLAMS
on the Half Shell, ½ Dozen **1.25**   Dozen **2.25**

CRAB FINGERS, Whole Crab Claws Completely
Shelled except for a "Handle" to hold
'em with! Delicious Seafood Dip **1.60**

CHILLED TOMATO JUICE .... .40

OCEAN-FRESH SHRIMP OR
OYSTER COCKTAIL SUPREME 1.50

ALASKAN KING CRABMEAT
COCKTAIL SUPREME 1.50

STEM CRYSTAL OF MIXED FRESH FRUITS
with Crown of Orange Ice .... .60

Soul Satisfying Soups

Served with Mixed Cracker Basket or Homebaked Bread and Butter

FAMOUS PIRATES' HOUSE OKRA GUMBO SOUP .... Bowl **.65** Cup **.45**
Superb with Scads of Shrimp and Crabmeat added .... Bowl **1.50** Cup **.95**

MISS EDNA'S SEAFOOD BISQUE - Something to Write Home About! Nourishing Nuggets of Fresh,
Flavorful Crabmeat and Plump Savannah Shrimp Swimming in a Skillful Blend of Cream of Tomato
and Pea Soup. Delicately Flavored with Sherry .... Bowl **1.60** Cup **1.10**

FRENCH ONION SOUP with Parmesan Toast Floats .... Bowl **.65** Cup **.45**

"Devilish Good Appetizers" and "Soul Satisfying Soups," not just "Appetizers and Soups." Good copy. Good selling.

Aperitifs

Pernod *(90°)* 1 45   Punt **e** Mes *on the rocks* 1 10

Sherry: Amontillado Club Dry, *Duff Gordon* 1 15

Pastis de Marseille, *Berger or Ricard* 1 35

Tio Pepe, *Gonzales Byass* 1 25

Vermouth Cassis 1 25

St. Raphael 1 10

Americano 1 20	Aquavit *(Snaps)* 1 20
Bitter Campari 1 20	Cardinal 1 25
Dubonnet *blonde or red* 1 10	Fernet Branca 1 00
Herbsaint 1 25	Kir═Vin Blanc Cassis 1 15
Lillet *white or red* 1 10	Margarita 1 50
Negroni 1 25	Ouzo, *Metaxa* 1 35

ḣORS Ɖ'OEUVRE

BAKED CHERRYSTONE CLAMS: *casino* 2 95	DUBLIN BAY PRAWNS *mustard sauce* 3 95
BAY CHERRYSTONE CLAMS on ½ shell 1 95	JUMBO LUMP CRAB MEAT COCKTAIL 3 25; *lamaze* 3 50
CRACKED DUNGENESS CRAB *mustard sauce* 3 25	MELON IN SEASON: Cantaloupe 1 35 Cranshaw 1 35
Imported Beluga Caviar, *jar* 4 50	Anchovies & Pimento *w/capers* 1 75
Whole California Grapefruit 1 25	Tomato or V-8 Juice Cocktail 85
Fresh New Brunswick Lobster Cocktail 3 75	Gulf White Shrimp Cocktail 2 35 *lamaze* 2 55
Half Avocado *Caesar* 1 50	Marinated Herring *sour cream* 1 50
Avocado Supreme *rémoulade* 1 50	Celery Hearts, Radishes & Mixed Olives 1 25

Honey Dew 1 35   Conchitas Con Parmesan 2 25

Snails *bourguigonne* (6) 2 50

Pascal Colorado Celery *w/roquefort* 1 50

Gulf White Shrimps *rémoulade* 2 55   *1000 Isle* 2 55

Soused Bismarck Herring Fillets 1 50

Hearts of Palm *vinaigrette* 1 75   Chopped Liver & Onions 1 50

*This listing of Aperitifs along with appetizers is a European custom that could
be adopted by more American food service operations.*

Beginning of the Journey

THE COCKTAIL SHAKER .... .45
With Juice on the Rocks

FRUITS EXOTIQUE ᴀᴜ KIRSH: .... .75
Fruits—mostly fresh from many places, bathed in Kirshwasser

MELONS OF THE SEASON .... .50

SHRIMP COCKTAIL EMERALD 1.15

CRAB MEAT COCKTAIL 1.45
The best of the Gulf in our Gribiche Sauce

A SYMPHONY OF SEAFOOD 1.65
Oysters, Crab Meat and Claws, Shrimps

CLAMS ON THE HALF SHELL 1.00

OYSTERS ON THE HALF SHELL 1.00

CASSOLETTE OF CRAB MEAT CRECY 1.85
Selected chunks of Crab Meat in a Sauce Piquante

BAKED OYSTERS MONSIEUR LE COMTE 1.25
With a puree of Mushroom and Wine Sauce

SNAILS BOURGUIGNONNE (6) 1.45
Les Escargots in Burgundy Butter

QUICHE LORRAINE 1.50
That excellent cheese pastry of the Continent

"Beautiful Soup so Rich and Green"

. . . Lewis Carrol

DOUBLE CONSOMME AMONTILLADO .... .65

BOULA BOULA .... .75
Turtle and Green Pea Soup with Sherry

THE ONION .... .75
Gratinee, of course, enhanced with Chablis

GASPACHO ᴅᴇ L'ESTRAMADOURE............. .60
The famous cold soup of Spain

BISQUE OF CRAYFISH .... .90
In true European style

This is a truly elegant selection of appetizers and soups
listed with elegant words and set in elegant type.

COCKTAIL OF FRESH FRUITS .60   TOMATO JUICE .50   HERRING *in Cream* 1.00
   Topped with sherbet & fresh mint   *or Horseradish Sauce*

      CHOPPED LIVER MAISON .85   LARGE LUMP CRABMEAT COCKTAIL 2.00

SHRIMP COCKTAIL 1.50   CLAMS *on Half Shell* 1.00   COCKTAIL *of* VARIOUS SHELLFISH 2.75

      IMPORTED PROSCIUTTO 2.00 *(With Melon 2.25)*   NOVA SCOTIA SALMON 2.25

MELON .75 *(whichever is best on the market)*   SMOKED BROOK TROUT 2.75

         IRANIAN BELUGA MALOSSOL "00" CAVIAR 6.50

Hot Appetizers

BAKED STUFFED CLAMS 1.50   SHRIMP SCAMPI 2.50

    LINGUINE, CLAM SAUCE 2.50   STUFFED BABY DANISH LOBSTER TAILS 3.00

        ESCARGOTS BOURGUIGNONNE 2.50   FETTUCCINE *(At Tableside)* 2.50

                LINGUINE, MEAT SAUCE 3.00

    GREEN NOODLES *ala Franco* 3.50   RISOTTO MILANESE 2.50

Soup

   SOUP *du Jour* .50   CONSOMME .50   FRENCH ONION SOUP *au Gratin* .75

         COLD VICHYSSOISE .60   CONSOMME MADRILENE .60

With a price range from 50¢ to $6.50, and a selection of both hot and cold appetizers and soups, this listing is complete and well presented.

SALADS

Salads are an accepted food item on the American menu. From a piece of lettuce with dressing on it to a complete meal, salads include a great number of food combinations with a variety of appeals. They help the dieter, are a favorite of women and are ideal for jaded summer appetites. But how do they fare on the menu? From the study shown on the charts on these pages, some interesting facts are revealed.

First, considering the kinds of salads listed a la carte and with dinner, we find that lettuce by itself, or with a few other similar vegetables—tossed greens, chef's salad, with tomato, etc.—is the number one salad in eating-out popularity. This probably corresponds with salad popularity in the home, making it a necessity item rather than creative menu merchandising. Fruit and shrimp salads are next in popularity, with cottage cheese following close behind. Combining tuna, crabmeat, lobster and other seafoods, it is apparent that seafood is a very popular salad ingredient, probably the most popular after the basic head of lettuce.

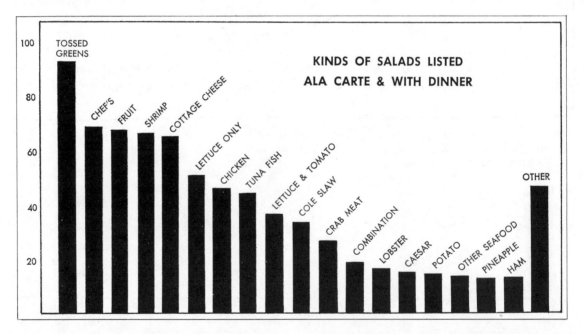

Next, considering the number of different salads listed a la carte and with dinner on the menu, we find that the most frequent listing is of one salad. This is most often the basic lettuce salad with dressing. The next highest number of salad selections put on the menu is four, and after that they break down rather evenly. It is interesting to note that there are more menus listing eight different kinds of salads than there are menus listing two kinds.

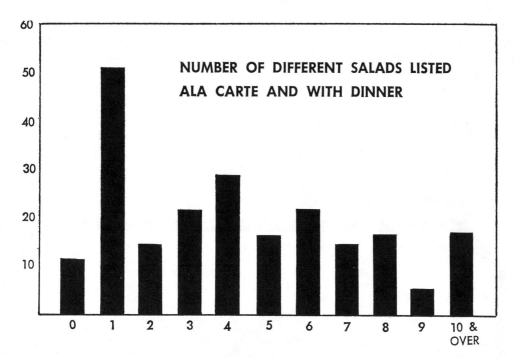

NUMBER OF DIFFERENT SALADS LISTED
ALA CARTE AND WITH DINNER

Finally we consider price. The number one price range is from 50¢ to 75¢, but the great majority of a la carte prices are $1.00 and above. A significant number are $2.00 and more, which makes the a la carte salad a very respectable entree.

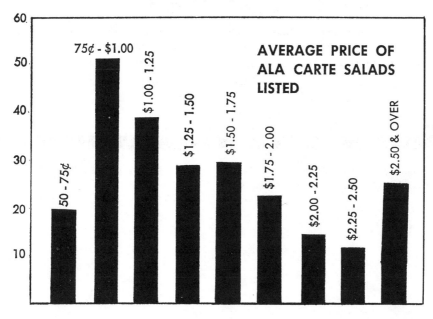

AVERAGE PRICE OF
ALA CARTE SALADS
LISTED

50 - 75¢
75¢ - $1.00
$1.00 - 1.25
$1.25 - 1.50
$1.50 - 1.75
$1.75 - 2.00
$2.00 - 2.25
$2.25 - 2.50
$2.50 & OVER

The important thing to remember when listing a la carte salads on the menu is to treat them like important entree items. This means setting the listing in readable size type. Do not crowd or set items too close together. And, above all, give your salads complete, descriptive, merchandising "sell" copy. Naming a salad does not identify it. You must include the ingredients; but don't just list them, use imagination, romanticise, and try to create appetite appeal.

While your menu is probably tailored to fit a particular clientele, comparison with the data shown on these charts could help you in your salad listing. Check and compare. Are you serving enough different salads? Are they the most popular salads? And last, but not least, are your prices right? Then, after you have determined what, how many and how much, check to see how you are listing salads on your menu. Is the type large and readable? Does the copy describe and merchandise? The right answer to all these questions can mean sales that brighten your profit picture.

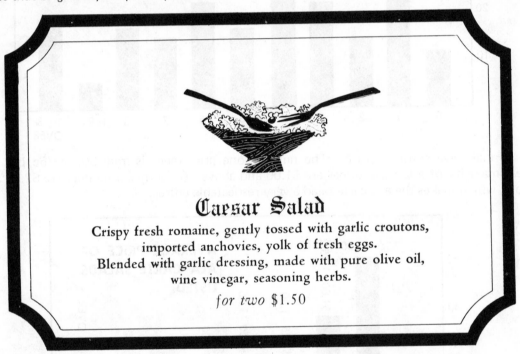

Certain salads like Caesar Salad are old standbys, but the salad menu is one place where it is easy and profitable to be creative.

Freshly-Made Salads

Fresh Shrimp Salad   2.50
Jumbo Gulf shrimp served whole on a bed of crisp salad greens, garnished with sliced tomatoes, cucumbers and ripe olives. Choose your own dressing

King Crabmeat Salad   2.25
Tender, bite size morsels of Alaskan King crabmeat served on a bed of lettuce with mayonnaise, dressing served separately and garnished with tomato, cucumber and black olives

Tuna Salad   1.75
Chunks of white meat tuna fish with tomato, pepper ring and radish, and crisp salad greens

Fresh Fruit Salad   1.75
Segments of chilled, fresh seasonal fruits served with cottage cheese and a delightfully blended dressing of mayonnaise, whipped cream and strawberries

Chef's Salad Bowl   1.75
A mound of garden fresh greens topped with julienne strips of ham, chicken and Swiss cheese, garnished with tomato, radish and pepper ring and dressing

Try Our Cold Meat Platter   2.25
A variety of sliced white meat of chicken, corned beef, sliced ham, imported Swiss cheese and tangy potato salad garnished with radishes and black olives, tomatoes, cucumbers.

Fresh Lobster Salad   4.50
Large pieces of succulent lobster meat imbeded in crisp lettuce and served with mayonnaise garnished with ripe olives, cucumber slices and pepper rings

the above served with rolls and butter

Salads are easy to describe. Just list the ingredients with a few adjectives thrown in. Be sure to also list salad dressing served with the salad.

a la carte

Weber's

California

CAROUSEL

Caesar Salad   1.75
*Bibb Lettuce
crisp parmesan cheese, olive oil and fresh lemon, combined with toast croutons, a touch of mustard and topped with anchovie filets*

a famous salad
Sarah Bernhardt   2.25
*Avocado pear, Shrimp,
Hard cooked egg on shredded lettuce
Chef garni   (In Season)*

all fresh fruits
California Salad Plate   1.95
with petite sandwiches   (In Season)

a great green salad
Julienne Salad   1.95
ham, turkey, swiss cheese

fresh Alaskan
King Crabmeat Salad   2.00
our own Louis dressing

an unusual salad
A Stuffed Tomato   1.75
with flaky tunafish

From Our Salad Bar

TRIPLE SALAD PLATE
Your choice of Chicken or Tuna Salad with molded fruit jello salad,
cottage cheese mound, green peppers, tomato, finger Sandwich   1.50

TROPICAL SALAD
Half Avacado with crabmeat and lobster, asparagus spears,
tomato on bed of lettuce   2.25

JUMBO TOMATO STUFFED WITH CHICKEN OR TUNA SALAD,
Mayonnaise garni with hard Boiled Egg,
green pepper rings, ripe olives, saratoga chips   1.75

NEW ORLEANS JUMBO SHRIMPS SALAD BOWL,
Tossed spring greens topped with succulent shrimps and garnished
with Hard Boiled Egg, Tomato wedges, 1000 Island Dresisng   2.10

THE SKIRVIN JUMBO SALAD BOWL
Tossed spring greens topped with julienne of Chicken,
Ham and Swiss Cheese, your choice of dressing   1.50

THE FRUIT PLATE
Selected fresh and preserved fruits on a bed of lettuce with a choice of
cottage cheese or sherbet, assorted finger sandwiches   1.50

These creative listings are sure to increase salad orders.

STEAK MARKETING SURVEY

A study of 242 menus of various types from food service operations across the U. S. gives some interesting information as to what, how many, what price and the degree of popularity of the various kinds of steaks that are listed on the menu. While your particular operation may make its steak selections on the basis of (1) availability and price of beef, (2) local preferences plus (3) past experience, the information shown on these charts can be a reference point from which you can compare, and if your menu does not measure up, perhaps some experimentation is called for.

Chart I shows the relative popularity of steaks by name as listed on the menu. Sirloin and filet mignon are the two leaders. Chopped steak (hamburger), if all of its variations including sandwiches were counted, would probably be number one. Also a N. Y. strip, if it is what is served on a steak sandwich and sometimes called a Kansas City steak, would have a higher rating.

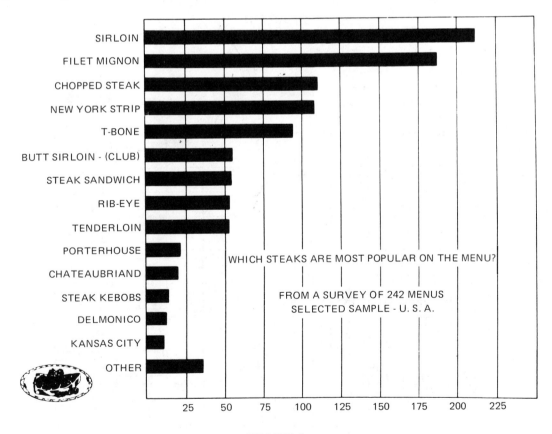

WHICH STEAKS ARE MOST POPULAR ON THE MENU?

FROM A SURVEY OF 242 MENUS
SELECTED SAMPLE - U. S. A.

CHART I

Chart II shows the number of different kinds of steaks listed on the menu. The largest number of menus list from one to seven different steaks with the peak at four. If you list four different steaks, you are average.

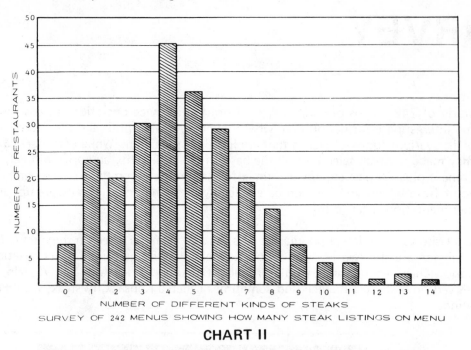

NUMBER OF DIFFERENT KINDS OF STEAKS

SURVEY OF 242 MENUS SHOWING HOW MANY STEAK LISTINGS ON MENU

CHART II

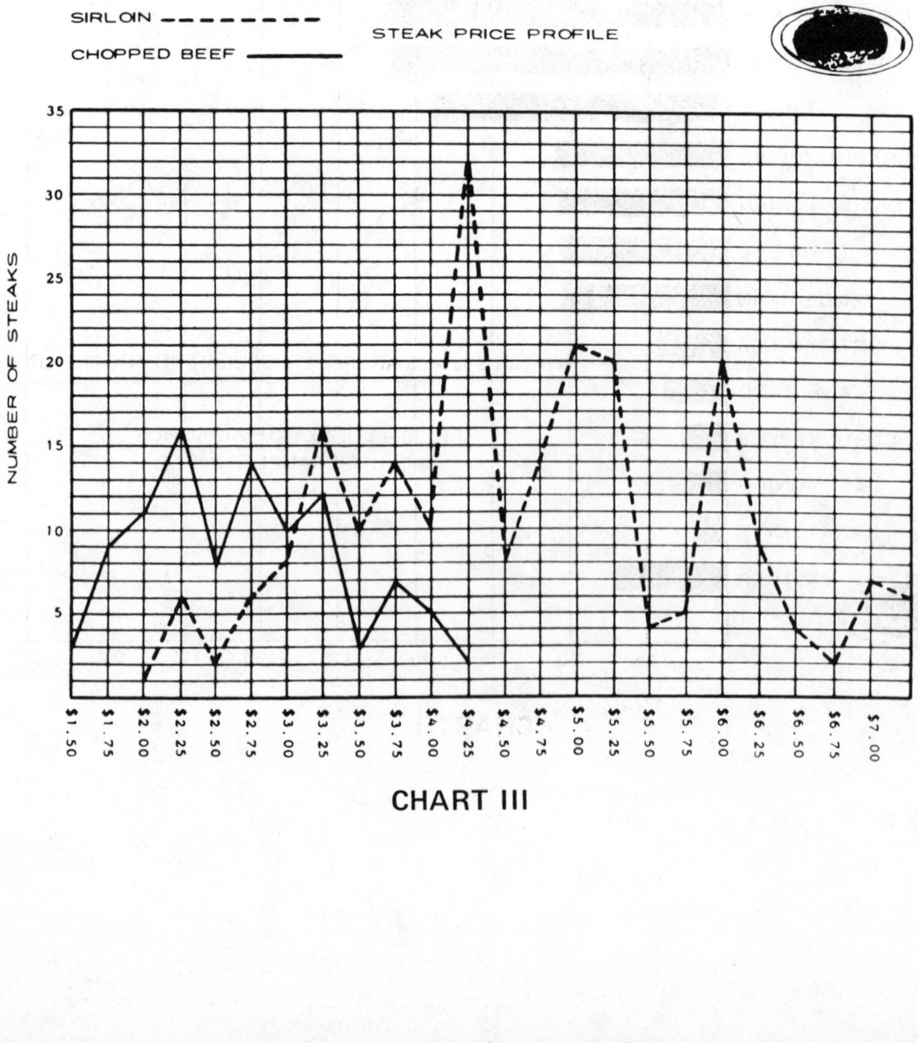

SIRLOIN – – – – – –   STEAK PRICE PROFILE

CHOPPED BEEF ———

CHART III

Charts III and IV show the price range of four popular steaks. The wide range shows that you can charge almost any price for a steak, depending on the quality of the meat and the quality of your restaurant.

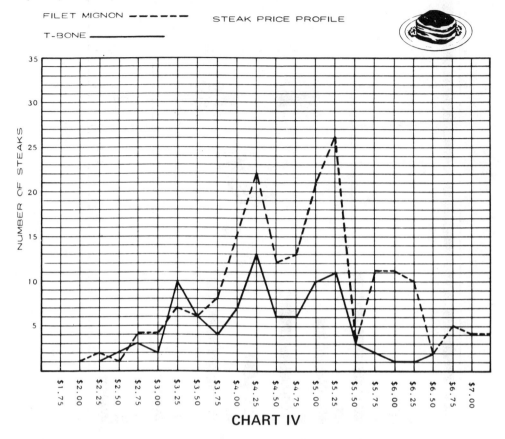

CHART IV

Chart V shows up a failing of most menus, a lack of descriptive steak copy.

CHART V

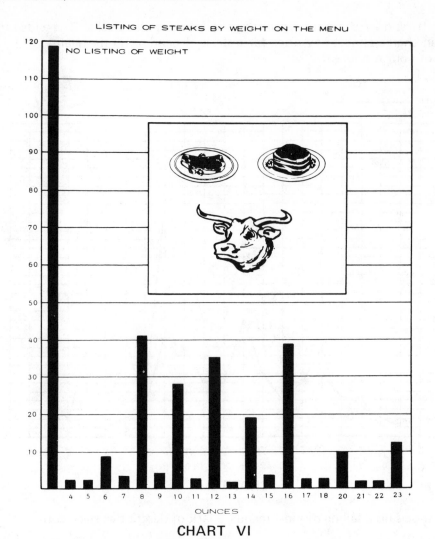

LISTING OF STEAKS BY WEIGHT ON THE MENU

CHART VI

Chart VI indicates the sizable percentage of operations that do not list steak weight on their menus.   Chart VII shows another copy defect, the failure to list the quality of your steaks.   Most restaurants serve good beef, Prime or Choice, but after spending good money to serve good meat, they fail to tell the customer.

INDICATION ON MENU OF QUALITY OF STEAK SERVED

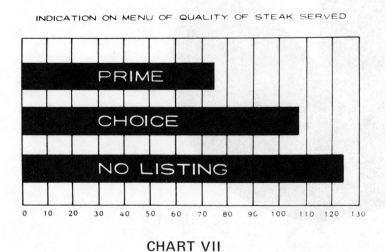

CHART VII

SEAFOOD SURVEY

Seafood is a highly popular menu item. Whether as an entree, appetizer or salad, when the public "eats out," it likes seafood. Perhaps the fuss, muss and smell of preparing it at home makes it more attractive in a food service operation. Besides, chefs seem to have a knack of preparing and serving seafood more attractively than the housewife does in the average home.

This seafood survey is information taken from 300 menus from across the country. They range from smaller, inexpensive table service restaurants to the most expensive "haute cuisine" places. But a surprising amount of uniformity exists in seafood service on the menu, even among a great variety of types and locations of eating establishments. The questions studied by the survey were:

    a.   Number of seafood entrees.
    b.   Popularity of seafood entrees (items listed most often).
    c.   Number of seafood appetizers.
    d.   Number of seafood salads.
    e.   Prices of certain seafood entrees.

Food service operations vary in their promotion of seafood entrees. Some specialize in seafood and have built impressive and well deserved reputations for their exceptional seafood cuisine. But, strangely enough, there seems to be hardly any food service, large or small, steak house or nationality specialty house that does not list at least one seafood item. This could be a carry-over from the "Fish on Friday" church ruling which the menu still reflects, but it is more likely a reflection of seafood popularity on the menu. As shown in Chart A, the number of seafood entrees starts at one (with 10 restaurants listing this number) and then peaks at the range of 4 to 7 seafood entrees. There is another big jump when the chart reaches over 11 seafood entrees. These are probably the operations specializing in or featuring seafood. One menu surveyed listed 26 seafood entrees!

NUMBER OF SEAFOOD ENTREES ON THE MENU

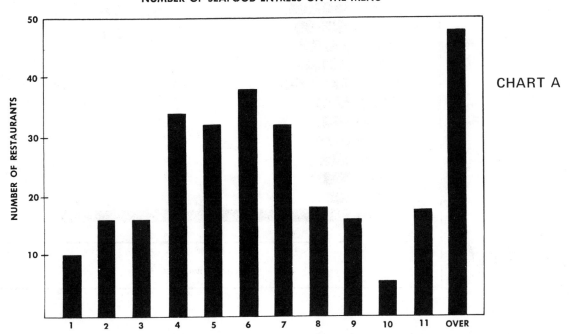

CHART A

The kind of seafood entrees a food service operation serves will vary, of course, somewhat with location. Establishments on the seacoast will serve a greater variety of local or unusual seafood, while some inland operations will serve fresh water fish not available on the seacoast. But, with modern transportation and marketing, location has become less a factor in the availability of seafood. Lobster is available in Keokuk, Iowa, as well as in Boston.

In fact, the pattern of popularity shown by Chart B is almost an indication that there is not enough variety in the menu listing. The same items tend to be on all menus. Shrimp takes first place, as shown in Chart B, for entree popularity. This, combined with its popularity as the number one appetizer item and as a very popular salad ingredient, makes shrimp king of the seafood listing on the menu. After shrimp, the other big seafood entree is lobster tails. Actually, lobster tails, combined with whole lobster, lobster newburgh and other lobster combinations or methods of preparation, equal or surpass shrimp on the entree portion of the menu. After shrimp and lobster, the popularity scale goes down from scallops, crab, seafood plate, oysters, fresh water trout all the way to filet of sole. There are no real surprises on seafood popularity except the overwhelming popularity of the first seven seafood items (shrimp through trout) compared with all of the many other kinds of seafood entrees.

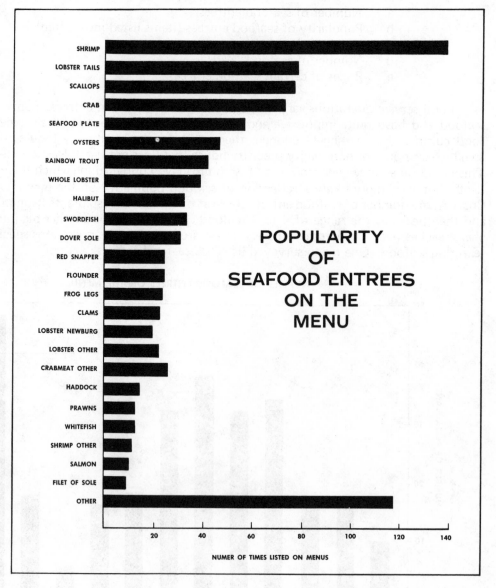

POPULARITY OF SEAFOOD ENTREES ON THE MENU

NUMBER OF TIMES LISTED ON MENUS

CHART B

The popularity of seafood as an entree item means that, when listed on the menu, it should be given top billing. It should be given good position, center of menu. It should be listed in large, clear, bold type. And it should have plenty of good descriptive, merchandising, sell copy. Seafood copy is not difficult to write if you follow these rules:

a.   Tell where the seafood comes from and some pertinent facts about it (from the warm waters of the Gulf or from the cold waters of the North Atlantic).

b.   Describe how it is prepared (broiled, baked, fried, cooked, special sauces and flavorings, etc.).

c.   How served (filled, whole, in shell, etc.).

d.   Use some tasty adjectives (juicy, tender, succulent, fresh, tangy, etc.).

Menu prices are a subject of constant concern for the food service operator. Whether he is charging enough or too much, not enough or what the market will bear are day to day questions which, of course, are related to costs, the market served and competitor's prices. In addition, food service has been operating in a period of rising costs and prices for some time. A Department of Agriculture study covering the last eight years shows that while prices for food eaten at home have risen 12%, prices for food eaten away from home have risen 26%. The main cost increase, of course, has been labor.

With regard to seafood entree prices on the menu, comparisons are difficult to make. Local variations in supply, the type of operation and the type of customer to whom it caters, plus local labor and other costs are all factors making comparisons difficult. But in spite of these difficulties, some examination of what restaurants are charging for some seafood items is possible. Chart No. 1 measures the prices charged for shrimp (as an entree prepared in any style), lobster tail and whole lobster. Shrimp entrees (in this study, at least) start

CHART 1

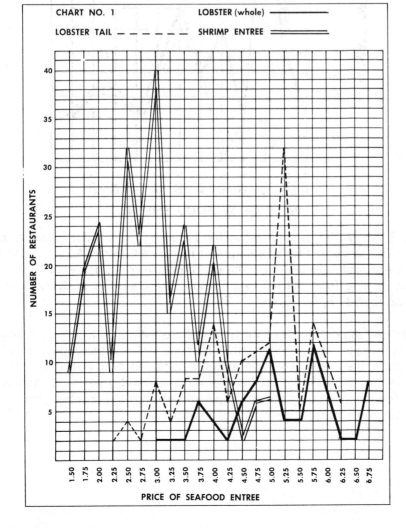

at $1.25 and go as high as $4.75. The peak is $2.75; most of the restaurants studied (40 of them) charge $2.75, with the lower and higher prices about equally on either side of this $2.75 peak. Lobster tails start at $2.00 and stop at $6.00 with three peaks—$3.75, $5.00 and $5.50. Whole lobsters start at $2.75 and run as high as $6.50. It is interesting to note that generally shrimp is less expensive than lobster tails and lobster tails are less expensive than whole lobster. But the most interesting, and possibly a more significant observation, is that some (quite a few, actually) restaurants charge more for shrimp than others do for lobster tails, while some charge more for lobster tails than others charge for the whole lobster.

Chart No. 2 shows prices for rainbow trout and scallops. The most common price for rainbow trout is $1.75, but $2.25 and $2.75 are also popular prices for this fish entree. Scallops seem to peak out at a $2.75 price with nearly as many below $2.75 as above.

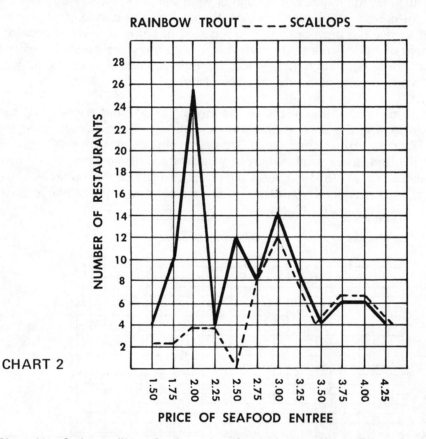

RAINBOW TROUT _ _ _ _ SCALLOPS _____

CHART 2

NUMBER OF RESTAURANTS

PRICE OF SEAFOOD ENTREE

Chart No. 3 shows filet of sole and seafood platter prices. Filet of sole reaches a price peak at $2.75. The range of filet of sole prices is from $1.25 to $4.25. Seafood platter is, of course, a more flexible menu item. The operator can make a special or a more modest entree item out of a seafood platter. As a result, there are five peaks on seafood platter prices—$1.75, $2.25, $3.25, $3.75 and $4.50.

Entrees are not the only area of the menu where seafood is featured. Many appetizers and salads use seafood as the basic element. Chart No. 4 shows the popularity of seafood as an appetizer item on the menu. To begin with, 22 restaurants did not list any seafood appetizer, but the vast majority (112) listed one or more seafood appetizers. Most menus listed at least one seafood appetizer (usually shrimp cocktail), but the number goes as high as nine and above, showing how popular seafood is as an appetizer.

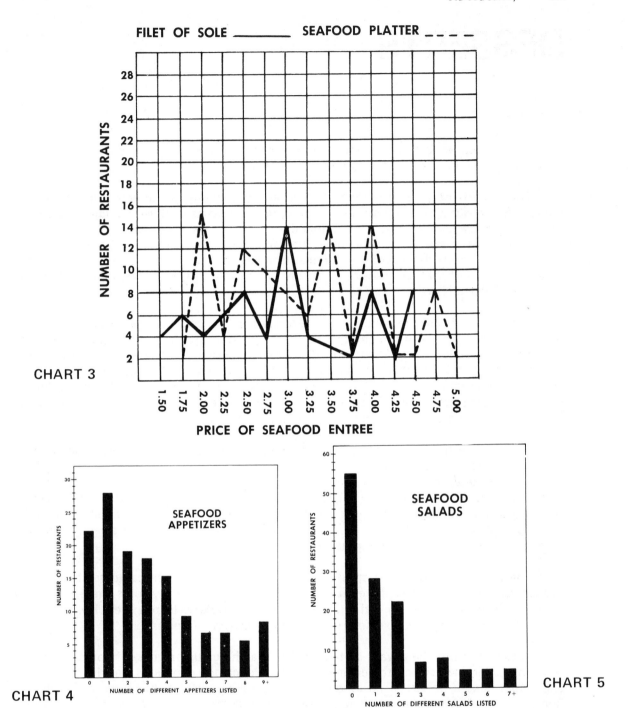

FILET OF SOLE _____   SEAFOOD PLATTER _ _ _ _

CHART 3

NUMBER OF RESTAURANTS

PRICE OF SEAFOOD ENTREE

SEAFOOD APPETIZERS

NUMBER OF RESTAURANTS

CHART 4

NUMBER OF DIFFERENT APPETIZERS LISTED

SEAFOOD SALADS

NUMBER OF RESTAURANTS

CHART 5

NUMBER OF DIFFERENT SALADS LISTED

    Chart No. 5 shows the popularity of seafood salads on the menu. And here too, while 55 restaurants listed no seafood salads, 65 did list some seafood salads. The number ranges from one seafood salad to seven and over. So while not as popular as the seafood appetizer and the seafood entrees, the seafood salad is still a popular item on the menu. Taken all together, of course, seafood is an extremely popular item on the menu in many departments. In fact, a good case can be made for giving seafood the number one position in menu popularity. Perhaps the popularity of seafood in the food service operation is due to the greater selection of items not too available in the average supermarket. Well described, well listed and merchandised on the menu, seafood (if well prepared and good to begin with) is one of the food service operator's best, money-making friends.

DESSERTS

A forgotten or side tracked after-thought on many menus, the dessert listing can be a profitable, check building part of any food service business.

The dessert listing on the menu gets a variety of treatment in any large selection of menus. Some eating places have a large selection of desserts, and list, merchandise and sell them in a big way, while other restaurants don't even list a single dessert. Yet the public is the same in both cases. And it is a public that eats cake, pie and ice cream at home. What is the reason for this wide disparity in emphasis on dessert merchandising from one operation to another? The final, real answer is probably unknown at this time, but some probable answers are examined here.

The "big" dinner menu allows for a leisurely meal. A cocktail, appetizer, and soup before the entree, wine with the entree, and dessert, coffee, after dinner drink and cigar after the entree. This is a true "continental" gourmet repast and many a fine restaurant that serves food and drink in this style has a good dessert listing. Yet many an elegant, supper club type restaurant that lists a $6.00 steak and a $7.00 seafood entree will neglect desserts entirely. A different group of people with different tastes? Again, we come back to the hard fact that these people eat desserts of all kinds at home.

Then there is the short order, fast food type operation. The claim here is made that the customer "does not have time." Or the food service operator will have mainly (or only) a luncheon business, and he will say, "I've tried selling and listing desserts, but my customers aren't interested, don't have time, I guess, or are watching their waistlines." Yet, some of the biggest, fast food, get 'em in, get 'em out operations have been built on a large selection of ice cream flavors (Howard Johnson's, for example). And what is ice cream if it is not a dessert, and probably the most popular dessert there is.

The real answer to the question of to whom, where and when can desserts be sold is probably to everybody, anywhere, at almost any time. To prove my point, there is no supermarket anywhere in America without a large selection of desserts, prepared, frozen, or in ingredient form, and there is no cafeteria without a selection of desserts.

The question of the always dieting, weight watching customer is, of course, very real. And after a big meal the customer suddenly becomes calorie conscious, decides to be a hero and denies himself dessert. The food industry has taken notice of this situation and for the home-food market supplies a variety of low-calorie desserts. But, so far, the food service business as a whole has done very little in this direction.

Judging from the wide variety of treatment for dessert listings on various menus, it is apparent that some operations do a big merchandising job and others do a very poor or casual dessert selling job. It would seem that those operations that want to sell more desserts usually find the right advertising-merchandising tools to do the job.

First, let's examine the various ways desserts can be listed on the menu. The first method is to have a separate dessert menu. This is usually a menu smaller than the regular entree menu with a listing of desserts and after dinner drinks. This separate menu usually permits a better dessert listing. It means more room to list more desserts, list them bigger, bolder and with more descriptive copy. Also, it allows for featuring of some "special" dessert items that the operation wants to sell in greater quantity.

One of the main advantages of a separate dessert menu is that the waitress or waiter can present the separate dessert menu to all customers after they have finished their entree. This should be done without asking the customer if he wants dessert. It is much better selling to present the dessert menu, assuming that a dessert is going to be ordered. The customer is at least more likely to look at the menu and consider ordering. There are various ways of listing desserts on the menu. The following are some layouts showing where desserts can be listed:

1.   A simple menu layout is the appetizer, entree, dessert sequence shown below in Figure A:

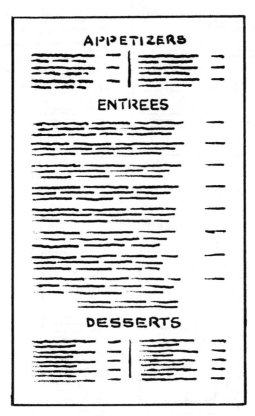

FIGURE A

2. Another layout is Figure B, (next page) a 4-panel (2 large, 1 small) 3-fold menu. The desserts are listed on panel 4. The opposite side of panel 4 can be the after dinner drink listing.

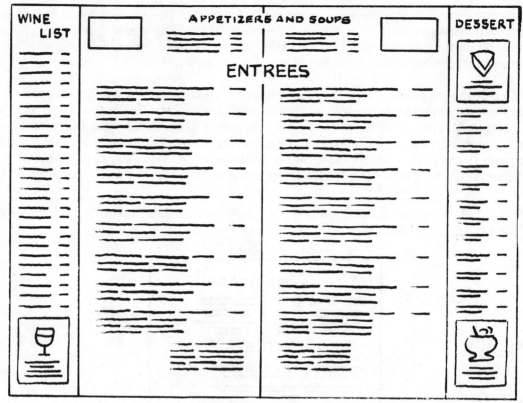

FIGURE B

3.   The back side of a 3-panel menu is shown in Figure C. This uses panel 1 for desserts and after dinner drinks. Notice that boxes in the two listings allow for special treatment of two desserts and two after dinner drinks.

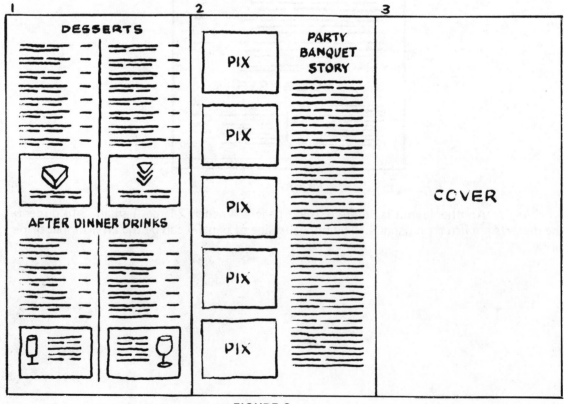

FIGURE C

4.   Another common layout solution to where to list desserts is shown below in Figure D. An 8-page menu (4-page cover, 4-page insert) leaves an entire page (page 4) for desserts and after dinner drinks.

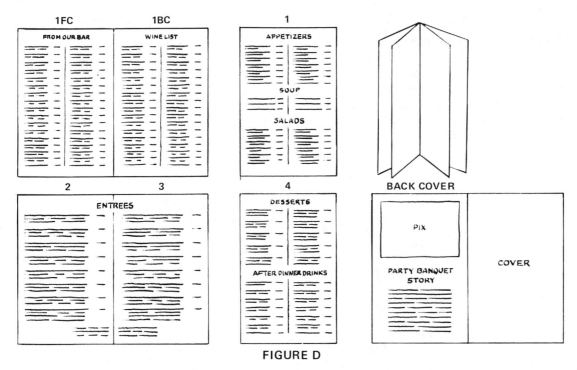

FIGURE D

After counting and classifying the dessert listing on 256 menus, some information about dessert popularity, prices, number, etc., is available and clear. The following charts are a graphic presentation of the information researched from menus all over the United States. Chart No. 1 is a study of the number of different desserts listed on the menu. The

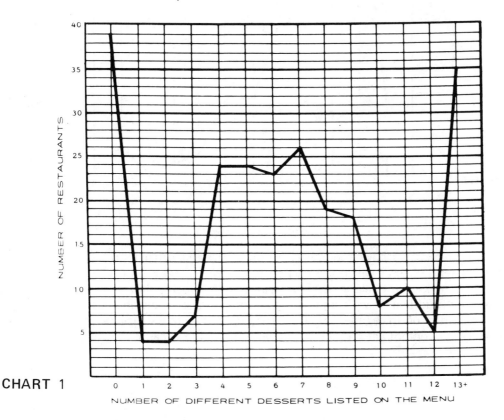

CHART 1

NUMBER OF DIFFERENT DESSERTS LISTED ON THE MENU

first observation is that 39 restaurants listed no desserts at all, while 35 restaurants listed 13 or more different desserts. This shows the wide range in dessert emphasis from one restaurant to another. The average range, however, is from 4 to 7 different items.

Chart No. 2 is a study of dessert prices. Starting from a range of 20¢ to 30¢ and ending with $1.20 and over, there obviously is a wide spread in dessert prices. But the price peaks very quickly at the 40¢ to 50¢ point showing that this is the most popular, most used price for desserts. The price is probably arrived at from experience as to what the customer will pay but the substantial number of desserts in the 40¢ to 50¢ range shows that there is room for maneuver in dessert prices. And since 40 restaurants out of 256 price desserts at $1.20 and over, it is obvious that expensive desserts are being sold.

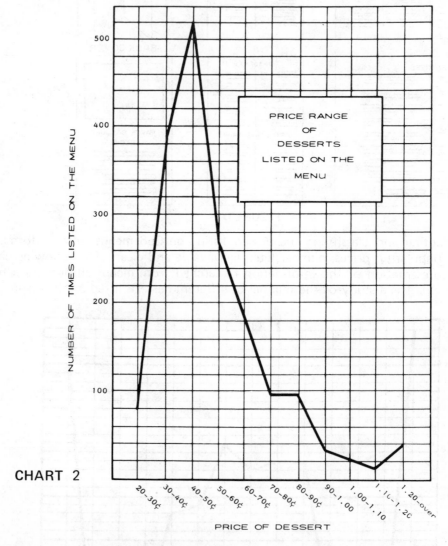

CHART 2

On Chart No. 3 we have a popularity poll of desserts other than pie, ice cream and fountain items and cheeses which are treated separately. Cheesecake rates highest on this chart with layer cake, fruit gelatin, parfaits, fruit and strawberry shortcake following in that order. Plain old pudding, if we combine the pudding, rice pudding and custard pudding, is, however, a big item on many menus. The fancy desserts—crepes suzettes, cherries jubilee, baked Alaska, etc., do not get on too many menus, probably because they are more difficult

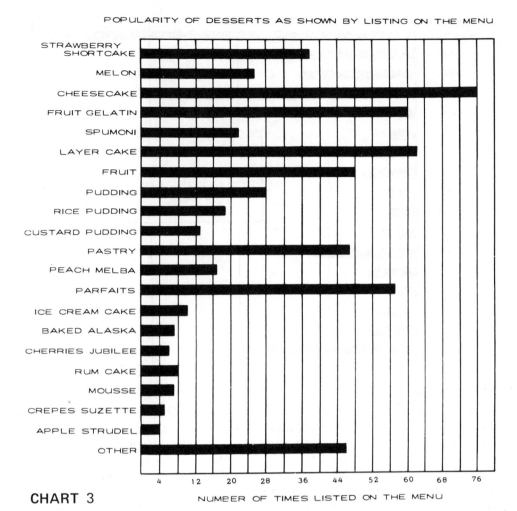

POPULARITY OF DESSERTS AS SHOWN BY LISTING ON THE MENU

CHART 3   NUMBER OF TIMES LISTED ON THE MENU

to make and serve. But if you want to upgrade your menu on the dessert end, this is the area where menu additions will be most noticeable.

There is nothing so American as pie, especially apple pie. Chart No. 4 shows pie popularity as shown by listings on the menu. Combined, the pie listing adds up to probably the number one item on the menu next to ice cream and its variations in the fountain menu. Too many menus, however, list assorted pies, fruit pies and cream pies. This is not good dessert merchandising. Nobody has ever eaten an assorted pie, and a fruit pie is either an apple, cherry or peach pie, etc. This method of listing, of course, is designed to fit a changing inventory of pies either bakery or home made. A better selling and merchandising practice is to feature a few specific pies big and feature them all the time on the menu. Many southern restaurants do a good job in this area with key lime pie and pecan pie.

The all time favorite, of course, is apple pie. And when combined with cheese or a la mode with ice cream, it is a formidable dessert item. Any operation that does not include apple pie on its menu is definitely bucking a trend. One aspect of pie listing that should be accented is that when you have "home made" pie, make a great deal of it on the menu. Do not mention it just casually in small type.

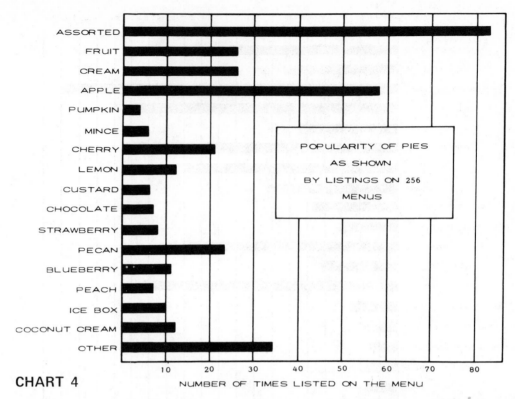

CHART 4

POPULARITY OF PIES AS SHOWN BY LISTINGS ON 256 MENUS

NUMBER OF TIMES LISTED ON THE MENU

Ice cream is probably number one as a dessert item in popularity, and when combined in all its variations—parfaits, sodas, sundaes, malts, sherbets, etc.–it becomes a really big menu dessert item. Chart No. 5 shows a sundae, that is ice cream with something added, chocolate sauce, nuts, etc., is offered more often than just plain ice cream. And after that sherbet follows as number 3 in popularity. One common fault of the listing of ice creams, sundaes, sodas and other fountain items is the failure to list flavors. Most food service operations serve more than one flavor of ice cream, yet they expect the customer to ask which flavors are available. This is poor selling. Decide on what flavors you wish to serve in all the fountain variations of ice cream, and then list them.

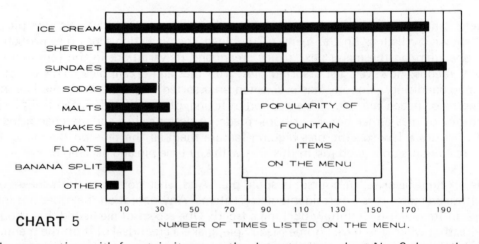

CHART 5

POPULARITY OF FOUNTAIN ITEMS ON THE MENU

NUMBER OF TIMES LISTED ON THE MENU.

In connection with fountain items on the dessert menu, chart No. 6 shows the separate fountain menu listing in relation to fountain items listed with the regular dessert listing. Less than 25% of the 256 menus studied had a separate fountain menu listing. In many cases this is a menu mistake. Fountain items are easy to store, make and serve (you don't have to be a well trained chef to make an ice cream sundae) and if listed separately, and in detail, they will be easier to order and easier to sell.

CHART 6

The type of establishment will often determine the emphasis on fountain items, but even a supper club or continental cuisine can feature ice cream desserts in the form of parfaits. The combination of ice cream and liqueur makes for a sophisticated sundae.

Cheese is not as popular a dessert item on American menus as it is on European menus. but it still has its place. Chart No. 7 gives a rundown on cheese popularity. The number one item, of course, is cheese and apple pie. While this is usually American or Cheddar cheese, here again many menus are remiss in not being specific as to the kind of cheese being served. "Cheese and crackers" and "cheese tray" are also poor ways to list cheese on the menu.

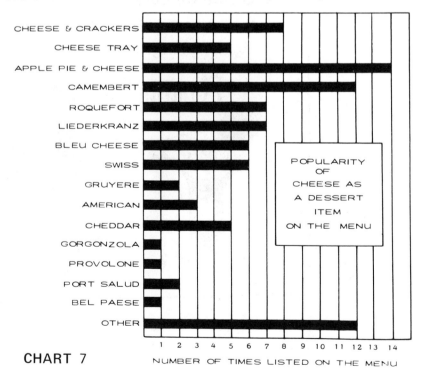

CHART 7

When the listing does get specific, it is Camembert that leads the list followed by Roquefort, Liederkranz and Blue Cheese.

This little study of desserts only begins to show some of the aspects and possibilities of desserts. Flaming desserts, for example, are popular in many dining rooms with fine cuisine. But whether large or small, spectacular or modest, the dessert, taking its place as "Tail End Charlie", should be always last, but never least.

That Little Extra Sweet

FRESH CUT PIE or CAKE 25
a la mode .10 extra

CHEESE CAKE 40
with FRUIT PRESERVES .10 extra

ICE CREAM or SHERBET 20

HOT FUDGE SUNDAE 45

ICE CREAM SUNDAE 40

1. **Creme de Menthe** ★ *parfait*   **.75**

2. **Creme de Cocoa** ★ *parfait*   **.75**

3. **Rum Nut Sundae** *aflame* .   **.75**

★ **Flavoraglow by Sparkler**

Flaming Desserts

1.   2.   3.

Clever graphics help sell both desserts, and special flaming ice cream desserts.

A Good Dinner Deserves a Good Dessert

BAKED ON THE PREMISES

From Our Bakers

PIES—Apple, Cherry, Blueberry, Lemon Meringue, Cocoanut Custard .... .25
   (Pumpkin, Mince in Season)

CAKES—French Layer, Cherry Crumb, Blueberry Crumb, Jelly Roll .... .25
   Open-Face Peach (In Season)

DANISH PASTRY—Cheese, Lemon, Cherry, Blueberry, Nut, Lekvar, Streusel,
     Apple, Apple Turnovers, Cinnamon Buns, Pineapple or Cinnamon

     Miniature Danish (Cheese or Lekvar), ... .25

     Cinnamon Bun Toasted .... .30

FRENCH PASTRY—Linzer Tortes, Pretzels, Palmiers, Poppy Seed Croissants ...... .25

COOKIES—Rich Butter, Mandel Bread, Bow Ties .... .25

From Our Chef

Jello, Whipped Cream . . .25	French Tapioca Pudding .25	Baked Cup Custard ... .25
Creamy Rice Pudding .25	Swiss Chocolate Pudding .... .25	Jumbo Baked Apple ... .40

From Our Fountain

Vanilla, Chocolate, Orange Sherbet and other Flavors of Ice Cream in Season...... .35
   with Rich Chocolate Sauce .... .50

From Our Pastry Chef

Country Club Pure Cream Cheese Cake..... .... .45
Blueberry, Cherry or Pineapple .... .55

Our Famous Toasted Cocoanut, Banana, Chocolate or Strawberry Whipped Cream Pie .40

STRUDEL—Apple, Cheese or Miniature Fruit and Nut .... .30

FRENCH PASTRIES (Filled Variety)—Chocolate Eclairs, Cream Puffs, Napoleons,
Butter Cream Squares, Whipped Cream Roll or Chocolate Whipped Cream Roll .35

BUTTER CREAM ROLL
.35

STRAWBERRY BOSTON
.35

SHORT CAKE
.50

FRESH STRAWBERRY TREATS

TARTS
.60

CONTINENTAL PASTRIES

Open Tarts: Cherry or Blueberry .... .35	Stars: Pineapple or Cherry .... .35
Pineapple or Peach Melba .... .30	Apple Dumplings .... .40
Seven Layer Cake .... .35	Rich Fudge Brownie .... .25

Almond Horns or Canoes .... .25

This pastry-oriented dessert listing features BAKED ON THE PREMISES plus photographs (in black and white, but still effective) that sell the pastry specials.

"Mammy's Famous Apple Pie"

.35   A la Mode   .55

Made from the choicest green apples, buttered and sugared with a heavy hand, and not as much as a pinch of spice that would alter the delicate blending of good ingredients, with pastry that is in perfect harmony, altogether produce a symphony of taste that has never been matched so perfectly.

Select some one of your pies and feature it with copy like this and you'll sell more.

If you have a Dessert Cart, sell it on the menu.

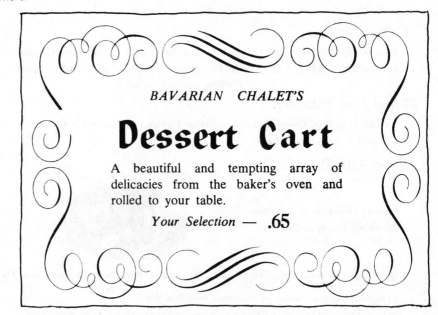

BAVARIAN CHALET'S

Dessert Cart

A beautiful and tempting array of delicacies from the baker's oven and rolled to your table.

Your Selection — .65

Flaming Desserts

CREPES SUZETTE (2) **$3.00**
The queen of desserts made and flamed at your table

BAKED ALASKA (for 2) 2.00
White cake flavored with brandy topped with ice cream and meringue. Flamed with imported liqueurs

CHERRIES FLAMBEE 1.50

Flaming Desserts deserve special treatment.

For Guests with a Specially Sweet Tooth may we recommend

Granny Clarke's Apple Pie
served with Ice Cream and
Fresh Dairy Cream

Delightful Chocolate Sauce
coating Vanilla Ice Cream
topped with Assorted Nuts
and Dairy Cream.

2/6   **3/-**

Ripe Blackberries poured
over Vanilla Ice Cream and
served with Dairy Cream

Fruit Salad served
with Ice Cream and
Fresh Dairy Cream.

3/-   **3/-**

Desserts

Crepes Dentelle Flambee

A Thin French Crepe, Filled with Creme Patisserie,
Diced Fruit Glacé
Marinated in Grand Marnier, Flambé with Rum
1.75

Omelette Surprise Marshall

A Mixture of French Ice Cream
on Sponge Cake Spiced with Rum
Covered with Meringue Served Flaming with Brandy
1.50

Pear Helene	*.60*	*Coupe aux Marrons*	*.80*
Bisquit Tortoni	*.80*	*Parfait Richmond*	*.65*
Meringue Glacee	*.75*	*Compote of Fruit*	*.65*

John Marshall Cream Pie   .40
Frosty Green Mountain   .75

Ice Cream: Chocolate, Vanilla, Pistachio .35

Beverages: Coffee Pot .25   Milk .20   Tea .25

PIECE DE RESISTANCE

STRAWBERRIES ROMANOFF **2.00**

A perfect blend of fresh strawberries, vanilla ice
cream and whipped cream. Prepared with Curacao
and Grand Marnier at your table.

Unusual desserts add sales appeal to any menu and help
build the check.

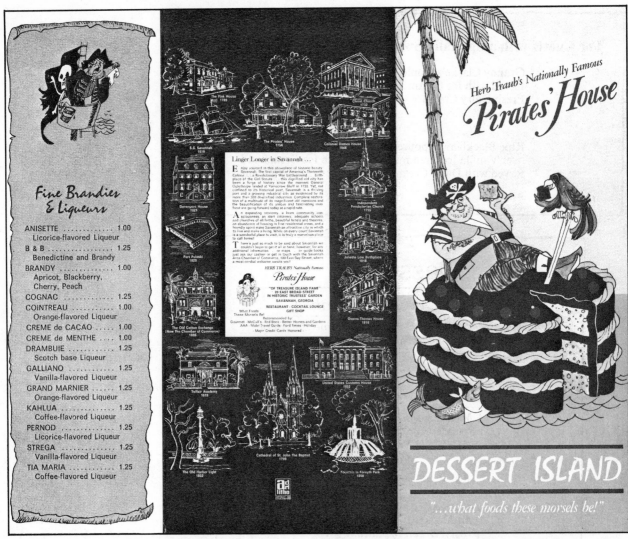

Cover design and general treatment is similar to big menu. This excellent Dessert Menu lists everything—desserts, ice cream dishes, children's desserts, flaming desserts, cakes, pies, after dinner drinks, dessert wines and fine brandies and liqueurs.

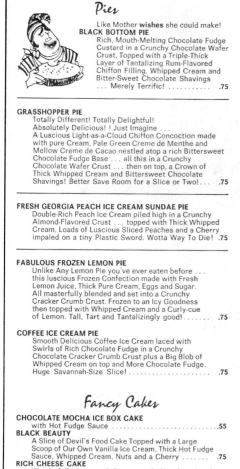

Pies

Like Mother **wishes** she could make!
BLACK BOTTOM PIE
Rich, Mouth-Melting Chocolate Fudge
Custard in a Crunchy Chocolate Wafer
Crust, Topped with a Triple-Thick
Layer of Tantalizing Rum-Flavored
Chiffon Filling, Whipped Cream and
Bitter-Sweet Chocolate Shavings
... Merely Terrific! .... .75

GRASSHOPPER PIE
Totally Different! Totally Delightful!
Absolutely Delicious! ! Just Imagine . . .
A Luscious Light-as-a-Cloud Chiffon Concoction made
with pure Cream, Pale Green Creme de Menthe and
Mellow Creme de Cacao nestled atop a rich Bittersweet
Chocolate Fudge Base . . . all this in a Crunchy
Chocolate Wafer Crust . . . then on top, a Crown of
Thick Whipped Cream and Bittersweet Chocolate
Shavings! Better Save Room for a Slice or Two! ... .75

FRESH GEORGIA PEACH ICE CREAM SUNDAE PIE
Double-Rich Peach Ice Cream piled high in a Crunchy
Almond-Flavored Crust . . . topped with Thick Whipped
Cream, Loads of Luscious Sliced Peaches and a Cherry
impaled on a tiny Plastic Sword. Wotta Way To Die! .75

FABULOUS FROZEN LEMON PIE
Unlike Any Lemon Pie you've ever eaten before . . .
this luscious Frozen Confection made with Fresh
Lemon Juice, Thick Pure Cream, Eggs and Sugar.
All masterfully blended and set into a Crunchy
Cracker Crumb Crust. Frozen to an Icy Goodness
then topped with Whipped Cream and a Curly-cue
of Lemon. Tall, Tart and Tantalizingly good! .... .75

COFFEE ICE CREAM PIE
Smooth Delicious Coffee Ice Cream laced with
Swirls of Rich Chocolate Fudge in a Crunchy
Chocolate Cracker Crumb Crust plus a Big Blob of
Whipped Cream on top and More Chocolate Fudge.
Huge Savannah-Size Slice! .... .75

Fancy Cakes

CHOCOLATE MOCHA ICE BOX CAKE
with Hot Fudge Sauce .... .55
BLACK BEAUTY
A Slice of Devil's Food Cake Topped with a Large
Scoop of Our Own Vanilla Ice Cream, Thick Hot Fudge
Sauce, Whipped Cream, Nuts and a Cherry .... .75
RICH CHEESE CAKE
Wonderfully moist and oh-so-smooth. Smothered with
Glazed Strawberries .... .75
CAROLINA TRIFLE
An Old Southern Dessert Made with Sherry-Flavored
Custard, Sponge Cake and Whipped Cream ...... .50

COPYRIGHT 1968 8-68

SPECTACULAR *Flaming Desserts*.

Prepared right at your table!
STRAWBERRY CREPE ELEGANTE
An oh-so-thin delicate French Crepe
heated in a Superb Fresh Strawberry
Syrup. Rolled around a Pirate-size
Portion of Thick Whipped Cream,
then submerged under a Sea of
Fresh Glazed Strawberries blazing
with Brandy. Crisp Toasted Almonds
give the Final Regal Touch! 1.50

CHERRIES JUBILEE
Dark, delicious Bing Cherries mixed with fine
Liqueurs. Blazed with Brandy and poured
flaming over a mountain of French Vanilla Ice
Cream. Delicious! ! ! 1.50
BANANA FOSTER
A Golden-ripe Banana sliced and simmered in a rich
Concoction of Butter, Brown Sugar and Banana Liqueur.
Set ablaze with Brandy then ladled over a huge dish
of Vanilla Ice Cream! 1.50
MERINGUE GLACE FLAMBE
A Melt-in-your-mouth Meringue Shell filled with
Vanilla Ice Cream. Topped with a Flaming Bittersweet
Chocolate Fudge Sauce that's loaded with Crisp
Toasted Almonds and laced with fine Liqueurs! ... 1.50

Ice Cream Concoctions

DANDY CANDY SUNDAE
Vanilla, Coffee, or Peppermint Stick Ice Cream
served with a Pitcher of Our Sensational Chocolate
Butter Pecan Candy Topping That Gets Cracklin'
Crisp as it hits the Ice Cream! .... .75
GIANT HOT FUDGE, BUTTERSCOTCH OR NESSELRODE .75
(Rum-Tutti Frutti) Sundae with Choice of Ice Cream
(Mmm . . . Take Some of our Delicious NESSELRODE
TOPPING Home. It's on Sale in the Gift Shop.)
ICE CREAM PECAN LOG
with Hot Fudge or Butterscotch Sauce .... .75
PARFAITS
Wonderful New Flavor Combinations Every Day ... .75
PIRATES' HOUSE ICE CREAM OR SHERBET
Delicious But Not Very Exciting
(Chocolate, Vanilla, Strawberry, Coffee, Peppermint
Stick Ice Cream — Pineapple or Orange Sherbet) .55
SENSATIONAL DO-IT-YOURSELF SUNDAE
For Those Who Like To Live Dangerously!
You'll get a tremendous Dish of Ice Cream.
Select any Three Flavors: Chocolate, Vanilla,
Strawberry, Coffee or Peppermint Stick plus
a lazy Susan loaded with Assorted Toppings,
Whipped Cream, Nuts and Cherries. From then
on it's up to you! 1.50

FUN FOR OUR *Little Pirates*
MERRY-GO-ROUND SUNDAE - A Big Scoop
of Vanilla Ice Cream Surrounded with
Animal Crackers and Topped with a Tiny
Umbrella That Really Works! ! .... .35
BLAZING ATOMIC SUNDAE - Order One
and Be Surprised. It's really
Supercalifragilisticexpialidotious ! ! .. .35
ICE CREAM OR SHERBET - Sprinkled All
Over with Little Candy Jewels! ! ...... .25

After Dinner Drinks

ANGEL'S KISS	1.25
Creme de Cacao & Cream	
BLACK RUSSIAN	1.50
Vodka & Kahlua	
(Coffee Liqueur)	
BRANDY ALEXANDER ..	1.50
Brandy, Creme de Cacao	
and Cream	
CREME de MENTHE	
FRAPPE	1.00
GRASSHOPPER	1.50
Creme de Menthe, Creme	
de Cacao & Cream	
IRISH COFFEE	
(served flaming)	1.75
Irish Whiskey, Coffee and	
Whipped Cream	
PINK LADY	1.25
Gin, Grenadine and Cream	
PINK SQUIRREL	1.25
Creme de Noyoux	
(Almond-flavored Liqueur)	
and Cream	
RUSTY NAIL	1.50
Scotch and Drambuie	
STINGER	1.50
Brandy and Creme	
de Menthe	

Dessert Wines

	Glass	Bottle
Christian Brothers		
Ruby Port	.50	3.50
Christian Brothers		
Sherry	.50	3.50
Christian Brothers		
Golden Sherry	.50	3.50
Taylor Port	.50	3.50
Taylor Cream		
Cream Sherry .	.50	3.50
Duff Gordon Nina		
(Medium Dry)	.60	4.50
Harvey's Gold		
Cap Port	.85	
Harvey's Bristol		
Cream	1.30	

*Besides good art and design handling, this dessert menu
has what seems the best copy possible. Everything is described and sold with a good selection of words. Note
also that ingredients in After Dinner Drinks are listed.*

At the End

Cherries Jubilee 1.75

Coconut Ice Cream .60   **Coconut Honey Ice Cream .60**

The Traders Rum Ice Cream with Praline Sauce **.75**

The Traders Ice Cream 1.10
(Fresh Cocoanut Ice Cream served with Flaming Kumquat Sauce)

Passion Fruit Sherbet .60   **Strawberries Puiwa** (in season) **1.75**

Tahitian Ice Cream 1.10
(Flaming mixture from the Islands blended with Rhum Baba
and Ice Cream)

Mangoes with Ice Cream .85   **Snow Ball .85**

Ginger Tea Ice Cream .60

Pineapple Sherbet .50   **Indian Mangoes .75**

Kona Ice Cream 1.10
(Tropical Fruits and Ice Cream Flambe with Trader Vic's Fruit Sauce)

Royal Tropical Fruit 1.25   **Hawaiian Papaya 1.00**

Hawaiian Pineapple 1.25   **Banana Fritters .75**

Camembert or Roquefort Cheese .75

The Luau Room is available for Private Parties

A South Seas type food service can offer a South Seas dessert listing and merchandise it as this listing does.

MAKE YOUR FOUNTAIN MENU A FOUNTAIN OF PROFITS

Ice cream is such a universally popular item on the American menu that it tends to be taken for granted. Yet the value of selling ice cream in all its various forms—plain, in flavors, in sundaes, sodas, malts, floats, shakes, with pies, cakes, etc., is proven daily by the success of such big operations as Howard Johnson's and Schraffts'. Even if you don't mention ice cream on the menu, customers will ask for it. Therefore, it is obvious that some time, effort and merchandising expertise will increase the sale of this part of your menu "sweet" selection.

The history of ice cream is unknown. It seems to have been more of a perfection than an invention. It began with flavored ices which were a favorite of the nobility as long ago as Alexander the Great in the 4th century B. C. Because of the difficulty of making ice cream before modern methods of refrigeration were developed, only the rich and noble had access to this food delicacy which is now commonplace. Charles I of England, for example, gave "hush money" to his chef so that ice cream would be reserved for exclusive use at the royal table. But the formula for ice cream could not be kept a secret, and the popularity as well as consumption of ice cream has spread. Even in early Colonial America, ice cream was known. Dolly Madison, for example, gave ice cream popularity plus the presidential stamp of approval by serving it at White House receptions. The development of other fountain combinations, sodas and sundaes, came later.

In the early 1800's, carbonated soda water was introduced as a "health water". Later, flavorings were added to make soft drinks, and then flavoring, cream and ice cream were added to create the first ice cream soda. Strangely enough, however, carbonated water was considered at one time by some people to be intoxicating! Various blue laws, therefore, outlawed the serving of sodas on Sunday. Some creative restaurateur or fountain operator got around the law by serving the ice cream and syrup flavorings without the carbonated water, on Sunday, and thus the "sundae" was born.

Another ice cream development was the ice cream cone. There are no statues to commemorate the memory of Ernest A. Homini, but there probably should be because at the St. Louis World's Fair in 1904, he introduced the ice cream cone. Another proof of the popularity of ice cream is the number of flavors on the market. There are reputed to be over 200 flavors. But while flavors come and go, plain old vanilla is still the public's number one favorite.

In terms of menu design and merchandising, there are two basic approaches to selling ice cream and fountain items. First, there is the type of food operation, usually a short order, fast food sandwich (hamburger-hot dog) set-up where the fountain listing is as important as the feature entrees. And then there is the more conventional, usually more expensive restaurant where ice cream is a dessert item. The two types of listings should get different treatment.

The short order menu should include the fountain items with the entree listings. This usually means a menu listing three basic offerings:

1.   Sandwiches (hamburgers, hot dogs, cheeseburgers, etc.)
2.   Entrees (chicken, fish, a small steak selection, chili, spaghetti).
3.   Sweets (pies, cakes, ice cream, sodas, sundaes, malts, etc.)

An important, integral part of this type of fountain menu listing is illustration. This usually means color illustrations of sodas, sundaes, malts, banana splits, etc. Depending on which items you want to sell the most of, it is vital that you feature and merchandise them.

The basic ways to feature fountain items are:

1.   Bolder, larger type.
2.   More descriptive copy.
3.   Color illustration.

If fountain items are a big part of your business or if you want to make them more important, you should use the following basic rules:

1.   List the flavors of all ice creams, sodas, sundaes, malts, shakes, and floats served.
2.   Use sub-headings to identify types of fountain items—SODAS, SUNDAES, MALTS, etc., especially if you have a big listing.

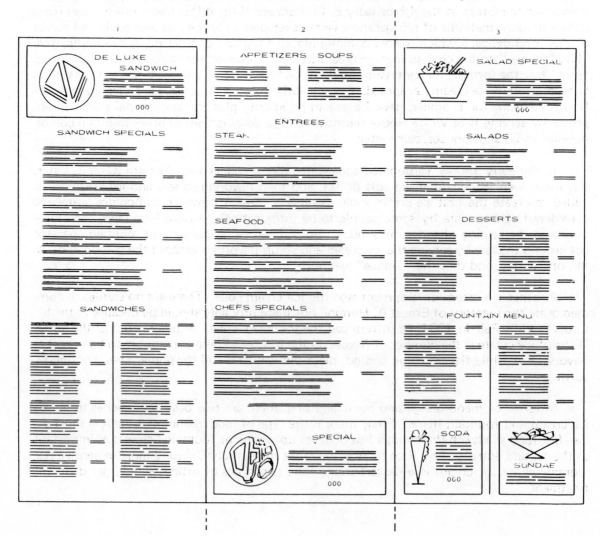

3.   Feature some fountain items.   Usually special sundaes—hot fudge, strawberry, chocolate nut, etc., or some fruit combination, banana split, etc.

If yours is a bigger, more conventional menu, you should list the ice cream and fountain items with the desserts. You can either list the fountain items under a separate heading or mix them with the desserts. But since they all function as after dinner items they should be listed together.

Since after dinner drinks are part of the after portion of the menu, desserts and drinks plus ice creams can be listed together. There are many liqueur and ice cream combinations that tie in the entire after part of the menu. Cherries Jubilee and a variety of parfaits are "naturals" for making an interesting and saleable dessert-ice cream-drink list. The important thing is to describe these items with good copy. Many people do not know how Cherries Jubilee or Baked Alaska are made or even the difference between a parfait and a sundae. You have to tell them.

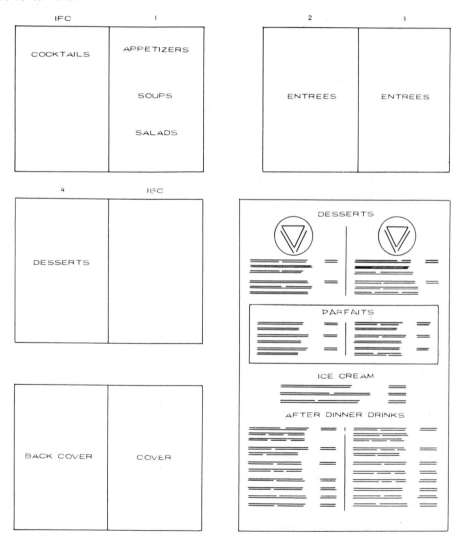

There are many creative ways to list and serve ice cream on the menu. One way is to allow guests to "Make Your Own Sundae". This is a selection of ice cream flavors served in a bowl with the sauces, syrups, nuts, fruits, etc., served on the side so that the customer can build his own ice cream concoction. Keith's Restaurant lists a selection of "Sweets" which shows unusual combinations of ice cream. They are as follows:

> CASSATA: Our very own recipe—layers of flavored ice cream with a delicious center of rich whipped cream blended with sherry, nuts and candied fruit.
> GREEN HEAVEN: Pineapple marinated in creme de menthe served with ice cream, nuts and whipped cream.
> CHERRIED DELIGHT: Cherries marinated in liqueur served with ice cream and nuts, and flavored with cherry brandy.

The Copper Hood Restaurant offers the TIKI HULA—A Volcano of Love—ice cream surrounded by pineapple chunks with coconut topping. And Mr. A's offers Baked Alaska L'Absinthe for Two or More. The Gourmet restaurant lists a real gourmet ice cream concoction—COUPE GOURMET—Mandarin orange, marrons, brandy and ice cream. And Tallino's, an Italian style restaurant, doesn't just offer the traditional Spumoni, it lists Spumoni with claret sauce. Even a Chinese restaurant can offer ice cream with a different twist. The Golden Pavillion, a well-known Chinese restaurant, lists GINGER ICE CREAM—a special blend of ginger roots and rich ice cream. The uses of ice cream on the menu are unlimited, as can be

---

Desserts

Parfait Creme de Menthe	.95	Chocolate Nut Sundae	.75
Parfait Creme de Cacoa	.95	Butterscotch Sundae	.75
Ron Rico Rum Parfait	.95	Pineapple Sundae	.75
Fresh Strawberry Parfait	.95	Strawberry Sundae	.75

Chocolate Parfait........ .95

Home Made Cheese Cake	.75
Hot Apple Pie with Cheese, Ice Cream or Whipped Cream	.75
Old-Fashioned Strawberry Plantation Surprise	.75
Roquefort, Bleu or Camembert Cheese	.75

Beverages *(with food)*

Coffee .25   Tea .25   Milk .25   Iced Coffee .25   Iced Tea .25

Entremets

Baked Alaska a L'Absinthe
  for Two or More   *per person 2.50*

Crêpes Suzette
  for Two or More   *per person 3.00*

Cherries Jubilée
  for Two or More   *per person 2.50*

Colossal Strawberries Giuseppe   1.95

Assorted French Pastries   .95

Ice Cream .65   Sherbet .65   Cheese Cake .85

Cream de Menthe Parfait   1.35

ICE CREAM

Colony Beach Special Ice Cream	.50
Ice Cream Rolled In Fresh Cocoanut or Chopped Pecan and Chocolate Sauce	.95
Make Your Own Sundae	1.00
Sherbet	.50
Cream de Menthe Parfait	1.25
Sundae	.75
Fruit Jello	.50

seen from the menus included on these pages. So, if your menu now lists only assorted ice creams, take a second look at your menu. It is most certain that by a little creative merchandising and effectively listing it on the menu, you can substantially increase your sales of ice cream in its many forms.

BLUM'S ICE CREAMS
Blum's delicious ice creams are super-rich

french vanilla	holland boy chocolate	turkish coffee
strawberry	coffee marshmallow	burnt almond
rocky road	double-double chocolate	peppermint stick

.50

FRESH FRUIT ICES, EUROPEAN
Tangy goodness of fresh fruits in light, sparkling freeze

strawberry	california orange	california lemon
raspberry		hawaiian pineapple

.50

BLUM'S SPECIAL SODAS
Scoops of Blum's ice creams in sparkling effervescence

french vanilla	cherry	pineapple mint
strawberry	holland boy chocolate	mint
red raspberry	bittersweet chocolate	turkish coffee
orange	mocha chocolate	caramel
lemon	chocolate mint	root beer
	pineapple	

Special Sodas .70   *Extra-Special .80

*With lavish additions of marshmallow, caramel or fudge sauce.

BLUM'S SHAKES AND MALTS
Irresistible flavors and heavenly creaminess

french vanilla	cherry	pineapple mint
strawberry	holland boy chocolate	mint
red raspberry	bittersweet chocolate	turkish coffee
orange	mocha chocolate	caramel
lemon	chocolate mint	root beer
pineapple	peanut butter	

Special Shakes .75   *Extra-Special .85
Special Malts .85   *Extra-Special .95

*With lavish additions of marshmallow, caramel or fudge sauce.

SPARKLING ICE CAPADES
Sun-ripened fruits captured in meltingly delicious ices

STRAWBERRY CRUSH, fresh strawberries and fresh strawberry ice floats, capped by raspberry ice.........75
RASPBERRY RAPTURE, the fresh-fruit deliciousness of raspberry ice and a rush of crushed raspberries........75
ORANGE SPARKLER, Blum's freshly-squeezed orange juice comes frozen with float of orange ice................75
LEMON CAPRICE, sunny pineapple juice adds the tang of grapefruit juice and floats scoops of fresh lemon ice....75

BLUM'S SUNDAES
Pure delight of Blum's matchless flavor in gigantic servings

holland boy chocolate	chocolate marshmallow	strawberry
bittersweet chocolate	caramel	raspberry
milk chocolate	caramel marshmallow	pineapple
chocolate mint	caramel pecan	pineapple mint
chocolate mocha	marshmallow	coffee
		fudge

.85

Small Dessert Sundaes (with meals) .60   A la Carte .65

BLUM'S SUNDAE BESTS
ALMONDETTE DIVINE
The unsurpassed Almondettes make a fitting sauce for fine ice cream

French vanilla ice cream glorified with the dark, caramel richness of Almondette Sauce, frilled with whipped cream and a rush of toasted almonds.

.95

> #### CUSTOMER'S FOLLY
> *The do-it-yourself sundae*
>
> Pick three of your favorite ice creams, three of your favorite sauces, (from the sundae list at top of page), fixings according to your fancy. Go on; live a little!
>
> 1.35

COF-FIESTA
The delectable pairing of coffee and chocolate

Coffee ice cream floating in rich chocolate sauce and whipped cream, topped with our own Koffee Krunch.

.85

HOT FUDGE OR HOT CARAMEL
Simply, purely perfection

French vanilla ice cream lavished with meltingly delicious hot fudge or caramel sauce, swirls of whipped cream.

.95

OLD FASHIONED BANANA SPLIT
...as created by our founder, Simon Blum

A big scoop of vanilla drenched with chocolate sauce... a big scoop of strawberry sauced with strawberry... a big scoop of chocolate drowned in marshmallow... waves of whipped cream, and nuts, and a banana (split).

1.35

GREAT BIG STRAWBERRY SMASH
Say, it's "smashing"!

Blum's own pound cake covered with strawberry sauce, piled with vanilla ice cream, heaped with fresh strawberry ice, topped with whipped cream and more strawberries.

1.65

See next page for parfaits

This menu—BLUM'S—is probably the most completely ice cream-oriented menu around. Any menu can be improved in the fountain department by using this one as a model, if not in whole at least in part.

BLUM'S PARFAITS

Incomparable blendings of exciting flavors
.85

EMERALD ISLE
Sure, and it warms the cockles of your heart!
A wallop of ice cream, a dollop of fudge sauce,
a flurry of mint and cocoanut, a halo of whipped cream.

FIDDLE FADDLE
Roundelay of favorite flavors and Blum's toppings
A delightful medley of chocolate and coffee ice creams,
coffee syrup, banana slices, whipped cream.

TING-A-LING TANG
The nip-up zip of citrus laced with the zing of raspberry
Orange ice in a sea of fresh-frozen raspberries and
marshmallow...lemon ice drenched with raspberry juice
and whipped cream...and pecans everywhere!

HOB NOB HILL
A tantare of favorite flavors crunched with almonds
Vanilla ice cream ladled over with chocolate and
marshmallow sauces...burnt almond ice cream with
a whipped cream float...a chopping of roasted almonds.

PEPPERMINT DRIZZLE
Vanilla ice cream layered between mint and chocolate
syrups...peppermintstick ice cream hushed with
marshmallow...vanilla ice cream, cold fudge
whipped cream, plus pecans and Thin Mint.
1.35

BLUM'S CAKES AND PIES

Cake* ... .55	A la mode ... .75

lemon krunch	pineapple custard	hazelnut
koffee krunch	cocoanut cream	chocolate fudge
chantilly	beverly brazil	cheesecake

Pie* ... .55	A la mode ... .75

lemon goddess	chocolate cream	fresh fruit
lemon meringue	cocoanut cream	french apple
boston cream	*Ask waitress for today's selections	

BLUM'S FAMOUS COFFEE-TOFFEE PIE
Creamy with richness, aromatic with coffee and chocolate
.75 a slice

BLUM'S FRENCH PASTRIES
Select from the delectable assortment on our pastry tray.
.55

BLUM'S DANISH PASTRY
Choose from our large, delicious variety.
.35

RAREBIT SANDWICHES
Your choice of ham, turkey, tuna or ground beef sandwiches
grilled until golden, topped with Welsh rarebit sauce.
Served with tossed green salad or cole slaw.
1.50

CUSTOM DELUXE SANDWICHES

CORNED BEEF NASHER, with Swiss cheese 1.35
DUKE OF WINDSOR, turkey, grilled pineapple, cheddar
cheese, avocado and Major Grey's Chutney 1.65
CLUBHOUSE, chicken, bacon, tomato and mayonnaise 1.75
COSMOPOLITAN, turkey, sugar-cured ham, Swiss cheese
with Russian Dressing 1.75

HOT SANDWICHES

beefburger ... .90	cheddarburger 1.00
(with onion pot) 1.05	frankly fabulous frankfurter .75
swissburger .. 1.25	with cheese .... .80

BEEFSTEAK-ON-A-BUN, tender steak served on Blum's bun
with beefsteak tomato slice and Blum's own onion pot 1.95

OPEN-FACE ROAST TURKEY SUPREME, served with a
rich supreme sauce, fluffy potatoes and cranberry sauce 1.75

REUBEN SANDWICH, grilled corned beef, Swiss cheese,
sauerkraut on rye with Russian dressing, potato salad 1.75

SHRIMP FONDUE, petite shrimp on grilled bread with Swiss
cheese sauce, bacon, avocado; cole slaw or green salad 2.25

MONTE CARLO, baked ham and cheese sandwich dipped in
egg batter, sauteed in butter. Served with small fresh fruit
salad with poppyseed dressing 1.75

MONTE CRISTO, baked ham, turkey and cheese sandwich
dipped in egg batter, sauteed in butter. Served with a small
fresh fruit salad with poppyseed dressing 1.95

SANDWICH FAVORITES

All sandwiches are served with cole slaw or potato salad.

sliced turkey 1.25	american cheese .... .85
baked sugar-cured	chopped egg .... .75
ham 1.10	lettuce and tomato... .75
corned beef 1.10	peanut butter and jelly .65
smoked tongue ..... .95	turkey and wisconsin
chicken salad 1.00	swiss cheese 1.35
tuna salad .... .95	fried ham and egg ... 1.25
wisconsin swiss	smoked tongue and
cheese .... .85	american cheese ... 1.15
liverwurst .... .75	ham and tomato..... 1.25
minced olive and nut . .85	bacon and tomato ... 1.25

See next page for salads

*It takes 6 full pages to list all of Blum's fountain items.
Menu is printed on inside covers and on a 4-page insert.
Pink Cover is illustrated with drawing of San Francisco
cable car. (See preceding page for first two pages.)*

BLUM'S CREATIVE SALADS

CANDIED BAKED APPLE SALAD

The delicious spiciness of our chilled and cinnamoned
baked apple is complemented by a circle of fresh fruits
and our marshmallow-nut dressing.

1.75

NICE FRUIT 'N ICE

Choice fresh fruit piled high with fresh pineapple sticks
and topped with Blum's incomparable fruit ices. This is
served with our distinguished poppyseed dressing
and date-nut finger sandwiches

1.75

KONA COAST CHICKEN SALAD

Pineapple shell brims with diced chicken salad and fresh
fruit jubilee gloriously garnished with grapes.

1.95

CALIFORNIA MEDLEY SALAD

Four salads in one. Chicken salad, seafood salad,
cottage cheese salad and fruit salad—
served with finger sandwiches.

2.25

COTTAGE FRUIT BOWL

Creamy cottage cheese is surrounded with a
delightful selection of fresh and prepared fruits.

1.45

IMPERIAL VALLEY SALAD

Crisp greens and fresh vegetables—the best
from the Salinas, Santa Clara and Imperial Valleys
make this salad which is topped with julienne ham,
turkey, two kinds of cheese and jumbo black olives.
Your choice of dressing.

2.35

SHRIMP OR CRAB LOUIS

Superb shellfish served on a bed of crisp lettuce, garnished
with hard-cooked egg, sliced tomatoes, ripe olives.
Louis dressing served on the side.

2.50

Remoulade sauce, .25 extra

PETITE LOUIS 1.85

From San Francisco's romantic past, a deliciously famous landmark,
the original BLUM'S, Polk at California Street (established 1890).
Ride the California Street Cable Car
right to the door of San Francisco's favorite store.

BEVERLY HILLS, CALIFORNIA

PALO ALTO'S STANFORD SHOPPING CENTER

SACRAMENTO AT CAPITOL SQUARE

SAN MATEO, CALIFORNIA

UNION SQUARE, SAN FRANCISCO

PASADENA, CALIFORNIA

I. MAGNIN, LOS ANGELES

FAIRMONT HOTEL, SAN FRANCISCO

THE CROSSROADS, SACRAMENTO

STONESTOWN, SAN FRANCISCO

PORTLAND

TOWN AND COUNTRY VILLAGE, SAN JOSE, CALIFORNIA

PALACE HOTEL, SAN FRANCISCO

SALEM PLAZA, OREGON

TOWN AND COUNTRY VILLAGE, SACRAMENTO

NEW YORK AT 59TH STREET

WEST COAST — 3-10-66

THE OLD TIME FOUNTAIN

All 2-K fountain creations are made to order. This takes a little time, but they're worth waiting for. Please do not ask for substitutions.

Double Dip Ice Cream Dish

Vanilla, Oldtime Chocolate, Strawberry, Coffee, Pistachio, Toasted Almond, Peppermint .... .50

Single-Dip Dish Ice Cream .... .30

SHERBET—Raspberry, Lemon, Pineapple .... Single .25; Double .40

Sherbet Bouquet .... .55

TINY TOT SUNDAE—1 Scoop Vanilla Ice Cream, Chocolate Top, Animal Crackers .... .40

CONES .... Single .20; Double .35

THICK MALTS AND SHAKES

Vanilla, Pineapple, Chocolate, Lemon, Coffee, Strawberry, or Cherry. Made with Ice Cream and Whole Milk ..... .45

With Egg .... .55

ICE CREAM SODAS

Vanilla, Chocolate, Strawberry, Pineapple, Lemon, Coffee or Cherry. Double dip and Whipped Cream .... .45

LEMON or LIME ADE— Made with Fizz Water .... .25

The truly luxurious ice cream you enjoy at 2-K is made from an exclusive formula. It is ours alone and is available only under the 2-K trademark, here in our restaurant and at better stores.
Take some home from the display case. Quart . $ .99

HOUSTONIAN

One of the World's Largest! 5 Scoops Ice Cream, Sliced Pineapple, 5 Sundae Toppings, Sliced Banana, Nuts, Whipped Cream, Cherry

95

HAWAIIAN

Vanilla and Strawberry Ice Cream, Pineapple and Strawberry Topping, Grated Coconut, Sliced Banana, Sliced Pineapple

70
Half Size— 50

CASEY JONES

A Fancy Sundae Choo-Choo Train. 3 Scoops Ice Cream, Strawberry, Pineapple, Chocolate Topping, with Banana Wheels, Marshmallows, Whipped Cream, Cherry

75

BANANA SPLIT

Vanilla, Chocolate, Strawberry Ice Cream, Topped with Fresh Frozen Strawberries, Pineapple and Chocolate on Banana Halves, Whipped Cream, Chopped Nuts, Cherry

75

GAY NINETIES

2 Scoops Vanilla Ice Cream on Banana Halves, Topped with Hot Fudge, Whipped Cream, Chopped Nuts.

70

ALASKAN PEAK

5 Scoops Ice Cream Covered with Marshmallow, 2 Whole Bananas and Coconut

(A Real Mountain)

95

BLACK AND WHITE

Sundae

Chocolate and Vanilla Ice Cream with Marshmallow and Chocolate Topping, Whipped Cream, Chopped Nuts, Cherry.

65

LOG CABIN

2 Scoops Coffee Ice Cream, Caramel Topping, Chopped Nuts and Salted Pretzel Sticks

65

SNOWBALL

Small Marshmallow Sundae Covered with Grated Coconut and Whipped Cream.

55

In addition to regular ice cream offerings, this listing includes some unusual ice cream specialties with appropriate copy and names.

Ye Pimlico Super Banana Bonanza. . . .   1.75
First a split ripe banana; second. three jumbo scoops of Creamy French ice cream covered with your choice of fresh fruit or hot fudge and topped with whipped cream and chopped nuts.

Emerald Isle 95
essence o' mint, a smackin' wallop o' the ice cream o' the month, cold chocolate fudge, a smitherin' o' shredded toasted coconut, charlotte russe, creme de menthe (for warmin' the cockles o' your heart) and right in the middle and atop it all, the bright green emerald isle. erin ga buy it!

Coconut Snoball 95
French vanilla ice cream with thick chocolate fudge topped with grated cocoanut.

The more unusual and creative the fountain menu, the more you can charge for it!

DESSERTS

✒ ICE HOUSE CREATIONS ✒

Ice Cream   Soft Serve Ice Cream   Sherbets .20
Vanilla, Chocolate, Strawberry, Coffee, Butter Pecan, Raspberry Sherbet

OLD FASHIONED ICE CREAM SODAS
Two Scoops of Ice Cream floating in Rich Smooth Syrups and Sparkling Soda
with Gobs of Whipped Cream .35

SHAKES AND MALTEDS .40
Spoon-Eatin' Thick — made with Soft Ice Creams. Served in the shaker it's mixed in

BANANA BANANZA .65
Mounds of Strawberry, Chocolate and Vanilla Ice Cream, Drenched with Pineapple
and Strawberry Fruit then Covered with Whipped Cream, Chopped Nuts and Cherries

SUNDAE FANTASIES .40
Fancifully made with Vanilla or Chocolate Ice Cream with Choice of Hot Chocolate Fudge,
Hot Butterscotch Fudge, Strawberry, Chocolate or Pineapple Sauce.
Topped with Whipped Cream and Maraschino Cherries

Table D'Hote

Assorted Sherbet Balls   Fresh Fruit Compote

Wild Mountain Blackberry Sundae

Vanilla, Chocolate or Peppermint Ice Cream

Kaphan's Fudge Pie Ala Mode

Kaphan's Blackbottom Pie

Lemon Glace   Coffee Sundae

Lemon Ice Box Pie

Ala Carte

Kaphan's Famous Ice Cream Pie . . .	.75
Frozen Rainbow Parfait w/Blackberries .	.70
Lemon Glace — Rich in Lemon w/Brandy .	.60
Coffee Sundae w/Coffee Liqueur . . .	.60
Parfaits — Chocolate, Caramel, Vin de Menthe — Coffee	.75
Kaphan's Famous Cheese Cake	.65
Topped with Blackberries.	.75
Pies — Fruit and Cream	.35

Desserts Flambes

Black Bing Cherries Jubilee	1.50
Rhum Ba Ba	1.00
Crepes Suzettes (Prepared Table Side). .	1.75
Strawberries or Peaches (in Season) . .	1.75
Bananas Kaphan's.	1.50

Cheeses

Roquefort	.50
Philadelphia Cream	.50
Camembert (Served with Toasted Crackers, and Guava Jelly)	.50

A complete dessert menu includes ice cream creations either with or without brandy and liqueurs.

YOUR LIQUOR LISTING SHOULD REFLECT CHANGING TASTES

How many different bottles of liquor to stock in your bar and cellar, and, therefore, how many different drinks to list on the menu is a very real and difficult problem for every food service operator. A large stock of bottled goods can represent a sizable financial investment. If this investment does not have a fast turnover, the money tied up becomes a considerable waste. The faster the turnover, the greater the return.

Trial and error, of course, will tell a food service operator a great deal. What sells will be reordered. But this practical kind of market research is not the complete answer to this problem. In the first place, trial and error can be expensive. Bottles gathering dust on a shelf tell a story, but at a cost. Also, by this method, the product never ordered and given a trial is a complete unknown to the operator.

Then, too, improper listing and merchandising on the menu can result in an improper consumption pattern within the restaurant. Any product, liquor or food, assuming it is a good product, can be sold if it is merchandised properly on the menu and in the restaurant, but the most popular food and drink items are easier to sell. It is these items that usually make up the backbone of the menu.

American drinking habits are changing. Scotch is less popular; wines and apertifs are gaining in popularity. The two-martini lunch is giving way to a one-white-wine with the midday meal. Special drinks such as the *Hurricane* (dark rum, fruit punch and lemon juice) and the *Apricot Glacier* (Southern Comfort, champagne and an apricot) are appearing more often in restaurants, and in the "Sun Belt"—Florida to California—the *Marguerita* with its tequila base is becoming increasingly popular.

GROWTH OF WINE CONSUMPTION

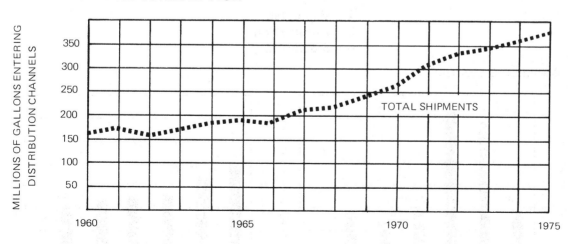

The fastest growing alcoholic beverages are wines, vodka, tequila and flavorful sweet drinks. This trend is likely to continue since these drinks are favored by the young. The older drinks such as blended whiskies and scotches are favored by older drinkers. Their popularity, therefore, is declining or remaining static. Younger drinkers are not acquiring a taste for whiskey.

The per-capita consumption of alcoholic beverages for Americans 14 years or older in 1975 was just under 2.7 gallons. This broke down into 12 fifths of 86 proof spirits, 12.5 fifths of wine, and 12.5 cases of beer. More women are drinking today than in the past, and there is more variety and less alcoholic content in the drinks consumed. Vodka, the most neutral and therefore the most mixable of spirits has become the most popular. It is only 80 proof, and recently most domestic spirits have been reduced to 80 proof (from 86 proof).

Throughout American history, and continuing through today, beer has constituted the largest single source of alcoholic intake, but wine is growing increasingly in popularity. In the past five years, wine consumption has increased by 37 percent—a faster rate of growth than any other alcoholic beverage. Most of this wine growth has been in *table* wines which average about 12 percent in alcoholic content, while fortified *dessert* wines with their higher 15 to 20 percent alcoholic content have declined in popularity.

The implications of the changes in American drinking habits are significant to the restaurant operator and his menu. First, most Americans are *moderate* drinkers. Only 9 percent are classified as heavy drinkers while 18 percent are counted as moderate drinkers and 31 percent are considered light drinkers. This leaves 42 percent as abstainers or infrequent drinkers. This emphasis on moderation plus the lower alcoholic content of the most popular beers and wines gives one indication. The growing popularity of vodka gives another, and the "special" cocktails gives a third.

For the menu planner and designer, every restaurant that serves alcoholic beverages should have a wine and beer list—either separate or as part of the food listing. The wine list should include wine by the glass, bottle or carafe. This latter wine is usually a "house" wine—white, red and rose—can be purchased by the barrel and is very profitable. A very popular wine drink is Sangria which is appearing on more and more wine lists and menus.

Relative to mixed drinks and cocktails the following are today's fifteen best sellers in bars and restaurants:

1. Martini
2. Manhattan
3. Whiskey Sour
4. Bloody Mary

TOP-SELLING LIQUORS

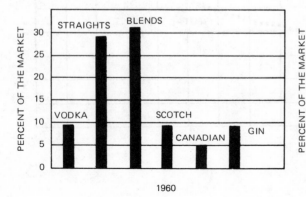

1960

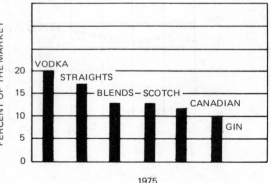

1975

5. Gimlet
6. Daiquiri
7. Collins
8. Old Fashioned
9. Margarita
10. Screwdriver
11. Bacardi
12. Stinger
13. Harvey Wallbanger
14. Gin and Tonic
15. Sombrero

While the two "old favorites," the Martini and the Manhattan still lead the list of cocktail favorites, there have been many new additions. Young adults—the postwar generation, now grown up—who were brought up on fruit juices and sodas, made these new drinks with provocative names popular mainly because they *taste* good.

There are also regional preferences where "new" drinks have appeared. The *Tequila Sunrise* (grenadine, tequila and orange juice) is popular in Los Angeles; the *Cool Teul* (Southern Comfort, tequila and orange juice) is common in Miami Beach; and the *Sombrero* (coffee liqueur and chilled milk) started in Boston and spread to other cities.

The key to these new "in" drinks is a special group of versatile liquors that mix very well with a variety of juices and sodas. These are rum, vodka, tequila plus a variety of liqueurs.

PER CAPITA BEER CONSUMPTION

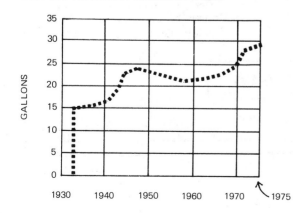

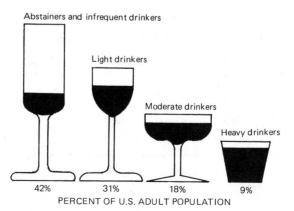

Try Our

Champagne Dinner

FOR TWO

Large Bottle of Champagne
served before or during meal

ANY TWO STEAKS
IN THE HOUSE

Tossed Salad

Baked Potato

Hot Rolls and

Pure Creamery Butter

*Don't leave yet. After Dinner ask
cashier for Complimentary Ticket
For two after dinner drinks in
our Lounge*

15⁰⁰

Selling food and liquor as a "package" is good merchandising.

NAME BRANDS

SCOTCH		OTHERS	
Black and White	60c	Sunny Brook	50c
Teachers	60c	Shenley	50c
Johnnie Walker Black	80c	Seagrams 7 Crown	50c
Cutty Sark	75c	Calverts Special	50c
J & B	75c	Walkers Deluxe	50c
White Label	75c	Old Crow	50c
Chevas Regal	80c	Cabin Still	50c
BONDS		Chapin & Gore	50c
Old Grandad	60c	Early Times	50c
Old Taylor	60c	Jack Daniels Bl.	70c
Old Fitzgerald	60c	Jack Daniels Gr.	60c

CANADIANS

Seagrams VO	60c	O.F.C.	60c
Canadian Club	60c	Windsor	50c

Brand names indicate that you serve good quality.

Tahitian Room

PLANTATION No. 2......**$1.10**
One of the Plantation's most
popular rum concoctions and we
personally recommend it

VIRGIN................. 1.25
For nostalgic memories of the islands
induced by Virgin Island Rums and
East Indian Special Rums

WAIKIKI................. 1.25
There's a Lei with this one

POLYNESIAN............. 1.25
It'll make you a shade darker, but
you feel lighter

HAWAIIAN COCKTAIL..... 1.25
Smooth, golden, brilliant and as
sparkling as an island Wahinee

VICTORY................. 1.25
Drop anchor, lads, while we
skillfully blend British Navy Rum,
Caribbean spices, Falernum and
Angostura

PARADISE COCKTAIL...... 1.25
You'll be looking for a full moon
after this one

FAR EAST COCKTAIL..... 1.25
Don't let the grenadine pull the
wool over your eyes. This is no
sissy drink

GILDED MAIDEN.......... 1.25
A beautiful golden drink with a
Midas touch—That is, after the nth
you're petrified

THREE DOTS AND A DASH. 1.25

151 COCKTAIL........... 1.25
The Atomic Bomb had something to
do with this drink—and don't say
we didn't tell you

HIBISCUS COCKTAIL...... 1.25
You know bartending is a lot of
hokum. You leave out one
ingredient or add another and give
the thing a different name and
you've got a new drink. Or have
you? Don't be fooled—This is just
another variation of the boss

SHARK'S TOOTH.......... 1.50
A suave disarmer, not for
missionaries

---

*For Your After-Dinner Pleasure
May We Suggest . . .*

IRISH COFFEE............ 1.25

ALEXANDERS............ 1.00

PINK LADY.............. 1.00

PINK SQUIRREL.......... 1.00

SALLY RAND—WITH FAN. 1.00

CRIKET................. 1.00

GRASSHOPPER........... 1.00

BEACHCOMBER.......... **$1.25**
A velvet beauty—for those who
know their way around the island
when the stars murmur of love

TAHITIAN............... 1.50
A serene blend of old Cuban Rums,
fruits and limes—Delicious

PLANTERS RUM PUNCH... 1.50
For luscious sipping, try one of
these sour-sweet deceivers—Not
as innocent as might at first
appear

**PLANTATION GOLD
COCKTAIL**................ 1.25
You pick the adjectives for THIS
event

COBRA'S FANG........... 1.25
(Not poison, but Oh! Oh!)

NEVER SAY DIE.......... 1.25
A favorite from igloo to isthmus
—A puisant potation and you can
say that again—or can you?

SKULL AND BONES....... 1.25
(HOLD on to your hair)

BARBADOS.............. 1.25
They're sneaky—but in a nice way

GREEN VALLEY........... 1.50
Fresh mint with gin fan to take
with you

SINGAPORE SLING........ 1.50

LOST HORIZON.......... 1.50
Ceremonial drink of island
friendship

TROPICAL SPLENDOR...... 1.50
A tall one—plenty ki-yi—
Connoisseurs paddle far for the
bouquet of this delicious Jamaica
Rum Punch

PLANTATION BOMBER No. 1 1.50
Take it easy—How did this one
get in here?

NUI NUI................. 1.75
Strong man he call for Zanzibar
—Prove 'um real drinker of the
juice of the cane

MISSIONARY DOWNFALL.. 1.50
A refreshing after-dinner sipper of
mint and pineapple crushed and
frapped with Cuban Rums

COFFEE GROG........... 1.25

BRANDY ICE............. 1.25
Brandy, ice cream

**CHILDREN'S TAHITIAN
FRUIT PUNCH**............. .50
A blend of fresh fruits and juices,
garnished with cherries, pineapple
and banana

TEST PILOT (Limit of Two)..**$1.50**
Name your target for tonight—
Hardy navigators favor this robust
rum punch

SCORPION.............. 1.50
You know this is the eighth sign
of the Zodiac, but numerically this
would be too many

FOG CUTTER............ 1.50
Especially for a foggy night

Q. B. COOLER........... 1.50
Virgin Island Rums, tropical fruit
juices, and the Plantation's
special blend

NAVY GROG (The Ship's In) 1.50

ZOMBI (Limit of Two)..... 1.75
Boss man say Zombi have big
reputationl Advise take it slow so
not go Bong, Bong, Bongo

RUM JULEP.............. 1.75
Very old and mellow liqueur. Rums
of marvelous bouquet and flavor,
freshened with mint—'Nuff said!

PINEAPPLE CUP (Pi-Yi).... 1.75
A real novelty—Crushed fruits
and light Cuban Rums served in
a hollowed-out baby pineapple

THE ZAMBA AND MAMBA 1.75
One-half of thisa and one-half of
thata—then use your imagination
—and shaka the maraccas for
another drink. A maraccas with
each drink.

MAI TAI................. 1.50

TROPICANA............. 1.75
Served in a large tropical beach
hat, and after embibing in this
drink, if you can still lift it, the
hat is yours, take it with you.

MARGARITA............. 1.25

Festive Bowls

*Ancient Polynesian ceremonial luau drinks were
served in festive communal bowls. We offer an
interpretation of the luau bowl.*

BLACK MAGIC BOWL
  For One.............**$1.50**
  For Two............. 2.75
  For Four............. 5.00
How to win handsome trader and keep
him under idyllic spell tonight.

**SHANGRA-LA POKA-
POKA BOWL**
  For Two............. 2.50
  For Four............. 4.50
It's like a journey to Shangra-La,
but you forgot you were there

---

*Most food service operations can take a lesson from the South Seas type restaurant.
They are really creative in their drink concoctions and the merchandising of them.*

Eat, Drink & be Merry, for Tomorrow Ye Diet!

Tall Cool Drinks

CUBA LIBRE Rum and Coca Cola .... .90
GIN BUCK Gin, Lemon Juice and Ginger Ale .... .90
GIN RICKEY Gin, Lemon Juice and Soda .... .90
JOHN COLLINS Bourbon, Lemon Juice and Sugar .... .90
TOM COLLINS Gin, Lemon Juice and Sugar .... .90
MIGHTY MULE Vodka, Lime Juice and 7-Up .... .90
PLANTER'S PUNCH Light Rum, Dark Rum,
Fruit Juices and Grenadine 1.50
SINGAPORE SLING Gin, Cherry Brandy, Fruit Juices and Sugar 1.50
SLOE GIN FIZZ Sloe Gin, Lemon Juice and Sugar .... .90
ZOMBIE Light Rum, Dark Rum, 151% Proof Rum,
Orange and Pineapple Juice 1.75

PLANTATION-SIZE MINT JULEP   2.25
in a Tall Frosted "Silver Cup" . . . The Epitome of Gracious Living
(Served only when fresh mint is available)

POTENT POTIONS THESE!
Two Sensational Specialties
Served in Novel Take-home Skull Mugs!

GIANT HOT BUTTERED RUM   2.50
Aflame with Fiery Grog (a double shot of Rum!)
in Pure Apple Cider. Plus Whole Cloves, a Cinnamon Stick
and Rich Creamery Butter Afloat!!!

POWER-PACKED PIRATE PUNCH   2.50
Tall, Cool and Fragrant with Light and Dark Rums,
Fresh Fruit Juices, Mellow Grenadine,
Orange Slices and Cherries.
Delightfully Refreshing! Refreshingly Different!

HOSTESS CITY SPECIAL   1.50
Made with Rum, Fresh Fruit Juices, Banana Liqueur
and Maraschino Cherries, Blended to a smooth Icy Slush
Served in a Tall, Beautifully Decorated Pirates' House
Tumbler that's yours to take home!

*Special drinks such as Plantation Size Mint Julep, Power
Packed Pirate Punch and Hostess City Special make this
listing unusual.*

CASA CARIOCA presents the

"Big Drink"

WHISKY BY THE POUND

¼ lb $ 1.60   ½ lb $ 3.20

¾ lb $ 4.80

1 lb $ 6.40

****

Mix your own Highballs

for a more exciting

and different evening

JUMBO SPECIALTIES (2 oz. base)

'67 SPECIAL 1.50
A blend of secret ingredients
guaranteed to ...

SIR JOHN A 1.50
A double size Manhattan

HI 'N.DRI 1.50
Double Martini with "Beefeater"

COUNTRY SQUIRE 1.35
Mansize Whiskey Sour —
with touch of Triple Sec

PLAYBOY OLD FASHIONED 1.50
Created with "Southern Comfort"

TATTOO 1.50
Blends of Rum and Fruit Juices

HENRY GUARD 1.50
Cherry Brandy, Southern Comfort

THE LATE RISER 1.50
Creme de Cacoa, Vodka,
one whole egg

Martini	70¢
Manhattan	70¢
Creme de Menthe Frappe	75¢
Dubonnet	75¢
Old Fashioned	75¢
Sloe Gin Fizz	80¢
Whiskey Sour	75¢
Tom Collins	75¢
Gibson	70¢
Vodkatini	70¢
Bloody Mary	75¢
B & B	95¢
Screwdriver	75¢
Orange Blossom	75¢
Vodka Collins	75¢
Bacardi	75¢
Daiquiri	75¢
Rob Roy	90¢
Side Car	90¢
Stinger	90¢
Brandy Alexander	95¢
Grasshopper	95¢
Pink Lady	95¢

The "Big Drink" can give your operation a big reputation. Whether 1-1/2 oz., or 2, or by the pound, if you serve a bigger cocktail or mixed drink, merchandise it on the menu.

GRASSHOPPER	.95
PINK SQUIRREL	.95
BRANDY ALEXANDER	.95
DAIQUIRI	
RUM, SUGAR, LEMON	.85
BACARDI	
RUM, GRENADINE, LEMON	.85
CUBA LIBRE	
RUM, COKE, LIME	.85
GIN RICKEY	
GIN, LIME, VICHY	.75
TOM COLLINS	
GIN, SUGAR, LEMON	.95
VODKA COLLINS	
VODKA, GRENADINE, LEMON	.95
SOUTHERN COMPORT MANHATTAN	
SO. COMFORT & IMP. S.W. VERMOUTH	.95
OLD FASHION	
WHISKEY, BITTERS, SUGAR, FRUIT	.85
PINK LADY	
GIN, CREAM, GRENADINE	.95
SLOE GIN FIZZ	
SLOE GIN, LEMON, SUGAR	.85
ROB ROY	
SCOTCH IMP. VERMOUTH	.95
SIDE CAR	
BRANDY, COINTREAU, LEMON	.95
VODKA MARTINI	.35
BATMAN	
SLOE GIN, VODKA, CHERRY BRANDY, LEMON JUICE, ORANGE JUICE, GRENADINE	1.50
STINGER	
BRANDY & CREME DE MENTHE	.95
FROZEN DAIQUIRI	1.50
BANANA DAIQUIRI	.95
IRISH COFFEE	
WITH MOUNDS OF WHIPPED CREAM	1.50

Illustrations sell the "big three", and listing of ingredients helps to sell the other cocktails in this listing.

AFTER DINNER DRINKS

To begin with, let us examine After Dinner Drinks on the menu from a merchandising-marketing standpoint, that is, popularity (which drinks are listed), number listed and price. The source of this information is a collection of 447 menus from all over the country. They include a variety of types and locations, but they all, of course, serve liquor.

Of the entire 447 menus examined, all of which listed liquor in some fashion—beer, wine, cocktails, etc.—only about half (53 per cent) listed After Dinner Drinks as a separate category on the menu. See Chart No. I. This indicates poor merchandising right off the bat by about half of the food service operators serving liquor. And of these 53 per cent who do realize that After Dinner Drinks are not the same as Cocktails (drinks before dinner), and Wines and Beers (drinks during dinner), but are actually ordered and consumed after the entree, either with desserts or as a substitute for desserts, only about 10 per cent listed these drinks in the proper place on the menu.

CHART NO. 1

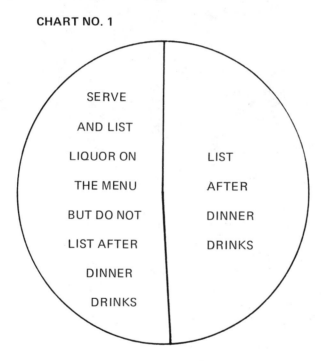

SERVE
AND LIST
LIQUOR ON
THE MENU
BUT DO NOT
LIST AFTER
DINNER
DRINKS

LIST
AFTER
DINNER
DRINKS

447 MENUS SURVEYED

Next, when an operation does list After Dinner Drinks, how many drinks get listed? The answer is shown in Chart No. II. There is some, but not a great deal of agreement here from establishment to establishment. A few list one or two. This is usually the operator who lists Irish Coffee (usually without any special treatment) with his other beverages, tea, milk, coffee, soft drinks, etc. The biggest category seems to offer a range of seven to twelve different After Dinner Drinks. There are, however, a sizable selection of dining rooms that list from fourteen to seventeen to even more, and these are also usually the operators who do a better job of selling these items on the menu.

CHART II

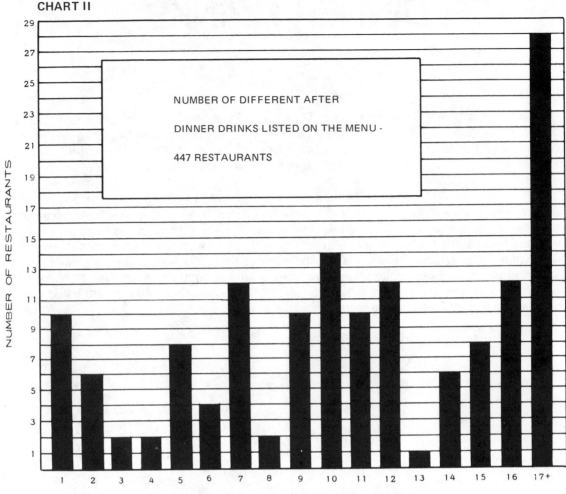

NUMBER OF DIFFERENT AFTER DINNER DRINKS LISTED ON THE MENU - 447 RESTAURANTS

NUMBER OF RESTAURANTS

NUMBER OF DIFFERENT AFTER DINNER DRINKS LISTED

As to price, what the food service operation charges for After Dinner Drinks, here too there is a spread. The kind of establishment makes a difference and the economic status of the customers is important, but most restaurants charge from 70¢ to $1.00. See Chart No. III. Reading this chart, allowance should be made for inflation. Add 5¢ to 10¢ depending upon the rate of cost of living increase in your area. Some restaurants charge even more than the popular $1.00 price, going up as high as $2.00 and even $3.00. Judging from this chart alone, it is obvious that After Dinner Drinks do add to the check and, therefore, add to profits.

Finally, we come to popularity. What are the most popular After Dinner Drinks as indicated by the number of times listed on the various menus examined? The three most popular drinks from this survey are (1) Creme de Menthe, (2) Irish Coffee, and (3) Drambuie. You may have local preferences, but across the country, more establishments list these three drinks. Of the cocktail type, After Dinner Drinks, Grasshopper, Stinger and Alexander are quite popular, and Benedictine plus B and B (Benedictine and Brandy) are also very popular. The Creme de Cacao is also a very popular drink. Of the "special" type of After Dinner Drinks, Galliano and Cherry Heering are very popular.

CHART III   WHAT RESTAURANTS CHARGE FOR AFTER DINNER DRINKS

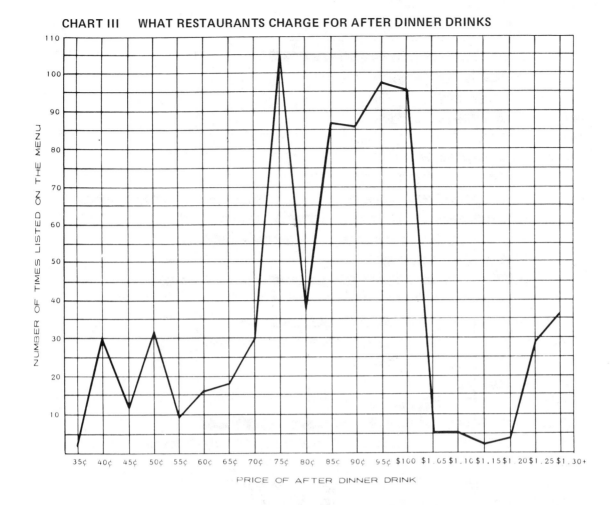

The more unusual, odd named and rather unknown After Dinner Drinks, such as Rusty Nail, Black Russian, Pink Squirrel, King Alphonso, are not listed too often. The reason probably is that they are not well known, and the average food service operator is not going to describe, merchandise and sell these drinks for that reason. This could be a mistake. Any drink, especially an unusual one, can be sold if it is featured on the menu. This means bigger, bolder type, more descriptive copy and an illustration, if at all possible. The result could be twofold. First, you will sell more of the drink and make more money, and second you will add to the reputation of your establishment by becoming known for your unusual, different drinks as well as your food listing.

The overall picture, as a result of this survey, is not one that the food service operations of America can be proud of with regard to After Dinner Drinks. They are the "Cinderellas of the Menu." They have a tremendous potential. But menu makers, designers and writers seem to "run out of steam" when they get to the end of the menu. This is unfortunate because these items of the bar inventory are easy to order, easy to store, easy to serve and easy to make a profit from. (See Chart IV.)

The use of the "after" portion of the menu is important. The waiter or waitress should not "ask" the customer if he wants dessert or an after dinner drink. At the end of the meal, the separate After Dinner menu, or the regular menu with the "after" part presented up, should be shown to all customers. This is positive selling and merchandising.

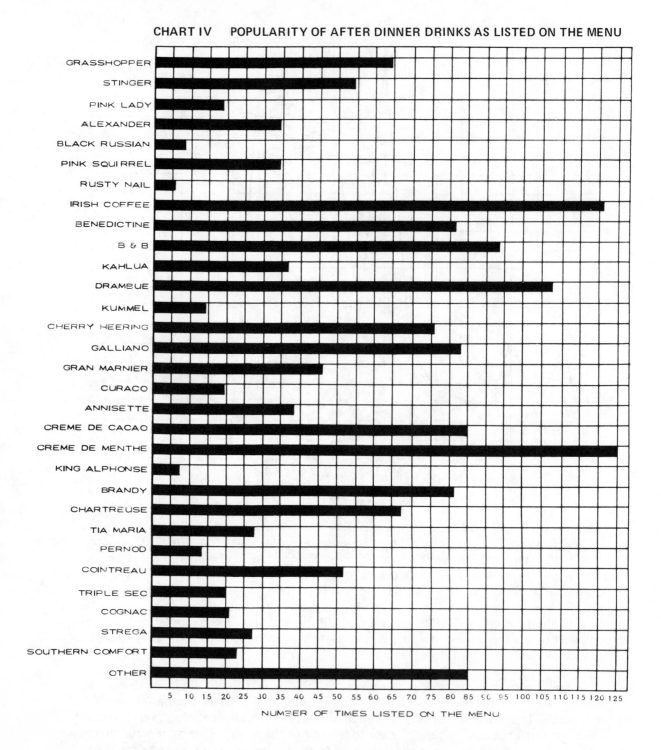

CHART IV   POPULARITY OF AFTER DINNER DRINKS AS LISTED ON THE MENU

NUMBER OF TIMES LISTED ON THE MENU

The "how" of listing after dinner drinks is largely a matter of copy. If the listing is in large, clear type on good paper, the main ingredient becomes copy. A main fault of most after dinner drink listings is that they do not describe the drinks. Most menus assume that the customer knows what a Black Russian or a Rusty Nail is, but this is a dangerous assumption.

The best way to sell is to describe. The following listing from Herb Traub's Pirate House with its one line descriptions is not fancy copy, but does tell the customer what the drink is.

After Dinner Drinks
Angel's Kiss. . .Creme de Cacao & Cream
Black Russian. . .Vodka & Kahlua (Coffee Liqueur)
Brandy Alexander. . .Brandy, Creme de Cacao and Cream
Creme de Menthe Frappe
Grasshopper. . .Creme de Menthe, Creme de Cacao & Cream
Irish Coffee (served flaming). . .Irish Whiskey, Coffee and
    Whipped Cream
Pink Lady. . .Gin, Grenadine and Cream
Pink Squirrel. . .Creme de Noyaux (Almond flavored liqueur)
    and Cream
Rusty Nail. . .Scotch and Drambuie
Stinger. . .Brandy and Creme de Menthe

The following list of dessert wines from the same menu is a typical selection:

Dessert Wines
Christian Brothers Ruby Port
Christian Brothers Sherry
Christian Brothers Golden Sherry
Taylor Port
Taylor Cream Sherry
Duff Gordon Nina (Medium Dry)
Harvey's Gold Cap Port
Harvey's Bristol Cream

Liqueurs, of course, can be combined with desserts to make especially "special" after-dinner treats. The easiest and most simple combination is liqueur and ice cream in the form of "Parfaits." The "Creme" liqueurs are especially effective in creating parfaits. A listing of available creme liqueurs follows:

Liqueur	Flavoring
Creme d'Ananas	Pineapple
Creme de Banane	Banana
Creme de Cacao	Cocoa
Creme de Cafe	Coffee
Creme de Cassis	Black Currant
Creme de Chocolat	Chocolate
Creme de Cumin	Caraway Seeds
Creme de Fraise	Strawberry
Creme de Framboise	Raspberry
Creme de Mandarine	Tangerine
Creme de Menthe	Peppermint
Creme de Moka	Coffee
Creme de Noyaux	Almond
Creme de Prunelle	Sloe
Creme de Roses	Rose
Creme de The	Tea
Creme de Vanille	Vanilla
Creme de Violette	Violet

In addition to ice cream, liqueurs can be added to bakery and fruit desserts. The uses and potential profits, therefore, of After Dinner Drinks are many, varied and worthy of consideration and exploitation.

Flaming After Dinner Drinks

ORANGE BRULOT EN CORBEILLE

Brandy, Spices and Coffee. Flame Brandy with Spices,
add Coffee and Pour into Orange Cup 2.00

IRISH COFFEE

Irish Whiskey, Creme de Cafe, Spices and Whipped Cream.
Flame Whiskey with Spices and pour into Glass
Top with Creme de Cafe and Whipped Cream. 1.75

POUSSE CAFE

Not Less Than Five Liqueurs Used.
Floated one atop the other without mixing. Flame and serve. 1.75

After Dinner Drinks

GRASSHOPPER *Green Creme de Menthe,*
White Creme de Cacao and Cream 1.50

PINK SQUIRREL *Creme de Noyaux,*
White Creme de Cacao and Cream 1.50

BANSHEE *White Creme de Cacao, Banana Liqueur and Cream* 1.50

SILVER DOLLAR *White Creme de Menthe, Banana Liqueur and Cream* .. 1.50

VELVET HAMMER *Cointreau, White Creme de Cacao and Cream* 1.50

GOLDEN DREAM *Galliano, Cointreau, Orange Juice and Cream* 1.50

GOLDEN CADILLAC *Galliano, White Creme de Cacao and Cream* 1.50

KING ALFONSO *Dark Creme de Cacao topped with Cream* 1.50

BLUE ANGEL *Sorry we can't Tell; But you will love it* 1.50

FLAMINGO *London Dry Gin, Grenadine and Cream* 1.50

RUSTY NAIL *Equal parts Scotch and Drambuie* 1.50

BRANDY ALEXANDER *Dark Creme de Cacao, Brandy and Cream* 1.50

In addition to a good selection of regular after dinner drinks,
this menu has three unusual flaming after dinner drinks.

After

To cap your seafood feast, linger over one of our tempting liqueurs . . . leisurely enjoying every sip. How about one now?

....

D. The "Halo" .... .95

Bewitching taste! A magic blend of apricot brandy with white creme de menthe, lemon juice and sugar. Served in a sugar rimmed cocktail glass.

E. Golden Cadillac 1.25

Tops! Equal parts of Galliano liqueur, creme de cacao, cream. Blended with crushed ice. Served in parfait glass. Savor leisurely!

F. Lace Curtain .... .85

Sip this tropical delight with a straw! A smooth frappe of creme de menthe and brandy. Served over shaved ice in cocktail glass.

After dinner drinks designed for a seafood menu.

If you have a special after dinner drink—give the recipe.

CAFE DON JUAN

For each guest, lightly coat the rim of an 8-ounce glass with lemon juice by rubbing with a slice of lemon. Dip the glass in sugar to coat the rim. Hold the glass over a flame, turning until the sugar melts and adheres to the rim. Then pour ¾ ounce of Bacardi Añojo Rum into glass and ignite over the flame, swirling the glass to keep liquid flaming for a few seconds. Add ¾ ounce of Kahlua to the flaming liquid in glass and let it continue flaming until sugar on rim turns brown. Almost fill glass with normal strength hot coffee and top with a heaping tablespoon of whipped cream. Sip the coffee through the cream.

"It should be sipped as if you are giving a soft kiss."

Descriptive copy that goes one step further.

LIQUEURS

APRICOT
Liqueur is made by steeping the fresh fruit in fine brandy for about one year, then straining and sweetening with sugar syrup.

BENEDICTINE (DOM)
Produced by the Benedictine Monks at Fecamp, France, from a secret formula since 1510. The liqueur was dedicated to God, with the Latin words "Deo Optimo Maximo," which means "to God, most good, most great." Benedictine is made from a large number of plants, seeds and herbs, some of which grow in the vicinity of Fecamp, and many that grow elsewhere, together with the finest brandy. Among the ingredients are: cloves, nutmeg, cinnamon, peppermint, angelica root, alpine mugwort, aromatic calamus, cardmon and flowers of arnica.

BENEDICTINE AND BRANDY (DOM)
This is the same liqueur as above, except that it has been mixed with fine old brandy.

DRAMBUIE
This is the most famous of the English liqueurs. Drambuie has a base of the very fine old Scotch whiskey. The other ingredients are honey, herbs and spices. It has been produced since 1745 and is called "Prince Charles Edwards Scotch Liqueur."

GRAND MARNIER
This is a blend of fine champagne cognac and orange curacao. World famous as an after-dinner liqueur.

CHARTREUSE, YELLOW OR GREEN
Grand Chartreuse is made at Voiron-Chartreuse, France, by the Chartreux Monks. This liqueur has been manufactured by the Chartreux Fathers since 1605, using a still-secret formula. It is reputed to have 130 different ingredients. Some of the main plants, roots, herbs and flowers used are: Melisse citronne, Hyssop flowers, dry peppermint, alpine mugwort, balsamite, thyme, anglica leaves and arnica flowers.

CHERRY HEERING
One of the finest liqueur brandies known throughout the world. It is made by steeping fresh sweet cherries in fine brandy for about one year.

COINTREAU
Cointreau is a brand of Triple Sec orange curacao and world famous as a liqueur and the base of the Side Car cocktail.

CREME DE CACAO
This is made from cocoa beans, cloves, mace and vanilla. It has a distinct chocolate flavor and is the main ingredient of the Alexander cocktail.

CREME DE MENTHE
A peppermint liqueur made from fresh mint leaves macerated in brandy spirits. This fine liqueur is made in three different colors: green, red and white. In recent years, this liqueur has become famous as one of the ingredients of the Stinger cocktail.

BRANDIES

APPLE JACK
CORONET V.S.Q.
COURVOISIER COGNAC
WILD CHERRY

3 STAR HENNESSY

MARTELL COGNAC

BLACKBERRY

After Dinner Drinks

.75 ANGEL'S TIP

Creme de Cacao, Cream and Half of Maraschino Cherry

.75 STINGER

Brandy and Creme de Menthe

.75 B & B

Benedictine D. O. M. and Brandy

.70 CREME DE MENTHE FRAFPE

Creme de Menthe over Cracked Ice with Maraschino Cherry

.85 COURVOISIER V. S. COGNAC

Made from grapes grown in the Charente District of France, the Principal City of which is Cognac

.50 BLACKBERRY BRANDY

Made from Blackberries aged in wood

.80 BENEDICTINE D.O.M.

A secret formula reputed to be a combination of Herb, Spices and fine brandy

.75 COINTREAU

Made from Triple Sec Orange Curacao

.60 CREME DE CACAO

Made from Cacao Beans, Spices and Vanilla

.75 GRASSHOPPER

Green Creme de Menthe, Creme de Cacao and Cream

.85 DRAMBUIE

A Liqueur made from Old Scotch Honey, Herbs, and Spices

.75 SOUTHERN COMFORT

A high proof liqueur made in U.S. from a secret formula reputed to have a brandy and whiskey base

.85 METAXA - 5 STAR BRANDY

Imported

.50 APRICOT

A Domestic Apricot Brandy

.75 HENNESSY THREE STAR

A fine imported French Cognac

.80 CAFE ROYAL

A cup of hot cafe with imported brandy

.70 MOUQUIN

Imported Brandies. 10 years old

.50 CREME DE MENTHE

Creme de Menthe

.50 CORONET V. S. Q.

Domestic Brandy

.75 CHERRY HERRING

A Liqueur made in Copenhagen, Denmark of cherry flavor

All Above Drinks Using Scotch, Bourbon, Canadian Whiskies, Imported Gins and Brandies — 15c Extra

All Above Drinks on the Rocks 15c Above Listed Price (Extra Portion)

This after dinner drink listing is a good selection of the more popular drinks, and all are completely described.

Slainte THE STORY OF IRISH COFFEE

A chef by the name of Joe Sheridan originated Irish Coffee at the famous Shannon Airport—back in 1938, when the flying boats were landing at Foynes. The passengers would come in by launch, shivering and shaking, fit to die with the cold.

"Surely," said Joe Sheridan, "we must invent a stirrup cup for the poor souls, and them not able to put their shivering hands in their pockets for a shilling to pay unless we warm them.

"What is more warming," said Joe, "than Irish Whiskey, smooth as a maiden's kiss. To take the chill from their poor shaking hands we will fill the glass with coffee, black as Cromwell's heart. We will top it off with a floating inch of Irish cream."

And so it was . . . and is today, in far off Dublin House! For Irish Coffee here is authentically Joe's— to the glasses themselves, straight from Shannon Airport. Remember this about good, properly made Irish Coffee like ours—one of them takes the chill off! Two of them set you to singing "Down went McGinty . . . "

And 'tis truly said that this is the most delectable drink to ever cross a discerning palate. Slainte!*

Slainte is Gaelic for "Good Health"

With copy like this, you'll sell a lot of Irish coffee!

PINK LADY
½ oz. Grenadine, 1¼ oz. Gin, ½ oz. lemon juice, ¾ oz. heavy cream. Shake with cracked ice and strain.

ANGEL'S TIP
Fill ¾ of Pony Glass with Creme de Cacao and on this float heavy cream. Top with cherry.

GRASSHOPPER
⅓ Green Creme de Menthe, ⅓ White Creme de Cacao, ⅓ light coffee cream, shake well with ice and strain.

STINGER
1 oz. brandy, ¾ oz. white creme de menthe. Shake well with cracked ice and strain. Serve on the rocks if you prefer.

ALEXANDER
½ oz. fresh cream, ½ oz. creme de cacao, 1½ oz. brandy, or gin shake well and serve.

DRAMBUIE
Fill ¾ of Pony Glass with Drambuie Liqueur and serve.

Enjoy one of these nine after you dine

BRANDY ICE
1 scoop ice cream, 1 oz. brandy. Blend together until firm. Serve in cocktail glass.

B & B
½ Benedictine, ½ Cognac. Fill liqueur glass and serve.

FRAPPE
Fill cocktail glass with fine ice. Add green creme de menthe and serve. If you prefer, serve on the rocks.

Created by Mastercraft, this listing of After Dinner Drinks, in color with the recipe for each drink, really sells.

A LA CARTE AND COMPLETE DINNER

There are two basic ways of listing and pricing the items on your menu—a la carte, with a separate price for every item on the menu, and complete dinner, a package deal where the appetizer, soup, potato, vegetable, beverage and dessert are included.

Very few food service operations have a menu that is completely an a la carte or completely a dinner menu. The most completely schizophrenic or divided menu is the one that has a complete, extensive a la carte menu and a counter-balancing extensive complete dinner menu. This means, in effect, that the customer can order almost every item on the menu either a la carte or as part of some gastronomic type of gourmet package deal.

The first result of this kind of menu is that it makes the menu look twice as big as it actually is since the restaurant is listing everything twice without increasing the load on the kitchen. The second result is that every item--steak, seafood, fowl or whatever--is listed with two prices which gives the customer a choice of the entree by itself (with no side dishes or extras or with those specific side dishes and extras he desires).

This price comparison, of course, can be like most comparisons--odious! The customer, it will be claimed by some, will be inclined toward the lower price. But the situation is not as simple as that. No customer wants to eat a steak, chicken or lobster completely by itself, so some additional extras will be ordered and, in effect, thereby build the check. The situation can become a game between the customer and the restaurateur over which is the better deal--the complete dinner package or a la carte plus extras.

The first important thing for the menu builder or food service operator to do is to remember that the complete dinner is a "package" and he should set it up as a package. Preferably at the beginning of the entree listing, but whether before, after (or a split combination of before and after), he should print clearly and in large readable type: "Dinner includes"--and list what "goes with" the entree. If you are selling a package, sell the whole package, not just the entree part of it.

The next thing to remember is that the a la carte part of the menu should be just that, a la carte. Many restaurateurs list a la carte entrees under an a la carte heading which includes enough side dishes--vegetable, salad, potato, etc.--to be a complete meal. This defeats the entire purpose of an a la carte listing and is poor merchandising.

Furthermore, it must be kept in mind that, if you have a fairly complete a la carte listing, as well as a dinner listing, you should have a complete a la carte listing of appetizers, salads, potatoes, vegetables, side dishes and desserts. In fact, many menus have complete dinners that are not actually complete. Either all or some of the desserts and appetizers are often not included in the dinner price.

Operators should be careful with regard to the price differential between a la carte and complete dinner. The difference should be the same for all entrees because the extras in the complete dinner package are the same. This may seem like a simple observation, but a surprising number of restaurateurs charge a variety of prices for the same extras in the complete dinner package.

The next problem for the menu builder is how to list the two prices, complete dinner and a la carte. One common method is to list the entrees with two prices right next to each other, a la carte price and complete dinner price. The other method, also common, is to have two separate and complete sections of the menu, a complete a la carte listing (with prices) and a separate and complete dinner listing (with prices). From a merchandising-selling point of view, the two separate listings, which makes direct price comparisons more difficult, is the better of the two methods.

The chart included with this article is a study of 257 menus showing the price differential between comparable a la carte and complete dinners. It will be noted that $1.00 is the most popular price differential with 75¢ as the next most common price difference. It would seem that too many food service operators are thinking in quarters and half dollars and their combinations rather than tailoring the menu to costs and a carefully calculated mark up. In these days of increasing costs and changing prices, 65¢ and 85¢ can make more sense in relation to a la carte and complete dinner prices than dividing the menu dollar into quarters.

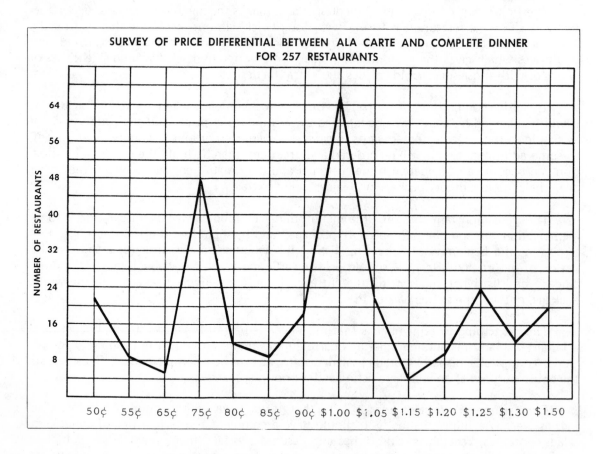

SURVEY OF PRICE DIFFERENTIAL BETWEEN ALA CARTE AND COMPLETE DINNER FOR 257 RESTAURANTS

Green Ridge Dinners

Complete Dinner Price Includes
a Choice of One
Cranberry Juice — Tomato Juice — V-8 Vegetable Juice — Half Grapefruit in Season
Anchovies on Lettuce — Grapefruit Juice — Turkey Soup — Clam Chowder — Fresh Fruit Cup with Sherbet —
Filet of Marinated Herring – Cherrystone Clams, Fresh Shrimp Cocktail or Oysters on the half shell in season 1.25 extra on all Dinners
Green Ridge Salad
Choice of Two
Creamy Whipped Potatoes — French Fried Potatoes — Hubbard Squash — Green Peas — Vegetable du Jour —
Cole Slaw — Sliced Tomatoes
Choice from our Dessert Menu — Coffee, Tea, Milk

	A LA CARTE	COMPLETE DINNER		A LA CARTE	COMPLETE DINNER
FABULOUS ROAST PRIME RIBS OF BEEF			**SAUTEED FRESH LOBSTER MEAT**		
Served Medium Rare Only, Thick Cut with			Sauteed in Pure Creamery Butter	4.95	5.90
Pop Over	5.50	6.45	**FRIED FRESH LOBSTER CHUNKS**		
ROAST PRIME RIBS OF BEEF			Deep Fried and Served with Drawn Butter .	4.95	5.90
Served Medium Rare Only, with Pop Over	4.50	5.45	**FRESH OPENED LOBSTER A LA NEWBURG**		
BROILED SIRLOIN STEAK — One Pound			En Casserole, Toast Points	4.95	5.90
A Large Boneless Cut of Choice Quality Beef	5.50	6.45	**BAKED STUFFED JUMBO SHRIMP**		
BROILED JUNIOR SIRLOIN STEAK — 3/4 lb.			Served with Drawn Butter	4.25	5.20
Boneless Cut of Choice Quality Beef	4.50	5.45	**FRIED FRESH JUMBO SHRIMP**		
BROILED TENDERLOIN STEAK			Dipped in Batter and Fried to a		
Tender and Juicy — Choice Quality Beef ..	4.95	5.90	Golden Brown	4.25	5.20
BROILED CHOPPED SIRLOIN STEAK			**FRIED FRESH CAPE SCALLOPS — Tartar Sauce**		
Fresh Ground Steer Beef Served with			Small Tender Scallops Fried to a		
Mushroom Sauce	2.65	3.60	Golden Brown	3.75	4.70
BREADED TENDERIZED FRESH VEAL CUTLET			**FRIED FRESH BABY SEA SCALLOPS**		
Served with Mushroom Sauce	2.75	3.70	Fried to a Golden Brown	2.95	3.90
BONELESS FRIED CHICKEN BREAST			**FRIED FRESH IPSWICH CLAMS — Tartar Sauce**		
Deep Fried and Served with Poulette Sauce	2.95	3.90	Small Clams Fried to a Golden Brown	2.95	3.90
FRIED FRESH NATIVE TURKEY BREAST			**BROILED SWORDFISH STEAK — Lemon Butter**		
Deep Fried and Served with Poulette Sauce	2.95	3.90	A Thick Slice of Fresh Swordfish, Broiled ..	3.25	4.20
FRIED CHICKEN LEG AND THIGH			**FRIED FRESH SEAFOOD PLATE**		
Fried to a Golden Brown	2.25	3.20	Shrimps — Clams — Cape Scallops	3.75	4.70
SAUTEED FRESH TURKEY LIVERS			**BROILED FRESH HALIBUT STEAK**		
En Casserole with Mushroom Sauce	1.95	2.90	A Thick Steak of Fresh Halibut,		
BROILED LIVE (1¼ to 1½ lb.) MAINE LOBSTER			Lemon Butter	3.25	4.20
Served with Drawn Butter	5.50	6.45			

This is an effective listing of both a la carte and Complete Dinner. A complete selling job is done on what the Complete Dinner consists of, and there is a real, big difference between it and the a la carte offerings with a corresponding price spread.

MENU PRICES

In the thirteen month period from October, 1975 to October, 1976 the U.S. city average consumer price index for restaurant meals went from 173.2 to 188.1, a substantial rise. The food at home index for that same period while it started out higher in October of 1975 (at 179.3), it dropped to 177.7 by March of 1976 and then began to rise again. By October of 1976, however, the food at home index had reached only 179.6.

The reason for the almost level price index for food at home is that meat, poultry and fish prices actually declined from an index of 192.9 in October, 1975 to 174.8 in October of 1976. This seems to have been enough to keep average food prices level even though the price index of dairy prices and fruits and vegetables rose significantly.

The fact that restaurant meal prices rose in spite of relatively stable food prices is significant for menu planners. It shows that most restaurant operators are on top of inflation and the increased cost of doing business. They keep their prices a jump or two ahead of inflation—on the average—and consistantly.

Restaurant operators, however, while they can use national price trends as a measuring device, conduct their business in a *local* environment. This means that local city or area economic conditions are also important to the menu planner.

There is, of course, a considerable difference in prices from city to city. In October of 1976, the consumer price index for food in Washington, D.C. was 188.2, while in the Los Angeles, Long Beach, California area it was only 173.7. Menu prices in Los Angeles reflect this food cost differential and are lower than in many other areas of the country.

FOOD CONSUMER PRICE INDEX BY CITY

OCTOBER, 1976

1967 = 100

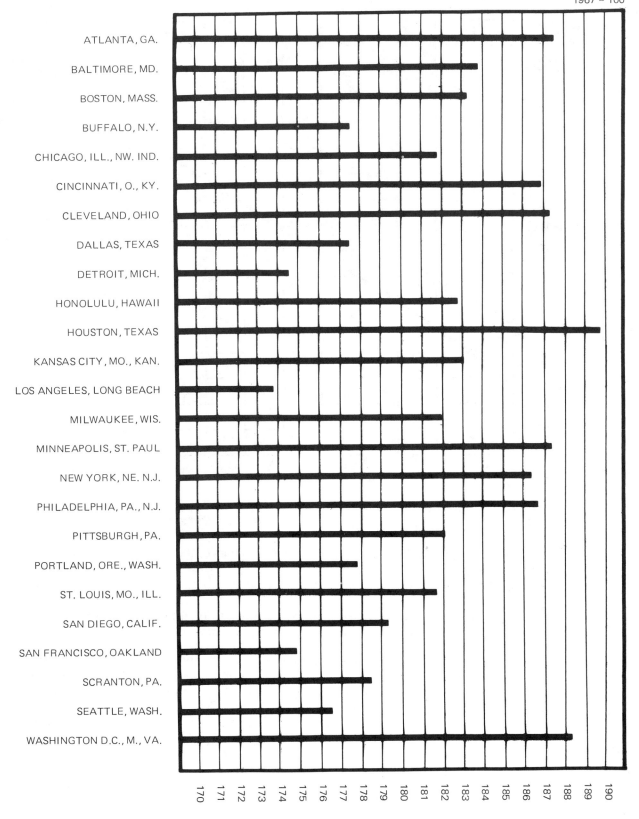

ATLANTA, GA.

BALTIMORE, MD.

BOSTON, MASS.

BUFFALO, N.Y.

CHICAGO, ILL., NW. IND.

CINCINNATI, O., KY.

CLEVELAND, OHIO

DALLAS, TEXAS

DETROIT, MICH.

HONOLULU, HAWAII

HOUSTON, TEXAS

KANSAS CITY, MO., KAN.

LOS ANGELES, LONG BEACH

MILWAUKEE, WIS.

MINNEAPOLIS, ST. PAUL

NEW YORK, NE. N.J.

PHILADELPHIA, PA., N.J.

PITTSBURGH, PA.

PORTLAND, ORE., WASH.

ST. LOUIS, MO., ILL.

SAN DIEGO, CALIF.

SAN FRANCISCO, OAKLAND

SCRANTON, PA.

SEATTLE, WASH.

WASHINGTON D.C., M., VA.

170 171 172 173 174 175 176 177 178 179 180 181 182 183 184 185 186 187 188 189 190

CONSUMER PRICE INDEX U.S. CITY AVERAGE

RESTAURANT MEALS ▬ ▬ ▬ ▬ ▬
FOOD AT HOME ▪▪▪▪▪▪▪▪▪▪▪▪▪▪▪

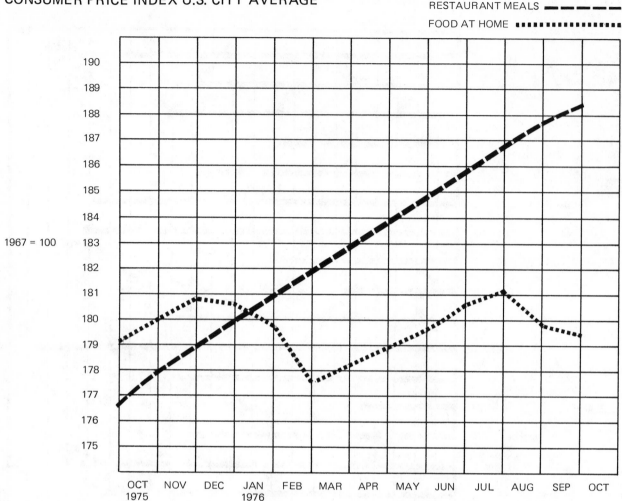

1967 = 100

In practical terms of menu design and printing, several factors must be taken into account to allow for rapid and constant change in menu prices as well as items. They are as follows:

Large menu-printing runs should be avoided.

The menu must be flexible—allowing for easy change on at least part of the menu.

Expensive color illustrations should be used with creativity.

Menu design flexibility can be achieved by the use of inserts, tip-ons and separate menus. Figure 1, for example, shows the use of a menu insert.

This is a four-page cover, usually of heavier, coated paper with a four-page insert of lighter, less expensive paper. The bar items—cocktails, bourbon, scotch, etc.—can be printed on the inside front cover, and the wine list can be printed on the inside back cover. Changes

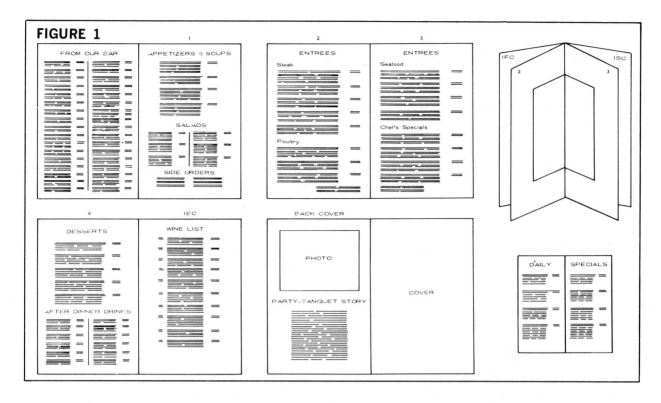

FIGURE 1

in alcoholic beverage prices have been slower than changes in food prices. But even here, these items and their prices could be on a tip-on which could be changed without throwing away the expensive menu covers.

The four-page insert is the main food listing.   Appetizers, soups and salads on page one, entrees on pages two and three, and desserts and after-dinner drinks on page four—all in ordering sequence. The fastest-changing items will be on pages two and three—the entrees. Desserts, appetizers and soups will not change as fast, therefore this side of the insert (pages one and four) can be preprinted in a certain amount, allowing for a quick change on page two and three.

In addition, a daily special insert can be printed up and bound into the center of the menu. This allows for even more flexibility in changes of price and item. Flexibility can also be achieved by the use of tip-ons (Figure 2).

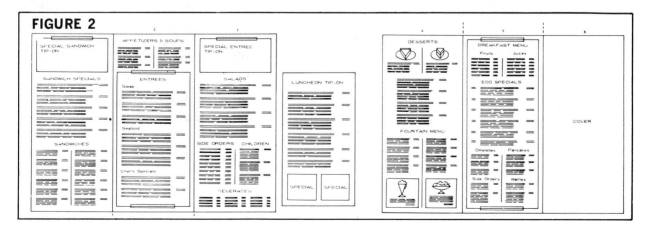

FIGURE 2

Figure 2 is a three-panel, two-fold menu with five tip-ons. On panel one sandwiches are listed, and space is allowed for a tip-on (sandwich special, steak sandwich, etc.). Soups and appetizers are listed at the top of panel two and space is allowed on the main portion of the menu for an entree tip-on. This allows for a daily or weekly change of the entree listing in both price and item selection. The luncheon entree tip-on can be substituted for the entree tip-on, so that this particular menu can function as both a lunch and dinner menu.

A variety of items can be listed on panel three—salads, side orders, children's menu, etc. Here also, space is allowed for another tip-on which can be used for another entree or salad special. Page four can be used for listing desserts and the fountain menu. These items can be on the permanent part of the menu, since their price does not change as often as other parts of the menu.

Panel five can be used for the breakfast menu listing. This can be either printed permanently on the menu or on a tip-on depending upon the amount of change anticipated in the cost of these items.

In addition to inserts and tip-ons, separate menus can give flexibility to your menu. The most common and useful separate menus are:

Wine List
Dessert (After Dinner) Menu
Children's Menu

Separate menus allow for price and item changes without changing or reprinting the entire menu. But if you use separate menus, be sure they function effectively and don't gather dust in a corner. The wine list should be presented to all customers, not just those who ask for it. Having it on the center of the table all the time solves this problem. And the dessert or after-dinner menu (including after-dinner drinks) should be presented to all customers when they finish their entree without asking if they want a dessert.

The most flexible menu of all, of course, in relation to rapidly changing prices and items is the one printed daily or even weekly. This is usually a less expensive menu printed on lighter, cheaper paper. It requires close association with a printer, if not a press in the restaurant itself, and it can be expensive over the long run. But the menus are new, crisp and clean every day, and advantage can be taken of bargains on the food market and nothing needs to be listed du jour. Everything for that day can be spelled out and featured.

Large menu-printing runs should be avoided in these days of rapidly changing food costs. The money saved by a larger printing of a menu is usually a false economy. What happens is that the restaurant operator will be slow in making both price and item changes because he has several thousand menus in the back room that he paid "good money" for. The result is that he probably loses twice the amount "saved" on the larger printing run because of his failure to keep up to date.

In line with this situation of large, expensive menu printings getting out of date as soon as they get off the press, color illustrations are a valuable merchandising tool and should be used. But when the cost of the photo, four-color separations (positives) and the printing are added up, the bill can be high, and to amortize the cost so that each menu will not cost $10.00, a large run is usually decided on, at least for the color part of the menu.

Here again, the problem can be solved. The color illustrations can be printed separately, either on a tip-on, gummed stock, etc. This allows for changes in color illustrations without changing the entire menu. Even chain or franchise operations which have a more legitimate reason for a large color printing run should investigate a more flexible menu. There are regional variations in taste, and an item illustrated in color on the menu may be a big seller in one city and a poor seller in another. But if 200,000 menus have been run off for the sake of "economy," there is no chance of making changes.

The key to menu design, production, and planning in today's economy is change. You must plan your menu for fast variations in prices, item popularity and food cost.

THE FLEXIBLE MENU

Living and doing business in an inflationary era and also a time of changing tastes as well as prices means that the menu must become more flexible to accommodate more rapid changes. A well designed, well printed menu can be an expensive item on a food service operations cost sheet, and to throw it away and reprint it after a few weeks because of price or item changes can be an expensive waste. To plan for this problem before it arises is to consider a flexible menu, one that is easy to change without major printing and design costs.

Recently, I read a novel where one of the central characters was a French restaurateur. He would go to the market every morning, buy produce and meat as it was available, go back to his restaurant, make out the menu for the day, and then write it in chalk on a large blackboard. This was his menu, and it was certainly flexible, designed for the best food buys of that day, plus immediate changes in price.

If, however, you have an average American food service operation, you have a printed menu, and it can be made flexible to suit almost any changing circumstances. The first flexible menu is the daily menu. This is a complete menu, printed daily on light, inexpensive paper and thrown away at the end of the day. If your menu is one with a great number of daily changes, this may be the answer to your problem.

FIGURE I

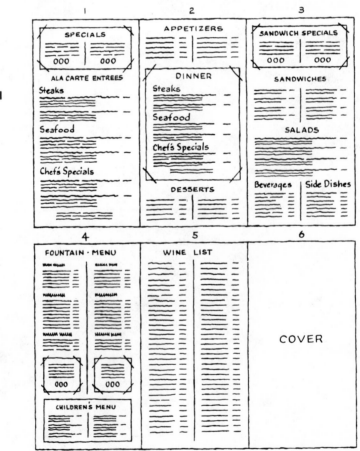

Most operations, however, do not change the entire menu daily, only parts of it. The answer to this problem is tip-ons and inserts for a permanent menu to allow for some items to change daily (or weekly) and other items to change less frequently. With diagrams, let's explore some of the flexibility possibilities.

Figure 1 is a typical 3-panel, 2-fold menu showing the tip-on possibilities which enable the menu builder to make changes without reprinting the entire menu. At the top of panel 1, where the a la carte entrees are listed, there is a tip-on for listing a la carte "specials." On panel 2 there is a large tip-on for the daily dinner entree listing. Note that the appetizers and desserts are not printed on the tip-on, but are on the regular, permanent menu. Usually, desserts and appetizers are more standard, and change less; therefore, they do not have to be changed daily.

On this particular example (Figure 2) we have used the back cover for the party-cold plate, low calorie specials, specialties of the house, etc.) could go here.

The back of the menu, panels 4 and 5, can be used for a variety of listings—fountain menu, children's menu, after-dinner menu (desserts and drinks), breakfast menu, wine list, from our bar listing, party-banquet story, take-outs, etc., etc. But here, also, flexibility can be added to the menu by tip-ons.

A word of caution, however, concerning menu tip-ons. Be sure they are printed with as much care (good typesetting and good printing) and on as good quality paper as the rest of the menu.

Figure 2 shows a common solution to the problem of the changing menu. This is a heavy, durable, coated cover with slow changing items and copy printed on it and with a four-page insert with the majority of the items that change the most printed on insert pages for easy replacement. These insert pages (including smaller, special insert pages for luncheon menu, specials, etc.) are usually bound to the hard cover with an attractive cord of silver or gold.

On this particular example (Figure 2) we have used the back cover for the party-banquet story with photos to illustrate our facilities. On the inside front cover, we have printed the wine list. The idea is to use this part of the menu for those parts of the menu that change the least over a period of time.

Do not, however, leave the back cover or the inside front and back covers blank. This is a waste of good selling, merchandising, advertising space.

On the large insert (pages 1, 2, 3 and 4) which is of lighter, less expensive, replaceable paper, list your appetizers, soups, salads (on page 1), your entrees (on pages 2 and 3) and your desserts and after-dinner drinks (on page 4). Even here, you can add greater flexibility to your menu. If, for example, your entrees change more often than your before-dinner items (appetizers, soups, salads) and your after-dinner items (desserts and after-dinner drinks), you can print up your center section on one side only (pages 1 and 4) and then print your center section (pages 2 and 3) as you need them.

In addition to the regular four-page insert that can be expanded to 8 or 12 pages, you can have a small four-page insert in this type of menu, printed on different colored paper (for variety in design and for getting attention), and on this insert you can print your luncheon menu, dinner or a la carte specials, late evening snacks, breakfast menu, or even wine list.

By the creative use of tip-ons, bindings and various types of paper, a flexible menu can be made that will accommodate the maximum change for the minimum amount of cost.

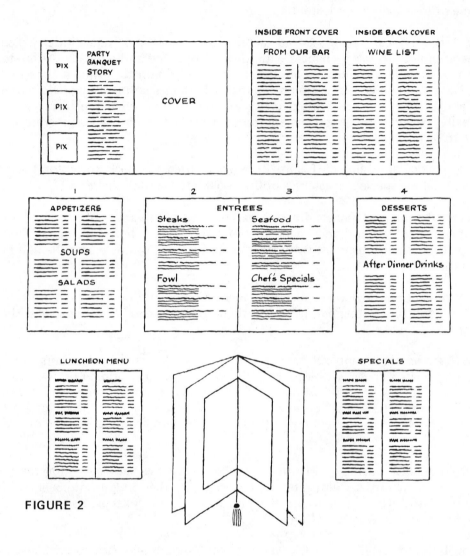

FIGURE 2

IS YOUR MENU BATTING IOOO?

"The pace at which various technological, social, political and economic changes are taking place has reduced the relevance of experience as a guide to many business judgments"

Herman Kahn

Together with TV, radio, your daily newspaper, weekly news magazine, trade journals, etc., your menu is a mass media. It is as common a method of communication as there is— read by some people three times a day, and by most once a day. Like any other mass medium of communication, it should be constantly checked and evaluated for marketing and merchandising effectiveness. Just as the three big TV networks constantly measure the sales and attention-getting effectiveness of their ads, commercials, copy themes, design style, etc., a food service operator must analyze the effectiveness of his menu.

The day of the "static" menu is over. Change is the only constant that can be depended on. The menu is the message, in more ways than one, for all food service operations. The MENU RATING FORM, Fig. A, is a marketing-merchandising measuring device to help you evaluate your menu. It is broken down into eight categories—Art and Design, Layout, Type, Copy, Merchandising, Marketing, Mechanical and Creativity.

Each of the sub-sections of this rating form is given a numerical score against which you can measure your menu. Take out your menu and measure its effectiveness. If any part of the rating form contains items (food or drink) that you do not serve, give yourself the top possible score for that portion of the rating. A perfect score would be 1,000, so see if your menu is batting 1,000! To help you evaluate your menu by use of the MENU RATING FORM, the following comments relative to each section of the form are made.

Art and Design

An attractive looking menu is important for a food service establishment just as attractive decor and service is important. But the design and art part of your menus is the easiest problem to solve. Just hire a professional designer or artist and you will get an attractive appearing menu. The style or appearance of your menu should match the decor and "life style" of your restaurant. If yours is an Old New England or Colonial style interior, the appearance of your menu should match this style; the type, art and illustrations should be of the right period, Early American. Similarly, if you run a Modern Supper Club type operation, the style of your menus should reflect this also with modern art and bright colors.

If your food operation is a "fast service" type, the design of your menu should reflect this. Usually, color illustrations are called for. Color photographs of the entrees, appetizers, salads, sandwiches and dessert can sell and influence the customer in a hurry. He looks, orders, eats and leaves, making room for another customer. Care should be taken, however, in the reproduction of color food photography. The reproduction must be accurate and appetizing looking. In addition, since color photography and reproduction are expensive, great care should be taken in this part of menu production. You will be required to "live" with your color illustrations for some time, even if you print them on tip-ons so that you can change them. Line drawings can add to the appearance of your menu, but do not overdo this type of graphics. They should add to the attractiveness without interfering with the menu's communication purpose.

Logical Layout

This is an important aspect of your menu, usually neglected by menu designers. Attention to this part of the menu can result in a better selling menu. First, your menu layout

---

A   MENU RATING FORM

	POSSIBLE SCORE	YOUR MENU
I. ART AND DESIGN:		
1. Menu is designed and artwork executed by competent, professional artist or designer	30	
2. Design, color and general appearance of menu matches decor, style and quality of restaurant	20	
3. Illustrations add to "sell" but do not hamper readability	10	
4. Color illustrations are "appetizing" appearing	10	
II. LAYOUT:		
1. Items are listed in following eating and drinking sequence:		
a. Foods—appetizers, soups, entrees, desserts (salad, sandwiches and side orders listed separate)	30	
b. Drinks—Cocktails (before dinner), Beer & Wine (with dinner), Brandies, Cordials, Liqueurs (after dinner, with desserts)	30	
2. Headings (Soup, Appetizers, Salads, Sandwiches, Entrees, Steaks, Seafood, Desserts, etc.) are used to separate categories of items on the menu for easier ordering	20	
3. Specials are given "Special" treatment—box or graphic device, bolder type, more descriptive copy, illustrations	30	
4. Layout is such that items you want to sell most of are given "top" or best position to catch the eye	30	
5. Tip-Ons do not cover any printed part of the menu	10	
6. Menu has no blank, unused pages	10	
III. TYPE:		
1. Type is big enough to be easily read by average person under lighting conditions prevailing in your restaurant	50	
2. Headings (Appetizers, Soups, Salads, Entrees, etc.) are in bigger, bolder, "different," type or lettering from rest of menu type	25	
3. A variety of type—caps and lower case is used	5	
4. Type style matches style of restaurant	5	
IV. COPY:		
1. Entrees are interestingly and appetizingly described with good *sell* copy that includes "how prepared" and special ingredients	50	
2. Expensive, "special" appetizers and soups are described	30	
3. All entree type salads are described (how made, ingredients) and salad dressings served are listed	20	
4. "Special" Sandwiches are described	20	
5. Quality of steaks (U.S. Choice or Prime) and weight (in ounces) is listed	10	

	POSSIBLE SCORE	YOUR MENU
6. Desserts are described with attractive, merchandising copy	25	
7. Cocktails and special After Dinner Drinks are described by ingredients and "how made"	20	
8. Wines are described with "wine and food" suggestions	20	
V. MERCHANDISING:		
1. Following basic information appears somewhere on menu: address, phone number, days open, meals served, hours of service and credit card policy	25	
2. Party, Banquet, Meeting Information	25	
3. Take-Out and/or Catering Information	20	
4. History of restaurant or community information	10	
5. Menu used as souvenir mailer or sold	10	
VI. MARKETING:		
1. High profit, bigger, more popular items are given better treatment—bolder type, more descriptive copy, illustration—than smaller, lower profit items	50	
2. All items on the menu have been checked within the last three months to eliminate slow, "dead" items	25	
3. Prices have been changed to meet changing prices within last thirty days	25	
4. Specials (daily, weekly, continental, gourmet, family, diet, etc.) are designed to attract customer plus make money for the restaurant	25	
VII. MECHANICAL:		
1. Paper menu is printed on is durable, practical, coated and grease-resistant on both sides	30	
2. Binding and tip-on devices are both practical and durable	10	
3. Tip-ons are of same quality (paper and printing) as rest of menu	10	
4. Printing is clean, sharp and of good quality	25	
5. Menu is big enough to accommodate all items listed allowing for easy reading and ordering plus room for descriptive copy and illustrations	40	
6. Menus are replaced before they become dirty and dog-eared	10	
VIII. CREATIVITY:		
1. Menu is unusual in design, color, and/or paperfold, cut or selection	75	
2. Copy is unusual, sparkling, and creative	75	
	POSSIBLE SCORE	YOUR MENU

should follow the logical eating and drinking sequence of a meal. In layout sequence, from top to bottom left to right, and in page or panel sequence, the food listing should start with Appetizers and Soups, then go to the Entrees and from there to Desserts. Such items as Sandwiches and Salads, if sold as entrees, should be given separate but important billing, but if Salads and Sandwiches are only sold as small items, they should not interfere with main entree billing.

Drinks also follow a logical ordering and consumption sequence. Before dinner, Cocktails and Aperitif Wines are consumed. With dinner, it is Wines and Beer, and after dinner it is Brandies, Cordials, Liqueurs and special after dinner cocktails that are consumed. This logical sequence means that your liquor listing should be in three different locations on the menu.

The three diagram layouts, Fig. B, C, and D, show menu layout variations that follow the logical ordering and consuming sequence. Fig. B is a simple, small, one-panel menu showing top to bottom layout-ordering sequence, Fig. C, a four-panel menu.

Fig. D shows a larger menu, the food sequence going from page 1 (Appetizers, Soups, Salads), pages 2 and 3 (Entrees) and page 4 (Desserts). Sandwiches and Cold Plates are given less important billing on this menu on the inside back cover.

Headings and sub-headings are important on your menu. Categories of food and drink on the menu—Appetizers, Soups, Salads, Sandwiches, Entrees, Desserts, Cocktails, Wines, Beers, etc., and Entree sub-heads such as Steak, Seafood, Fowl, Chef's Specials, etc., help to identify, make for easier ordering and help sell.

Be sure that your "Specials", the big items that you want to sell most of get special treatment. This means good position on the menu; some graphic device (box, panel, border); bolder, bigger type than the rest of the menu; more detailed descriptive copy and, if possible, an illustration, line drawing or color photo.

Where you list your items does make a difference. The first or top item on any listing usually outsells the subsequent items listed, and on a 2-page or 2-panel menu, the items listed on page 2 get more action. Experimentation and study will tell where what you want to sell, sells best. Also, be sure that tip-ons do not cover any printed portion of your menu, and if you have any blank pages or panels on your menu, take a hard look. You can probably merchandise something or some extra service on those blank pages.

Type Size and Styles

The words that communicate your message on your menu are set in type. The most important aspect of that type is that it is big enough and bold enough so that the average customer (who may not have 20/20 vision, and may not have his glasses with him) can easily read your menu under whatever your lighting conditions are, bright or dark. There should be space between lines and listing; overcrowding makes your menu hard to read. Care should be given to type selection (style, size and variety) for appearance and readability.

Copy That Sells

What you say about what you serve is another important aspect of your menu. This does not mean that you have to write long, involved paragraphs of copy. A few well chosen words are enough. These include how the item is prepared, the quality and special features of it, special sauces and condiments, etc. Entrees are not the only items that need description. Expensive, fancy appetizers and most soups need descriptive copy. Entree type salads should be described (ingredients plus how made), and salad dressings served should be listed.

To sell your wine, you have to use words on your menu, words that tell what wine types (red, white, rosé, champagne) go with what food categories (beef, fowl, seafood, etc.) as well as some description of the wine—imported, American, dry or sweet, special character-

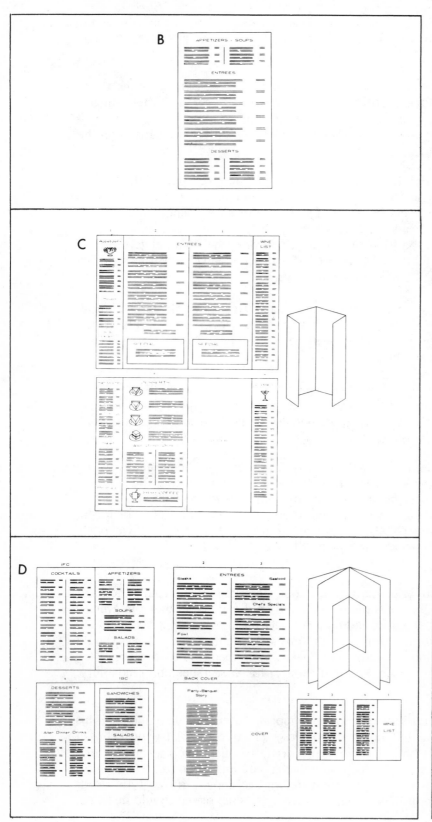

This restaurant "tells all" on its menu—from days open, size of motel, meeting rooms, sauna, swimming pool, outside dining, location and limousine service. As both a restaurant and motel, they sell everything.

Many restaurants serve martinis, but most don't merchandise them. This one is topped with scotch, not vermouth, and given a special name.

Foreign entrees need descriptive copy more than conventional American entrees, but don't always get it.

istics, etc. The customer's wine knowledge is usually limited, so he needs all the help you can give him.

Merchandising

Besides selling food and drink, your menu can communicate other things—basic information plus whatever extra services you have. To begin with, the basic facts—address, phone number, days open, meals served, hours of service, should be listed somewhere on the menu. Your credit card policy, even if you don't honor credit cards, should be explained. If banquets, parties and meetings are a part of your business, feature these services. But be complete. List the number of people you can accommodate, how many banquet rooms available, who to contact and the phone number. Take-Outs and Catering Service can also be merchandised on the menu. For all of these menu extras—banquets, take-outs, catering, photographs help to describe your facilities, services and products.

Finally, the menu can do double merchandising duty if it is designed to function as a mailer or souvenir give-away; or if it's an expensive menu, sell it.

Marketing and Menus

What you list on the menu, what you charge for it, and what items you feature is the focal point of your entire food and beverage operation. Here, constant menu item popularity checks plus intelligent cost analysis is imperative. Don't hesitate to change your menu to fit new costs and changing public taste. Saving on printing, typesetting and design costs by keeping your old menu "as is" too long can be the most expensive economy you can practice. And take a hard look at what you are featuring. Reliable marketing information is available, and if you don't use it, your competition will.

Mechanical Aspects

The physical make-up of your menu is basic. First there is the paper it is printed on. Many menus indicate that not enough time, care and concern has been spent on the right paper selection. Decide in advance how long you want your menu to last and then print it on the right paper—heavy coated (on both sides), durable, if you want it to last a long time —but on lighter, less expensive paper if you use a daily, short term menu. The other mechanical parts of your menu, bindings, plastic clip-on holders, and the tip-ons themselves should be good quality. Many food service operations will design, print and produce an attractive, effective, quality menu and then attach a poorly printed "daily special" tip-on, done on a typewriter, on cheap paper, which spoils the entire effect of the menu.

Another mechanical aspect of the menu that's important is its size. Many menus are physically too small. When too many items are jammed together on the menu, nothing functions the way it should. The listing becomes hard to read; big, expensive, high profit items get lost among small, unimportant items. And the confused customer ends up asking the waitress, "What's good?"

Creative Menus Get Attention

Finally, is your menu different? Is it really creative, or does it look like every other menu? Here's where good, professional menu service can be of help. A really exceptional menu will have unusual design, good use of color, exciting paper selection plus an unusual shape or fold. In addition to design creativity, the basic idea plus copy can make a menu. Customers usually have time to read as well as look at a menu, therefore, an unusual, creative menu will advertise your operation as unusual and creative both in service and cuisine.

If your menu self analysis through the use of the MENU RATING FORM leads to a less than desirable score, if your menu is not batting 1,000, or if you don't trust your own analysis, send your menu to INSTITUTIONS/VF Magazine's Menu Merchandising Service. The menu you save could be your own!

HOW TO USE CLIP ART

The clip art in this section is provided for use on the menu. It can be used as cover art or internal decoration. Included are an assortment of styles and subjects relative to food as served on the menu, plus headings—steak, appetizers, seafood, etc.—in special, unusual styles that may not be available to your printer, as well as some hand lettered headings.

The pages of clip art are perforated and can be removed easily from the menu book. They can be used by your printer or layout artist in the same size as printed or can be enlarged or reduced. They can be printed in black or in a second color—red, blue, brown, etc. They can also be reversed (white line on a black or colored background). For use on the inside of the menu, a drawing of a fish can head up the seafood section, a steak illustration can enliven the steak listing and the figure of a chef can help identify chef's specials.

Some cautions should be observed in using artwork on the menu:

First, it should not be overdone. Remember, you are primarily communicating and selling. Art and decoration should make the message more attractive and pleasant but should not be so dominant as to interfere with the printed word.

Second, try to select pieces of art work that are similar so that your menu does not look like a hodge-podge of unrelated visual elements.

And, third, select drawings, headings (as well as type) that match the style, decor and cuisine of your operation. If yours is old-fashioned New England decor, choose your clip art accordingly or if yours is a more modern up-to-date atmosphere, illustrate your menu with art in a corresponding modern style.

All of the clip art is in "line." This means that it is easy and inexpensive to reproduce. It can be printed by both the letter-press and offset methods. And it will reproduce well on any kind of paper or plastic with all standard inks.

For use as cover art, it is often effective to take small artwork and blow it up large, both positive and reverse (negative), through photostats to see what it looks like. In other cases, for use on inside pages, the actual drawing may be cut out and pasted right on the layout or typesetter's galley. Since there is artwork on both sides of the page, however, be careful that you do not destroy art you may want to use later. A photostat of one side will save it if you wish to keep it for later use.

STEAK

Martini

Tom Collins

Old Fashioned

Grasshopper

Manhattan

soup

DINNER

desserts

LUNCHEON

entrees

salads

dinner menu

beverages

appetizers
and cocktails

365

Wine List

wine list

Wine List

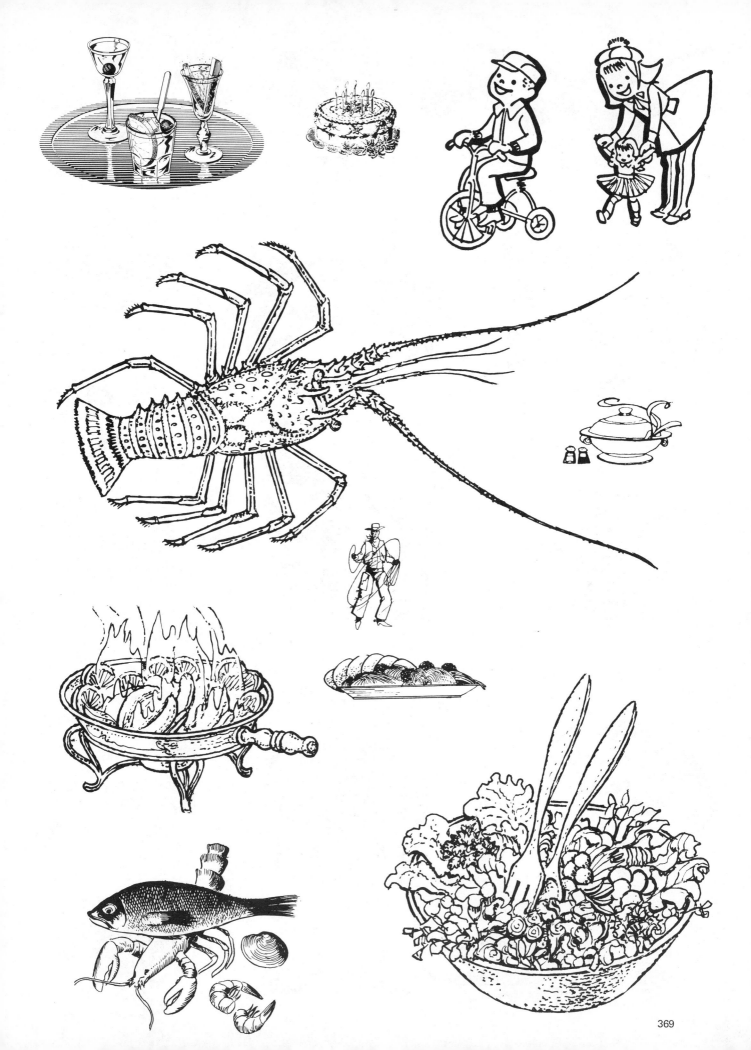

Special today

WINE LIST

CHEF'S SUGGESTIONS

CHILDREN'S PLATES

SIDE ORDERS

SANDWICHES

APPETIZERS

BEVERAGES

SALADS

SEAFOOD

EGG DISHES

STEAKS & CHOPS

DESSERTS

MENU

menu

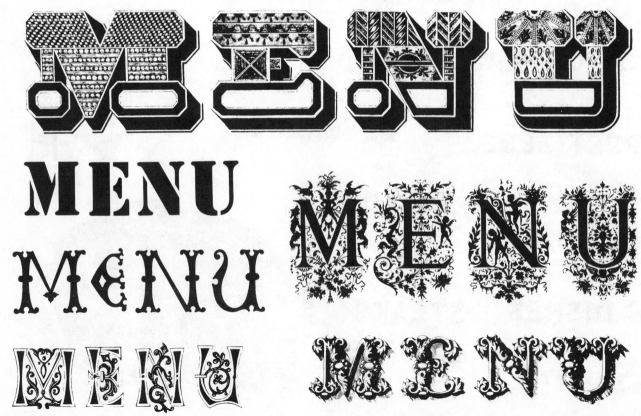

MENU

MENU

MENU

MENU

MENU

MENU

Soups Dinner Appetizers

Flaming Dishes

from the Silver Skillet

Champagne Desserts Desserts

Kiddie Korner Specials Cocktail

Complete Dinners Ala Carte

Ala Carte Features Suggestions

Sandwiches Appetizers

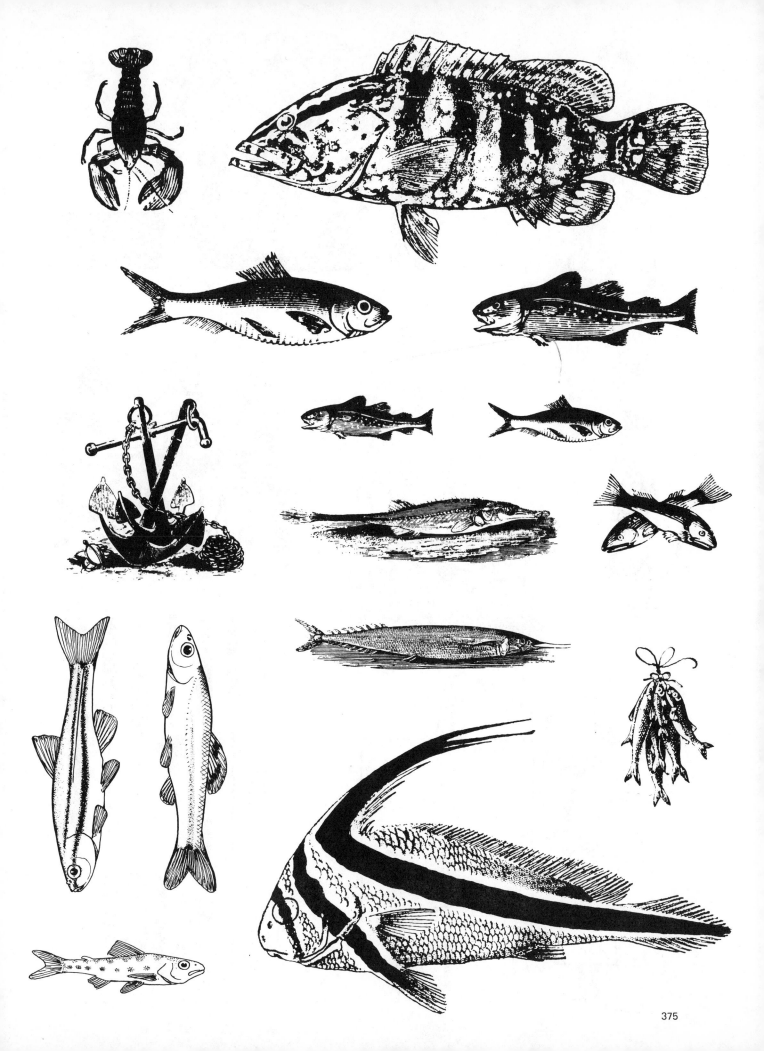

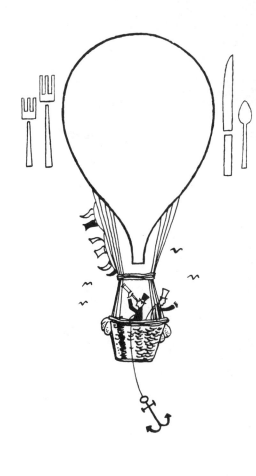

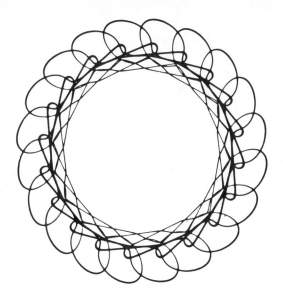
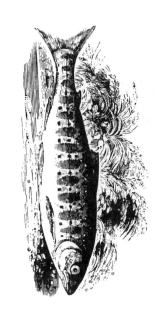

MENU

menu

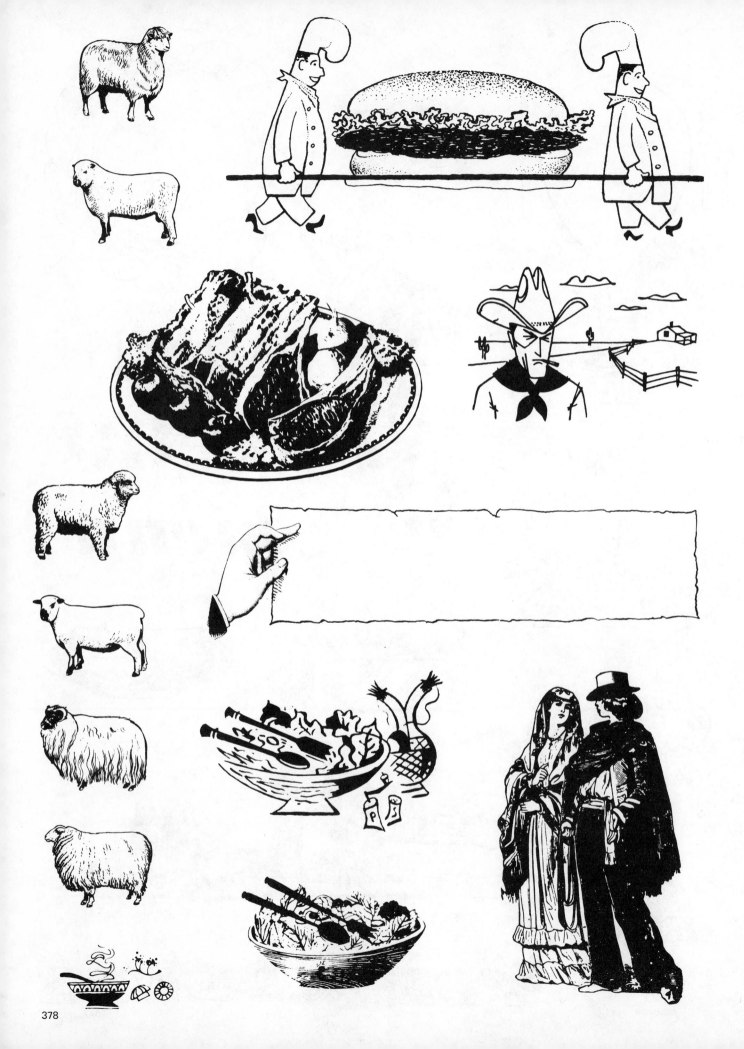

Chef's Specials

Dinners	Luncheon Specials

Red Dinner Wines
"Best with All Red Meats and Full-flavored Dishes"

White Dinner Wines
"Preferred with Seafood, Fowl and Other Light Entrees"

Pink Dinner Wines
"The Most Versatile of Wines, Good with All Foods"

Sparkling Wines
"Delicious and So Festive for All Special Occasions"

Soups

POULTRY

Chef's
Specials

Sandwich Plates

French Fries

Sandwiches

Fruits & Melons

Salads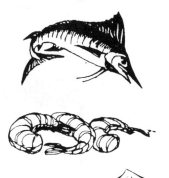

Beverages & Juices

 Desserts

Fountain

Seafoods

always
in
season

Salad Plates

From Our Broiler

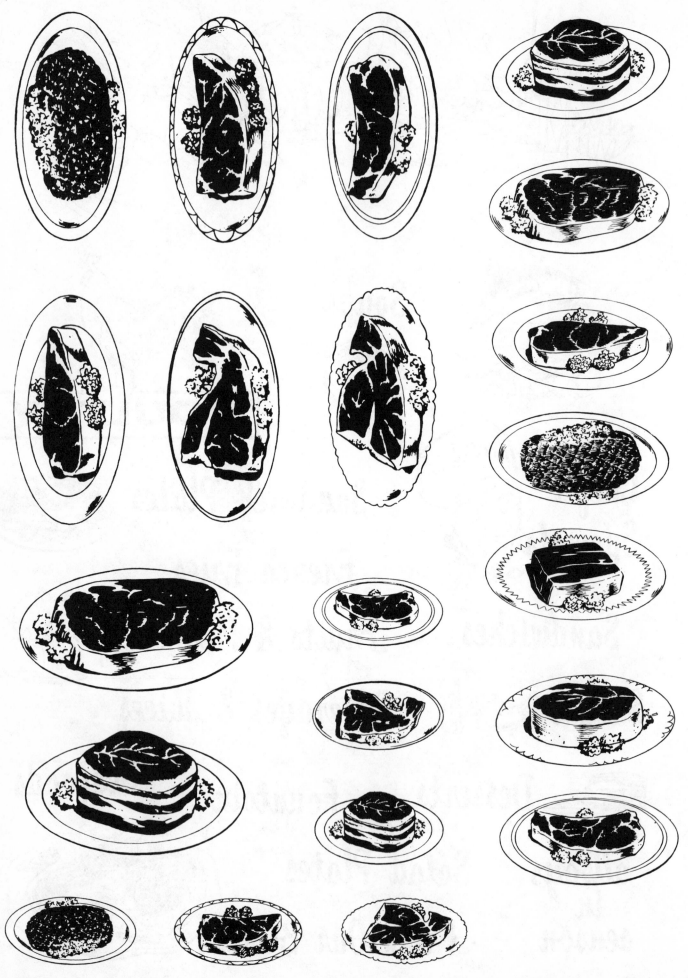

OUR SPECIALS OF THE WEEK

MONDAYS

WEDNESDAYS

SATURDAYS

Chef's Specials

Luncheon

Specials Dinners

wine list